THE SENSORY ORDER

AND OTHER WRITINGS ON THE FOUNDATIONS

OF THEORETICAL PSYCHOLOGY

F. A. HAYEK

THE COLLECTED WORKS OF

F. A. Hayek

THE SENSORY ORDER

AND OTHER WRITINGS ON

THE FOUNDATIONS OF THEORETICAL

PSYCHOLOGY

F. A. HAYEK

Edited by Viktor J. Vanberg

Liberty Fund

This book is published by Liberty Fund, Inc., a foundation established to encourage study of the ideal of a society of free and responsible individuals.

The cuneiform inscription that serves as our logo and as a design element in Liberty Fund books is the earliest-known written appearance of the word "freedom" (*amagi*), or "liberty." It is taken from a clay document written about 2300 B.C. in the Sumerian city-state of Lagash.

The Sensory Order and Other Writings on the Foundations of Theoretical Psychology is volume 14 of The Collected Works of F. A. Hayek, published by The University of Chicago Press.

This 2023 Liberty Fund paperback edition of *The Sensory Order and Other Writings on the Foundations of Theoretical Psychology* is licensed by The University of Chicago Press, Chicago, Illinois, U.S.A., and published by arrangement with Routledge, a member of the Taylor & Francis Group, an Informa Business.

23   24   25   26   27   P   5   4   3   2   1

Library of Congress Cataloging-in-Publication Data
can be found on the Library of Congress website
at https://lccn.loc.gov/2023020891.

Liberty Fund, Inc.
11301 North Meridian Street
Carmel, Indiana 46032
libertyfund.org

This book is printed on paper that is acid-free and meets the requirements of the American National Standard for Permanence of Paper for Printed Library Materials, Z39.48-1992. ♾

Cover design by Erin Kirk, Watkinsville, Georgia
Printed and bound by Sheridan Books, Inc., Chelsea, Michigan

THE COLLECTED WORKS OF F. A. HAYEK

Founding Editor: W. W. Bartley III
General Editor: Bruce Caldwell

*The University of Chicago Press edition
was published with the support of*

The Hoover Institution on War, Revolution,
and Peace, Stanford University

The Cato Institute

The Earhart Foundation

The Pierre F. and Enid Goodrich Foundation

The Heritage Foundation

The Morris Foundation, Little Rock

CONTENTS

EDITORIAL FOREWORD

This new edition of *The Sensory Order* is supplemented by four texts that are directly related to what the subtitle describes as Hayek's *Inquiry into the Foundations of Theoretical Psychology*.

Firstly, "Contributions to a Theory of How Consciousness Develops" is the English translation, published here for the first time, of a paper entitled "Beiträge zur Theorie der Entwicklung des Bewußtseins," which Hayek wrote as a student in 1920 before he decided to pursue degrees in law and in economics rather than in psychology. Even though, as Hayek notes in his preface to *The Sensory Order*, "the basic idea then conceived has continued to occupy me," it was only in the second half of the 1940s that he took up again the subject addressed in his student days' essay, to expand the arguments he had outlined there into a book-length manuscript. The title he originally chose for this project, *What Is Mind?*, he changed for the 1952 publication to *The Sensory Order*. Secondly, this volume includes the English translation, also published here for the first time, of a lecture Hayek had delivered in 1949 at a conference in the Tyrolean village Alpbach. Because this lecture, entitled "Das Wesen des Geistigen," consists of a brief summary of the core ideas Hayek had developed in *What Is Mind?*, the latter title has also been chosen for the English version published here instead of a literal translation of the original German title. The third supplemental text, "Within Systems and About Systems: A Statement of Some Problems of a Theory of Communication," is a previously unpublished fragment of a paper Hayek had started to work on in 1952 in which he sought to further clarify issues addressed in *The Sensory Order*, but which he left uncompleted. Finally, the fourth supplement included here, "*The Sensory Order* after 25 Years," is Hayek's contribution, originally published in 1982, to a conference on Cognition and the Symbolic Process, which was held in 1977 at Pennsylvania State University. Professor Walter B. Weimer, who organized at this conference a panel that had *The Sensory Order* as its special subject, deserves credit for having contributed to the increase in interest Hayek's *Inquiry into the Foundations of Theoretical Psychology* enjoys since the 1980s, after decades during which it was largely ignored.

In order to maintain the character of the contributions collected here as single documents, the references are listed separately for each of them. Following the practice in other volumes of *The Collected Works*, obvious typographical and other errors are silently corrected. Where words appear in different spelling they have been changed to the standard format (e.g. "centre" to "center," "fibre" to "fiber," "behaviour" to "behavior," "colour" to "color"). For consistency with the other contributions in the volume, "gestalt" in *The Sensory Order* has been changed to "Gestalt." All other changes from the original texts are explicitly noted.

This is the occasion to express my gratitude to a number of persons from whose encouragement and support I greatly benefitted in preparing this edition. First and foremost I am indebted to my spouse, Monika Vanberg. During my entire academic career she has been the first person to read, and critically comment on, virtually all of my writings. Without her "imprimatur" no manuscript was ever sent to the publisher—which does not mean, of course, that she should be held responsible for any remaining deficiencies. As important as her encouragement and support have been for all of my earlier work, they have been a far more essential help for me in preparing this edition. Monika took on the tedious task of several rounds of proofreading all the texts. She provided valuable comments and suggestions to my introduction, and I immensely benefitted from the opportunity to discuss with her all the editor's footnotes in this volume.

I am particularly grateful to Mrs. Ursula Mayer, of Walter Eucken Institut, for her never tiring and always friendly support in librarian matters. She always found ways to retrieve for me even the most difficult-to-locate sources, and especially some of Hayek's early references surely fell into this category. Thanks are also due to Dr. Grete Heinz for her masterly translation of Hayek's 1920 paper and his Alpbach lecture. Working with her on this project was a rewarding experience. I gratefully acknowledge helpful comments and suggestions from two anonymous referees. Last but not least I wish to thank the general editor of *The Collected Works*, Bruce Caldwell, for his generous support in archival and other matters as well as for his patience during the many years he had to wait for the completion of this volume.

Viktor J. Vanberg

THE "KNOWLEDGE PROBLEM" AS THE INTEGRATING THEME OF F. A. HAYEK'S OEUVRE

An Introduction to *The Sensory Order*

by Victor J. Vanberg

Among F. A. Hayek's numerous publications, *The Sensory Order* (hereafter *TSO*) is undoubtedly the most unusual. After all, from someone known as an economist and social philosopher, one would hardly expect a treatise on the "Foundations of Theoretical Psychology." And, indeed, to Hayek's disappointment, for the first decades after its appearance, *TSO* received hardly any attention, neither from psychologists nor from social scientists. Psychologists did not suspect Hayek, the social theorist, to have anything important to contribute to their discipline, and Hayek's colleagues in the social sciences did not expect his thoughts on "theoretical psychology" to be of relevance to their concerns.

True, several early reviewers took notice,[1] and Hayek received a number of personal reactions from friends and colleagues. A sympathetic response to the unpublished typescript came from Ludwig von Bertalanffy.[2] Erwin Schrödinger[3] expressed his general agreement but voiced some reservations.[4] John C. Eccles pointed to the complementarity of Hayek's thoughts and his own neurophysiological theory but expressed his skepticism "in respect to

---

[1] See Boring 1953; Chisholm 1954; Grenell 1954; Hamlyn 1954; Kneale 1954; Sprott 1954.

[2] Letter, L. v. Bertalanffy to F. A. Hayek, June 22, 1950, Hayek papers, box 12, folder 4, Hoover Institution Archives, Stanford University, California (from here on abbreviated as HIA).

[3] Erwin Schrödinger (1887–1961), the Austrian physicist and philosopher of science and recipient of the 1933 Nobel Prize in Physics, had been known to Hayek as the son of one of his father's fellow botanists (Hayek 1994, 139; Kreuzer 1983, 9).

[4] Letter, E. Schrödinger to F. A. Hayek, October 24, 1952, Hayek papers, box 48, folder 37, HIA. Schrödinger objected to Hayek's claim that an "isomorphism" exists between the "neural order" and the "phenomenal order" (see *TSO* 2.2ff.), arguing in favor of a "psychophysical parallelism." In an interview, when asked about Schrödinger's response to *TSO*, Hayek answered: "To my great surprise, he was the one man who seemed to have fully understood *TSO*. But of course he was working on just this sort of problem. I had known Schrödinger when he was a *Gymnasiast*. His father was an amateur botanist as well as an industrialist. He was a member of my father's circle, who regularly met at our house. Sometimes young Schrödinger came along; he was about five or six years my senior" (Hayek 1984, 139).

the main thesis" of the book.[5] In a long, encouraging letter, John Z. Young[6] noted the affinity of Hayek's thoughts to Donald O. Hebb's neurophysiological theory,[7] and in a short letter, Hebb acknowledged the agreement in the "general direction" of their respective approaches.[8] Yet all this fell far short of what Hayek had hoped for,[9] and as he expressly stated, most disappointing for him was the reserved response of the two persons whose opinion he cared particularly about: Karl Popper and Konrad Lorenz.[10]

A turning point in the reception of *TSO*—reflected with some delay in the citation counts[11]—came in the 1980s, and it was Walter B. Weimer,[12] a psychologist at Pennsylvania State University, who played some role in this.[13] Weimer, who had come across Hayek's book and recognized its relevance for the ongoing debate in cognitive psychology,[14] wrote a letter to Hayek in the fall of 1976 saying: "Nearly a quarter of a century ago you published *TSO*. Now

---

[5] Letter, J. C. Eccles to F. A. Hayek, April 8, 1953, Hayek papers, box 18, folder 4, HIA. Similar to Schrödinger's critique, Eccles objected to Hayek's "isomorphism-thesis," insisting, instead, on a "dualism" of neural and mental phenomena.

[6] John Zachary Young (1907–97) was an English neurophysiologist who studied the central nervous system and the functions of the brain.

[7] Letter, J. Z. Young to F. A. Hayek, January 7, 1953, Hayek papers, box 60, folder 21, HIA. In the opening paragraph of his letter, Young notes: "It seems to me that you describe approximately the position that Hebb adopts, but in many ways more clearly."

[8] Letter, D. O. Hebb to F. A. Hayek, November 26, 1952, Hayek papers, box 24, folder 1, HIA.

[9] Hayek (this volume, p. 389): "Although my book had at first a few sensible and sympathetic reviews . . . I have since practically no indication of any response to my theses by the psychological profession."

[10] Letter, F. A. Hayek to R. Riedl, March 19, 1984, Hayek papers, box 46, folder 12, HIA. In a letter to B. Weimer of January 16, 1983 (Hayek papers, box 57, folder 2, HIA), Hayek noted in reference to Popper: "But what most worried me was that he never would show any sympathy with the argument of *TSO* which he more or less, though politely, rejected, without giving any reasons."

[11] In the mid-1990s the annual citation numbers jump from the single digits to the double digits, moving close to fifty in 2009.

[12] W. N. Butos (2010b, 2f.): "It was chiefly cognitive psychologist Walter B. Weimer who should be credited for bringing Hayek's cognitive work before a larger audience and making the case for its wider significance for economics and social theories generally."

[13] An article by Rosemary Agnito, which appeared in 1975 in the journal *Behaviorism*, may also have helped attract the attention of cognitive psychologists to Hayek's treatise. Agnito (1975, 162) begins her paper by saying: "During the fifties an extremely perceptive work in theoretical psychology appeared in this country which provided an account of mind defined as a process of classification. . . . This study has been largely ignored in the philosophical community despite its revealing insights into such fundamental epistemological and psychological concerns as memory, learning, behavior and the status of conscious activity, among others. I am referring to Friedrich Hayek's work, *TSO*."

[14] Weimer (2011, xxvi) recollects that he skimmed through Hayek's book as an undergraduate in 1962 but that it was "The Primacy of the Abstract" ([1969] 2014) that made him "actually read *TSO*."

psychologists are quite slow, especially in recognizing anything of significance, but a few of us have taken notice of your work and the opinion is beginning to form that you have written a prolegomenon which is necessary for any future cognitive psychology."[15] The specific purpose of Weimer's letter was to invite Hayek to a conference on "cognition and the symbolic process."[16] As he phrased it, "if there were any way in which we could persuade you to attend, and/or present some of your ideas, it would delight us and help spread the interest in your 'other' research."[17] The proceedings of the conference, which was held in May 1977 at Pennsylvania State University, including a panel on *TSO*, were finally published in 1982, with Weimer's "Introduction to the Theoretical Psychology of *TSO*" (Weimer 1982) and Hayek's contribution, "*The Sensory Order* after 25 Years."[18]

Most significant for the increase in the attention *TSO* gained was the recognition Hayek's contribution to theoretical psychology received from two prominent neuroscientists, Gerald Edelman[19] and Joaquin M. Fuster.[20] Fuster, a professor for Psychiatry and Biobehavioral Sciences at UCLA, had, already in the spring of 1976, written a letter to Hayek in which he stated:

> For almost twenty years I have been engaged in research on the central nervous system at the University of California. . . . It is becoming obvious that the principles of classical sensory physiology (neurons specializing in external feature detection, etc.) are no longer applicable to the neuronal transactions that take place at cortical level. Instead, it appears that the theoretical

[15] Letter, W. B. Weimer to F. A. Hayek, October 21, 1976, Hayek papers, box 57, folder 2, HIA. In a follow-up letter of December 20, 1976 (ibid.), Weimer notes: "I shall send you by surface mail some papers I have written recently that refer to *TSO*, so you can get an idea of how at least one psychologist uses (perhaps misuses!) your ideas. I think you will be amazed at how little the field has progressed in some areas."

[16] In the original conference flyer the purpose of the symposium was described as: "Recognizing the current revolution within cognitive psychology . . . and . . . to crystallize . . . research proposals for where cognitive psychology ought to go in the future" (Marsh 2011b, xix).

[17] Ibid.

[18] F. A. Hayek, "*The Sensory Order* after 25 Years," in *Cognition and the Symbolic Processes*, vol. 2, ed. W. B. Weimer and D. S. Palermo (Hillsdale, NJ: Lawrence Erlbaum, 1982), 287–93. Reprinted in this volume, pp. 382–389.

[19] Edelman (1982, 24; 1987, 24): "I must say that I have been deeply gratified by reading a book of which I had not been aware when I wrote my little essay on group selection theory. It was written by the economist Friedrich von Hayek. . . . At the time I did not know who von Hayek was; I was deeply impressed, and found out subsequently that he had won the Nobel Prize in Economics."

[20] Fuster (2011, 4f.): "Only now, more than half a century after the publication of his theoretical book (Hayek 1952), is the reaction to Hayek's argument beginning to be heard. And it's a positive reaction, now supported by facts. . . . Now, belatedly reacting to his book, we can confidently say that modern facts speak eloquently for his theory."

principles enunciated by you in "*TSO*" are remarkably useful for understanding the neural and behavioral phenomena that we are observing. The concept of sensory "classification," as you utilize it in your theoretical discourse, is the most appropriate that I have encountered for interpreting a variety of experimental data related to visual representation in the inferotemporal cortex. In fact, I have adopted your theoretical approach as part of the rationale for a new series of investigations of cortical neuron discharge which I am now undertaking.[21]

In his 1995 book, *Memory in the Cerebral Cortex*, Fuster publicly praised Hayek's pioneering contribution to cognitive neuroscience:

> The first proponent of cortical memory networks on a major scale was neither a neuroscientist nor a computer scientist but, curiously, a Viennese economist: Friedrich von Hayek (1899–1992). . . . Although devoid of mathematical elaboration, Hayek's model clearly contains most of the elements of those later models of associative memory . . . that, with their algorithms, have not come any closer than it does to solving those problems in a neutrally plausible manner. It is truly amazing that, with much less neuroscientific knowledge available, Hayek's model comes closer, in some respects, to being neurophysiologically verifiable than those models developed 50 to 60 years after his. (Fuster 1995, 87ff.)[22]

In similar terms Gerald M. Edelman, recipient of the 1972 Nobel Prize in Physiology or Medicine, expressed his admiration for "Friedrich von Hayek, an economist who, as a young man, thought quite a bit about how the brain

---

[21] Letter, J. M. Fuster to F. A. Hayek, May 3, 1976, Hayek papers, box 21, folder 9, HIA. In a follow-up letter of June 2, 1976 (ibid.), Fuster states: "Modern neuroscience, on dealing with cortical function, is in fact abandoning the old deterministic-localizationist ideas in favor of probabilistic concepts and Gestalt concepts as you used them in *TSO*. Your argument is as valid now as it was when it was first presented, with the difference that now we have more empirical support for it."

[22] See also Fuster 1997, 451: "Friedrich Hayek . . . seems to have been the first to postulate what is the core of this paper, namely, the idea of memory and perception represented in widely distributed networks of interconnected cortical cells. Subsequently this idea has received theoretical support, however tangential, from the fields of cognitive psychology, connectionism and artificial intelligence. Empirically, it is well supported by the physiological study and neuroimaging of working memory."—Fuster (2011, 6): "Hayek started out by proposing a brain-based theory of perception, but ended up by proposing a brain-based theory of the mind. For many years, sensory physiologists have attempted to do the same, but have become mired in the reductionism of sensory psychophysics and neuron physiology, unable to rise above them to build a conscious mind, which, like Hayek's perception, is made of relationships, history, and an ever-evolving cerebral cortex. They never came to grips, as he did, with the fact that the cognitive code is essentially a relational code."

works" (Edelman 2004, 22). Having read *TSO* he remarked in 1982 about its author: "What impressed me most is his understanding that the key to the problem of perception is to comprehend the nature of classification. . . . I think the essence of his analysis still remains with us; the problem of perception, at the level of its necessary conditions, is a problem of classification."[23]

It seems that the recognition Hayek's psychological thoughts found in cognitive neuroscience[24] was needed to alert economists to the fact that *TSO* may also deserve to be taken seriously by scholars whose primary interest is in Hayek's economics and social philosophy. Even if it is still, as Caldwell diagnosed in 1997, "particularly among economists, Hayek's least appreciated book" (1856), economists have begun to take notice of *TSO*—including Nobel Laureates Douglass North and Vernon Smith[25]—and the literature devoted to the subject is growing.[26] Essentially two issues figure prominently in this literature. This is, on the one hand, the question of how Hayek's contribution is to be assessed in light of the context of modern neuroscience and, on

---

[23] Edelman 1982, 24f.; 1987, 24f. See also Edelman 2004, 22: "The point to be stressed is that, while synaptic change is essential for the functioning of memory, memory is a system property that also depends on specific neuro-anatomical connections. . . . Various patterns have been found for the so-called synaptic rules governing these changes, following the initial proposals of Donald Hebb, a psychologist, and Friedrich von Hayek, an economist who, as a young man, thought quite a bit about how the brain works. These scholars suggested that an increase in synaptic efficacy would occur when pre- and postsynaptic neurons fired in close temporal order."

[24] On this see also Birner 1999, 51, fn.; Marsh 2010, 122f., 142f.; Basar 2005.

[25] North 2005, 32ff.; V. L. Smith 2003, 1070f. Vernon Smith is counted among the founders of *neuroeconomics*, a subfield of behavioral economics that aims at improving the "economic model of man" by using neuroscientific methods and insights. With its interest in neural mechanisms, the field is, as Vernon Smith notes, apparently related to the project Hayek pursued with *TSO*. Because of its concentration on the use of brain imaging techniques and its ambition to use "data from brain imaging . . . [for] grounding economic choice in neural detail" (Camerer 2008, 44), however, neuroeconomics guides its research efforts in a direction quite different from the explanatory goal Hayek pursued. Hayek's interest was not in explaining the "neural details" of particular kinds of choices, a project which, in view of the complexity of human choice, he would have considered illusionary. In the context of Hayek's work, the insights outlined in *TSO* are of significance as a theoretical foundation for his inquiry into "how knowledge is acquired and communicated," the central question that, in his view, economic theory has to answer (on this see below, section 4) in order to be able to provide an adequate explanation of the principles that govern the formation and evolution of social order.

[26] See, in particular, the two essay collections edited by Butos (2010a) and Marsh (2011a). Butos, who had been a student of W. Weimer, was among the earliest economists to make *TSO* the principal subject of publications. See Butos 1997; Butos and Koppl 1993, 2006; Butos and McQuade 2002; McQuade and Butos 2005. Other contributions to the discussion on *TSO* include Yeager (1984) 2011; Bouillon 1991; Herrmann-Pillath 1992; Streit 1993; Birner 1994, 1999; de Vries 1994; Tuerck 1995; B. Smith 1997; Rizello 1999; Horwitz 2000; G. R. Steele 2002; Boettke and Subrick 2002; De Vecchi 2003; Caldwell 2004b; Vanberg 2004a; Gaus 2006; Feser 2006; Sprich 2008. J. W. Lindemans (2011) provides an excellent summary and discussion of *TSO*.

the other hand, the issue whether, and if so to what extent, Hayek's thoughts on the "Foundations of Theoretical Psychology" must be regarded as an integral and foundational part of his oeuvre, a part that is important for a deeper understanding of his economic and social philosophy. As the present edition of *TSO* is part of Hayek's *Collected Works*, it seems appropriate to concentrate in this introduction on the second issue. My aim is to show that *TSO* has, indeed, its systematic and highly significant place in the development of the socioeconomic paradigm that Hayek elaborated over the six decades of his active literary production. Before I turn to this task (in sections 4ff.), I shall first take a look at the genesis of *TSO* (section 1), its central problem (section 2), and its theoretical core (section 3).

1. The Origins and the Writing of TSO

With his reference to the fact that Hayek, "as a young man, thought quite a bit about how the brain works," Edelman alludes to the essay "Beiträge zur Theorie der Entwicklung des Bewußtseins" that Hayek wrote in 1920, but that remained unpublished until quite recently.[27] Hayek refers to this essay in his preface when he describes *TSO* as "the outcome of an idea which suggested itself to me as a very young man when I was still uncertain whether to become an economist or a psychologist" (115),[28] adding: "The paper in which as a student more than thirty years ago I first tried to sketch these ideas, and which lies before me as I write, I was certainly wise not to attempt to publish at the time, even though it contains the whole principle of the theory I am now putting forward" (115).[29]

On several occasions Hayek has commented on the circumstances under which he wrote the essay, the purpose of which he described as "an attempt to create a basis for a general physiological explanation of consciousness phenomena by investigating the simplest conscious experiences, particularly those of a sensory nature, and explaining them in terms of the operation of established physiological laws" (321). In interviews he recalled that he "wrote most

---

[27] The German original was published for the first time in Hayek (1952) 2006. The English translation, "Contributions to a Theory of How Consciousness Develops," has been prepared for this volume by Grete Heinz (this volume, pp. 321–347).

[28] Otherwise unspecified page numbers refer to the present volume.

[29] That Hayek may have unsuccessfully tried to get his essay published may be concluded from a remark he made in an unpublished interview with W. W. Bartley, dated "St. Blasien, June 11, 1984": "As early as '21 I had submitted it to the publisher Deuticke in Vienna. I had shown it to Stöhr; I still possess somewhere the large envelope with my name on top of it which Stöhr sent it out in." (This and other unpublished interviews cited in the editor's introduction are used with the permission of the Hayek estate and Stephen Kresge.) On Stöhr see below, fn. 39.

of that first draft" in the winter of 1919–20 in Zurich,[30] where he "worked for a few weeks in the laboratory of the brain anatomist von Monakow,[31] tracing fiber bundles through the different parts of the human brain" (Hayek 1994, 64), and audited lectures at the University of Zurich.[32]

Hayek's early interest in physiological psychology,[33] an area that seems far remote from the subjects of the works that made him famous, appears less surprising in light of his family background (Hayek 1994, 37ff.). As he described it: "I come from a purely biological tradition. My grandfather was . . . gymnasial professor in biology; my father was a botanist. My two brothers, one became an anatomist, the other a chemist."[34] Late in his life, Hayek would come to speak of himself as a "verpatzter Biologe"—a "would-be biologist"—who had been induced by the circumstances after WWI to shift his interest from his family's natural science background to economics.[35] One

---

[30] Unpublished interview with W. W. Bartley, dated "London, March 28, 1983." As Hayek notes, the stay in Zurich was occasioned by the fact that "the University of Vienna closed down, because there was no coal to heat" (ibid.). Hayek reports that the visit to Zurich as well as a visit "on an estate in Norway . . . in late August and September 1920 . . . were made possible by invitations from my father's fellow botanists who . . . wanted to help the son of a friend who had recently returned from war and not only needed some feeding up but was also suffering from malaria" (Hayek 1994, 63). On his war experience Hayek (ibid., 45) reports: "I joined a field artillery regiment at Vienna in March 1917, and after a little over seven months' training was sent . . . to the Italian front where I served for a little over a year. . . . Like most of my comrades, I managed to contract an infection of malaria . . . so that I finally returned to Vienna towards the middle of November of 1918 in a somewhat weakened state."

[31] Constantin von Monakow (1853–1930) was a Russian-born Swiss neuropathologist who taught at the University of Zurich, from 1885 as "Privatdozent" and from 1994 as Professor. In 1886 he founded an institute for brain anatomy that was officially established as a university unit in 1910.

[32] Hayek (1994, 63f.) recalls: "The most lasting effect of my auditing . . . was that a young lecturer talked at some length of a new book (*Erkenntnislehre*) . . . whom after my return to Vienna I soon discovered to be identical with the newly appointed professor of philosophy, Moritz Schlick, who was the first to persuade me that philosophy could make sense, which until then I had found only in the works of Ernst Mach." Moritz Schlick (1882–1936) was a German physicist and philosopher. He was the founder and leader of the Vienna Circle. Having completed his doctoral dissertation under Max Planck at the University of Berlin in 1904 he held positions at the Universities of Rostock and Kiel before, in 1922, he took the chair of Naturphilosophie at the University of Vienna, previously held by Ernst Mach. Schlick's book *Allgemeine Erkenntnislehre* was published in 1918 (Berlin: Verlag von Julius Springer). An English translation, *General Theory of Knowledge*, was published in 1974 (New York: Springer Verlag). On M. Schlick see also below, p. 12.

[33] Hayek (1994, 62) speaks of "my brief but intense concern with the problems of physiological psychology, which took up a considerable part of my interest in 1919 and 1920."

[34] Unpublished interview with W. W. Bartley, dated "London, March 28, 1983."

[35] Letter, F. A. Hayek to R. Riedl, October 18, 1979, Hayek papers, box 46, folder 12, HIA; letter, F. A. Hayek to M. Koch, February 1983, Hayek papers, box 31, folder 10, HIA; letter, F. A. Hayek to E. Mayr, December 14, 1983, Hayek papers, box 37, folder 24, HIA.

of the circumstances that caused his shift in interest was, as Hayek (1994, 44) puts it, the fact that the "great disturbances of war got me more interested in economics," combined with his coming across Carl Menger's *Grundsätze der Volkswirtschaftslehre*,[36] the book that is generally considered the founding treatise of the Austrian tradition in economics.[37] Another was the fact that psychology was only "very badly represented at the university."[38] As Hayek (this volume, p. 382) recalls: "For a young man returning from World War I to enter the University of Vienna, with his interests having been drawn by those events from the family background of biology to social and philosophical issues, there were at the moment just no teaching in psychology available."[39] Furthermore, as far as career prospects are concerned, he reckoned that "law and economics gave one a chance of an occupation" (Hayek 1994, 44).

It was thus, in Hayek's (1983b, 271) own account, "for practical reasons" that he decided to study law with economics as part of the curriculum,[40] and to give up the research interests that he had pursued in his *Beiträge* paper. "In September 1920," he recalls, "when I had to start systematic work for the main law examination, I put the draft of that essay away—I thought at the time, for a short while; however, I did not concern myself again seriously with these problems until about 1946" (1994, 62). After he earned his law degree

[36] Wien: Braumüller, 1871.

[37] Hayek (1983b, 174): "I think the decisive influence was really World War I, particularly the experience of serving in a multinational army. . . . It was during the war service in Italy that I more or less decided to do economics. But I really got hooked when I found [Carl] Menger's *Grundsätze* such a fascinating book, so satisfying."

[38] Hayek 1983b, 476. Hayek (ibid.) adds: "Finally, I got definitely hooked by economics by becoming acquainted with a particular tradition through the textbook of Carl Menger, which was wholly satisfactory to me. I could step into an existing tradition, while my psychological ideas did not fit into any established tradition. It would not have given me easy access to an academic career. So I became an economist, although the psychological ideas continued to occupy me."

[39] Hayek (1994, 44): "While I was at the university, I was still in doubt between economics and psychology. . . . After the death of Stöhr, there wasn't even anyone teaching psychology. What psychology I knew, I got myself from books." About Stöhr (see also above, fn. 29) Hayek said in his interview with W. W. Bartley (London, March 28, 1983): "The only man who had any understanding was a man called Adolf Stöhr, who was visibly dying; as I once put it, it was equally painful for him to give lectures as it was to listen to him. But I had great admiration for him, and gave him the first draft of my *Sensory Order* to look at. And I owe it to him that I had confidence to continue with it. I believe the only course of lectures of his I heard, he had to break off, and died soon after." See also Hayek 1994, 62; this volume, p. 382, fn. 2.

[40] Hayek (1994, 62): "I was of course supposed to study law, and economics constituted merely one subject in one of the three major exams for the final (doctor's) examination. Yet though I not only passed most of the exams with distinction but also succeeded . . . to take the degree after three years (in November 1921) instead of the usual four, my main interests were long divided between psychology and economics." See also Kreuzer (1983, 15): "Though I studied law as the main subject . . . I essentially divided the time between psychology and economics, such that law always remained somewhat of a minor matter" (my translation—Ed.).

in 1921 he had "to think about earning a living." As he put it: even though "the fascination of physiological psychology never quite left me, . . . for the next 25 years—struggling to get on as an economist (and rapidly forgetting my law)—I could devote no time to following the development in psychology" (this volume, p. 384).

What, in Hayek's (1994, 126) own account, revived his interest in his "old ideas on theoretical psychology" was his "work on the methodology of the social sciences . . . done during the early years of the war."[41] This revived interest is reflected, in particular, in chapter 2, "The Problem and the Method of the Natural Sciences," and chapter 5, "The Objectivism of the Scientistic Approach," of his essay "Scientism and the Study of Society" that was originally published between 1942 and 1944 in three parts in *Economica*.[42] A core argument implied in his 1920 essay, and carefully elaborated in *TSO*, is summarized in the following passage:

> It is that not only those mental entities, such as "concepts" or "ideas," which are commonly recognized as "abstractions," but *all* mental phenomena, sense perceptions and images as well as the more abstract "concepts" and "ideas," must be regarded as acts of classification performed by the brain. This is, of course, merely another way of saying that the qualities which we perceive are not properties of the objects but ways in which we (individually or as a race) have learned to group or classify external stimuli. (Hayek [1942–44] 2010, 111)

Before he actually came to devote significant time, though, to his "old ideas on theoretical psychology," Hayek got occupied with a different project—a project, he thought, the circumstances of the time required of him: the writing of what was to become his most famous book, *The Road to Serfdom*.

As Hayek ([1944] 2007, 39) reports in the preface to the 1956 edition of *The Road to Serfdom*, what induced him to write the book was his growing concern in the late 1930s that English public opinion "completely misconceived" the nature of the Nazi and other totalitarian movements.[43] In the preface to

---

[41] Hayek (this volume, p. 384): "In the early 1940s, I had done a study of what I christened 'scientism'—that is, an examination of the harmful effects that the physics model had had on the methodology of the social sciences—and in this work had been driven both to rely in some measure on the results of my unpublished work in psychology and to think further about some of the problems with which I had dealt in it."

[42] Now in Hayek 2010, 74–166. Caldwell (2004a, 341) speaks of the *Scientism* essay as a "transition piece" that involved two different, but later gradually intertwining, programs. One of these led to *TSO*, the other to *The Constitution of Liberty*.

[43] In the preface to the 1976 edition, Hayek ([1944] 2007, 53) explains: "This book, written in my spare time from 1940 to 1943 . . . was caused by my annoyance with the complete misinterpretation in English 'progressive' circles of the character of the Nazi movement, an annoyance

the original 1944 edition (ibid., 37) he explicitly emphasized that it was meant as a "political book," the writing of which he had regarded "as a duty which I could not evade," even though he anticipated that it might "prejudice the reception of the more strictly academic work to which all my inclinations lead me."

The extraordinary, and for Hayek unexpected, public attention that *The Road to Serfdom* found,[44] especially in the United States,[45] brought Hayek numerous invitations and got him occupied in a series of public lectures, including a most successful lecture tour in 1945 in the United States.[46] Though, as he notes, "the financial temptation to do more semi-popular writing and lecturing was considerable" (Hayek 1994, 125), it was in this situation that Hayek came to the decision to seriously return to the psychology project he had abandoned in 1920. In retrospect he explained his decision as follows:

> I felt that this sort of popular lecturing and writing had a corrupting effect on one's mind and that in the long run I would do more for the political ideals I cared for if I stuck to strictly academic activities. . . . Some of my more leftish acquaintances (with considerable cheek) gave me to understand that in their opinion I had ceased to be a scientist and had become a propagandist. (1994, 125)

> After *The Road to Serfdom* I felt that I had so discredited myself professionally, I didn't want to give offense again. I wanted to be accepted in the scientific community. To do something purely scientific and independent of my economic view. (ibid., 152)

> At any rate, I decided that I would reward myself for what seemed to me a duty performed by completely disregarding for a time what was expected of me and doing exclusively what happened to interest me most at the moment. These were the old ideas on theoretical psychology, which had been revived

---

which led me from a memorandum to the then director of the London School of Economics, Sir William Beveridge, through an article in the *Contemporary Review* of 1938, which at the request of Professor Harry G. Gideonse of the University of Chicago I enlarged for publication in his Public Policy Pamphlets, and which, finally and reluctantly, . . . I expanded into this tract for the times." For the publication in the Public Policy Pamphlets see Hayek (1939) 1997.

[44] See Ebenstein 2001, 128ff.; 2003, 117ff.; Hennecke 2000, 182ff.

[45] As Hayek ([1944] 2007, 39) acknowledges in the foreword to the 1956 paperback edition, *The Road to Serfdom* owed its popularity in the United States not least to a condensed version published in 1945 in *Reader's Digest.*

[46] In the preface to the 1976 edition, Hayek ([1944] 2007, 55) remarks: "I have long resented being more widely known by what I regarded as a pamphlet for the time than by my strictly scientific work."

by the work on the methodology of the social sciences I had done during the early years of the war. (ibid., 125f.)[47]

Hayek seriously resumed work on the psychology project "in the spring and early summer of 1946" while he spent "two months each at the University of Chicago and Stanford University" (ibid., 125).[48] In December of 1947 he completed the second draft, entitled *What Is Mind? An Essay in Theoretical Psychology*,[49] of what was to become *TSO*, and in November of 1948 he noted in a letter that he was hoping to finish the final draft "this winter."[50] Yet he would be working on the book project for a few more years. In the summer of 1949 he presented a paper, *Das Wesen des Geistigen*, at the European Forum Alpbach in the Tyrolean Alps, in which he summarized the core message of his book.[51] Looking back in 1984 he recalls: "I brought a practically finished manuscript for *TSO* to Chicago when I moved there. The rest was revising."[52]

---

[47] Hayek (this volume, p. 384): "Only after I had . . . established a certain reputation as an economist—and had made myself unpopular with the majority of my fellow economists through an attack on socialism . . .—did I feel that I could afford to take out the old manuscript and see what I could do with it."

[48] From a letter he wrote to Otto Neurath (dated July 21, 1945, Hayek papers, box 40, folder 7, HIA) one can conclude that Hayek already started working on the psychology project in the summer of 1945. In his letter he writes: "I don't know yet whether before I am ready to start on the discussion you suggested I shall not ask you for your comments on what I am at the moment entirely engrossed in (an attempt to elaborate the psychological implications of the early part of my Sientism articles—or rather an attempt to re-state certain ideas I had formed on this subject a very long time ago)—at the moment at any rate I feel quite unable to give my mind to anything but these questions, but, of course, nothing may come of it." The "discussion" Hayek refers to is a project that Neurath had tried for some time to get an obviously reluctant Hayek to agree to. Neurath wanted it to be a definitive debate on their long-standing and fundamental disagreements on methodological issues. Otto Neurath died a few months after Hayek's letter, on December 22, 1945, and the discussion was never realized.

[49] Hayek papers, box 128, folder 35, HIA. On the title page it says in brackets: "Second draft up to chapter III, para 2, first draft thereafter; completed December 25, 1947." The first draft, entitled "What Is Mind? A working hypothesis on the origin of sensory qualities and abstract concepts" (Hayek papers, box 128, folder 34, HIA) lists 1945 as the year of completion.

[50] In a letter to John U. Nef (dated November 15, 1948, Hayek papers, box 39, folder 39, HIA), Hayek notes: "I hope you will not be disappointed by my book on mind when it appears. It . . . attempts to show in principle how in the physiological sphere an order may be created which is analogous to the order of mental events. . . . But I have been working on this on and off for something like twenty-eight years and the fourth and I hope final draft which I am trying to complete this winter ought to be fairly respectable." John U. Nef (1899–1988), an economic historian, was a cofounder of the Committee on Social Thought at the University of Chicago and instrumental in getting Hayek to join the Committee in 1950.

[51] An English translation, prepared by Dr. Grete Heinz, is included in the present volume, pp. 348–360. Bruce Caldwell (2004a, 261, fn. 2) briefly comments on the Alpbach lecture.

[52] Unpublished interview with W. W. Bartley, November 1984, Freiburg.

2. TSO: *Its Central Problem*

As noted above, one of the reasons for Hayek's decision to seek a career in economics instead of physiological psychology, his primary field of interest, was that when he was studying at the University of Vienna between 1918 and 1920, there was "just no teaching in psychology available" (this volume, p. 382). This was also the reason why he had to get his "knowledge of psychology from the books" (ibid.). Among the readings he chose—"without much guidance," as he notes[53]—he lists Wilhelm Wundt, William James, Johannes Müller, and Hermann von Helmholtz, emphasizing though that "the decisive stimulus for taking up the problem on which I soon started to work came from Ernst Mach" (ibid.).[54] In a short paper that he contributed to a conference on occasion of the fiftieth anniversary of Mach's death, Hayek ([1967b] 1992, 172ff.) reports:

> I no longer remember exactly how I happened to come across Mach almost immediately on my return from the battle lines in November 1918. . . . I know that I had been very engrossed in Mach's *Populärwissenschaftliche Vorlesungen, Die Mechanik in ihrer Entwicklung*, and particularly his *Analyse der Empfindungen* . . . . I was stimulated by Mach's work to study psychology and the physiology of the senses.[55]

After having taught physics for twenty-eight years at Charles University in Prague, Ernst Mach had come to the University of Vienna in 1895 to take the newly created chair in the History and Theory of Inductive Sciences. Mach's philosophy of science strongly influenced a number of young academics who formed the nucleus of what would later became known as the Vienna Circle (*Wiener Kreis*), a group that formed around Moritz Schlick, who joined the University of Vienna in 1922, taking the chair originally held by Mach.[56]

---

[53] This volume, p. 115.

[54] See also Hayek 1994, 62, and this volume, p. 382f., where Hayek includes G. E. Müller instead of Johannes Müller in his list. On the two Müllers, see below, preface, fn. 10; *TSO*, 1.32, fn. 17. On Ernst Mach—of whom Hayek (this volume, p. 383) speaks as "an only recently dead physicist to whose writings turned most of the young scientists, who then arrogantly regarded all non-positivist philosophy as absurd nonsense"—see below, preface, fn. 10.

[55] See Mach 1883, 1885, 1896.

[56] Between Mach and Schlick, the chair was held by L. Boltzmann and A. Stöhr (Kraft 1968, 1). Several members of the group founded the Ernst Mach Society (*Verein Ernst Mach*) in 1928 in honor of Ernst Mach. In 1929 the so-called "manifesto of the Vienna Circle" (*Wissenschaftliche Weltauffassung. Der Wiener Kreis*) was published, dedicated to Schlick in gratitude for his decision to refuse an offer from the University of Bonn and to remain in Vienna (Kraft 1968, 3).

Though Hayek developed his views on scientific method under the influence of Mach's philosophy[57] and was in close contact with members of the Vienna Circle,[58] it is his dissent with one of Mach's central tenets and his opposition to the positivism of his followers that is at the heart of his own physiological-psychological approach. Hayek has described his dissent with Mach as follows:

> Mach in his famous book *The Analysis of Sensations* explains or assumes that while all our individual sensations have an original pure quality, they are constantly modified by experience. There is only an original order and then the experiential change. Which led me to the conclusion that if you can show that experience can change the thing, why need there be an original quality? The original quality may have arisen in the same fashion.[59]

While agreeing with Mach's view on the relational or connectionist nature of sense perceptions, what Hayek objected to was the claim that "pure, simple sensations are the elements of our entire sensory perceptions" (Hayek [1967b] 1992, 174). A consistent application of Mach's own analysis rendered, as he put it, the concept of such "elements" superfluous.

[57] Hayek ([1967b] 1992, 174): "One might say that for a young man interested in philosophical questions who came to the University of Vienna right after the war . . . and for whom orthodox philosophy was not appealing, Mach offered the only viable alternative."

[58] Hayek ([1943] 2014, 78f.): "Not only was my first technical training largely scientific in the narrow sense of the word but also what little training I had in philosophy or scientific method was entirely in the school of Ernst Mach and later of the logical positivists."—Hayek (1983b, 16ff.): "I think my introduction to what I now almost hesitate to call philosophy—scientific method, I think, is a better description—was through Machian philosophy. It . . . dominated discussion in Vienna. . . . While I was still at the university, this very interesting figure, Moritz Schlick, became one of the professors of philosophy. It was the beginning of the Vienna circle, of which I was, of course, never a member, but whose members were in close contact with us. . . . What dissuaded me is that the social scientists, the science specialists in the tradition of Otto Neurath, just were so extreme and so naïve on economics; it was actually through them that I became aware that positivism was just misleading in the social sciences. I owe it to Neurath's extreme position that I recognized it wouldn't do. And it took me a long time, really, to emancipate myself from it." Elsewhere Hayek ([1967b] 1992, 174) notes about Neurath: "Another stumbling block was that he [Mach] was being exploited too explicitly to support a socialist approach . . . particularly by Otto Neurath, one of the founders of the later Vienna circle. Neurath hoped to convert Mach's positivism . . . into a physicalism or, as he called it at times, a scientism." On Hayek's aversion to Neurath's physicalism see also Hayek, this volume, p. 301 fn. 15; and Kreuzer 1983, 13.

[59] Hayek—North/Skousen interview (1985). Quoted from Ebenstein 2003, 134f. Hayek supplements the quoted statement by the comment: "So it was only a step beyond Mach, which turns against him with the result that my own psychology developed. In this sense I began from the same thing on which the logical positivist [movement]—Schlick, Neurath, Carnap, and so on—developed from Vienna; but split at the base, led us apart very much. But these two apparently absolutely contrary trends come from a common initial viewpoint" (ibid.).

I had the revelation that Mach's concept of 'simple and pure sensations' in his sensory psychology was actually meaningless. Since Mach had qualified so many of the connections between sensations as "relations," I was finally forced to conclude that the whole structure of the sensory world was derived from "relations" and that one might therefore throw out altogether the concept of pure and simple sensations, which plays such a large role in Mach. (ibid.)[60]

Against a Machian "absolute theory of sensations," Hayek proposes in his 1920 paper a "relative theory of sensations" according to which "we can never speak of a psychic atom or element: each consciousness content is relative and changeable" (this volume, p. 332). "The psychic content of an impulse," so he argues, "depends not on the impulse as such but on how it resonates with other impulses. . . . For this reason this content is not fully predetermined and unchanging. On the contrary, it is perpetually in flux and is dependent on the individual's entire past" (ibid.).[61]

In contrast to Mach—for whom the "only 'things' we know are sensations (sense data): colors, sounds, temperatures, pressures, odours, time and space sensations"[62]—Hayek insists on the need to distinguish between a *physical* and a *phenomenal* world, between the external world of objective facts and the inner world of our subjective experience.[63] The need to draw this distinction, so Hayek argues, has been made apparent by the "progress of the physical sciences," which, in "order to be able to give a satisfactory account of the regu-

[60] Hayek recalls here the conclusion he had already drawn in the concluding sentences of his 1920 paper (this volume, p. 347). See also Hayek's remark in his preface to *TSO* (this volume, p. 118) and in his "*The Sensory Order* after 25 Years" (this volume, p. 383).

[61] Arguing against the concept of unchangeable "elementary sensations," Hayek stresses that all sensations, including the most elementary, are based on past experience and that "the apparatus by means of which we learn about the external world is itself a product of a kind of experience" (*TSO*, 8.1 [here and from now on citations from *TSO* will be identified by paragraph numbers]), the experience accumulated in the evolutionary past of the species.

[62] De Vries 1994, 316f. De Vries (ibid.) quotes Mach's statement "Bodies do not produce sensations, but complexes of sensations make up bodies." On Mach's view that "colors, sounds, spaces, times, . . . are provisionally the ultimate elements, whose given connections it is our business to investigate," see Bartley 1987, 11ff. See also Popper ([1953b] 1989, 173): "Mach . . . believed in . . . the view that physical things are bundles, or complexes, or constructs of phenomenal *qualities*, of particular experienced colors, noises, etc.; Mach . . . suggests that there is nothing at all behind them."

[63] Of the theory developed in *TSO*, Hayek says that by "destroying the conception of elementary and constant sensations as ultimate constituents of the world, it restores the necessity of a belief in an objective world which is different from that presented to us by our senses" (*TSO*, 8.37).

larities existing in the physical world . . . have been forced . . . more and more to disregard the way in which these objects appear to us" (*TSO*, 1.6).[64] While in the phenomenal or sensory order[65] events are classified in terms of their *effects on our senses* (i.e., "according to their sense properties such as colors, sounds, odours, feelings of touch, etc." [*TSO*, 1.7]), the physical sciences classify the same events in terms of their *effects on each other*.[66]

In his *Scientism* essay of the early 1940s, which marked his first return to his abandoned psychology project, Hayek (2010) paid considerable attention to the issue of the difference between the ways in which "our senses arrange external stimuli" (84) and the ways in which physical science organizes "all our experience of the external world" (87).[67] To the extent that science "replaces the system of classification which our sense qualities represent" (83) we must realize, Hayek argued, that "although there will usually exist some objective justification why we regard certain things as similar, this need not always be the case" (112), "that things which appear to us the same do not always behave in the same manner, and that things which appear different to us sometimes

[64] "By saying that there 'exists' an 'objective' world different from the phenomenal world we are merely stating that it is possible to construct an order or classification of events which is different from that which our senses show us and which enables us to give a more consistent account of the behavior of the different events in that world" (*TSO*, 8.29). It is worth noting that Konrad Lorenz in a 1941 article, of which Hayek probably knew, has argued similarly: "The reproductions of the world by our forms of intuition and categories break down as soon as they are required to give a somewhat closer representation of their objects, as is the case in wave mechanics and nuclear physics" (Lorenz [1941] 1982, 128). I shall return to Lorenz's article and its significance for Hayek's arguments below, pp. 42f.

[65] Hayek (*TSO*, 1.10) notes that he employs "the term 'sensory' as equivalent to phenomenal, especially (as in the title of this book) in the phrase 'sensory order.'"

[66] Hayek (2010, 84): "This process of reclassifying 'objects' which our senses have already classified in one way . . . is, perhaps, the most characteristic aspect of the procedure of the natural sciences. The whole history of modern Science proves to be a process of progressive emancipation from our innate classification of the external stimuli till in the end they completely disappear. . . . The new world which man thus creates in his mind, and which consists entirely of entities which cannot be perceived by our senses, is yet in a definite way related to the world of our senses. It serves, indeed, to explain the world of our senses."—"The point which we mainly wanted to stress was that what men know or think about the external world or about themselves, their concepts and even the subjective qualities of their sense perceptions are to Science never ultimate reality, data to be accepted. . . . The concepts which men actually employ, the way in which they see nature, is to the scientist necessarily a provisional affair and his task is to change this picture, to change the concepts in use so as to be able to make more definite and more certain statements about the new classes of events" (ibid., 86).

[67] See Hayek 2010, 81ff., 88ff.,108ff. Hayek (ibid., 84) quotes in this context L. S. Stebbing's (*Thinking to Some Purpose*,1939, 107) statement that "physical science has now reached a stage of development that renders it impossible to express observable occurrences in language appropriate to what is perceived by our senses." On Stebbing see below, fn. 134.

prove in all other respects to behave in the same way" (83).[68] The difference that, in this sense, exists between the physical order and the phenomenal order is, according to Hayek, "an important empirical fact which, on the one hand, demands explanation (a task for psychology) and which, on the other hand, must be accepted as a basic datum in our study of people's conduct" (109).[69]

As Hayek emphasizes, the fact that in pursuit of their explanatory ambitions the physical sciences have come to disregard more and more the way our senses perceive the world does, of course, not mean that the phenomenal or sensory order simply vanishes as a subject of scientific inquiry.[70] Instead, its study "has become the exclusive task of psychology" (*TSO*, 1.17), the task of explaining why "that apparatus of classification . . . which our senses constitute" (Hayek 2010, 104) makes us perceive events as it does, and what this means for the study of human action.[71] It is this very issue—the question of how it is that we come to form in our mind a "sensory picture of the world" that serves "to guide us more or less successfully in our environment" (this volume, p. 383)—that *TSO* is meant to address. As Hayek puts it, "the central problem of this book" (*TSO*, 1.10) is to explain the relation between the "microcosm" in the brain and the "macrocosm" of the external world. In paragraph 1.49 of *TSO*, he provides a concise statement of this problem:

> *What we call 'mind' is thus a particular order of a set of events taking place in some organism and in some manner related to but not identical with the physical order of events in the environment.* The problem which the existence of mental phenomena raises is therefore how in a part of the physical order (namely an organism) a subsystem can be formed which in some sense (yet to be more fully defined) may be said to reflect some features of the physical order as a whole, and

---

[68] Hayek (2010, 85 fn.): "We have no evidence for the assumption that the things in the external world in their relation to each other differ or are similar in the way our senses suggest to us. In fact we have in many instances evidence to the contrary."

[69] Hayek (2010, 113): "Although we should know that a different arrangement of the facts of nature is more appropriate for explaining external events, in interpreting human action we should still have to use the classification in which these facts appear in the minds of the acting people."

[70] Hayek (this volume, p. 351): "The elimination of sensory qualities from the physical world view does not simultaneously eliminate them as a scientific problem. . . . At the same time that the system of sensory qualities disappears from physics, it becomes a problem in psychology."

[71] Hayek (*TSO*, 1.13): "The task of the physical sciences is to replace that classification of events which our senses perform but which proves inadequate to describe the regularities in these events, by a classification which will put us in a better position to do so. The task of theoretical psychology is the converse one of explaining why these events, which on the basis of their relations to each other can be arranged in a certain (physical) order, manifest a different order in their effect on our senses." In retrospect Hayek (this volume, p. 387) has called this statement "perhaps the most basic contention in my book."

which thereby enables the organism which contains such a partial reproduction of the environmental order to behave appropriately towards its surroundings.[72]

3. TSO: *Its Theoretical Core*

When he returned to his student-days project in the 1940s and examined the psychological literature, Hayek found to his surprise, so he reports, that *on the purely theoretical level* the issue he had been concerned with "had remained pretty much in the same state" (preface, this volume, p. 119).[73] He felt thereby encouraged in his belief that, though an outsider, he may have something of importance to say, at least as far as the "statement of the problem" and "the general principles of its solution" are concerned (this volume, p. 120).

As Hayek (this volume, p. 382) has noted in retrospect, what motivated his own theoretical outlook was his initial rejection of an, in his view, naïve empiricism, in particular the claim that "experience begins with the reception of sensory data possessing constant qualities which either reflect . . . or are uniquely correlated with . . . attributes of the elements of the physical world" (*TSO*, 8.3). Such a naïve empiricism ignored, in his view, the very question that must be answered once we acknowledge that there is no "original pure core of sensations" (*TSO*, 2.15), namely how "a given physical situation is transformed into a certain phenomenal picture" (*TSO*, 1.19).[74] Answering this question requires us, he specifies (*TSO*, 2.7), to account for the relations between three different "orders":

1. The physical order of the external world, or the physical stimuli . . .
2. The neural order of the fibers, and of the impulses proceeding in these fibers . . .
3. The mental or phenomenal order of sensations (and other mental qualities).

---

[72] In his lecture "What Is Mind?" (this volume, p. 351), Hayek notes: "Once we . . . manage to show how an organism within nature learns to differentiate or organize in a particular way what goes on in his surroundings, as we do with our senses, the larger part of our problem will have been solved."

[73] See also Hayek, this volume, p. 384.

[74] "Psychology must . . . try to reconstruct the process by which the organism classifies the physical events in the manner which is familiar to us as the order of sensory qualities" (*TSO*, 1.21). In § 14 of the 1947 typescript "What Is Mind?," Hayek had noted: "Any real attempt to link our knowledge of mental processes with our scientific picture of the physical world must therefore start from a description of the physical stimuli . . . and would then have to proceed to show how our nervous system differentiates between these stimuli in the manner which is familiar to us from our experience of sensory qualities."

In other words, according to Hayek, what needs to be explained is how the effects that physical stimuli cause in the nervous system (the "neural order") give rise to the sensations of our subjective experience.[75]

The explanation Hayek proposed in his 1920 typescript and elaborated more fully in *TSO* falls, in the terminology of modern psychology, under the rubric "connectionism."[76] Hayek's principle claim has been summarized by Gerald Edelman (1987, 25) as follows:

> He made a quite fruitful suggestion, made contemporaneously by the psychologist Donald Hebb, that whatever kind of encounter the sensory system has with the world, a corresponding event between a particular cell in the brain and some other cell carrying the information from the outside world must result in reinforcement of the connection between those two cells. These days, this is known as a Hebbesian synapse, but von Hayek quite independently came upon the idea.[77]

Already in his 1920 paper (this volume, p. 324) Hayek had stated this claim quite explicitly:

---

[75] In similar terms, G. Edelman (2004, xiii) describes as the aim of his own explanatory project: "A scientific analysis of consciousness must answer the question: How can the firing of neurons give rise to subjective sensations, thoughts, and emotions? To some, the two domains are so disparate as to be irreconcilable. A scientific explanation must provide a causal account of the connection between these two domains so that properties in one domain may be understood in terms of events in the other. This is the task I have set myself in this small book."

[76] G. Gaus (2006, 248): "Hayek is recognized today as an early neural network modeler. Neural network theory, or connectionism, can be seen as a development of the associationist psychologies . . . according to which thoughts are connected by the laws of association (such as similarity, continuity, and so on). . . . Unlike traditional associationism, connectionism abjures any appeal to primitive qualitative differences between sensations and thoughts. Connectionist systems are composed purely of neurons [and] . . . qualitative differences . . . are the result of a complex pattern of neural activation." On the relation between his own theoretical outlook and "the basic ideas of the old association psychology," Hayek (*TSO*, 7.16) comments: "Our view agrees, of course, with associationism in the endeavor to trace all mental properties to connections established by experience between certain elements. It differs from it by regarding the elements between which such connections are established as not themselves mental in character but as material events which only through those connections are arranged in a new order in which they obtain the special significance characteristic of mental events."

[77] On D. O. Hebb see below, preface, fn. 12. Hebb (1949, 62, 70) summarizes the principal claims of his theory as follows: "When an axon of cell A is near enough to excite a cell B and repeatedly or persistently takes part in firing it, some growth process or metabolic change takes place in one or both cells that A's efficiency, as one of the cells firing B, is increased. . . . The general idea is . . . that any two cells or systems of cells that are repeatedly active at the same time will tend to become 'associated,' so that activity in one facilitates activity in the other." Hayek notes in the preface (this volume, p. 120) that the final version of *TSO* "was practically finished" when Hebb's *The Organization of Behavior* appeared. While he acknowledged that Hebb with "much greater technical competence . . . worked out the physiological details," Hayek credits his own book with stating "the general principles of the theory" more clearly.

> The simultaneous excitation of two ganglion cells in the brain forges a permanent connection between the two cells, so that future excitation of one cell also stimulates the other cell. . . . Keeping in mind that organisms are never bombarded by just a single stimulus but always by a large number of stimuli, and that on these occasions linkages are always created between ganglion cells, we realize that during an individual's entire life span each of these cells nearly continuously acquires new linkages, that old linkages are reinforced as well. . . . Each ganglion cell thus has a large number of unique linkages, so that a whole network of linkages will spread between the cells, whose ordering will reflect the relative strength or weakness of the linkages.

The brain is in Hayek's account a vast network of connections among a myriad of cells, "connections through which impulses are transmitted" and which "are created as a result of the simultaneous occurrence of sensory impulses" (*TSO*, 2.47). The linkages between the neurons reflect in their strength (i.e., their probability to transmit excitations from one cell to another) "the relative frequency with which in the history of the organism the different groups of internal and external stimuli have acted together" (*TSO*, 3.34).[78] Against the view that mental qualities are "originally attached to . . . the individual physiological impulses," he maintains that these qualities are "determined by the system of connections," and the individual impulse is given its distinctive quality by its position "in the whole system of . . . connections" (*TSO*, 2.49).[79]

The "history of the organism" of which Hayek speaks is meant to include the "combined experience" (*TSO*, 2.16) of the individual and the species.[80] It includes the experience the individual accumulates during its personal history as well as the "experience" the species has accumulated during its evolutionary past. The first is embodied in patterns of linkages in its central nervous system, the second is incorporated in the organism's genetic endowment, in particular in the sensory organs (i.e., the apparatus through which the individual can only gain experience).[81] The system of connections between nerve

---

[78] The phrase "internal and external stimuli" refers to the fact that the "'physical environment' within which the central nervous system operates includes the *milieu intérieur*, i.e., the organism itself in so far as it acts independently of the higher nervous centres" (*TSO*, 2.49).

[79] When *TSO* was published, it was this claim that distinguished, in Hayek's view, his "theory of the determination of mental qualities . . . from the position taken by practically all current psychological theories" (*TSO*, 2.49). In a footnote he added: "The closest approximation to the theory developed here seems to have been reached by D. O. Hebb, 1949, a work which came to my knowledge only after the present book was completed in all essentials."

[80] "The whole sensory order can be conceived as having been built up by the experience of the race or the individual, i.e. it is based on the retention of connections between effects exercised upon them by the external world" (*TSO*, 5.15).

[81] Hayek notes that, when applied to the evolution of the species, the term "experience" is "somewhat ambiguous and misleading, because it suggests the occurrence of sensory qualities,

cells that determines how an organism records newly arriving stimuli is thus composed of "innate" linkages, reflecting the heritage of the species' evolutionary past, and of "learned" linkages, reflecting the individual's personal history.[82]

Central to Hayek's connectionist theory of the mind is the notion that the "transmission of impulses from neuron to neuron within the central nervous system" can be "conceived as constituting an *apparatus of classification*" (*TSO*, 2.48).[83] The manner in which, according to the relative strengths of the respective linkages, impulses are transmitted within the system of connections provides, so Hayek conjectures, the answer to the question of how the neural system is "capable of performing such discrimination in its responses to stimuli as we know our mind in fact to perform" (*TSO*, 2.31). The differentiation—or classification[84]—of stimuli occurs by the different paths the impulses that the stimuli trigger "travel" from neuron to neuron within the neural system, in correspondence to the strength of the respective linkages.

The classification that occurs by the transmission of impulses along different paths in the central nervous system can be repeated on "many superimposed levels of connections" (*TSO*, 3.3). Impulses "which do not uniquely correspond to particular stimulations of sensory receptors but which represent merely common qualities attributed to the primary impulses . . . will," so Hayek argues, "in turn become the object of further processes of classification; the classes for which they stand will be further grouped into classes of classes, and this process can be repeated on many successive levels" (*TSO*, 3.54). Speaking of "the whole hierarchy of the apparatus of classification which culminates in the conscious mind," (*TSO*, 5.31) he concludes that the central nervous system can thus be interpreted "as an apparatus of multiple classification . . . on many levels . . . , applied in the first instance to all sensory perception but in principle to all the kinds of mental entities . . . that we

---

while the phenomenon with which we are concerned is a kind of pre-sensory experience which only creates the apparatus which later makes qualitative distinctions possible" (*TSO*, 5.7).

[82] "The creation of connections, or experience, arranges originally meaningless physiological processes whereby stimuli are recorded in the brain by way of connections of different strengths into a structural network within which they occupy a specific position contingent on the conditions of their occurrence. . . . It is experience that creates and enlarges this system. The processes taking place within it refer back to prior relationships between experiences. One might justly say that each human being thinks with his past" (this volume, p. 329).

[83] Emphasis added. Such transmission, Hayek adds, "may either take place between different neurons carrying primary impulses, or between such neurons and other ('internuncial') neurons which are not directly connected with receptor organs" (*TSO*, 2.48).

[84] "By 'classification' we shall mean a process in which on each occasion on which a certain recurring event happens it produces the same specific effect. . . . All the different events which whenever they occur produce the same effect will be said to be events of the same class" (*TSO*, 2.34).

find to occur in the mental universe."[85] Such different mental phenomena "as sensation, perception, concepts, and ideas" have, according to Hayek (2010, 111, fn.), all "in common that they are classifications of possible external stimuli (or complexes of such stimuli)."[86] The same principle, he posits—namely the classification of impulses in the central nervous system—can thus help explain all kinds of behavioral phenomena from simple reflexes to conscious action.[87]

If the neural system is conceived as an apparatus of classification, it follows that what an organism can perceive must be limited by the capacity of its classificatory apparatus. Whether and how stimuli arriving from the external world are recorded is contingent in the first place on the nature of the sensory organs: the organism can only perceive what its innate sensory apparatus is capable of recording.[88] It is limited also by the system of connections that incorporates the individual's past experiences.[89] Perception is thus always *selective* and *interpretative*. It is *selective* in singling out only those aspects of a complex reality that the organism's—inborn and learned—classificatory apparatus is capable of recording. And it is *interpretative* in the sense of locating stimuli within the framework of an experience-based system of connections.[90]

---

[85] Hayek, this volume, p. 385. In the 1947 typescript *What Is Mind?* (§ 371), Hayek states: "If . . . we regard the phenomena variously known as discrimination and equivalence, generalization and abstraction . . . as the essential types of mental phenomena, and show how they all can be regarded as different manifestations of the same process of classification . . . , we are in fact already very near an explanation of the principle involved." See also below, *TSO*, 7.2.

[86] "The operation of both the senses and the intellect are equally based on acts of classification (or reclassification) performed by the central nervous system" (*TSO*, 5.19).—"The formation of abstract concepts thus constitutes a repetition on a higher level of the same kind of process of classification by which the differences between the sensory qualities are determined" (*TSO*, 6.47).

[87] As Hayek puts it, between simple reflexes "as the one ideal type and the other extreme of the 'voluntary' or 'conscious' responses there exists probably a continuous range of connections between stimuli and responses of intermediate types in which processes of classification take place" (*TSO*, 4.27).—"While the full and detailed classification of sensory impulses, . . . which we know from conscious experience, is effected mainly at the highest centers, we must assume a more limited classification on somewhat similar principles to take place already on the lower levels, where certainly no conscious experience is associated with it" (*TSO*, 5.31).—"There . . . exist many forms intermediate between fully conscious and fully unconscious mental events which make this difference one of degree" (*TSO*, 6.6).

[88] "The organism possesses receptor organs which are sensitive for only certain kinds of external events but not for others; and these receptor organs which it does possess also do not sharply distinguish between stimuli which are physically different. . . . Which external events are recorded at all, and how they will be recorded, will thus depend on the given structure of the organism as it has been shaped by the process of evolution" (*TSO*, 5.20).

[89] "The conscious mind can know of the external world only in terms of the classes which earlier experience has created" (*TSO*, 6.45).

[90] His whole theory, Hayek notes, "might indeed be said . . . [to be] no more than an extension and systematic development of the widely held view that every sensation contains elements

Accordingly, so Hayek (2010, 111) concludes, "the qualities which we perceive are not properties of the objects but ways in which we . . . have learned to group or classify external stimuli. To perceive is to assign a familiar category (or categories): we could not perceive anything completely different from everything else we have perceived before."

The system of connections that reflects the evolutionary past of the species and the learning history of the individual gains its significance, as Hayek reasons, from the fact that it enables organisms "within themselves to reproduce (or 'build models of') some of the relations which exist between events in their environment" (*TSO*, 1.20).[91] The process of classification and reclassification produces in the central nervous system an—however imperfect— "internal representation" of the external world that serves the organism as guide in the environment in which it lives.[92] As experience accumulates, the internal representation—or, as Hayek calls it, "the microcosm in the brain" (*TSO*, 5.19)—is more and more adapted to relevant contingencies in the environment—or again, as Hayek calls it, "the macrocosm of the external world" (ibid.), the criterion of "relevance" being "the pragmatic needs of the individual and the species" (*TSO*, 6.47).[93] Hayek speaks of a "gradual approximation" of the mental order "to the order which in the external world exists between the stimuli evoking the impulses which 'represent' them in the nervous system" (*TSO*, 5.19).

The adaptation of the "microcosm in the brain" to the "macrocosm of the external world" occurs through the strengthening or weakening of connections, according to how well they work in guiding action. Connections that lead to expectations from which "rewarding" behavioral consequences result are thereby reinforced while disappointed expectations result in a weakening of the respective connections.[94] The apparatus of classification, which the system of connections constitutes, is thus constantly evolving in a process of continuous reorganization or reclassification.[95] It is subject to ever new revisions

---

of interpretation based on learning, an extension by which the *whole* of the sensory qualities is accounted for as such an interpretation" (*TSO*, 2.17).

[91] "The connections formed by the linkages between different impulses will evidently reproduce certain regularities in the occurrence of the external stimuli acting on the organism" (*TSO*, 5.17).

[92] "This 'classification' . . . of the stimuli by the organism can be said to 'reproduce' the 'objective' relations between those stimuli in the physical world" (*TSO*, 5.19).

[93] "The structure of connections in the nervous system is modified by every new action exercised upon it by the external world" (*TSO*, 5.66).

[94] "The experience that the classification based on past linkages does not always work, i.e. does not always lead to valid predictions, forces us to revise that classification" (*TSO*, 8.14).

[95] "The reclassification, or breaking up of the classes formed by . . . our discrimination of sensory qualities, and the replacement of these classes by new classes . . . will occur whenever the expectations resulting from the existing classification are disappointed, or when beliefs so far held are disproved by new experiences. The immediate effects of such conflicting experiences

that, as Hayek puts it, are "forced on us because we find that the classification of objects and events which our senses effect is only a rough and imperfect approximation to a reproduction of the differences between the physical objects which would enable us correctly to predict their behavior" (*TSO*, 6.47).

In reference to the "microcosm in the brain" that reproduces the "macrocosm of the external world," Hayek distinguishes more specifically between what he terms the "map" and the "model." While both are "reproductions of relations between events in the outside world" (*TSO*, 5.41), they provide, as Hayek emphasizes, different kinds of information about the "macrocosm." The "map" designates "the semi-permanent apparatus of classification" (*TSO*, 5.89), reflecting "the relationships between various kinds of events in the external world, which the linkages will gradually produce in the higher nervous centers" (*TSO*, 5.26). It provides "a theory of how the world works" (*TSO*, 5.89), representing "the kind of world in which the organism has existed in the past, or the different *kinds* of stimuli which have acquired significance for it" (*TSO*, 5.42). By contrast, the "model" represents and provides "information about the particular environment in which the organism is placed at the moment" (ibid.). While the "map" provides information about *general properties* of the kind of world in which the organism lives, the "model" provides information about the *specific circumstances* the organism finds itself confronted with in particular situations. Or, in Hayek's wording, "the 'map,' the semi-permanent apparatus of classification, provides the different generic elements from which the models of particular situations are built" (*TSO*, 5.89).[96]

By combining the theory about "how the world works" with the information about the specifics of particular situations, the organism is able to build an internal representation or model of its environment which, as Hayek puts it, will "constantly tend to run ahead of the situation," anticipating "future events in the environments" (*TSO*, 5.58).[97] The internal representations can serve to guide behavior by not only representing "the actually existing environment; but also . . . the changes to be expected in that environment" (*TSO*, 5.59).[98] Summarizing his argument, Hayek notes:

---

will be to introduce inconsistent elements into the model of the external world; and such inconsistencies can be eliminated only if what formerly were treated as elements of the same class are now treated as elements of different classes" (*TSO*, 8.15).

[96] In reference to "the model" Hayek notes: "Its nature is, of course, limited by the possibilities which the structural 'map' provides, by the connections or channels which exist" (*TSO*, 5.44).

[97] "Correct anticipation of future events in the environment . . . implies that there exists inside the structure a system of relationships between events caused by the external circumstances which is in some measure structurally equivalent to the system of relationships which exists between those external events. Such an internal structure which reproduces some of the relations between the outside events we have called a model" (*TSO*, 5.85).

[98] "This representation of the possible results following from the existing position will, of course, be constantly checked and corrected by the newly arriving sensory signals which record the actual development in the environment" (*TSO*, 5.58).

The representation of the existing situation in fact cannot be separated from, and has no significance apart from, the representation of the consequences to which it is likely to lead. Even on a pre-conscious level the organism must live as much in a world of expectation as in a world of "fact," and most responses to a given stimulus are probably determined only *via* fairly complex processes of "trying out" on the model the effects to be expected from alternative courses of action. (*TSO*, 5.61)

Hayek's arguments on the role that internal representations or models of the external world play in guiding behavior are of particular interest with regard to the question on which the following sections will focus: the significance of *TSO* in providing a theoretical foundation for Hayek's socioeconomic theory. As I will seek to demonstrate, the notion of behavior-guiding "internal models" is at the very core of Hayek's theory of rule-governed behavior, which in turn is at the center of his thoughts on social order and cultural evolution.

4. TSO *and the "Knowledge Problem"*

As noted before, to Hayek's disappointment his work on the "Foundations of Theoretical Psychology" for a long time found only marginal attention, among psychologists as well as among his academic peers in the social sciences. Even scholars with a particular interest in Hayek's work have only recently begun to look more closely at his treatise on cognitive theory that, on the surface, appears so far apart from the main body of his socioeconomic and political-philosophical oeuvre. In fact, among them there is still some controversy about the significance of *TSO* for a full appreciation of Hayek's theoretical heritage.

Authors such as Edward Feser and William Butos, who have specifically published on *TSO*, voice skepticism in this regard. In Feser's (2006, 287) view, "its status as the 'foundation' for Hayek's economics and politics has . . . been exaggerated," and in his editor's introduction to a volume specifically dedicated to the subject, Butos (2010b, 10) notes that "the relevance of Hayek's cognitive theory for social theory remains controversial and unsettled." In the same volume, Daniel D'Amico and Peter Boettke (2010, 358), admitting that "it is important to read Hayek in full in order to digest the complete message of his work," argue that "it is an overstatement to herald *TSO* as an essential foundation of Hayek's economics."[99]

---

[99] D'Amico and Boettke (2010, 358) add: "We do not think that Hayek's own thinking was developed in this manner, nor is such a foundational arrangement essential to understanding

Other commentators have taken the opposite view. In reference to *TSO*, Walter Weimer speaks of "the essential continuity in Hayek's thought" (1982, 241), noting that the "psychology" contained in it "is part and parcel" of his economics (Weimer 2011, xxvi). Jack Birner, one of the first economists who took notice of *TSO*, posits that without Hayek's cognitive theory "most of the rest of his work cannot be understood" (Birner 1999, 44). For John Gray (1984, 3), a "careful investigation of its argument is indispensable for any adequate understanding of Hayek's work." Leland Yeager ([1984] 2011) holds that "fully appreciating Hayek's work requires knowing of his interest in psychology." For Raimondo Cubeddu (2002, 128), *TSO* constitutes "the theoretical link between Hayek's different interests within the social sciences" and it "is fundamental in understanding the evolution of his ideas." Similarly, for Gerald Steele (2002, 387), who has written extensively on the subject, it is "a basis for the fullest understanding of Hayek's intellectual contribution in economics, epistemology, ethics, jurisprudence and politics." And Steven Horwitz (2000, 23) considers Hayek's treatise on theoretical psychology "crucial for understanding his economics and politics."

I submit that if Hayek were to judge between the two groups of commentators, he would clearly side with the latter. Looking back at the development of his thought, he has repeatedly stressed how important, in his assessment, his excursion into the foundations of theoretical psychology has been. Referring to his 1920 paper that he wrote when he was "still uncertain whether to become an economist or a psychologist," he notes in his preface to *TSO*: "But though my work has led me away from psychology, the basic idea then conceived has continued to occupy me; . . . it has often proved helpful in dealing with the problems of the methods of the social sciences."[100] Years later, responding to an interviewer's suggestion that "*TSO* is not really independent" of his economics, Hayek said: "Of course. One sees this in retrospect rather than while one is doing it. I must say that the insights I gained . . . both from the first stage in 1920 or later in the 1940s . . . shaped my thinking. But it works both ways. What I'd done in economics helped me to do this biological work as much as the opposite" (Hayek 1984, 153). His most detailed comment on this issue appears, hidden in a footnote, in his epilogue to the third volume of *Law, Legislation and Liberty*:

Hayek's general theory." They suggest "the alternative position—it is Hayek's vision of the working of the economy that is the key to understanding his theoretical psychology" (ibid., 360). The reversal of the "foundational" status is in apparent conflict, though, with the simple fact that Hayek drafted his cognitive theory before he decided, for pragmatic reasons (see above, p. 8), to seek a degree in economics and law instead of continuing his study of psychology.

[100] This volume, p. 115. Bruce Caldwell (1997, 1856) reports that in a letter to John Nef on November 6, 1948, Hayek had described his work on what was to become *TSO* as "the most important thing I have yet done."

My colleagues in the social sciences generally find my study on *TSO* . . . uninteresting or indigestible. But the work on it has helped me greatly to clear my mind on much that is very relevant to social theory. My conception of evolution, of a spontaneous order and of the methods and limits of our endeavors to explain complex phenomena have been formed largely in the course of the work on that book. As I was using the work I had done in my student days on theoretical psychology in forming my views on the methodology of the social science, so the working out of my earlier ideas on psychology with the help of what I had learned in the social science helped me greatly in all my later scientific development. It involved the sort of radical departure from received thinking of which one is more capable at the age of 21 than later. (Hayek 1979, 199f., fn. 26)

In the remainder of this introduction, my aim is to detail the reasons why *TSO* indeed provides, as characterized by Hayek himself, an essential *foundation* of his comprehensive social theory, covering economics, law, politics, and philosophy.[101] As I shall argue, the essential link that connects his contributions in these fields with his thoughts on the "Foundations of Theoretical Psychology" must be seen in the role that the so-called "knowledge problem" plays as the focal theme around which Hayek's oeuvre revolves. In emphasizing the intrinsic link between *TSO* and Hayek's concern with the "knowledge problem," I am in agreement with Bruce Caldwell (1997, 1856), who argues likewise that "the book provides a theoretical basis for the 'limitations of knowledge' theme that has been recurrent in Hayek's work."[102]

It has often been observed that Hayek's concern with the "knowledge problem" is the underlying theme of his entire work,[103] a theme that he prominently addressed in his Nobel lecture, "The Pretense of Knowledge" ([1975] 2014). Equally often observed has been the fact that Hayek first explicitly addressed the "knowledge problem" in "Economics and Knowledge," the presidential address he presented in November of 1936 to the London Economics Club and subsequently published in the February 1937 issue of *Economica*.[104] In

---

[101] In his previously (see above, fn. 10) quoted letter to Walter Weimer of January 16, 1983 (Hayek papers, box 57, folder 2, HIA), in which he expressed his disappointment about Karl Popper's unsympathetic reaction to *TSO*, Hayek states: "For me . . . it is becoming more and more clear that it is the foundation of all my thinking."

[102] For Caldwell (ibid., 1873), it is "a key for comprehending the nature and extent of Hayek's divergence from mainstream economics." See also Caldwell 2004b.

[103] Walter Weimer (1982, 263) holds that "Hayek is at all times an epistemologist, especially when doing technical economics, and even in his historical and popular writings. The subject matter of epistemology is the theory of knowledge—its nature, manner of acquisition, and how it is embodied."

[104] Now published in F. A. Hayek, *The Market and Other Orders*, ed. Bruce Caldwell, vol. XV of *The Collected Works of F. A. Hayek* (Chicago: University of Chicago Press, 2014), 57–76.

September of 1936, two months prior to delivering his presidential address, Hayek had presented a lecture in German under the same title, "Wirschafts-theorie und Wissen," in Vienna. Alfred Schütz, who had attended the lecture, sent Hayek an extensive comment,[105] along with a letter dated October 15, 1936, in which he mentions that Hayek had "kindly given" him the manuscript.[106] Schütz also sent his comment to Ludwig von Mises, Felix Kaufmann, and Fritz Machlup,[107] which may indicate that they also had attended Hayek's lecture. Hayek knew Kaufmann and Machlup as well as Schütz from his time in Vienna as coparticipants in a private discussion group, called *Geistkreis*, and as participants in the Mises seminar, which Hayek joined in 1924 after his return from his fifteen-month-long study-visit to New York.[108] Reporting on his memories of the Mises seminar, Hayek ([1963a] 1992, 27) specifically mentions "Felix Kaufmann, who was mainly a philosopher," and "Alfred Schütz, who was mainly a sociologist," for giving the discussions in the seminar "their special character."[109] Another member of the *Geistkreis* and participant in the Mises seminar was Oskar Morgenstern.[110] He had published in 1934 an essay, "Vollkommene Voraussicht und wirtschaftliches Gleichgewicht,"[111] in which he discussed the role of the perfect knowledge assumption in economic theory, addressing a theme that, as Bruce Caldwell (2014, 3f.) notes, several economists debated at the time, and that Hayek takes up in his "Economics and Knowledge," citing Morgenstern's essay.[112]

The role that "Economics and Knowledge" plays in connecting *TSO* with Hayek's subsequent research agenda is the subject of the following section.

---

[105] See Schütz 2010.

[106] The German manuscript appears to have been lost. The essay "Wirtschaftstheorie und Wissen" included in the German edition (published in 1952) of *Individualism and Economic Order* (Hayek 1948) is listed as a translation of the *Economica* article without any reference to a German draft.

[107] See the editors' report on Schütz's comments, in Schütz 2010, 91.

[108] Caldwell 2004a, 140f., 150.

[109] Hayek ([1963a] 1992, 32): "Through Schütz we all became familiar with Max Weber and Husserl's phenomenology (which I, however, never understood . . .)."

[110] In retrospect Hayek (1994, 58) said about the participants in the *Geistkreis*: "Nearly all of them are now in America: Max Mintz, Erik Vögelin, Alfred Schütz, Walter Fröhlich, Felix Kaufmann, and, of those who joined later, Gottfried Haberler, Oskar Morgenstern, Fritz Machlup, and Friedrich Engel-Janosi. In part it was the same circle who also met in Mises's *Privatseminar*, when I believe I was for the first time admitted." About Mises's "*Privatseminar* which he held in the evening at his office," Hayek (ibid., 69) notes that it was during "the middle twenties . . . much the most important center of economic discussion at Vienna."

[111] Oskar Morgenstern, "Vollkommene Voraussicht und wirtschaftliches Gleichgewicht," *Zeitschrift für Nationalökonomie* 6 (1934): 337–57. An English translation, "Perfect Foresight and Economic Equilibrium," appeared in *Selected Economic Writings of Oskar Morgenstern* (New York: New York University Press, 1976), 169–83.

[112] Hayek (1937) 2014, 65.

5. *"Economics and Knowledge"*

In Hayek's (1983b, 226) own assessment, "Economics and Knowledge" marked the "decisive point of the change" in the development of his scholarly interests. What caused this change was, as he recalls, his "editing various essays on socialist planning" (ibid., 79) for the volume *Collectivist Economic Planning*.[113] While working on this project he became "increasingly interested in the philosophical and methodological questions" (ibid.) that he then started to pursue, first documented in his 1936 presidential address to the Economics Club at the London School of Economics (LSE).[114] In an interview, conducted in 1978, Hayek reports:

> It was really the beginning of my looking at things in a new light. If you asked me, I would say that up until that moment I was developing conventional ideas. With the '37 lecture to the Economics Club in London, my Presidential Address, which is "Economics and Knowledge," I started my own way of thinking. . . . And it was with a feeling of sudden illumination, sudden enlightenment that I—I wrote that lecture in a certain excitement. I was aware that I was putting down things which were fairly well known in a new form, and perhaps it was the most exciting moment in my career when I saw it in print. (Hayek 1983b, 425f.)[115]

Hayek had reason to sense "a certain excitement" in writing that lecture because the argument he developed there posed a fundamental challenge to the "formal economic analysis" (Hayek [1937] 2014, 57) that was gain-

[113] F. A. Hayek, ed., *Collectivist Economic Planning: Critical Studies on the Possibilities of Socialism* (London: Routledge and Sons, 1935). To this volume Hayek contributed two essays, "The Nature and History of the Problem" and "The Present State of the Debate," now published in F. A. Hayek, *Socialism and War—Essays, Documents, Reviews*, ed. Bruce Caldwell, vol. 10 of *The Collected Works of F. A. Hayek* (Chicago: University of Chicago Press, 1997), 53–84, 89–116.

[114] Hayek (1983b, 225f.) once answered: "It really began with my doing that volume on collectivist economic planning, which was originally merely caused by the fact that I found that certain new insights which were known on the Continent had not reached the English-speaking world yet. . . . Being forced to explain this development on the Continent in the introduction and the conclusion of this volume, which contained translations, I was curiously enough driven not only into political philosophy but into an analysis of the methodological misconceptions of economics."

[115] See also Hayek (1965) 2014, 49f.: "This brings me to what in my personal development was the starting point of all these reflections, and which may explain why, though at one time a very pure and narrow economic theorist, I was led from technical economics into all kinds of questions usually regarded as philosophical. When I look back, it seems to have all begun . . . with an essay on 'Economics and Knowledge' in which I examined what seemed to me some of the central difficulties of pure economic theory."

ing increasing acceptance in a profession eager to prove its status as a "true science." Right at the beginning, Hayek states this challenge quite clearly:

> Indeed, my main contention will be that the tautologies, of which formal equilibrium analysis in economics essentially consists, can be turned into propositions which tell us anything about causation in the real world only in so far as we are able to fill those formal propositions with definite statements about how knowledge is acquired and communicated. In short, I shall contend that the empirical element in economic theory—the only part which is concerned not merely with implications but with causes and effects and which leads therefore to conclusions which, at any rate in principle, are capable of verification—consists of propositions about the acquisition of knowledge. (ibid.)

Hayek's principal objection against "formal equilibrium analysis" is that it presumes individuals to be "quasi omniscient" (ibid., 68), thus relying on the "highly unrealistic . . . assumption of perfect knowledge" ([1961] 2014, 415). By starting from "the assumption that people's *knowledge* corresponds with the objective *facts*" it "habitually disregards," so Hayek ([1945a] 2014, 104) charges, "an essential part of the phenomena with which we have to deal: the unavoidable imperfection of man's knowledge."[116] Together with the perfect-knowledge assumption, Hayek rejects its twin, "the bogy of the 'economic man' and . . . [the] assumption of a strictly rational behavior" ([1946] 2010, 57), that, as he puts it, "celebrated figment" ([1960] 2011, 120) and "skeleton in our cupboard" ([1937] 2014, 68).

Even though, in "Economics and Knowledge," Hayek ([1937] 2014, 60, fn.) only passingly refers to Ludwig von Mises's claim of the a priori foundation of economic theory, in writing this lecture he was surely aware of the fact that what he argued there was in direct conflict with core tenets of his former mentor's teaching. In retrospect he has said about his 1936 lecture that it "was a gentle attempt to persuade Mises to give up the *a priori* claim" (1983b, 58).[117] As Hayek (1994, 64) reports, it was after his graduation in October of

---

[116] Hayek ([1963b] 2014, 437): "The ignorance with which we have to cope . . . we can assume away only at the peril of making our problem disappear (as has happened to some parts of equilibrium analysis)." Throughout his work Hayek emphasizes the fundamental challenge that the "constitutional limitation of man's knowledge" ([1946] 2010, 59) poses for economic theory. In varying terms he speaks of the "inevitable imperfection of the human mind" ([1942–44] 2010, 105), of "man's unavoidable ignorance" ([1960] 2011, 73), "the insuperable limits to his knowledge" ([1975] 2014, 372), or of "our constitutional ignorance" (1976, 8).

[117] In a letter of 1981, quoted by B. Caldwell (2004a, 420), Hayek said: "The main intention of my 1936 lecture was to explain gently to Mises why I could not accept his a priorism." See Vanberg 2004a, 158ff., for a discussion of Mises's priorism.

1921 that he had first met Ludwig von Mises, who was, at the time, director at the *Abrechnungsamt*, a temporary government office within the chamber of commerce charged with settling prewar debt. Equipped with a letter of rec- ommendation by his doctoral advisor Friedrich von Wieser, Hayek contacted Mises in search of a job, successfully. "Once I was employed in that office," he recalls, "our contacts rapidly became close, and for the following eight years Mises was unquestionably the personal contact from whom I profited most, not only by way of intellectual stimulation but also his direct assistance in my career" (ibid., 68).[118]

Even though, as he notes, "in the conventional sense [Mises] was never my teacher," Hayek (1994, 68) emphasizes that from him he had "probably learnt more than from any other man." He also speaks of Mises as "a scholar whom I greatly admire and to whom I owe much inspiration" ([1961] 2014, 384). Nevertheless, Hayek apparently never shared Mises's methodological view of economics as a praxeological discipline, based on "aprioristic reason- ing" (Mises 1990, 29).[119] By insisting "that the whole theory of human action, including all economic theory, is of such an *a priori* character," Mises tends to overlook, so Hayek ([1961] 2014, 384) charges, "that this logical ground- work does not yet provide an explanation of how things actually happen but stands to such an explanation of the real events in about the same relation as mathematics stands to physics." Implicitly Hayek accuses Mises's a priorism of the same deficiency for which he blames formal equilibrium analysis with its assumption of perfect knowledge, namely that it "prevents us from asking all the important questions" which an "empirical science of economics" (ibid., 415) must answer, that it "systematically leaves out what is our main task to explain" ([1945a] 2014, 104).[120]

In quite similar terms as in "Economics and Knowledge," Hayek speaks in

---

[118] Hayek (1994, 69): "It was also Mises to whom I owe the creation of the Austrian Institute for Business Cycle Research, conceived by him, I believe, largely for the purpose of providing scope for me after he had failed to get me as a sort of scientific assistant into the chamber of commerce."

[119] Hayek ([1988] 1992, 158): "I must admit that often I myself did not initially think his argu- ments were completely convincing and only slowly learned that he was mostly right. . . . And today, considering the kind of battle that he had to lead, I also understand that he was driven to certain exaggerations, like that of the a priori character of economic theory, where I could not follow him." In the above (fn. 117) mentioned letter of 1981, Hayek declares: "I was *never* an a priorist" (quoted from Caldwell 2004a, 421).

[120] Hayek ([1961] 2014, 415): "In the task of explaining why events conform to a certain pat- tern, that is, in the empirical science of economics, the assumption of perfect knowledge ought to have no place. To use it at this stage is to assume away the chief problem. . . . The theory of market equilibrium which starts from the assumption of perfect knowledge possessed by the partners in the market largely begs the questions it ought to answer by assuming away what need to be explained."

his famous 1945 article, "The Use of Knowledge in Society," of the need for an *empirical* science of economics to explain the "process by which knowledge is constantly communicated and acquired" ([1945a] 2014, 104). In raising the question of how knowledge is acquired and communicated, he points to the fact that two aspects of the "knowledge problem" need to be distinguished—two aspects that may be contrasted as the *individual* and the *social* dimension of the knowledge problem. There is, on the one hand, the question of how individuals learn what they need to know in order to navigate the world in which they live. And there is, on the other hand, the question of how multitudes of individuals with partial and imperfect knowledge can effectively coordinate their actions and cooperate with each other.

The two questions call for two interrelated but separable lines of research, both of which Hayek has made significant contributions to.[121] The *social* aspect of the knowledge problem is naturally the principal subject of economics as a *social science*, a fact that Hayek emphasizes when he says about his essay "Economics and Knowledge":

> Its main concern was that the task of economic theory was to explain how an overall social order of economic activity was achieved which utilized a large amount of knowledge which was not concentrated in any one mind but existed only as the separate knowledge of thousands or millions of different individuals. ([1965] 2014, 50)

Accordingly, Hayek devotes much of his work to what he describes as "the really central problem of economics as a social science. The problem . . . is how the spontaneous interaction of a number of people, each possessing only bits of knowledge brings about a state of affairs . . . which could be brought about by deliberate direction only by somebody who possessed the combined knowledge of all those individuals" ([1937] 2014, 72f.).[122]

Not being concerned with this issue, *TSO* is clearly not an *integral* part of economics as a *social* science. Its importance lies in the fact that it provides an essential *theoretical foundation* for an economics that, if it is to qualify as an *em-*

---

[121] J. Birner (1999, 60) argues similarly when he posits that "'Economics and Knowledge' of 1937 may be considered as linking the two branches of Hayek's research programme," his critique of "the reduction . . . of all economic behavior . . . to the pure logic of choice" being the first branch, and his interpretation of the price system as a "system of communication" the second.

[122] Hayek ([1937] 2014, 72): "Clearly there is here a problem of the division of knowledge which is quite analogous to . . . the problem of the division of labour."—Hayek ([1945a] 2014, 104): "The practical problem, however, arises precisely because these facts are never so given to a single mind, and because, in consequence, it is necessary that in the solution of the problem knowledge should be used that is dispersed among many people."

pirical science, must start, as Hayek (ibid., 77) puts it, from "empirical propositions . . . about how people will learn," propositions which "are of a fundamentally different nature from those of formal analysis."[123] This is what Hayek (ibid., 69) insists on when he posits: "But the assumptions or hypotheses, which we have to introduce when we want to explain the social process, concern the relation of the thought of an individual to the external world, the question to what extent and how his knowledge corresponds to the external facts. And the hypotheses must necessarily run in terms of assertions about causal connections, about how experience creates knowledge."

Since the question of how an individual's knowledge "should ever come to correspond to the objective data"[124] is the principal theme of *TSO*, it is surprising that nowhere in "Economics and Knowledge" Hayek draws on the ideas developed in his 1920 draft paper which, in his account, already "contains the whole principle of the theory" (this volume, p. 115).[125] It is also surprising that, after stressing the indispensable role of empirical "propositions about how people learn," Hayek ([1937] 2014, 77) adds: "I do not mean to suggest that there opens here and now a wide field for empirical research. I very much doubt whether such investigation would teach us anything new." As Caldwell[126] has noted, one wonders how this statement should be interpreted. It could be meant only to say that, as a matter of pragmatic division of labor, economics as a social science leaves the empirical study of individual behavior to psychology and concentrates on social phenomena that result from human *interaction*. In support of this interpretation, one might refer to Hayek's ([1943] 2014, 86) statement: "The misunderstanding is that the social sciences aim at explaining individual behavior. . . . The social sciences do in fact nothing of the sort. If conscious action can be 'explained,' this is a task for psychology, but not for economics or . . . any other social science."

---

[123] Hayek ([1937] 2014, 69): "The significant point here is that it is these . . . hypotheses or assumptions that people do learn from experience, and about how they acquire knowledge, which constitute the empirical content of our propositions about what happens in the real world. . . . The important point . . . is that the nature of these hypotheses is in many respects rather different from the more general assumptions from which the Pure Logic of Choice starts."

[124] Hayek ([1937] 2014, 63): "There seems to be no possible doubt that these two concepts of 'data,' on the one hand, in the sense of the objective real facts, as the observing economists is supposed to know them, and, on the other, in the subjective sense, as things known to the person whose behavior we try to explain, are really fundamentally different and ought to be carefully distinguished. And, as we shall see, the question why the data in the subjective sense of the term should ever come to correspond to the objective data is one of the main problems we have to answer."

[125] Birner (1999, 60): "Hayek's statement about 'how knowledge is acquired and communicated' is another occasion where one would expect him to have applied his earlier psychological theory. But surprisingly, again he does no such thing."

[126] Caldwell 2013, 6f.

Yet some of his comments on the status of the pure logic of choice sound as if what he objects to is only its application in the social realm, not its role in the study of individual human action. This seems, for instance, implied when Hayek says that his 1937 article was

> an attempt to persuade Mises himself that when he asserted that the market theory was a priori, he was wrong; that what was a priori was only the logic of individual action, but the moment you passed from this to the interaction among many people, you entered into the empirical field. (Hayek 1994, 72)[127]

There seems to be a tension, or even inconsistency, between, on the one side, Hayek's emphasis on the need for empirical hypotheses "about how experience creates knowledge" and, on the other side, his concession that in the study of individual action the pure logic of choice has its legitimate place, even though, as he says, it "does not explain any facts" (Hayek [1942–44] 2010, 103, fn. 6).[128] Since, as Hayek asserts, the analysis of social phenomena has to start from assumptions about individual human action,[129] it is difficult to see how one can arrive at an *empirical* social theory if the assumptions from which one has to start do "not explain any facts."[130] The puzzling tension or inconsistency in Hayek's arguments deserves to be more closely examined. It directly bears on the often, and controversially, discussed issue whether it was

---

[127] Hayek (1983b, 58): "I believe it was in that same article on economics and knowledge where I make the point that while the analysis of individual planning is in a way an a priori system of logic, the empirical element enters in people learning what other people do."—Hayek ([1968a] 1992, 55f.): "Against this [Mises's a priorism] the present writer . . . contended that while it was true that the pure logic of choice by which the Austrian theory interpreted individual action was indeed purely deductive, as soon as the explanation moved to the interpersonal activities of the market, the crucial processes were those by which information was transmitted among individuals, and as such were purely empirical (Mises never explicitly rejected this criticism but no longer was prepared to reconstruct his by then fully developed system)." See also Hayek's ([1961] 2014, 415) emphasis on the critical juncture "when we pass from the logical analysis of a single plan of resource allocation to the explanation of the action of many men."

[128] Hayek ([1943] 2014, 90): "The . . . theories of the social sciences do not consist of 'laws' in the sense of empirical rules about the behavior of objects definable in physical terms. All that the theory of the social sciences attempts is to provide a technique of reasoning which assists us in connecting individual facts, but which like logic and mathematics, is not about the facts. It can, therefore, . . . never be verified or falsified by reference to facts."

[129] As Hayek ([1946] 2010, 52) notes about a "true individualism": "But its basic contention is . . . that there is no other way toward an understanding of social phenomena but through our understanding of individual action directed toward other people and guided by their expected behavior."

[130] Hayek ([1961] 2014, 284): "To give such an account of the causal mechanism which produces the order [of economic affairs] is clearly a task for an empirical science and can never be solved by the deductive methods of pure logic."

his reading of Karl Popper's *Logik der Forschung* that led Hayek in his 1936 lecture to move away from Mises's a priorism.[131]

6. K. R. Popper and the "Pure Logic of Choice"

As Hayek recalls, it was during a visit in Vienna that Gottfried Haberler drew his attention to Karl Popper's *Logik der Forschung*[132] (*The Logic of Scientific Discovery*).[133] His first personal encounter with Popper came in 1935 in London, when they were introduced to each other by Susan Stebbing, a philosopher at Bedford College, University of London, who had read a copy of the manuscript of *Logik der Forschung* and had invited Popper to give lectures in London.[134] About their encounter Popper (1997, 311) reports:

> My lifelong friendship with Fritz Hayek began in September or October of 1935, when I knocked at the door of his study here in the LSE. . . . Having just arrived in London for the first time, I felt anything but confident. Yet Hayek received me with more than friendliness. He assured me that he had been told by his friend Gottfried Haberler that he must read a book that I had published a year earlier in Vienna. So I gave him a copy; and he assured that he would read it at once and that, if I came back next week, he would have read it. And when I came back again after a week, he really had read it (except for a chapter on quantum mechanics)—and with great care.

Hayek's reading of Popper's book left its mark, evident by the fact that, in the above-quoted (p. 29) passage from "Economics and Knowledge," he added as a footnote to the term "verification": "Or rather falsification (cf. K. R. Popper, *Logik der Forschung*, [Vienna, 1935], *passim*)" (Hayek [1937] 2014, 57). This reference may seem to indicate that, indeed, "'Economics and Knowledge' . . . , a turning point in his career, reflects *Logik*'s influence."[135] Yet, from repeated comments he has made, it is obvious that Hayek embraced Popper's arguments as a message that confirmed his preexisting methodolog-

---

[131] See, in particular, the controversy between Bruce Caldwell (1988; 1992a; 1992b; 2004a, 409ff.) and Terence Hutchison (1981, 210–19; 1992).

[132] Hayek 1994, 50; Kreuzer 1983, 17f.

[133] *Die Logik der Forschung* was published in the autumn of 1934 (with the imprint "1935"). The English translation was first published in 1959.

[134] Hacohen 2000, 215, fn. 7; 311; 317, fn. 93. Popper (1974a, 85) recalls: "I received . . . an invitation from Professor Susan Stebbing of Bedford College, London. I came to England in the autumn of 1935 to give two lectures at Bedford College."

[135] Colin Simkin, *Popper's Views on Natural and Social Science* (Leiden: Brill, 1993), 2. (Quoted from Hacohen 2000, 318, fn. 95.)

ical views, not as a new revelation he needed to be converted to. As he once put it:

> I was a Popperian before he published *The Logic of Scientific Discovery*. We were both, in the 1920s, constantly arguing with two types of people—Marxists and Freudians—who both claimed that their theories were, in their nature, irrefutable. Now the claim that a scientific theory should be beyond the possibility of refutation is, of course, very irritating. This led Popper to the conclusion that a theory that cannot be refuted is, by definition, not scientific. When Popper stated that in detail, I just embraced his view as a statement of what I was feeling. And that is why ever since his *Logik der Forschung* first came out in 1934, I have been a complete adherent to his general theory of methodology. (Weimer-Hayek Discussion 1982, 323)[136]

One wonders how Hayek can, on the one hand, argue that the "analysis of individual planning is in a way an a priori system of logic" (1983b, 58) while, on the other hand, he endorses Popper's argument "that the test of empirical science was that it could be refuted."[137]

Intriguingly, one finds a similarly puzzling combination of arguments on Popper's side. Popper had read "Economics and Knowledge," according to Hacohen (2000, 365), in the fall of 1937, and, as strange as it may seem, it converted him to a Mises-type praxeological a priorism, the very view that Hayek had meant to refute in his essay.[138] In 1963, Popper ([1963a] 1994, 154) introduced a lecture at Harvard University's Department of Economics on "the status of the rationality principle in the social sciences" by saying: "My views on the methodology of the social sciences are the result of my admiration for economic theory: I began to develop them, some twenty-five years

---

[136] In his above-quoted (fn. 10) letter of January 16, 1983, to B. Weimer (Hayek papers, box 57, folder 2, HIA), Hayek notes in reference to Popper: "When he spelled out the conception of a hypothetico-deductive method at which I had already arrived, in a manner of which I would have never been capable, I swallowed it whole."

[137] Having mentioned the common experience that he and Popper had had in the 1920s in Vienna with Marxists and Freudians, Hayek (1983b, 18f.) said about Popper's book: "It had just come out a few weeks before. . . . And to me it was so satisfactory because it confirmed this certain view I had already formed due to an experience very similar to Karl Popper's. . . . And that led me, already, to the understanding of what became Popper's main systematic point: that the test of empirical science was that it could be refuted, and that any system which claimed it was irrefutable was by definition not scientific. I was not a trained philosopher; I didn't elaborate this. It was sufficient for me to have recognized this, but when I found this thing explicitly argued and justified in Popper, I just accepted the Popperian philosophy for spelling out what I had always felt."

[138] Hacohen (2000, 367): "Popper . . . liked Hayek's exploration of the logic of choice. It probably invited his first reflections on social science models."

ago, by trying to generalize the method of theoretical economics." In a foot-note he added: "I was particularly impressed by Hayek's formulation that eco-nomics is the 'logic of choice' (Cp., for example, F. A. von Hayek, 'Economics and Knowledge' . . .). This led me to my formulation of the 'logic of the situa-tion.' . . . This seemed to me to embrace, for example, the logic of choice and the logic of historical problem situations" (ibid., 181, fn. 1).[139]

In light of Karl Popper's general falsificationist methodology, it is astound-ing how similar his "*situational logic* or *situational analysis*" (Popper 1972, 178) is to the praxeological a priorism of Ludwig von Mises,[140] who explicitly rejected Popper's falsificationism.[141] According to Mises, praxeology as a "general theory of human choice" (Mises 1949, 3) is a priori because it "starts from the a priori category of action and develops out of it all that it contains" (Mises [1962] 2006, 36).[142] He explicitly stresses that it is not "part of psychology" (Mises 1990, 21) and asserts:

> All its theorems are products of deductive reasoning. . . . Into the chain of praxeological reasoning the praxeologist introduces certain assumptions concerning the environment in which an action takes place. Then he tries to find out how these special conditions affect the result to which his reasoning must lead. (Mises 1990, 39f.)

It sounds not all too different when Popper describes his situational analysis as "a method which . . . replaces psychological explanations by . . . consider-ations mainly of a logical character" (ibid., 178), noting that

> it is the central point of situational analysis that we need, in order to "ani-mate" it, no more than the assumption that the various persons or agents act *adequately*, or *appropriately*—that is to say, in accordance with the situation. . . . Thus there is only one "animating" law involved—the principle of acting

[139] Popper (1974a, 93): "The . . . method of situational analysis, which I first added to *The Pov-erty* in 1938, and later explained more fully in Chapter 14 of *The Open Society*, was developed from what I had previously called the 'zero method.' The main point here was an attempt *to general-ize the method of economic theory (marginal utility theory) so as to become applicable to the other social sciences.*"

[140] For a closer examination of Mises's a priorism, see Vanberg 2004a, 158ff., and of Popper's situational logic, see Vanberg 2002, 19ff. The similarities between the two views are examined in Vanberg 1975, 85–94, 109–20.

[141] Mises ([1962] 2006, 63): "If one accepts the terminology . . . of Popper, a theory or hypoth-esis is 'unscientific' if in principle it cannot be refuted by experience. Consequently, all a pri-ori theories, including mathematics and praxeology, are 'unscientific.' This is merely verbal quibble."

[142] Mises (1949, 68): "Praxeology—and consequently economics too—is a deductive system. It draws its strength from the starting point of its deductions, from the category of action."

according to the situation, which is clearly an almost empty principle. It is known in the literature under the name "rationality principle." . . . It does not play the role of an empirical explanatory theory, of a testable hypothesis. (Popper [1963a] 1994, 169)

If there is a difference between Mises's praxiological a priorism and Popper's situational analysis, it does not concern their common claim that social analysis is a matter of logical deduction from unquestionable premises.[143] They differ in what they posit as their unquestionable premises. Popper ([1957] 1994, 141) appears to take the assumption of *objective* rationality as the start point of his situational logic when he says:

[By] the method of logical or rational reconstruction . . . I mean the method of constructing a model on the assumption of complete rationality (and perhaps also on the assumption of the possession of complete information) on the part of all the individuals concerned. . . . An example of this method is the . . . model behavior to be expected on the basis of the "pure logic of choice," as described by the equations of economics.[144]

By contrast, when Mises (1949, 18) insists that "human action is necessarily always rational," he is careful to emphasize that his claim is strictly about *subjective* rationality. As he puts it:

It is a fact that human reason is not infallible and that man very often errs in selecting and applying means. An action unsuited to the end sought falls short of expectation. It is contrary to purpose, but it is rational, i.e., the outcome of . . . an attempt—although an ineffectual attempt—to attain a definite goal. (ibid., 20)

Particularly puzzling about Hayek's ambiguous comments on, and Popper's explicit endorsement of, the "pure logic of choice" is the fact that both authors have proposed *empirical* theories of human learning and action that may provide a much more adequate behavioral foundation for an *empirical* social science than the "a priori category of action" or the "nearly empty rationality principle." In Hayek's case this is, of course, his theory of the human

[143] Popper ([1963a] 1994, 171): "The rationality principle does not play the role of an empirical or psychological proposition, and, more especially . . . it is not treated in the social sciences as subject to any kind of test."

[144] Popper ([1963a] 1994, 169): "The situation, as I use this term, already contains all the relevant aims and all the available relevant knowledge, especially of the various possible means for realizing these aims."

mind laid out in detail in the present volume,[145] a theory that he had already outlined in his 1920 paper—before he came into contact with Mises and his praxeological a priorism—and that he has drawn on in a number of his post-*TSO* essays.[146] In Popper's case, this is his evolutionary theory of the growth of knowledge, a founding contribution to evolutionary epistemology,[147] a research program which also counts Hayek among its founders.[148] The following section takes a closer look at the similarities between central arguments in *TSO* and core tenets of Popper's "Darwinian theory of the growth of knowledge" (Popper 1972, 261).

7. TSO *and Evolutionary Epistemology*

There exists, in fact, as John Gray (1984, 11) has put it, a "striking similarity between Popper's later views and those expounded by Hayek in *The Sensory Order*," a similarity that lets one wonder why, as Hayek has complained,

[145] In his *Scientism* essay, Hayek ([1942–44] 2010, 112f.) implicitly refers to the subject of *TSO* when he argues: "It is important to observe that our contention is not that such an attempt to explain the principle of how our mind or our brain transforms physical facts into mental entities is impossible. Once we recognize this as a process of classification there is no reason why we should not learn to understand the principle on which it operates. . . . Our argument is, rather, in the first instance, that for the task of the social sciences such an explanation of the formation of mental entities and their relation to the physical facts which they represent is unnecessary, and that such an explanation would help us in no way in our task; and, second, that such an explanation, also conceivable, is . . . unlikely to be ever more than an 'explanation of the principle' on which this apparatus of classification works."—"The problem of explaining mental processes by physical ones is entirely distinct from the problems of the social sciences, it is a problem for physiological psychology. But whether it is solved or not, for the social sciences the given mental entities must provide the starting point, whether their formation has been explained or not" (ibid., 113f.).

This statement suffers from similar ambiguities as Hayek's above-quoted comments on the pure logic of choice. It could be meant to say that, as a matter of a pragmatic division of labor, the social sciences leave the task of "explaining mental processes" to psychology. Taking "mental entities" as "starting point" in the sense of building social science explanations on a psychological behavioral foundation is, however, something entirely different from building them on a "pure logic of choice." In its ambiguity, Hayek's statement allows for both interpretations.

[146] Hayek (1955) 2014; (1963b) 2014; (1964b) 2014; (1965) 2014; (1969) 2014.

[147] D. T. Campbell (1974c, 450) credits Popper with being "the modern founder and leading advocate of a natural selection theory."

[148] In his survey of the field, W. W. Bartley (1987, 20f.) lists Popper and Hayek among its "founders," along with D. T. Campbell, Ernst Mayr, and Konrad Lorenz. C. Hermann-Pillath (1992, 147) notes: "Hayek's book on *The Sensory Order* ought to be regarded as one of the most creative and innovative attempts to develop a biologically founded epistemology. . . . More particularly, Hayek provided the starting points for a full-fledged evolutionary epistemology that simultaneously analyzes phylogenetic and ontogenetic aspects of human cognition present in the development of the neural structures."

Popper "never would show any sympathy with the argument of *TSO*."[149] It is obviously Popper's contribution to evolutionary epistemology that Gray has in mind when he speaks of his "later views." Donald Campbell (1974c, 450f.), who coined the term "evolutionary epistemology," summarizes the core tenet of this research program as follows: All knowledge processes (i.e., processes that lead to knowledge gains) can be interpreted as instances of the "variation and selective retention process of evolutionary adaptation."[150]

Popper's Darwinian epistemology is a straightforward generalization of his falsificationist methodology—according to which the growth of scientific knowledge is a matter of *conjecture* and *refutation*—from its original field of application to "the view of the evolution of life as a process of trial and error-elimination" (Popper 1972, 255). As Popper puts it: "From the amoeba to Einstein, the growth of knowledge is always the same: we try to solve our problems, and to obtain, by a process of elimination, something approaching adequacy in our tentative solutions" (ibid., 262).[151]

At the core of Popper's "conjecture and refutation" outlook is the assumption that conjectures must come first for knowledge to be gained, that all *"acquired knowledge, all learning, consists of the modification . . . of some form of knowledge . . . which was there previously"* (ibid., 71). There are, as Popper emphasizes, no "pure" observations:[152]

---

[149] Hayek in his letter to Walter Weimer of January 16, 1983 (see above, fn. 10).

[150] Campbell (ibid., 413): "Evolution—even in its biological aspects—is a knowledge process, and . . . the natural selection paradigm for such knowledge increments can be generalized to other epistemic activities such as learning, thought, and science." In a letter to Donald Campbell of January 4, 1978 (Hayek papers, box 14, folder 2, HIA), Hayek wrote: "There are perhaps few greater pleasures for a scholar than to discover an evolutionary trend in the scientific literature of another field which is running parallel to efforts one has been pursuing for years. . . . I am, of course, referring to your presidential address of 1975 which has only just come to my notice. . . . It seems to me that it is high time that the two distinct developments . . . found together. In my case, although I have of course dabbled in psychology (*The Sensory Order*), my inspiration is . . . largely from the political tradition." In his response letter to Hayek of April 28, 1978 (Hayek papers, box 14, folder 2, HIA), Campbell noted: "During the years 1950–53, I was a 35-year old assistant professor of psychology at the University of Chicago, and was your guest for lunch at the Quadrangle Club at least once. I was reading *The Sensory Order* at that time."

[151] Popper (1972, 242): "All *organisms* are constantly . . . *engaged in problem-solving* . . . . Problem-solving always proceeds by the method of trial and error; new reactions, new forms, new organs, new modes of behavior, new hypotheses, are tentatively put forward and controlled by error-elimination."—"We solve our problems tentatively proposing various competing theories and hypotheses . . . and submitting them . . . to empirical tests, for the purpose of error elimination" (ibid., 239f.).—"Epistemology becomes . . . the theory of the growth of knowledge. It becomes the theory of problem-solving or, in other words, of the construction . . . and critical testing of competing conjectural theories" (ibid., 142).

[152] Popper ([1963b] 1994, 86): "There is no such thing as a 'pure' observation, that is to say, an observation without a theoretical component. All observation . . . is an interpretation of facts in the light of some theory or other."

An observation is always preceded by a particular interest, a question, or a problem—in short, by something theoretical. After all, we can put every question in the form of a hypothesis or conjecture to which we add: "Is this so? Yes or no?" Thus we can assert that every observation is preceded by a problem, a hypothesis, . . . by something theoretical or speculative. This is why observations are always selective, and why they presuppose something like a principle of selection.[153]

The growth of knowledge is, in this account, driven by disappointments of what we expected, disappointments which "force us to correct our system of expectations" (Popper [1948a] 1972, 344).

Hayek emphasizes the very same outlook—later he would speak of it as "the primacy of the abstract"[154]—in *TSO* when he states that "*all* we know about the world is of the nature of theories and all 'experience' can do is to change these theories" (*TSO*, 6.37).[155] In a footnote,[156] Hayek credits Popper with the "idea," yet even if in his way of putting it he may have been inspired by Popper's arguments—in its *substance* the "idea" is obviously a principal ingredient of his theory of the mind as an apparatus of classification and reclassification.[157] It is clearly implied, for instance, when he argues that sensory perception is "always an interpretation" (*TSO*, 6.36) and "in a sense 'abstract'" (*TSO*, 6.39).[158]

What is true for the notion that we can never observe "the inexhaustible totality of everything"[159] but that all perception is theory-guided, occurs in the

[153] Popper (1948a) 1972, 342f. "The hypothesis (or expectation, or theory, or whatever we may call it) precedes the observation, even though an observation that refutes a certain hypothesis may stimulate a new (and therefore a temporally later) hypothesis" (ibid., 346).

[154] Hayek ([1969] 2014, 322): "The formation of abstractions ought to be regarded not as actions of the mind but rather as something which happens to the mind. . . . This implies that the richness of the sensory world in which we live, and which defies exhaustive analysis by our mind, is not the starting point from which the mind derives abstractions, but the product of a great range of abstractions which the mind must possess in order to be capable of experiencing that richness of the particular."

[155] Hayek ([1969] 2014, 321): "What I have been arguing is in some way related to . . . Karl Popper's argument . . . that the capacity to generalize comes first and the hypotheses are then tested and confirmed or refuted according to their effectiveness as guides to action."

[156] "I owe this way of putting it to my friend K. R. Popper, who, however, may not entirely agree with this use I am making of his idea" (*TSO*, 6.37, fn.).

[157] In his essay "The Theory of Complex Phenomena," which he contributed to a volume in honor of Karl Popper, Hayek ([1964b] 2014, 248, fn. 4) notes: "See . . . on the general point that all perception involves a theory or hypothesis my book *The Sensory Order*."

[158] "Every sensation, even the 'purest,' must . . . be regarded as an interpretation of an event in the light of the past experience of the individual or the species" (*TSO*, 8.4).

[159] Hayek (1942–44) 2010, 132. "All perception of reality, including the simplest sensations, involves a classification of the object according to some property or properties" (ibid., 130).—"All

light of preexisting expectations, is equally true for the notion that all growth of knowledge, or learning proceeds by the evolutionary principle of selection by consequences. Both are integral parts of the theory outlined in *TSO*. Where Popper speaks of disappointments requiring corrections in our system of expectations, Hayek speaks of the "reclassification" that is needed "whenever the expectations resulting from the existing classification are disappointed, or when beliefs so far held are disproved by new experiences" (*TSO*, 8.15).[160]

Like Popper,[161] Hayek distinguishes between two sources of the "system of expectations" or, in his terms, of the "conjectures" embodied in the "past linkages." They reflect, on the one hand, the experience accumulated by the individual during its own learning history and, on the other hand, the experience accumulated by the species in the course of its evolutionary past.[162] The "principle which determines the formation of the mental order," Hayek argues, "may operate either in the ontogenetic or in the phylogenetic process . . . processes which take place in the evolution of the species and in that of the individual" (*TSO*, 5.3). These processes are governed by the evolutionary principle of *selection by consequences*, or, as he puts it, are "determined by the accidents of evolution, the physiological capacities and the pragmatic needs of the individual and the species" (*TSO*, 6.47).[163]

The fact that the "apparatus by means of which we learn about the external world" (*TSO*, 8.1) is a product of individual learning as well as of the species' evolutionary past, has, as Hayek points out, an important implication. It means that the "experience" on which our perception of the world is based is in part embodied as genetically coded information in our sense organs, and thus *prior* to our sensory perceptions. Hayek speaks in this regard of "presensory experience" (*TSO*, 8.2) and explains:

---

we can perceive of external events are therefore only such properties of these events as they possess as members of classes which have been formed by past 'linkages'" (*TSO*, 6.37).

[160] "The experience that the classification based on the past linkages does not always work, i.e., does not always lead to valid predictions, forces us to revise that classification" (*TSO*, 8.14).

[161] Popper ([1948a] 1972, 347): "Ontogenetically (that is, with respect to the development of the individual organism) we thus regress to the state of the expectations of a newborn child; phylogenetically (with respect to the evolution of the race, the phylum) we get to the state of expectations of unicellular organisms." The "expectations" embodied in our organs can, as Popper (1972, 146) notes, be regarded as "the biological predecessors of linguistically formulated theories."

[162] See above, p. 22.

[163] Hayek ([1969] 2014, 32): "It seems to me that the organism first develops new potentialities of action and that only afterwards does experience select and confirm those which are useful as adaptations to typical characteristics of its environment."—Hayek ([1942–44] 2010, 86, fn. 8): "The classification of the stimuli in our central nervous system is probably highly 'pragmatic' in the sense that it . . . stresses those relations . . . which in the course of evolution have proved significant for the survival of the species."

A certain part at least of what we know at any moment about the external world is therefore not learned by sensory experience, but is rather implicit in the means through which we can obtain such experience; it is determined by the order of the apparatus of classification which has been built up by pre-sensory linkages. (*TSO*, 8.10)

In his arguments on "pre-sensory experience," Hayek was surely influenced by Konrad Lorenz, whose 1942 article "Die angeborenen Formen möglicher Erfahrung" ("The Inborn Forms of Possible Experience") Hayek refers to in *TSO*.[164] The relation between Hayek's thoughts on pre-sensory experience and Lorenz's arguments deserves a closer look because it helps to clarify the nature of what John Gray (1984, 13) has referred to as "Hayek's Kantianism."[165]

In 1940 Lorenz was appointed—by, as he puts it, "one of the virtually incredible acts of fate" (Lorenz 1985, 266)—to the chair at the University of Königsberg, which had once been held by Immanuel Kant. As a "counterattack," so he recalls, to critique from Kantians because of his, a biologist's, "controversial position in Immanuel Kant's chair" (ibid., 272), he wrote his paper "Kant's Lehre vom Apriorischen im Lichte moderner Biologie" ("Kant's Doctrine of the A Priori in the Light of Contemporary Biology"), in which he proposed a naturalistic, evolutionary interpretation of Kant's a priori categories.[166] Lorenz introduced the paper by saying:

For Kant, the categories of space, time, causality, etc., are givens, established a priori, determining the form of all of our experience, and indeed making experience possible. For Kant, the validity of these primary principles of reason is absolute. . . . The biologist convinced of the fact of the great creative events of evolution asks of Kant . . : Is not human reason with all its categories and forms of intuition something that has organically evolved . . . , just as the human brain? (Lorenz [1941] 1982, 121f.)

Noting that it "is the duty of the natural scientist to attempt a natural explanation" (ibid., 122), Lorenz argues:

The a priori which determines the forms of appearance of the real things of the world is, in short, an organ, or more precisely the functioning of an

---

[164] Hayek refers to Lorenz in the context of drawing a "distinction between the part of the mental order which for the individual is determined by its inherited constitution and the part which for it may be regarded as being of experiential origin" (*TSO*, 5.3).

[165] A central theme of Gray's book is the claim that the "entirety of Hayek's work . . . is informed by a distinctly Kantian approach" (Gray 1984, 5).

[166] Lorenz (1985, 272): "This daring and even foolhardy attack on transcendental idealism was not published until . . . after I had been recruited into the German army." The paper was published in 1942.

organ. We come closer to understanding the a priori if we confront it with the questions asked of everything organic. . . . These questions are, first, how does it preserve the species; second, what is its genealogical origin; third, what natural causes make it possible? . . . Our categories and forms of perception, fixed prior to individual experience, are adapted to the external world for exactly the same reasons as the hoof of the horse is already adapted to the ground of the steppe before the horse is born and the fin of the fish is adapted to the water before the fish hatches. (ibid., 124f.)[167]

In an autobiographical essay, looking back at his 1941 article, Lorenz asks the question "What Kant would have thought of the *a priori*, if he had been familiar with the facts of evolution" (Lorenz 1985, 272),[168] and he supposes that Kant "would, without any objection, have taken the view held by what we call evolutionary epistemology" (ibid.).[169]

Lorenz with his "naturalistic interpretation of human reason" (Lorenz [1941] 1982, 141) and Hayek with his concept of "pre-sensory experience" are obviously fully in agreement in their interpretation of Kant's a priori categories. They both acknowledge, as Lorenz (1985, 272) puts it, that Kant "was right in contending that our forms of ideation and our categories of thought . . . are not individually acquired by learning," but they insist that what is *a priori for the individual* is *a posteriori for the species* and can, as such, be

---

[167] H. C. Plotkin (1982, 6): "The Lorenzian position expresses a powerful conception of any adaptation comprising some form of organization that is congruent with the environmental order to which it is relative. Such congruence can only come about through the gaining and storing of information about the environment, including a programme for the translation of this information into appropriate phenotypic traits."

[168] Lorenz (1985, 270f.): "To any thinker thoroughly familiar with the fact of evolution, it is a matter of course that the organization which enables us to perceive the external world, the sensory organization as well as that of our central nervous system . . . has evolved in interaction with and in adaptation to the outer reality that surrounds us. . . . Kant's question, how it is to be explained that our a prioristic categories of thought and form of ideation fit adequately the external world, receives an easy and even banal answer on an evolutionary basis."

[169] Referring to Popper and Campbell as representatives of the research program of evolutionary epistemology, Lorenz justly claims that he "was the first to put it into word" (1985, 272). See Falk 1993 for a more detailed discussion of Lorenz's pioneering contribution to evolutionary psychology. In a language similar to Popper's, Lorenz argues in his 1941 article that the "a priori forms of thought and intuition . . . just as any other organic adaptation . . . are for us 'inherited working hypotheses'" ([1941] 1982, 133). He notes "that the categorical forms of intuition and categories have proved themselves as working hypotheses in the coping of our species with the absolute reality of the environment" (ibid., 128). Like Popper, Lorenz had been a student of Karl Bühler ("Within Systems," § 39, this volume, p. 375, fn. 7). He mentions that he had "studied psychology at Karl Bühler's institute" (Lorenz 1985, 266) in Vienna and noted: "At an early age, thanks to the tuition of Karl Bühler, I had thoroughly understood that knowing an object results from an interaction between an organization within the observer and an object in the outer world, both of which are equally real" (ibid., 271).

explained naturalistically.[170] About the significance of this outlook for "pure empiricism," Hayek says:

> It agrees with empiricism in assuming that all our knowledge stems from experience. But . . . a large part of this knowledge stems from a strange kind of experience: one that antecedes conscious sensation and perception and that first creates that order of nerve stimuli that gives them a conscious value or significance. Conscious experience thus presupposes the existence of an order which is indeed created by a sort of pre-conscious or pre-perceptive experience, but which itself is not accessible by conscious experience. . . . Kant's categories are here resurrected as ordering principles that the organism does indeed acquire via the kind of impact of the outside world that I call pre-perceptive experience.[171]

8. The "Primacy of the Abstract," Subjectivism, and the Method of "Understanding"

The fact, asserted by Hayek along with his fellow evolutionary psychologists, that man's perception of the external world is guided by "working hypotheses," which reflect the genetically coded evolutionary experience of the species—Hayek's pre-sensory experience—and the memory-coded learning experience of the individual, has important implications for the explanation of human action. Just as we cannot *observe* the "inexhaustible totality of everything," we cannot *respond* to the "inexhaustible totality of everything," and just as "working hypotheses" selectively guide our sensory perceptions, conjectures about relevant contingencies operative in the environment in which we live guide our responses to external events. In other words, the "primacy of the abstract" governs our perceptions as well as our actions.

The connection between the primacy of the abstract in *perception* and in *action* constitutes a direct link between *TSO* and a most central theme in Hayek's work, the role of *rules* in guiding man's actions in a complex world.[172]

---

[170] Noting that, by contrast to Kant's understanding, "Hayek's a priori knowledge is . . . fallible," J. W. Lindemans (2011, 153) states: "Hence, contrary to Gray, I conclude that Hayek's 'general philosophy' was *not* Kantian." Lindemans refers, in particular, to Hayek's assertion that what for the individual is a priori knowledge must not also be "true of the physical world" (*TSO*, 8.12). S. Scheall (2015) contrasts Hayek's "fallibilist concept of the a priori" with Mises's "absolutist a priorism."

[171] "What Is Mind?," this volume, p. 357.

[172] Looking back after twenty-five years, Hayek noted that when, after having abandoned his 1920 paper, he returned to the project in 1946, he started from "the conviction that the different attributes of mental entities—conscious or not—could be reduced to differences in effects as guides to human action" (this volume, p. 384).

The "relation between the rules of perception and the rules of action" (Hayek [1962b] 2014, 247)[173] is an issue to which Hayek repeatedly returns in his writings (often with references to *TSO*), as the following sample of quotations documents. Speaking of man as "a rule-following animal,"[174] he says in *Law, Legislation and Liberty*:

> Abstractions will here be regarded . . . as the basis of man's capacity to move successfully in a world very imperfectly known to him. . . . The main purpose of our stress on the rules which govern our actions is to bring out the central importance of the abstract character of all mental processes. (1973b, 30)

In "The Primacy of the Abstract" he argues:

> All sensory experience, perceptions, images, concepts, etc. derive their particular qualitative properties from the rules of action which they put into operation. . . . The chief points I want to drive home here are that the primary characteristic of an organism is a capacity to govern its actions by rules . . . ; that in this sense its actions must be governed by abstract categories . . . ; and that what we call mind is essentially a system of such rules conjointly determining particular actions. ([1969] 2014, 320f.)

In "Kinds of Rationalism" Hayek writes:

> In all our thinking we are guided (or even operated) by rules of which we are not aware, and . . . our conscious reason can therefore always take account only of some of the circumstances which determine our actions. ([1965] 2014, 45)

And in *The Constitution of Liberty* one reads:

> Abstraction occurs whenever an individual responds in the same manner to circumstances that have only some features in common. Men generally act in accordance with abstract rules in this sense. . . . Even . . . their conscious thinking and acting are probably still guided by a great many of such

---

[173] Hayek ([1967c] 2014, 278): "The term 'rule' is used for a statement by which a regularity of the conduct of individuals can be described, irrespective of whether such a rule is 'known' to the individual in any other sense than that they normally act in accordance with it."

[174] Hayek (1973b, 11): "Man is as much a rule-following animal as a purpose-seeking one. And he is successful . . . because his thinking and acting are governed by rules which have by a process of selection been evolved." In a similar spirit, Darwin (1974, 84) put down in his notebook: "Animals may be called 'creatures of instinct' with some slight dash of reason so men are called 'creatures of reason,' more appropriately they would be '*creatures of habit*.'"

abstract rules which they obey without being able to formulate them. ([1960] 2011, 217)

In Hayek's account, the "role of rules" is an essential aspect of the "knowledge problem," the focal theme around which, as noted before, the main body of his work revolves.[175] In varying terms Hayek speaks of rules as an adaptation "to the irremediable limitations of our knowledge" ([1968c] 1978, 72), to man's "ignorance of most of the particular facts of his surroundings" (1973b, 30), and as "a device for coping with our constitutional ignorance" (1976, 8), "a device we have learned to use because our reason is insufficient to master the full detail of complex reality" ([1960] 2011, 127).[176] Rules can serve as guides for action because they incorporate knowledge about relevant contingencies in the external world, knowledge that reflects the "learning history" of the individual (memory-coded rules) and of the species (genetically coded rules).[177] The knowledge embodied in rules consists in this sense of "working hypotheses"[178] about the kinds of effects that can be expected from alternative ways of responding to events in the environment. As Hayek (1973b, 18) puts it: "Knowledge of the world is knowledge of what one *must* do or not do in certain kinds of circumstances."[179]

In *TSO* Hayek explains in detail how the mind's apparatus of classification operates as "a model-building apparatus" (*TSO*, 5.90), creating "an internal structure which reproduces some of the relations between the outside events" (*TSO*, 5.85). The "classifying system," he argues, "may in this sense be regarded as embodying a theory of the external world."[180] As a product of

---

[175] The significance Hayek attributed to this theme is also reflected in the fact that in 1966 he organized "a symposium on unconscious rules governing conscious action" (Caldwell 2014, 24).

[176] Hayek (1973b, 30): "We never act, and could never act, in full consideration of all the facts of a particular situation, but always by singling out as relevant only some aspect of it." The "whole rationale of the phenomenon of rule-guided action," Hayek (1976, 20) posits, derives from "the significance of rules as an adaptation to this inescapable ignorance of most of the particular circumstances which determine the effects of our actions."

[177] Hayek (1973b, 31) speaks of knowledge that "has become incorporated in the schemata of thought which guide us."

[178] Hayek ([1962b] 2014, 246f.): "They [the rules] will often determine or limit the range of possibilities within which the choice is made consciously. By eliminating certain kinds of action altogether and providing certain routine ways of achieving the object, they merely restrict the alternatives on which a conscious choice is required. . . . Thus, even decisions which have been carefully considered will in part be determined by rules of which the acting person is not aware. Like scientific laws, the rules which guide an individual's action are better seen as determining what he will not do rather than what he will do."

[179] Hayek ([1969] 2014, 320): "What this amounts to is that all the 'knowledge' of the external world which such an organism possesses consists in the action patterns which the stimuli tend to evoke, or, with special reference to the human mind, that what we call knowledge is primarily a system of rules of action."

[180] "Within Systems," § 12, this volume, p. 366.

phylogenetic and ontogenetic "learning," the model or theory is shaped by the evolutionary principle of selection by consequences. The hypotheses of which it consists are "tested and confirmed or refuted according to their effectiveness as guides to action" (Hayek [1969] 2014, 321).[181] While the theory or model is itself the product of selection by consequences, the brain as a system that "within itself contains a model guiding its actions" (*TSO*, 5.91) can, in a sense, apply the very same evolutionary principle in a *forward-looking* sense, selecting among potential alternative courses of actions in terms of their *anticipated* consequences.[182] As Hayek ([1967c] 2014, 285) states: "The unique attribute of the brain is that it can produce a representative model on which alternative actions and their consequences can be tried out beforehand."[183] In the next section I shall take a closer look at this "unique attribute of the brain" and its relevance for the explanation of intentional, *purposive* action. First, however, I want to examine the relation between Hayek's view of the mind as a "model-building apparatus" and his emphasis on *subjectivism* as a distinguishing feature of the social sciences.

Hayek accuses strict behaviorists of a "naïve realism" ([1941] 2010, 261) that ignores the fact that individuals' responses to external events depend on their "internal structure" (i.e., the theory or model embodied in the mind's classifying system). The ambition of a pure empiricism to "entirely dispense with any knowledge of the subjectively experienced mental qualities, and . . . to confine itself to the study of bodily responses to physical stimuli" (*TSO*, 1.76) is, so he charges, fundamentally misguided as a methodological "approach to the study of man and society."[184] The fact that "there is a process of multiple classification inserted between stimulus and response (*TSO*, 2.24), Hayek argues, requires us to recognize that "we cannot hope to account for observed behavior without reconstructing the 'intervening process of the

---

[181] Hayek ([1969] 2014, 321): "It seems to me that the organism first develops new potentialities for actions and that only afterwards does experience select and confirm those which are useful as adaptations to typical characteristics of its environment. There will thus be gradually developed by natural selection a repertoire of action types adapted to standard features of the environment."

[182] Hayek added his above-quoted (p. 1) complaint about his social science colleagues' disinterest in *TSO* as a footnote to a remark he made in his epilogue to *Law, Legislation and Liberty* about learnt rules that involve "classifications of different kinds of objects" and which "include a sort of model of the environment that enabled man to predict and anticipate in action external events" (1979, 157).

[183] "Even on the pre-conscious level the organism must live as much in a world of expectations as in a world of 'fact,' and most responses to a given stimulus are probably determined only *via* fairly complex processes of 'trying out' on the model the effects to be expected from alternative courses of action" (*TSO*, 5.61).

[184] Hayek ([1942–44] 2010, 108): "The attitude which, for want of a better term, we shall call the 'objectivism' of the scientistic approach to the study of man and society, has found its most characteristic expression in the various attempts to dispense with our subjective knowledge of the working of the human mind."

brain'" (*TSO*, 2.23).[185] As he censures, the advocates of a strict behaviorism or empiricism are "always and inevitably inconsistent in their procedure" because they "invariably describe the external stimuli which elicit behavior not in terms of their physical properties but in terms of their sensory attributes" (*TSO*, 1.77).[186] In fact, Hayek notes, such an empiricism may be said to be "from its own point of view . . . not radical and consistent enough" (*TSO*, 1.79), because in "confining itself to the study of man's behavior in the phenomenal world" it treats "the main manifestation of mind as a datum rather than as something requiring explanation" (*TSO*, 1.84).

From the necessity to distinguish between "the phenomenal (sensory, subjective, or behavioral)" and the "objective, physical, scientific, etc." world (Hayek [1962b] 2014, 242), Hayek concludes that we need to draw a distinction between the "subjectivist approach of the social sciences and the objectivist approach of the natural sciences" ([1942–44] 2010, 92).[187] In his comments on how, exactly, their "subjectivism"[188] sets the social sciences apart from the natural sciences, he is, however, by no means entirely unambiguous,[189] a fact that has, as Bruce Caldwell (2014, 7, fn. 15) notes, "led to various interpretations of his ideas in the secondary literature." This is, in particular, true for his

---

[185] "The peculiar character of such a classifying system consists in the fact that in a clearly definable sense it will respond, not to the external facts, but to the representations of the facts. . . . All this is of course merely a consequence of the fact that the effects of an external event pass through a series of connecting links and that the effects of different events will be the same or different according as their consequences pass through the same or different connecting links" ("Within System," § 22; this volume, p. 369f.).

[186] Hayek ([1942–44] 2010, 109): "A behaviorist or physicalist, to be consistent, ought not to begin by observing the reactions of people to what our senses tell us are similar objects; he ought to confine himself to studying the reactions to stimuli which are identical in a strictly physical sense."

[187] Caldwell (2014, 6) interprets this as follows: "Hayek's key argument is that the facts of the social sciences differ from those of the natural sciences and therefore require a different method for understanding them."

[188] In reference to "the advance of subjectivism," Hayek ([1942–44] 2010, 97) notes: "All disciplines which deal with the results of conscious human action . . . must start from what men think and mean to do: from the fact that the individuals which compose society are guided in their actions by a classification of things or events according to a system of sense qualities and of concepts . . . which we know because we, too, are men; and that the concrete knowledge which different individuals possess will differ in important respects. Not only man's action toward external objects but also the relations between men and all the social institutions can be understood only by what men think about them."

[189] Hayek ([1942–44] 2010, 94): "And it is probably no exaggeration to say that every important advance in economic theory during the last hundred years was a further step in the consistent application of subjectivism." It sounds almost as an endorsement of Mises's methodological views when Hayek adds in a footnote that this development "has probably been carried out most consistently by Ludwig von Mises," including Mises's a priorism among the "characteristic features of his theories" that "follow directly . . . from this central position" (ibid., fn. 7).

comments on the methodological status of the method of "understanding" (*Verstehen*).[190] What in this regard he exactly wants to claim is, for instance, not easy to determine from statements such as this one:

> We have yet to consider more closely the role which the perception of the meaning of other people's action must play in the scientific explanation of the interaction of men. The problem which arises here is known in the discussion of the methodology of the social sciences as that of *Verstehen* (understanding). We have seen that this understanding of the meaning of actions is of the same kind as the understanding of communication (i.e., of action intended to be understood). . . . The theoretical social sciences . . . endeavor to reconstruct the individual's reasoning from the data which to him are provided by the recognition of the actions of others as meaningful wholes. ([1962b] 2014, 248f.)

It helps to get a clearer view of the issue that is at stake if one keeps two things apart: on the one hand, the role that "understanding" plays in people's everyday life, and, on the other hand, the role it can play in scientific inquiry.

Hayek ([1943] 2014, 83) refers to the role of "understanding" in everyday life when he notes that we "constantly act on the assumption that we can . . . interpret other people's action on the analogy of our own mind."[191] From the fact that in ordinary life "we generally act successfully on the basis of such 'understanding' of the conduct of others" (Hayek [1962b] 2014, 238), we cannot conclude, however, that such "understanding" can also serve as an explanatory tool "for the purposes of the social sciences."[192] This is not only so, as Hayek ([1942–44] 2010, 112) points out, because "although there will usually exist some objective justification why we regard certain things as similar, this need not always be the case," a problem that will become more significant "as we go from interpreting the actions of men very much like ourselves to men who live in a very different environment" ([1943] 2014, 85).[193] More importantly, it is not so because there is a fundamental difference

---

[190] Hayek ([1942–44] 2010, 89): "Our procedure is based on the experience that other people as a rule . . . classify their sense impressions as we do. But we not only know this. It would be impossible to explain or understand human action without making use of this knowledge."

[191] Hayek ([1963b] 2014, 442): "The undeniable fact is that we generally recognize the actions of other people as intelligible or having meaning. All human intercourse, above all, all communication, but also all recognition of the action of others as being directed to a purpose and therefore forming a significant link in the structure of social relationships, rests on this capacity."

[192] This is what Hayek ([1943] 2014, 82) may seem to suggest when he speaks of our interpretation of human action as "purposive or meaningful, whether we do so in ordinary life or for the purposes of the social sciences."

[193] Hayek ([1962b] 2014, 245): "Intelligibility is certainly a matter of degree and it is commonplace that people who are more alike also understand each other better. Yet this does not

between the "intuitive understanding" that can guide our everyday conduct and a scientific explanation that must be explicated in terms of arguments, the validity of which can be intersubjectively examined. Hayek ([1964a] 1992, 148f.) hints at this difference when he notes that "our capacity for 'comprehending' human action undoubtedly adds information which we can use in explaining it," and then adds that we need to distinguish, though, the "comprehension which can furnish the basis of a theory from the emphatic 'understanding' sometimes claimed as the basis of explanation."[194]

The undisputed fact that the social sciences, different from the natural sciences, have to account in their explanations for the subjective component in human behavior does not dispense "economics as an empirical science" (Hayek [1937] 2014, 68) from the requirement to state its explanations in terms of refutable conjectures. How is one then to interpret Hayek's ([1942–44] 2010, 114) dictum that the method of the natural sciences loses "its raison d'être . . . where we try to understand human beings"? Given his endorsement of Popper's falsificationist methodology,[195] it would surely have been inconsistent for him to subscribe to a methodological dualism that draws a principal dividing line between the natural and the social sciences. I suppose that, viewed in the wider context of Hayek's writings, the quoted dictum should be read as a rejection of an approach that he labels "scientism," not as the claim that explanations of the social sciences are exempt from the falsifiability standard. In other words, I propose the following interpretation of Hayek's admittedly ambiguous reasoning about the role of "subjectivism": In the social sciences, the method of the natural sciences loses its raison d'être in so far as its limitation to "objective facts, defined in physical terms" is concerned. Yet it

---

alter the fact that even in the limiting case of . . . understanding between men of different cultural background . . . intelligibility of communication and other acts rests on a partial similarity of mental structure."

[194] Hayek seems to distance himself from both the scientism of the "objectivists" as well as from the claims made for "understanding" as a special methodology, when he notes: "While the one side claimed that our data were not only based on observation but on the same kind of observation as in physics, observation of events which could be defined in terms of sensory elements, the other side claimed that we had to resort to a special procedure of understanding (*Verstehen*) which was sometimes represented as if it were not observation. Neither of these attitudes seems to me to do justice to what is a real problem" ([1963b] 2014, 442).

[195] Popper ([1968] 1972, 185): "I oppose the attempt to proclaim the method of understanding as the characteristic of the humanities, the mark by which we may distinguish them from the natural sciences." To critics who might characterize his view as "scientistic," Popper answers in a footnote (ibid., fn. 35): "The term 'scientism' meant originally 'the slavish imitation of the method and language of [natural] science' . . . ; it was introduced in this sense by Hayek. . . . I suggested its use as a name for the aping of what is widely *mistaken* for the method of science; and Hayek now agrees (in his Preface to his *Studies in Philosophy, Politics, and Economics* . . .) that the methods actually practiced by natural scientists are different from 'what most of them told us . . . and urged the representatives of other disciplines to imitate.'"

does not lose its raison d'être in so far as the requirement of falsifiability is concerned. Intuitive "understanding" may serve as a heuristic device in the formation of testable explanatory conjectures, but it cannot be a substitute for such conjectures.

However one may judge the textual evidence of Hayek's explicit methodological statements,[196] though, most significant is the fact that with his conception of the mind as an apparatus of classification and its corollary, the focus on rule-following behavior, Hayek has laid the theoretical foundation for an intersubjective account of subjective human action in terms of refutable conjectures. At the core of this account is his argument that "understanding" and rule-following are closely connected. In Hayek's account, intuitive understanding of other people's actions is possible because—respectively, to the extent that—we are guided in our own behavior by the same rules. We "understand" another person's action because we can subsume it under a rule.[197] Or, as Hayek ([1962b] 2014, 234) puts it, "our capacity to recognize other people's actions as meaningful . . . must be based on the possession of highly abstract rules governing our actions, although we are not aware of their existence and even less capable of articulating them in words."[198]

As Hayek suggests, in our everyday conduct we surely need not be aware of the rules on which our understanding of other people's actions is based.[199] Yet, as noted before, such intuitive understanding cannot be a substitute for a scientific explanation stated in terms of refutable conjectures. If understanding and rule-following are interconnected as Hayek posits, one should conclude that such an explanation must *explicate* the rules on which actions are conjectured to be based. Explaining actions—by contrast to intuitively understanding them—would mean explicitly "stating the rules governing the actions

---

[196] Caldwell (2004b, 252, fn. 8) notes in reference to Hayek's "subjectivism": "I sometimes have labeled his approach 'scientific subjectivism'; in my opinion, Hayek was trying to provide a basis in natural science for the use of an intentionalist, subjectivist approach in the social sciences."

[197] This is, I suppose, the most defendable interpretation of Hayek's arguments. The reverse— that we can subsume other people's actions under rules because we can "understand" them— may seem to be implied when Hayek ([1942–44] 2010, 94f.) argues: "Unless we can understand what the acting people mean by their actions any attempt to explain them, that is, to subsume them under rules which connect similar situations with similar actions, is bound to fail." A possible reading of this statement is that our intuitive understanding may serve as a heuristic device for explicating the rules on which it is based.

[198] Hayek ([1962b] 2014, 249): "Our capacity to recognize action as following rules and having meaning rests on ourselves already being equipped with these rules. This 'knowledge by acquaintance' presupposes therefore that some of the rules in terms of which we perceive and act are the same as those by which the conduct of those whose actions we interpret is guided."

[199] Hayek ([1968c] 1978, 81): "Men may 'know how' to act, and the manner of their action may be correctly described by an articulated rule, without their explicitly 'knowing that' the rule is such and such; that is, they need not be able to state the rule in words in order to conform to it in their actions or to recognize whether others have or have not done so."

of which the actors will usually be unaware" (ibid., 233). The conjecture that person A does X because she faces a situation of type S and follows a rule according to which in situations of this type X is the appropriate thing to do, can be intersubjectively examined in two regards. Its general claim that in situations of type S the person will adopt, as a rule, actions of type X is refutable, and so is its specific claim that the person faces a situation of type S. What distinguishes our scientific explanations of actions from our intuitive understanding is that the former explicates as testable conjectures the rules that the latter tacitly imputes. In our everyday conduct, our rule-imputing intuition allows us to understand how others acted, as well as to predict how they will act in certain kinds of situations. In fact, one may interpret understanding as a kind of retroactive prediction, saying that, given the situation a person was in, we would have expected her to act as she did. In our efforts to provide a scientific account, we explain and predict actions in terms of refutable conjectures, explicating the rules on which these actions are supposed to be based. This is what Hayek ([1968c] 1978, 81) refers to when he states that "a rule may effectively govern action in the sense that from knowing it we can predict how people will act, without it being known as a verbal formula to the actors."

9. "The Causal Determination of Purposive Action"[200]

In his often quoted statement that "man is as much a rule-following animal as a purpose-seeking one" Hayek (1973b, 11) appears to draw a distinction between *rule-following conduct* and *purposive action*, which raises the issue of whether explaining the latter requires a different approach than the naturalistic outlook, discussed in the previous section, that Hayek proposes for the former. After all, there appears to be an obvious difference between the backward-looking logic of explaining actions in terms of rules acquired in the *past*, and the forward-looking logic of explaining them in terms of goals as aimed-at *future* states. On the undisputable fact that conscious, purposeful action is *goal-directed* or guided by *intentions*, Mises ([1962] 2006, 6) based his verdict: "The natural sciences are causality research; the sciences of human action are teleological."

At the very beginning of this introduction, I mentioned that to Hayek's great disappointment his friend Karl Popper "never would show any sympathy with the argument of *TSO* which he more or less, though politely, rejected."[201]

---

[200] In a letter to Gottfried Haberler (letter of February 23, 1957, Hayek papers, box 16, folder 1, HIA), Hayek says he had chosen this title for a paper he planned to write up "in the summer." Bruce Caldwell (2004a, 301, note 17) notes that he has been unable to locate the paper in the Hayek archive.

[201] See above, fn. 10.

In the present context—the issue of how intention-guided, purpose-seeking action can be explained—it is instructive to take a closer look at Popper's reservations about *TSO*, and his ensuing exchange with Hayek. Upon its publication, Hayek had sent Popper a copy of *TSO* to which the latter responded in a letter, dated December 2, 1952, saying:

> I am not sure whether one could describe your theory as a causal theory of the sensory order. I think, indeed, that one can. But then, it would also be the sketch of a causal theory of the mind. But I think I can show that a causal theory of the mind cannot be true (although I cannot show this of the sensory order); more precisely, I think I can show the impossibility of a causal theory of the human language (although I cannot show the impossibility of a causal theory of perception). I am writing a paper on the impossibility of a causal theory of the human language, and its bearing upon the body-mind problem,[202] which must be finished in ten days. I shall send you a copy as soon as it is typed.[203]

The paper Popper referred to is his "Language and the Body-Mind Problem," published in 1953; the very first sentence reads: "This is a paper on the impossibility of a physicalist causal theory of the human language" (Popper [1953a] 1989, 293). Building on Karl Bühler's distinction between different functions of language,[204] Popper arrives in this article at the conclusion that *"no causal physical theory of the descriptive and argumentative functions of language is possible"* (ibid., 298), a claim on which he essentially based his objection to Hayek's ambition to develop a causal theory of mental phenomena.[205] Hayek responded to Popper's critique in a letter, dated December 7, 1952:

[202] Hayek refers to this problem at the very beginning of *TSO* (1.2): "The traditional heading under which our problem has been discussed in the past is that of the 'relation' between mind and body, or between mental and physical events. It can also be described by the question of 'What is mind?' or 'What is the place of mind in the realm of nature?'"

[203] Hayek papers, box 44, folder 1, HIA. Hayek must surely have told Popper about the ideas he was developing in *TSO* while he was still his colleague at the LSE and in correspondence after he had moved to Chicago. An indication of this is that in a letter to Hayek, dated September 10, 1952 (Hayek papers, box 44, folder 1, HIA), in which he speaks about his work on the "body-mind problem," Popper inserts the remark: "Note: There *may* be thus a causal theory of the sensory order but not of human thought."

[204] Popper did his doctoral dissertation with Karl Bühler. For more details see below, "Within Systems," § 39, fn. 7.

[205] In retrospect Hayek (1983b, 255f.) has said about the problem he had tried to answer in *TSO*: "That problem is what determines the difference between the different sensory qualities. The attempt was to reduce it to a system of causal connections—associations, you might say—in which the quality of a particular sensation . . . is really its position in a system of potential connections leading up to actions."

I am . . . much looking forward to the arrival of the MS of your article which I expect will clear up some of the points in your letter which, because they are scarcely more than brief hints, I do not fully understand. It all depends on what you mean by a "causal explanation." Would you regard what I call an "explanation of the principle" a causal explanation at all? If your argument were intended merely to prove that we can never explain why at a particular moment such and such sensations, mental processes, etc. take place I should agree. If, on the other hand you were intending to deny that it can be explained how physical processes can be arranged in the general kind of order which is characteristic of mental phenomena, it would need a great deal to convince me.

In a follow-up letter, dated January 19, 1953, Popper restated his critique, noting:

As to my comments on your book, they are, as far as critique is concerned, implicit in my paper. I think you have made a splendid effort towards a theory of the sub-linguistic (= sub-human ((descriptive)) language) level of mind; but I believe that no physiological approach (although most important) can be sufficient to explain the descriptive and argumentative functions of language. Or in other words, there can be no causal or physiological theory of reason.[206]

Hayek, in turn, in his letter to Popper of February 3, 1953, restated his argument about "explanations of the principle":

I have only just got Bühler's book out of the library and of course not yet had time to read it (you have of course drawn my attention to it earlier, but its size has always acted as a deterrent). I am convinced that the hierarchy idea in his classification of language functions is sound. And how far this hierarchic character of the language functions makes an explanation of the higher functions impossible depends on what we require of an explanation. As you know, I regard myself a full explanation of the higher function as impossible. But I still feel that an "explanation of the principle" . . . might be possible. . . . On the whole I would like to say, that although your article helped me a good deal to get further with my own thinking on these problems, it has not really convinced me. Or perhaps I should say, I am not really certain what you are asserting.[207]

---

[206] Hayek papers, box 44, folder 1, HIA.
[207] Hayek papers, box 44, folder 1, HIA.

Obviously, for Hayek it was not at all clear what Popper's arguments on "the impossibility of a causal theory of the human language" amounted to and, in particular, what bearing they might have on his own project. Nevertheless, the respect he had for his friend's opinion seems to have motivated Hayek to make an effort to respond to Popper's challenge. As Hayek had mentioned in his letter to Popper of December 7, 1952, he was working at the time on a paper dealing with the problem of "the distinction between what we can say 'within a system' and what we can say 'about a system.'"[208] Apparently prompted by Popper's objections, Hayek included in the draft paper he was writing, and which he subtitled "A Statement of Some Problems of a Theory of Communication," a section entitled "Program of Further Discussion," in which he sought to deal with Bühler's theory of language functions. The paper, under the title "Within Systems and About Systems," which was never finished and remained an unpublished fragment,[209] is included in its incomplete form in the present volume (pp. 361–381).[210]

As Hayek has said in retrospect, he abandoned the project because he found it "excrutiately difficult,"[211] a fact taken by commentators like Jack Birner and Edward Feser as evidence of his failure to answer Popper's challenge.[212] It is surely true that "Hayek never addressed Popper's arguments in any of his published works" (Feser 2011, 74). Yet it seems to me rather doubtful whether his "failure" to answer Popper's claim about the impossibility of a causal explanation of the "higher functions of language" is of much relevance for the principal subject of *TSO*. As Hayek politely indicated in his response to Popper's critique, it is far from clear what Popper's claim exactly

---

[208] Immediately following the above-quoted passage, Hayek says in his letter of December 7, 1952: "Of course, my analysis of a particular problem raises the most far-reaching philosophical problems. I am now for months puzzling about what just now seems to me the most general problem of all and which at the moment I describe for myself as the distinction between what we can say 'within a system' and what we can say 'about a system.' I am convinced that this is a most important problem, since ever since I began to see it clearly I meet it constantly in all sorts of different connections, but though I have made some little headway it is one of the most difficult and elusive problems I have ever tackled."

[209] The section "Program of Further Discussion" appears at the end of the fragment, §§ 36ff., this volume, pp. 374ff.

[210] According to Caldwell (2004a, 301, fn. 17), Hayek decided to break up the unfinished paper into parts to be used in other publications, such as his "Degrees of Explanation" (Hayek [1955] 2014).

[211] Letter, F. A. Hayek to Walter Weimer, December 29, 1983, Hayek papers, box 57, folder 2, HIA.

[212] Birner (2009, 189): "The abrupt end of the manuscript is consistent with Hayek's comment that he abandoned work on the paper; he had failed to explain one or more higher functions of language within his own theory—as Popper had predicted." See also Feser 2011, 74, 92ff.

entails.[213] More importantly, it is even less clear what its bearing is on Hayek's project to propose a naturalistic account of how men learn about the world in ways that allow them to successfully navigate the problem environment they are facing. More tangible and of direct relevance for Hayek's project, though, is an issue that Popper raises in connection with his argument on language functions, namely whether *intentions* as mental states can be accounted for in causal terms,[214] an issue that Hayek had addressed in his "Within Systems" paper before turning to the issue of communication.[215] My discussion here will focus on this issue, leaving the communications issue aside.

Rejecting Popper's "impossible to explain" claim, Hayek pursues an explanatory ambition that he clearly states in § 24 of "Within Systems." In reference to the mind's internal representation of the external world, he says:

> That the map of the environment (as it has been called in *The Sensory Order*) which guides the action of the system, is, as it were, a four-dimensional map which includes a time-dimension, is of crucial importance for the causal explanation of a feature which appears to be common to all structures which we describe as "minds." This is the property to which we refer by such terms as "intention," "purpose," "aim," "need," or "desire." Though we must not use any of these "mental" terms until we have succeeded in adequately defining them in terms of our causal system, this is clearly necessary if we are to substantiate the claim that we can supply at least an explanation of the principle on which "mind" operates.[216]

At the heart of the controversy between Hayek and Popper is the issue of whether mental states—such as intentions, purposes, and goals—can, as Hayek posits, in principle, be explained in terms of physical states or whether, as Popper holds, this is in principle impossible. For Popper such mental states are autonomous forces that act upon the physical world. Referring to his article "Language and the Body-Mind Problem," he notes in his letter to Hayek of January 19, 1953: "It is a plea for interactionism,"[217] and in his follow-up

---

[213] In fact, in light of the methodological views that are generally associated with his name, including his dictum that we cannot know our future knowledge, it seems strange for Popper to erect ex ante such principal limits to what can be explained. Much more congenial to his own methodological paradigm, one might consider what Konrad Lorenz (1950, 223), like Popper a student of Karl Bühler (see above, fn. 169), has said about such "impossible to explain" claims: "The legitimate answer to this is obviously that no man can know to what extent causal analysis is going to succeed in explaining the process of life."

[214] Popper ([1953a] 1989, 293): "In arguing with other people . . . , we cannot but attribute to them intentions, and this means, mental states."

[215] "Within Systems," §§ 5, 24, 25, 32–36; this volume, pp. 363, 370–71, 373–74.

[216] This volume, p. 370.

[217] Hayek papers, box 44, folder 1, HIA.

letter of January 26 he adds: "I am sure not only that . . . [mental states exist], but that they *interact* with physical states."[218] By contrast, for Hayek mental states cannot be separated from physical states as an independent force but must be accounted for in terms of the same principles that govern the physical world.[219] In his letter of February 3, 1953, Hayek responds to Popper's argument about mental states interacting with physical states:

> My difficulty with your "*interactionism*" is that it seems to presuppose something like a mental "substance" to which I cannot attach any meaning. . . . My inability of understanding what are the two entities between which you postulate "interaction" is real. I have no objection against your saying that the former can never (in principle) be described in physical terms and that therefore a "reduction" of the whole world into "nothing but" events described in observational terms will forever be impossible. I say so much in my book. But to say that we shall never be able to say what particular physical events correspond to particular mental events does not mean that the whole range of mental events is not conceivable as an order of physical events—more complex than any we can ever describe in detail, but not requiring a kind of substance or action with which we are not familiar in the physical world.[220]

Hayek draws a distinction between two kinds of explanations that allows him to specify where he agrees and where he disagrees with Popper. This is the distinction, which I shall discuss in more detail in the next section, between, as he calls it, an "explanation of the principle" and a "full or detailed explanation."[221] Hayek agrees with Popper's argument insofar as he speaks of "our inherent incapacity to explain mental processes in detail or to derive them from material processes" and explicitly concedes: "we will never be able to reduce particular mental processes to specific material processes."[222] In this sense he acknowledges that "for practical purposes we shall always have to adopt a dualistic view" (*TSO*, 8.46).[223] Yet, disagreeing with Popper, he denies

---

[218] Hayek papers, box 44, folder 1, HIA. Popper ([1953a] 1989, 298): "There is no reason (except a mistaken physical determinism) why mental states and physical states should not interact. . . . If we act through being influenced by the grasp of abstract relationships, we initiate physical causal chains which have no sufficient *physical* causal antecedents."

[219] As C. Herrmann-Pillath (1992, 148) observes: "Critical rationalism as evolutionary epistemology is now confronted with a serious clash of tension between Hayek's psychoneural monism and Popper's dualistic interactionism."

[220] Hayek papers, box 44, folder 1, HIA.

[221] "What Is Mind?," this volume, p. 358.

[222] "What Is Mind?," this volume, p. 360.

[223] Butos and Koppl (2006, 33) interpret Hayek's arguments as an "explicit defense of methodological dualism." In my reading this is not what Hayek means to imply when he notes that "for

"any ultimate dualism of the forces governing the realms of the mind and that of the physical world respectively" (ibid.) and seeks to explain mental phenomena "by the operation of processes of the same kind as those which we observe in the material world" (*TSO*, 8.40).[224]

Rather than adopting a materialist view, Hayek argues, his antidualism "is less materialistic than the dualistic theories which postulate a distinct mind 'substance'" (ibid.). Instead of "viewing the mind as a special 'substance' that is different from matter," the antidualist theory he advocates conceives of the mind as "an order that reveals itself in the relations between material things."[225] As Hayek puts it:

> An account of mental phenomena which avoids the conception of a distinct mental substance is therefore the opposite of materialistic, because it does not attribute to mind any property which we derive from our acquaintance with matter. In being content to regard mind as a peculiar order of events, different from the order of events which we encounter in the physical world, but determined by the same kind of forces as those that rule in the world, it is indeed the only theory which is not materialistic. (*TSO*, 8.43)

The "particular order of events," as Hayek defines the mind, is, as noted above (pp. 17ff.), the "neural order of the fibers, and of the impulses proceeding in these fibers," which constitutes the "mental or phenomenal order of sensations." He could have meant it as a direct response to Popper's dualism when Hayek summarizes as the "conclusion" of his theory "that the two orders are . . . identical and that to postulate a separate set of terms for the mental order would be redundant" (*TSO*, 2.11), and also when he states:

> The contention that all the attributes of sensory qualities (and of mental qualities) are relations to other such qualities, and that the totality of these relations between mental qualities exhausts all there is to be said about the mental order, corresponds of course, (perhaps we should say follows from) the conception of mind itself as an order of events. (*TSO*, 1.105)

To conceive of the mind as an order of neural events means, as Hayek notes, to explicitly distinguish between the physical properties the individual neural events will "possess by themselves" and the properties that they will possess "solely as a result of their position in the order of inter-connected neural events" (*TSO*, 2.27). By contrast to their physical properties of neural

---

practical purposes we shall always have to adopt a dualistic view" (*TSO*, 8.46). He explicitly says: "My theory is antidualist" ("What Is Mind?," this volume, p. 358).

[224] "What Is Mind?," this volume, p. 349.

[225] "What Is Mind?," this volume, p. 358.

events (i.e., "those properties which will appear if they are placed in a variety of experimental relations to different other kinds of events") their "mental properties are those which they possess only as a part of the particular structure and which may be largely independent of the former" (*TSO*, 2.29).[226]

Without explicitly using the term, in effect Hayek invokes the category of *information* when he stresses the properties that neural events possess as parts of a relational structure. As noted above (pp. 22f.), Hayek's main argument about the formation of the neural order is that a system of "connections formed by the linkages between different impulses" (*TSO*, 5.17) constitutes an internal representation of external events in the environment.[227] In other words, the neural order shaped by the experience of the species and the individual is a carrier of information about the environment that can serve in guiding behavior. This is, of course, in line with what has been said above (pp. 46ff.) about Hayek's arguments on knowledge embodied in the *rules* that govern our perceptions and our actions. In the present context, the argument that the neural order is a carrier of information is of particular significance because it provides the cue to Hayek's proposal for a causal explanation of intentional, purposeful action.

Because it is very much in line with, and helps to arrive at a better understanding of, Hayek's arguments, it is instructive to take first a brief look at what the evolutionary biologist Ernst Mayr has said about the causal explanation of goal-directed behavior.[228] Mayr, who, like Hayek, is counted among the founders of modern evolutionary epistemology,[229] has proposed to use the term "teleonomic" to describe purposeful, goal-directed action in order to avoid the ambiguities that are notoriously invoked when such behavior is said to require a "teleological" as opposed to a causal explanation. His central claim is that a "teleonomic process or behavior is one that owes its goal

---

[226] "It is at least conceivable that the particular kind of order which we call mind might be built up from any one of several kinds of different elements—electrical, chemical, or what not" (*TSO*, 2.29).—"That a particular order of events or objects is something different from all the individual events taken separately is the significant fact behind the endless and unprofitable talk about the whole being greater than the mere sum of its parts. . . . An order involves elements *plus* certain relations between them. . . . The capacity of entering into such a relation is, of course, a property of the elements" (*TSO*, 2.30).

[227] "In *The Sensory Order* it has been shown how the formation of connections ('linkages') between simultaneously occurring representations of external events will build up such a structure which is capable of classifying external actions according to the effects which the corresponding external events will produce in the environment" ("Within Systems," this volume, p. 366).

[228] Ernst Mayr deserves credit for having developed the "biological theory" Hayek calls for when he says: "An adequate account of the highly purposive character of the action of the central nervous system would require as its foundation a more generally accepted biological theory of the nature of adaptive and purposive processes than is yet available" (*TSO*, 4.5). For a more detailed discussion of Mayr's approach and its affinity to Hayek's theory of rule-following behavior, see Vanberg 2002, 15ff; 2004a, 176ff.; 2004b, 11ff.

[229] See fn. 148 above.

directedness to the operation of a program" (Mayr 1982b, 24).[230] Borrowing the term from the language of information theory, Mayr defines a "program" as "*coded or prearranged information that controls a process (or behavior) leading it toward a given end*" (ibid., 27),[231] noting that the "the existence of teleonomic programs—unmoved movers—is one of the most profound differences between the living and the inanimate world" (ibid., 35).

Mayr's principal message is that looking at goal-directed behavior as teleonomic, program-based behavior provides the foundation for a causal explanation of purposiveness and intentionality, because "a program (1) is something material and (2) exists prior to the initiation of the teleonomic process" (ibid., 27).[232] When we speak of a causal explanation of goal-directed behavior it is important, as Mayr notes, to distinguish between *proximate* causes, the behavior-guiding role of existing programs, and *ultimate* causes, the forces that have produced or shaped these programs.[233] In Mayr's (ibid., 30) words:

> The ultimate causes for the efficiency and seeming purposefulness of these living systems were explained by Darwin in 1859. The adaptiveness of these systems is the result of millions of generations of natural selection. . . . Proximate and ultimate causes must be carefully separated in the discussion of

---

[230] Mayr (1982b, 23) distinguishes "teleonomic processes in living nature," such as the goal-directed behavior of a predator chasing its prey or purposeful human action, from "teleomatic processes in inanimate nature," such as radioactive decay or a ball rolling down a slope, that are not controlled by a program. As Mayr (1988, 45) notes: "The occurrence of goal-directed processes is perhaps the most characteristic feature of the world of living organisms."

[231] Mayr (1992, 129): "There is a strict equivalence between the 'program' of the information theorists, and the genetic and somatic programs of the biologists."—Mayr (1982b, 27f.): "My definition of 'program' is deliberately chosen in such a way as to avoid drawing a line between seemingly 'purposive' behavior in organisms and in manmade machines. . . . The origin of a program is quite irrelevant for the definition. It can be a product of evolution, as are all genetic programs, or it can be the acquired information of an open program, or it can be a manmade device."—Mayr (1988, 31): "The purposive action of an individual, insofar as it is based on the properties of its genetic code, therefore is no more nor less purposive than the actions of a computer that has been programmed to respond appropriately to various inputs. It is, if I may say so, a purely mechanical purposiveness."

[232] Mayr (1982b, 27): "The programs that control processes in organisms are either entirely laid down in the DNA of the genotype ('closed programs') or constituted in such a way that they can incorporate additional information ('open programs') acquired through learning, conditioning, or through experience. . . . Most behavior, particularly in higher animals, is controlled by open programs."

[233] Mayr (1961, 1503): "Ultimate causes . . . are causes that have a history and that have been incorporated into the system through thousands of generations of natural selection. It is evident that the functional biologist would be concerned with analysis of the proximate causes, while the evolutionary biologist would be concerned with analysis of the ultimate causes. . . . Proximate causes govern the responses of the individual (and his organs) to immediate factors of the environment while ultimate causes are responsible for the evolution of the particular DNA code of information with which every individual or every species is endowed."

teleological systems. . . . A system is capable of performing teleological processes because it was programmed to function in this manner.

Though Hayek does not use the term "program,"[234] his thoughts on "the causal determination of purposive action" are perfectly compatible with Mayr's account, and could be easily translated into Mayr's language.[235] The notion of "coded information that controls behavior" that Mayr captures with the term "program" is implied when Hayek speaks of "maps," "models," or "dispositions" that can guide behavior "by representations of the consequences of different kinds of behavior" (*TSO*, 5.68).[236] And like Mayr, Hayek regards the coded information to which these concepts refer as the cue to a naturalistic, causal explanation of purposive, intentional behavior. As he puts it:

> The structure of representations . . . or . . . the map of the environment (as it has been called in *The Sensory Order*) which guides the action of the system, . . . is of crucial importance for the causal explanation of a feature which appears to be common to all structures which we describe as "minds." This is the property to which we refer by such terms as "intention," "purpose," "aim," "need" or "desire."[237]

> The adaptive and purposive behavior of the organism is accounted for by the existence of the "model" of the environment formed by the pattern of impulses in the nervous system. . . . If the model can pre-form or predict the effects of different courses of action, and pre-select among the effects

[234] It is worth noting, though, that D. T. Campbell and K. Lorenz, who are also counted among the founders of evolutionary epistemology, use the term in the same sense as Mayr. Lorenz (1985, 280) speaks of "phylogenetically programmed behavior mechanisms" and "phylogenetic programming" (ibid., 281), stating: "In fact, everything learned must have as its foundation a phylogenetically provided program if . . . appropriate species-preserving behavior patterns are to be produced" (ibid., 279). Referring to his "effort to put 'the problem of knowledge' into a behavioristic framework which takes full cognizance of man's status as a biological product of an evolutionary development," Campbell (1987b, 92, fn. 2) notes: "In this perspective, any process providing a stored program for organismic adaptation in external environments is included as a knowledge process, and any gain in the adequacy of such a program is regarded as a gain in knowledge."

[235] In her summary of *TSO*, R. Agnito (1975) speaks of Hayek's account of the "mind as including neurological information processing" (171) and notes: "Ultimately, then, information pertains to physiological connections in relationship to whatever is 'out there.' . . . In other words, this complex structure of functional connections (or linkages) may be viewed as a programmed tendency to interpret or evaluate external events which affect the organism" (165).

[236] "In building models of the course of events which may take place in the environment, it will not only be representations of actual or present events in the environment but also representations of potential or future events in that environment which will determine the responses of the system" ("Within Systems," § 13 and 23; this volume, pp. 366f. and 370).

[237] "Within Systems," § 24; this volume, p. 370.

of alternative courses those which in the existing state of the organism are "desirable," there is no reason why it should not also be capable of directing the organism towards the particular course of action which has thus been "mapped out" for it. (*TSO*, 5.68)[238]

Like Mayr, Hayek also notes the analogy between the coded information stored—as "programs" or as "maps" and "models"[239]—in living organisms and in man-made machines when he argues:

That such guidance by a model which reproduces, and experimentally tries out, the possibilities offered by a given situation, can produce action which is purposive to any desired degree, is shown by the fact that machines could be produced on this principle . . . which show all the characteristics of purposive behavior. Such machines, however, are still comparatively primitive . . . compared with the central nervous system. . . . But although for this reason such machines cannot be described as brains, with regard to the purposiveness they differ from a brain merely in degree not in kind. (*TSO*, 5.75)[240]

This also means, as Hayek points out, that purposiveness does not require consciousness:

It is notoriously difficult to discuss purposive behavior without employing terms which suggest the presence of conscious mental states. The phenomenon of purposive action, however, does not presuppose the existence of an elaborate mental order like the one which we know from conscious experience, and still less the presence of consciousness itself. Some degree of purposiveness can be attained by structures infinitely more simple than those which constitute the mental order. (*TSO*, 576)[241]

Hayek attributes the "intellectual difficulty" in recognizing the causal nature of, in Mayr's terms, "teleonomic processes" to the fact that such processes appear "to involve a reversal of causation: the effect which is at first

[238] As a qualification Hayek notes: "There will, in general, also exist more than one possible goal of the desired kind, and more than one way of achieving any one goal. The determination of purposive action involves, therefore, a further process of selection among the various different courses of action which might satisfy the initiating urge" (*TSO*, 5.70).

[239] On Hayek's use of the terms "map" and "model," see above, pp. 23f.

[240] In reference to the internal representation of the environment, Hayek notes: "For much of our argument it will even be irrelevant whether this structure has formed itself as a result of the experience of the system, or whether it has been given to the system by a designer" ("Within Systems," § 13; this volume, p. 367).

[241] By contrast, Popper ([1982] 1994, 17) states: "My hypothesis is that the original task of consciousness was to anticipate success and failure in problem-solving and to signal to the organism . . . whether it was on the right or wrong path to the solution of the problem."

represented as the end of the represented chain of actions is then assumed to become the cause of this same chain of actions being actually carried out."[242] Yet the "intellectual difficulty" should be easy to overcome if one considers the example of unsuccessful actions which amply illustrate that what causes an action is obviously not the *effect* it actually produces but the purposes or intentions that motivated it (i.e., mental states that *precede* the action).[243]

Instead of the concepts "map" and "model," Hayek has preferred to use in later publications the term "disposition" when discussing the issue of purposiveness and intentionality.[244] In retrospect, he has even said with disappointment that in rereading *TSO* he discovered that he had used "the term *disposition* only a few times in connection with my discussion of purpose and intention," adding: "It seems to me now that I could have greatly simplified my exposition in the book if I had throughout used the term *disposition*."[245] One may doubt whether this is actually the case. After all, with the term "disposition," Hayek circumscribes in essence the very same thing for which he had used in *TSO* the terms "map" and "model." And it does not seem to add more clarity when he speaks of dispositions "as adaptations to typical features of the environment" (Hayek [1969] 2014, 319), and when he relates the concept to the fact "that all the 'knowledge' of the external world . . . consists in the action patterns which the stimuli tend to evoke" (ibid., 320).[246] What, instead, might have truly "simplified the exposition" is if Hayek had had at his disposal the terminology that Mayr has suggested.

10. Complex Phenomena and "Explanations of the Principle"

In the above-quoted letter of December 7, 1952, in which he responded to Popper's claim that "a causal theory of the mind cannot be true," Hayek

---

[242] "Within Systems," § 30; this volume, p. 372. K. Lorenz (1950, 228) has commented on the difference between our intuitive understanding of purposive action and its scientific explanation: "It is a fateful misunderstanding to believe that the teleological 'understanding' of behavior . . . makes it superfluous to gain insight into its causation."

[243] "The conception that a system selects a particular course of action because this course of action is represented as producing an effect towards which the system is disposed at the moment implies that this course of action and its successive effects must first be represented in their temporal order" ("Within Systems," § 29; this volume, p. 372).

[244] Hayek ([1969] 2014, 321): "In the sphere of action what I have called 'the primacy of the abstract' would then merely mean that the disposition for a kind of action possessing certain properties comes first and the particular action is determined by the superimposition of many such dispositions."

[245] This volume, p. 386.

[246] Hayek (1973b, 75): "*Rule* in this context means simply a propensity or disposition to act or not to act in a certain manner. . . . Any such rule will always operate in combination and often in competition with other rules or dispositions and with particular impulses."

noted: "It all depends on what you mean by a 'causal explanation.' Would you regard what I call an 'explanation of the principle' a causal explanation at all?" In retrospect he specified what he had meant to achieve in *TSO* as follows:

> You could, in theory, reproduce a sort of map of how one stimulus evokes other stimuli and then further stimuli which can, in principle, reproduce all the mental processes. I say "in principle" because it is much too complicated ever to do it. It led me, incidentally to the distinction between an explanation of the principle and an explanation of the detail . . . which I really developed in my psychological work and then applied to economics. (1983b, 256)

Hayek leaves no doubt that the theory advanced in *TSO* does not aim at "fully explaining any particular mental act" (*TSO*, 1.01). As he puts it:

> When we claim to provide an "explanation" this will never mean more than an "explanation of the principle" by which the phenomena of the kind in question can be produced. . . . Though we may be able to explain the general character of the processes at work, their operation may be so complicated in detail as to place their full description forever beyond the power of the human mind. (*TSO*, 2.18)[247]

The limits that are set to our ability to provide a causal theory of the mind translate into limits of our ability to explain human action. Hayek emphasizes that when he speaks of a "causal determination of purposive action" he does not mean to claim that one can explain or predict specific actions, but only means to assert that in the realm of human action principles of causation are at work of which we can seek to gain a general understanding. The distinction between an explanation of the principle and a "full or detailed explanation"[248] means here that, although we may know the general principles that determine human action, "it will never be possible for us to explain or predict . . . why the human mind under certain circumstances will lead us to certain actions rather than to others."[249] The reason is that, because "the whole history of the

[247] Hayek ([1969] 2014, 326): "And although . . . a complete reduction of the subjectively experienced mental qualities to exhaustively defined places in a network of physical relations is in principle impossible for us, . . . we can at least arrive at . . . a limited 'explanation of the principles' involved." See also "Within Systems," § 35; this volume, pp. 373f.
[248] Hayek ([1961] 2014, 376): "By a full explanation I mean here a statement which enables us to derive from ascertainable facts a precise prediction of particular events. Such prediction will be possible only if we can ascertain (and preferably also control) all the circumstances which influence those events."
[249] "What Is Mind?," this volume, p. 358.

organism" (*TSO*, 5.66) will determine its actions, the complexity of all the particular circumstances which exert their influence over the organism's history makes such specific explanation or prediction illusionary.[250] Summarizing his argument, Hayek ([1964b] 2014, 272f.) states:

> We may . . . well be able to establish that every single action of a human being is the necessary result of the inherited structure of his body (particularly of its nervous system) and of all the external influences which have acted upon it since birth. . . . The chief fact would continue to be, in spite of our knowledge of the principle on which the human mind works, that we should not be able to state the full set of particular facts which brought it about that the individual did a particular thing at a particular time. The individual personality would remain for us as much a unique and unaccountable phenomenon which we might hope to influence in a desirable direction by such empirically developed practices as praise and blame, but whose specific actions we could generally not predict and control, because we could not obtain the information on all the particular facts which determined it.[251]

About the conclusion that follows for the study of social phenomena, Hayek ([1961] 2014, 377) says:

> Even if we assume that in principle everybody's action is determined by the combined effect of his inherited constitution, all his past experience, and his knowledge of his environment at the moment when he acts, we clearly can never know all these facts for all the men who form part of any particular social structure. Their individual action must therefore remain largely unpredictable. . . . It has often been contended that the unpredictability of individual conduct must . . . make all significant theoretical knowledge of society impossible. I . . . turn to the task of showing how in the case of the relatively complex structures of society it is still possible to arrive at some useful, though limited, theoretical generalizations.

In the next section, I shall examine the role that the concept of the explanations of the principle, to which he implicitly refers here, plays in Hayek's

---

[250] Hayek ([1969] 2014, 269): "The very insight which theory provides, for example, that almost any event in the course of a man's life may have some effect on almost any of his future actions, makes it impossible that we translate our theoretical knowledge into predictions of specific events."

[251] A "system organized on the principles here described will . . . , as a result of its own operations, . . . scarcely ever respond twice in exactly the same manner to the same external conditions. And it will as a result of 'experience' acquire the capacity of performing entirely new actions" (*TSO*, 5.65).

economic and social theory. Before doing so, two issues that Hayek addresses in the concluding chapter of *TSO*, "Philosophical Consequences," deserve at least a brief look. This is, on the one hand, the issue whether there are limits to the explanation of mental phenomena that go beyond the problems posed by the complexity of the subject, and, on the other hand, the issue of what the claim that human action is "causally determined" implies for the concept of "free will."

Hayek refers to the latter issue in the title, "The Division of the Sciences and the 'Freedom of the Will,'" of the very last section of *TSO*,[252] but he only briefly discusses it directly in one paragraph of this section where, in reference to "the age-old controversy about the 'freedom of will,'" he argues:

> Even though we may know the general principle by which all human action is causally determined by physical processes, this would not mean that to us a particular human action can ever be recognizable as the necessary result of a particular set of physical circumstances. To us human decisions must always appear as the result of the whole of a human personality. (*TSO*, 8.93)[253]

More directly and extensively than in *TSO*, Hayek has addressed the issue of "determinism and free will" in later publications, in particular in chapter 5, "Responsibility and Freedom," of *The Constitution of Liberty* ([1960] 2011, 133ff.). His concern there is with the question of what the assumption, argued for in *TSO*, that human action is causally determined means for the ideal of a free society with its foundational principle of individual responsibility.[254] The presumption that to adopt a deterministic view means to deny the freedom of will and, in consequence, to reject the principle that persons can, and should, be held accountable for what they do, he counters with arguments that are worth quoting at some length:

> The difficulties that people have had concerning the meaning of voluntary action and responsibility do not at all spring from any necessary consequence of the belief that human action is causally determined but are the

---

[252] This volume, p. 300.

[253] Hayek ([1962a] 1967, 232): "We can certainly not say that a particular conscious act of any man is the necessary result of particular circumstances that we can specify—leaving out his peculiar individuality built up by the whole of his history."—"Conscious experiences have . . . justly been compared to mountain tops rising above the clouds which, while alone visible, yet presuppose an invisible substructure determining their positions relative to each other" (*TSO*, 6.21). On the subject of "free will," Hayek had noted already in his 1920 paper: "The question of free will depends on what one means by an individual who is the subject of free will. If the individual, as argued here, is identified with his self, his consciousness and memory, the question is easily resolved" (this volume, p. 340).

[254] For a more extensive discussion of Hayek's arguments, see Vanberg 2011.

result of an intellectual muddle. . . . It appears that the assertion that the will is free has as little meaning as its denial and that the whole issue is a phantom problem, a dispute about words in which the contestants have not made clear what an affirmative or a negative answer would imply. . . . As has often been shown, the conception of responsibility rests, in fact, on a deterministic view, while only the construction of a metaphysical "self" that stands outside the whole chain of cause and effect and therefore could be treated as uninfluenced by praise or blame could justify man's exemption from responsibility. . . . The conduct of a person at any moment . . . will be determined by the joint effects of his inherited constitution and all his accumulated experience. . . . What the determinist position asserts is that those accumulated effects of heredity and past experience constitute the whole of the individual personality, that there is no other "self" or "I" whose dispositions cannot be affected by external or material influences. . . . It is just because there is no separate "self" that stands outside the chain of causation that there is also no "self" that we could not reasonably try to influence by reward or punishment. (Hayek [1960] 2011, 136f.)[255]

Hayek's principal conclusion is that, as a constitutive principle of a free society, the belief in individual responsibility is not meant as a factual claim about what made persons act as they did in particular instances but, instead, as a normative principle, a social convention guiding an individual's conduct.

We assign responsibility to a man, not in order to say that as he was he might have acted differently, but in order to make him different. . . . Of the effects in the particular instance we may never be sure, but we believe that, in general, the knowledge that he will be held responsible will influence a person's conduct in a desirable direction. In this sense the assigning of responsibility does not involve the assertion of a fact. It is rather of the nature of a convention intended to make people observe certain rules. (Hayek [1960] 2011, 138)[256]

[255] As an aside, it may be noted that Ludwig von Mises (1949, 46) has criticized the "metaphysical sense" of the term "free will" in similar terms: "Individual man is the product of a long line of zoological evolution which has shaped his physiological inheritance. . . . The innate and inherited biological qualities and all that life has worked upon him make a man what he is at any instant of his pilgrimage. . . . His will is not 'free' in the metaphysical sense of the term. It is determined by his background and all the influences to which he himself and his ancestors were exposed."

[256] Hayek ([1962a] 1967, 232f.): "Free societies have always been societies in which the belief in individual responsibility has been strong. . . . By a curious confusion it has come to be thought that this belief in individual responsibility has been refuted by growing insight into the manner in which events generally, and human action in particular, are determined by certain classes of causes. . . . Of our generic knowledge as to how human action can be influenced we make use in

Concerning the second issue, the "limits to explanation" of mental phenomena, Hayek distinguishes between "practical limits" posed by the mere fact of complexity and "an absolute limit." He mentions the formation of waves as an example that illustrates the problem of mere practical limits. In this case, even if we may "possess full theoretical knowledge of the mechanism by which waves are formed . . . we shall probably never be able to predict the shape and movements of the wave that shall form on the ocean at a particular place and moment of time" (*TSO*, 8.66). In the sphere of mental processes, Hayek posits, we encounter, though, additional difficulties:

> Apart from these practical limits to explanation, which we may hope continuously to push further back, there also exists, however, an absolute limit to what the human brain can ever accomplish by way of explanation. (*TSO*, 8.67)

> There appear to exist reasons which should make for man a *full* explanation of his own processes of thought absolutely impossible, because this conception involves . . . a contradiction. (*TSO*, 2.19)

Referring to his interpretation of the mind as an "apparatus of classification," Hayek specifies these reasons as follows:

> Any apparatus of classification must possess a structure of a higher degree of complexity than is possessed by the objects which it classifies; . . . therefore, the capacity of any explaining agent must be limited to objects with a structure possessing a degree of complexity lower than its own. If this is correct, it means that no explaining agent can ever explain objects of its own kind, or of its own degree of complexity, and, therefore . . . the human brain can never fully explain its own operation. (*TSO*, 8.69)

It is apparent that Hayek has attributed considerable importance to this argument about an absolute limit to the explanation of mental phenomena, an argument he had already stated in his *Scientism* essay.[257] He not only comments on it at some length in *TSO*, but returns to it repeatedly in his later

---

assessing praise and blame—which we do for the purpose of making people behave in a desirable fashion. It is on this limited determinism . . . that the belief in responsibility is based, . . . the chief device which society has developed to assure decent conduct—the pressure of opinion making people observe the rules of the game. . . . We shall never build up a successful free society without that pressure of praise and blame which treats the individual as responsible for his conduct and also makes him bear the consequences of even innocent error."

[257] Hayek (1942–44) 2010, 113.

publications.[258] It is, however, not at all obvious whether any relevant *practical* implications follow from this argument for the explanatory project that Hayek pursues in *TSO*, namely to provide an understanding for how human beings acquire the knowledge of the world they need to successfully deal with the problems they face. Even less obvious is what relevant practical implications could follow for the explanatory tasks that Hayek seeks to address with his economic and social theory. In fact, Hayek himself suggests that there may be no such relevant practical implication when, in his "The Theory of Complex Phenomena," he states in reference to the "absolute impossibility . . . of a mind fully explaining itself":

> It is not relevant here because the practical limits determined by the impossibility of ascertaining all the relevant data lie so far inside the logical limits that the latter have little relevance to what in fact we can do. ([1964b] 2014, 269f.)

For Hayek, quite obviously, the practically relevant limits to explanation are those that the *complexity* of their subject poses for the study of "phenomena like mind and society" ([1963b] 2014, 429).

As noted above, in his *Scientism* essay, Hayek had drawn a distinction between the "subjectivist approach of the social sciences and the objectivist approach of the natural sciences" ([1942–44] 2010, 92). With the contrast "subjectivist vs. objectivist," Hayek may seem to imply—and has been interpreted to imply—that the natural and the social sciences are separated by a fundamental methodological divide. By shifting the focus to the complexity issue, Hayek comes to draw a distinction that has nothing to do with fundamental differences in scientific methodology, but is about differences in the limits to explanation that sciences face according to the complexity of the

---

[258] See "Within Systems," § 1; this volume, p. 361f. Hayek ([1961] 2014, 376): "I happen to think that so far as the human mind is the object of scientific study, there are indeed demonstrable limits to what explanation can achieve—demonstrable, because they are a logical consequence of what we mean by explanation." In "Rules, Perception and Intelligibility," Hayek ([1962b] 2014) extensively discusses "the impossibility of ever explaining a mind of the complexity of our own" (ibid., 251), admitting that he is "not able to supply a strict proof" (ibid.) of this claim. Taking up the issue in "*The Sensory Order* after 25 Years" (this volume, p. 388), he also notes that the proof for the impossibility claim provided in *TSO* "may be inadequate." He refers to the "theory of sets" of the Russian-born German mathematician Georg Cantor (1845–1918) and to the "Gödel theorem," named after the Austrian-American mathematician and logician Kurt Gödel (1906–78), as contributions that indirectly support his conjecture that the brain can never fully explain itself ([1962b] 2014, 252). For a discussion of Hayek's reference to the Gödel theorem, see D. Tuerck 1995, 286f.

phenomena they study.[259] As Bruce Caldwell (2014, 15; 2004b, 248f.) reports, it was after reading an article by the mathematician Warren Weaver (1948), "Science and Complexity," that Hayek came to distinguish between sciences of *relatively simple* and sciences of *complex* phenomena, instead of contrasting, as he had done in the *Scientism* essay, the social with the natural sciences.[260]

In "Degrees of Explanation," where he first introduces the noted distinction, Hayek prominently refers to Weaver's article, noting that the problems of complexity to which his own "discussion refers are of the kind which Warren Weaver has described as 'problems of organized complexity.'"[261] Weaver's concept allowed Hayek to further specify his earlier critique of "scientism" as an attitude that he blamed for "the harmful effects that the physics model had had on the methodology of the social sciences" (this volume, p. 384). The belief that classical physics, because it "is the most highly developed of all the empirical sciences . . . ought to be held up to all others for imitation," should, as Hayek ([1955] 2014, 195) now argues, not "make us overlook . . . that the procedure of some of the other sciences, 'natural' or 'social,' may differ from that of physics." Physics, Hayek notes, owes its success to the fact that in its field "the number of significantly connected variables of different kinds is sufficiently small to enable us to study them as if they formed a closed system for which we can observe and control all the determining factors" (ibid.,

---

[259] In the preface to his "Studies in Philosophy, Politics and Economics," which he dedicated to Karl Popper, Hayek states: "Readers of some of my earlier writings may notice a slight change in the tone of my discussion of the attitude which I then called 'scientism.' The reason for this is that Sir Karl Popper has taught me that natural scientists did not really do what most of them not only told us that they did but also urged the representatives of other disciplines to imitate. The difference between the two groups of disciplines has thereby been greatly narrowed and I keep up the argument only because so many social scientists are still trying to imitate what they wrongly believe to be the methods of the natural sciences" (Hayek 1967d, viii).

[260] In his article, Weaver distinguishes between three kinds of problems sciences deal with: problems of *simplicity*, problems of *disorganized complexity*, and problems of *organized complexity*. He refers to pre-1900 physical science as a paradigmatic example of a science "largely concerned with two-variable *problems of simplicity*" (1948, 537). By contrast, he argues, post-1900 physics, like thermodynamics, deals with problems of *disorganized complexity*, problems in which "the number of variables is very large" and "the behavior of all the individual variables" is unknown, in which, however, "the system as a whole possesses certain orderly . . . properties" that can be analyzed by statistical methods (ibid., 538). The distinguishing characteristic feature of "the life sciences" (ibid., 536) must, according to Weaver, be seen in the fact that they are concerned with problems of *organized complexity*, "problems which involve dealing simultaneously with a sizable number of factors which are interrelated into an organic whole" (ibid., 539). "These problems," Weaver notes, "are just too complicated to yield to the old nineteenth-century techniques which were so dramatically successful on two-, three-, or four-variable problems of simplicity. These new problems, moreover, cannot be handled with the statistical techniques so effective in describing average behavior in problems of disorganized complexity" (ibid., 540).

[261] Hayek (1955) 2014, 195, fn. 2. References to Weaver also appear in Hayek (1961) 2014, 378; (1975) 2014, 365; (1973a) 1992, 103.

195f.). The situation is, however, categorically different in sciences that deal with complex phenomena, as "in biology or in the social sciences."[262]

As Hayek points out, the above-mentioned example of the formation of waves illustrates that, in its "applied" branches as opposed to its "pure" theory, physics also faces the chief problem that disciplines dealing with complex phenomena encounter,[263] the difficulty of "ascertaining all the data determining a particular manifestation of the phenomena in question" (Hayek [1964b] 2014, 263).[264] In such cases, physics is no less limited to *explanations of the principle* or *pattern prediction* than sciences of complex phenomena generally.[265] These limits to explanation assume, however, as Hayek (ibid., 260) emphasizes, "much greater importance when we turn . . . to the more complex phenomena of life, of mind, and of society."[266] We encounter, he argues, an

---

[262] Hayek ([1968a] 1992, 56) points to "the differences that must inevitably exist among disciplines that deal with relatively simple phenomena, like mechanics, which necessarily were the first to be very successful and which for this reason came to be regarded as paradigms that other disciplines ought to imitate, and the sciences of highly complex phenomena". See also Hayek (1961) 2014, 377.

[263] Problems of complexity "become increasingly prominent as we turn from the 'pure' theory of physics to disciplines like astrophysics or the various branches of geophysics (seismology, meteorology, geology, oceanography, etc.) which are sometimes described as 'applied sciences'" (Hayek [1955] 2014, 198).

[264] Hayek footnotes this statement with a reference to *TSO*, 8.66–8.86. See also Hayek (1975) 2014, 370: "The difficulties which we encounter in [sciences of complex phenomena] . . . are not . . . difficulties about formulating theories for the explanation of the observed events. . . . They are due to the chief problem which arises when we apply our theories to any particular situation in the real world. A theory of essentially complex phenomena must refer to a large number of particular facts; and to derive a prediction from it, we have to ascertain all these particular facts."—Hayek ([1963b] 2014, 438): "The theory of ocean tides is simple; its application to the tides at a particular place may be of insuperable complexity."

[265] Hayek seeks to avoid a too simplistic interpretation of what he means by "explanation of the principle" when he states: "The difference between such 'explanations of the principle' and more detailed explanations is, of course, merely one of the degree of generality, and strictly speaking no explanation can be more than an explanation of the principle. It will be convenient, however, to reserve the name 'explanation of the principle' for explanations of a high degree of generality, and to contrast them with explanations of the detail" (*TSO*, 8.59). See also Hayek (1964b) 2014, 258: "A theory will always define only a kind (or class) of patterns, and the particular manifestation of the pattern to be expected will depend on the particular circumstances (the 'initial and marginal conditions' to which, for the purposes of this article, we shall refer as 'data'). How much in fact we shall be able to predict will depend on how many of those data we can ascertain."

[266] Already in his *Scientism* essay, Hayek ([1942–44] 2010, 106) had argued: "The distinction between an explanation of the principle on which a phenomenon is produced and an explanation which enables us to predict the precise result is of great importance for the understanding of the theoretical methods of the social sciences. It arises, I believe, also elsewhere, for example in biology and certainly in psychology." See also Hayek 1973b, 41: "When we turn from mechanical to such 'more highly organized' or essentially complex phenomena as we encounter in the realms of life, mind and society . . . we have to deal with 'grown' structures with a degree

---

"increasing complexity as we proceed from the inanimate to the ('more highly organized') animate and social phenomena" (ibid., 261),[267] or, in Weaver's terminology, as we move from phenomena of disorganized complexity to phenomena of organized complexity.

An important difference between the two kinds of phenomena concerns the applicability of statistical methods in order to deal with the difficulties that arise because of the large number of the individual elements that are involved. Such statistical methods are applicable to phenomena of disorganized complexity in inanimate nature but not to phenomena of organized complexity, because here the very differences between the individual elements matter, differences which statistical methods eliminate. As Hayek argues:

> Organized complexity here means that the character of the structures showing it depends not only on the properties of the individual elements of which they are composed, and the relative frequency with which they occur, but also on the manner in which the individual elements are connected with each other. In the explanation of the working of such structures we can for this reason not replace the information about the individual elements by statistical information. (Hayek [1975] 2014, 365)

> Statistics . . . avoids the problem of complexity by substituting for the information on the individual elements information on the frequency with which their different properties occur in classes of such elements, and it deliberately disregards the fact that the relative position of the different elements in a structure may matter. . . . It is . . . for this reason irrelevant to the solution of problems in which it is the relations between individual elements with different attributes which matters. (Hayek [1964b] 2014, 265)[268]

---

of complexity which they have assumed and could assume only because they were produced by spontaneous ordering forces."

[267] Hayek ([1963b] 2014, 438): "It is, of course, a commonplace that as we move from mechanics through the other branches of physics through inorganic and organic chemistry to the 'more highly organized' systems of biology we move in an ascending order of essential complexity."—Hayek ([1961] 2014, 376): "As we move from the comparatively simple phenomena of inanimate nature to the increasingly complex ones of life and society, we may have to . . . be content with results which are much more limited in their predictive content than is the case in the physical sciences."

[268] Hayek ([1961] 2014, 377): "In general in the social sciences [we can] not resort . . . to those techniques which the physical sciences employ in those instances where they cannot obtain sufficient information about the individual elements of a system: namely to rely on information about the probability or frequency with which particular attributes occur among a class of events."—Hayek ([1964b] 2014, 270): "Most of the phenomena in which we are interested . . . could not occur at all unless . . . the overall pattern that will form itself is determined by the significantly different behavior of the different individuals so that the obstacle of obtaining the rel-

Hayek has repeatedly referred to "the Darwinian theory of evolution by natural selection" as a paradigmatic example of a theory that, dealing with phenomena of organized complexity, is limited to explanations of the principle.[269] It is, therefore, worth quoting what the above-mentioned evolutionary biologist Ernst Mayr has said about the differences that separate biology from physics. It nicely complements and supports Hayek's view on complexity and explanations of the principle when Mayr (1988, 34) locates "one of the major differences between biology and the physical sciences" in the "uniqueness of biological entities and phenomena," and when he argues:

> This uniqueness of biological individuals means that we must approach groups of biological entities in a very different spirit from the way we deal with groups of identical inorganic entities. . . . He who does not understand the uniqueness of individuals is unable to understand the working of natural selection. (Mayr 1982a, 46f.)

About the spirit in which one should deal with groups of unique biological entities, and which he calls *population thinking*, Mayr says:

> For those who have accepted population thinking, the variation from individual to individual within the population is the reality of nature, whereas the mean value (the "type") is only a statistical abstraction. . . . There is nothing in inanimate nature that corresponds to biopopulations, and this perhaps explains why philosophers whose background is in mathematics or physics seem to have a difficult time understanding this concept. The ability to make the switch from essentialist thinking to population thinking is what made the theory of evolution through natural selection possible. (Mayr 1988, 15)[270]

---

evant data cannot be overcome by treating them as members of a statistical collective." See also Hayek (1963b) 2014, 438.

[269] Hayek ([1964b] 2014, 266): "Probably the best illustration of a theory of complex phenomena which is of great value, although it describes merely a general pattern whose detail we can never fill in, is the Darwinian theory of evolution of natural selection. . . . The basic conception of the theory is exceedingly simple and it is only in its application to the concrete circumstances that its extraordinary fertility and the range of phenomena for which it can account manifests itself. The basic proposition which has this far-reaching implication is that a mechanism of reproduction with transmittable variations and competitive selection of those which prove to have a better chance of survival will in the course of time produce a great variety of structures adapted to continuous adjustment to the environment and to each other." See also Hayek (1955) 2014, 203; 1973b, 16, 23f.; "Within Systems," § 6, this volume, p. 362.

[270] Mayr (1988, 1): "The further the study of biological systems advanced during the past 200 years, the more evident it became how different living systems are from inanimate systems. . . . If a physicist says 'ice floats on water,' his statement is true of any piece of ice and any body

As noted above, Mayr (1982b, 35) sees "one of the most profound differ-ences between the living and the inanimate world" in the role that *encoded infor-mation* plays in controlling the behavior of living beings. While, so he argues, all "processes in organisms, from the interaction of molecules to the complex functions of the brain," not different from processes in the rest of nature, obey physical laws, "organisms differ from inanimate matter . . . in the organiza-tion of their systems and especially in the possession of coded information" (Mayr 1988, 2). The fact that their genetic program "incorporates the 'expe-rience' of all ancestors," Mayr emphasizes, "makes organisms historical phe-nomena" (ibid., 16).[271] And it is, as he posits, their "historicity" that constitutes "a clear-cut difference between the levels of complexity in living and in inani-mate nature" (ibid., 60).

Mayr's argument on the significance of coded information supports Hayek's claim that the complexity of their subject matter distinguishes the sciences "of life, of mind and of society" from physics, and it helps to answer an objection that Popper has raised against Hayek's claim. In reference to a passage in the latter's *Scientism* essay,[272] Popper ([1957] 1994, 139f.) argues:

> There is no doubt that the analysis of any concrete social situation is made extremely difficult by its complexity. But the same holds for any concrete physical situation. . . . In fact, there are good reasons, not only for the belief that social science is less complicated than physics, but also for the belief that concrete social situations are in general less complicated than concrete physical situations. For in most social situations, if not in all, there is an ele-ment of *rationality*.

Popper is surely right in insisting that "concrete physical situations"—such as Hayek's example of the formation of waves at a specific place and time—can be extremely complex. Yet when with his reference to "*rational-ity*" he invokes, by implication, his model of the "logic of the situation,"[273] he

---

of water. The members of a class usually lack the individuality that is so characteristic of the organic world, were each individual is unique . . . and each evolutionary event is unique."

[271] Mayr (1988, 2): "The entire ontogeny as well as the physiological processes and the behav-ior of organisms are directly or indirectly controlled by the information encoded in the genes. There is nothing in any nonliving (except man-made) system that corresponds to the genotype, a system that has selectively stored vital information during the billions of years that life has existed on the earth."

[272] Popper refers to Hayek's ([1942–44] 2010, 106) statement that "our knowledge of the prin-ciple by which . . . phenomena are produced will rarely if ever enable us to predict the precise result of any concrete situation."

[273] See above, pp. 36ff.

tacitly defines away the additional complexity that the social sciences have to deal with because the agents populating the social world are, in Mayr's words, "historical phenomena," whose behavior is governed by encoded information, reflecting their individual learning history. To explain social phenomena in terms of the "logic of the situation" means to ignore the fact that the individuals involved, because of differences in their learning histories, will behave differently in "objectively" identical situations. Again, in Mayr's words, it means to look at individuals as "types" rather than in the spirit of population thinking. Or, to use Weaver's distinction, in denying that, in terms of the complexity of the phenomena they have to deal with, the social sciences differ from the physical sciences, Popper ignores the difference between phenomena of disorganized complexity and phenomena of organized complexity.

Since, as mentioned above,[274] Popper considered his "logic of the situation" as an attempt "to generalize the method of theoretical economics," it is worth noting that, immediately following the passage to which Popper refers in his above-quoted remark, Hayek ([1942–44] 2010, 106f.) points to general equilibrium theory as a paradigm example of an explanation of the principle:

> The best illustration [of an explanation of the principle] in the field of the social sciences is probably the general theory of prices as represented, for example, by the Walrasian or Paretian system of equations. These systems show merely the principle of coherence between the prices of the various types of commodities of which the system is composed; but without the knowledge of the numerical values of all the constants which occur in it and which we never do know, this does not enable us to predict the precise results which any particular change will have.

It is somewhat surprising that in this assessment of the status of general equilibrium theory Hayek remains silent about the problem of the behavioral model, the perfect-knowledge assumption that "animates" the Walrasian system. After all, it is because of this assumption that, in his "Economics and Knowledge," he speaks of the "tautologies of which formal equilibrium analysis in economics essentially consists" ([1937] 2014, 57). It is an assumption that, like the rationality assumption in Popper's logic of the situation, treats individuals as "types," eliminating their uniqueness as "historical phenomena." In pointing to the Walrasian system as an illustration of the distinction between an explanation of the principle and an explanation of the detail,[275] Hayek obviously wants to draw attention to an issue that is different from,

---

[274] See p. 36.
[275] See also Hayek (1973a) 1992, 103.

but supplements, his concern in "Economics and Knowledge." His emphasis here is on the fact that in dealing with the organized complexity, as in the case of market phenomena, we must distinguish between *mathematization* and *quantification*. In a footnote to the above-quoted passage, Hayek adds the comment:

> Pareto himself has clearly seen this. After stating the nature of the factors determining the prices in his system of equations, he adds (*Manuel d'économie politique*, 2d ed. [1927], pp. 233–34): "It may be mentioned here that this determination has by no means the purpose of arriving at a numerical calculation of prices. . . . If one really could know all these equations, the only means to solve them which is available to human powers is to observe the practical solution given by the market." ([1942–44] 2010, 107, fn. 9)[276]

In general terms Hayek notes on this issue a few pages later in the *Scientism* essay:

> It should, perhaps, be emphasized that there is no necessary connection between the use of mathematics in the social sciences and the attempts to measure social phenomena. . . . Mathematics may be—and in economics probably is—absolutely indispensable to describe certain types of complex structural relationships, though there may be no chance of ever knowing the numerical values of the concrete magnitudes. (ibid., 114, fn. 10)

About "the chief value of mathematics for economics," by contrast to "a widespread misconception," he has later said:

> It consists *not* in the fact that it enables us to make economics quantitative, but on the contrary that it enables us to disregard the quantitative aspects and to give precise descriptions of abstract patterns irrespective of the particular magnitudes in which they manifest themselves. ([1963b] 2014, 441)[277]

Instead of taking quantification as the hallmark of scientific achievement, so Hayek ([1975] 2014, 371) posits, economists must come to terms with the fact that, because they deal with "phenomena where organized complexity rules," their "capacity to predict will be confined to . . . general characteristics of the events to be expected." Because they exclude certain logically possible

---

[276] See also Hayek (1963b) 2014, 441; (1964b) 2014, 270f; (1975) 2014, 366; Weimer-Hayek Discussion 1982, 326f.
[277] See also Hayek (1961) 2014, 379.

outcomes,[278] such pattern predictions satisfy, as Hayek emphasizes, Popper's falsifiability criterion,[279] yet their empirical content and, accordingly, their falsifiability will necessarily be relatively small.[280]

Hayek's conclusion is that economists must come to acknowledge that the complexity of their subject matter requires them "deliberately to cultivate the techniques of explanation of the principle" ([1955] 2014, 212). The latter, he notes, is surely a less powerful instrument than a full explanation, but "it is more powerful in the sense that it can be applied to fields to which the other procedure, for the time being or permanently, cannot be applied at all" (ibid.). Having to be content with explanations of the principle is a fate that, Hayek posits, economics shares with all sciences that have to deal with complex phenomena, a fate which even physics, "the discipline which was at least able to start with the relatively simple," (ibid., 211) may come to face.

> Even physics, as it ceases to treat of a few connected events as if they were closed systems, . . . will increasingly have to face the same difficulties with which we are familiar from the biological and social sciences. This would mean that because of the nature of its subject physics comes only at a later stage up against the same sort of obstacle which other disciplines have met earlier. (ibid.)[281]

[278] Hayek ([1942–44] 2010, 106): "While we can explain the principle on which certain phenomena are produced and can from this knowledge exclude the possibility of certain results, for example, of certain events occurring together, our knowledge will in a sense be only negative."

[279] Hayek ([1975] 2014, 371): "Often all that we shall be able to predict will be some abstract characteristics of the pattern that will appear. . . . Yet, as I am anxious to repeat, we will still achieve predictions which can be falsified and which therefore are of empirical significance."—Hayek ([1964b] 2014, 263): "The prediction that a pattern of a certain kind will appear in defined circumstances is a falsifiable (and therefore empirical) statement."

[280] Hayek ([1964b] 2014, 264): "Such a theory will, of course, in Popper's terms, be one of small empirical content, because it enables us to predict or explain only certain general features of a situation which may be compatible with a great many particular circumstances, . . . and the possibility of falsifying it [will be] correspondingly small. But as in many fields this will be for the present, or perhaps forever, all the theoretical knowledge we can achieve, it will nevertheless extend the range of the possible advance of scientific knowledge." The limited falsifiability has, as Hayek ([1955] 2014, 210) posits, an important implication: "Because such theories are difficult to disprove, the elimination of inferior rival theories will be a slow affair, bound up closely with the argumentative skill and persuasiveness of those who employ them. There can be no crucial experiments which decide between them. There will be opportunities for grave abuses: possibilities for pretentious, over-elaborate theories which no simple test but only the good sense of those equally competent in the field can refute."

[281] Hayek ([1964b] 2014, 264): "The advance of science will thus have to proceed in two different directions: while it is certainly desirable to make our theories as falsifiable as possible, we must also push forward into fields where, as we advance, the degree of falsifiability necessarily decreases. This is the price we have to pay for an advance into the field of complex phenomena."

11. *"Systems within Systems"*

As his arguments, reported in the previous section, suggest, it is, in Hayek's view, the concept of *organized complexity* along with its twin concept, the *explanation of the principle*, that constitutes the systematic link between his theory of the mind and his social theory, in particular his outlook at the market.[282] The obvious similarities that exist between them, both in terms of their general methodology and their substantive conjectures, have been commented on by a number of authors,[283] as well as the fact that Hayek's concern with the knowledge problem provides the key to the "continuity between his cognitive psychology and his general market theory."[284] Indeed Hayek has expressly emphasized this very connection between his psychology and his social theory:

> In both cases we have complex phenomena in which there is a need for a method of utilizing widely dispersed knowledge. The essential point is that each member (neuron, or buyer, or seller) is induced to do what in the total circumstances benefits the system.[285]

[282] Hayek ([1964b] 2014, 269): "It should not be difficult now to recognize the similar limitations applying to theoretical explanations of the phenomena of mind and society. One of the chief results so far achieved by theoretical work in these fields seems to me to be the demonstration that here individual events regularly depend on so many concrete circumstances that we shall never in fact be in a position to assert them all; and that in consequence . . . the ideal of prediction and control must largely remain beyond our reach."

[283] B. Smith (1997, 23): "Hayek shows . . . that the central idea behind the connectionist paradigm is at home not only in psychology and neurology but also in the sphere of economics. For the mind, from the perspective of *The Sensory Order*, turns out to be a dynamic, relational affair that is in many respects analogous to a market process." W. N. Butos and T. J. McQuade (2002, 114) elaborate on the "fundamental similarities in his explanatory schemata for cognitive and market theories." B. Caldwell (2004a, 296) notes that Hayek's notion of rule-based orders "has analogues both in the formation of the market order and in the formation of the mental order."

[284] Butos and McQuade 2002, 114. Weimer (1982, 254f.): "The 'stuff' of our thinking'—that is, knowledge—is thus a key to Hayek's work; the remarkable *economy* of knowledge that results from the division of knowledge in complex phenomena is central to both his economic analysis and his psychology."

[285] Weimer-Hayek Discussion 1982, 325. Referring to *TSO*, the neuroscientist J. M. Fuster (2011, 9) speaks in a similar spirit about the analogies between the human brain and the spontaneous order of the market: "All the items of memory and knowledge in our brain constitute a massive system of relational encoding and communication. Most importantly, . . . knowledge is dispersed and distributed in the cerebral cortex much as it is in the marketplace among individuals. . . . Thus, current cognitive neuroscience not only confirms Hayek's hypotheses on the brain/mind relation but also incorporates gradually into the cerebral cortex some of the same principles of operation that he and other liberal economists tell us govern the behavior of individuals in an economic system as complex as the human brain. . . . In neither of the two is a 'central executive' necessary."—"Finally, our cortex serves our individual goals with more knowledge than we are aware of. . . . Inasmuch as we may derive individual benefit from intuitive knowledge, and inasmuch as our intuitive knowledge may serve our fellow humans, it

Hayek takes care, though, to warn against carrying the analogy between brain and market too far. The brain, while in itself a polycentric order, acts as "the directing center" for an organism, providing the organism with "the possibility of trying out beforehand on a model the various alternative complexes of actions and selecting from them the most promising before action is taken" (Hayek [1967c] 2014, 285).[286] By contrast, the market neither contains nor acts as such a "directing center," but is a self-contained spontaneous order.[287]

With his methodological arguments on the study of complex phenomena, and with his theoretical contributions to mind and society as spontaneous orders, Hayek can be, and has been,[288] justly regarded as a pioneer in a research field that, more recently, has become known under the label "complex adaptive systems."[289] It is significant that one of the main contributors to this field, John H. Holland, acknowledges as a major source of inspiration D. O. Hebb's *The Organization of Behavior*,[290] the very book that Hayek names in the preface to *TSO* as containing "a theory of sensation which in many respects is similar" to his own.[291] This may be a reason why, as a reviewer of Holland's book *Hidden Order* (1995) has put it, Hayek's and Holland's approaches are "wonderfully complementary,"[292] even though the latter apparently did not

---

is entirely possible that there is in our brain an 'invisible hand' sustaining that larger one that Adam Smith proposed for society at large" (ibid., 10).

[286] Hayek ([1967c] 2014, 285): "The structure which the brain directs may have a repertoire of possible patterns of actions, . . . but if it actually had to take that action before it was tried out on a model, it might discover its harmful effects only when it was too late and it might be destroyed as a result."

[287] Hayek ([1967c] 2014, 286): "Although the brain may be organized on principles similar to those on which a society is organized, society is not a brain and must not be represented as a sort of super-brain, because . . . the ordering task is not deputized to any part in which a model is performed."

[288] Vaughn 1999. According to S. Horwitz (2010, 384), "'complex adaptive systems' is the right over-arching metaphor for Hayek's thought."

[289] For insightful discussions of *TSO* as an inspiration for an "adaptive system theory of social orders," see McQuade 2006 and McQuade and Butos 2009.

[290] Holland (1998, 19): "For my part, I had been inspired by a lecture . . . on Hebb's 1949 neuropsychological theory of learned behavior. Hebb's object had been to build a theory of behavior based on the interactions of neurons in the central nervous system."

[291] This volume, p. 120f. See also above, fn. 79.

[292] Miller (1996, 59): "Holland calls that discipline-in-formation the study of 'complex adaptive systems,' or *cas*. Like economists F. A. Hayek and Herbert Simon, he was one of the field's earliest contributors—and one of the best. Although Holland developed his ideas without knowledge of Hayek's work, the two scholars are wonderfully complementary. . . . Taking different paths, Hayek and Holland came to a common notion of the territory they were exploring. Hayek also called for a new discipline to study *cas*, which he called 'spontaneous orders.' . . . The interdisciplinary investigation Holland is pursuing into the nature of spontaneously ordering evolutionary learning systems is the research program Hayek had earlier proposed."

know of Hayek's much earlier work in the field. A very brief look at Holland's theoretical outlook may suffice here to document its proximity to core tenets of Hayek's approach that I have examined in this introduction.[293]

Holland (1992, 18) defines "complex adaptive systems" (*cas*), of which the central nervous system and the market are paradigm examples, as systems that "change and reorganize their component parts to adapt themselves to the problems posed by the environment." Such systems consist of a multitude of interacting "adaptive agents," agents that "are diverse rather than standard, and both their behavior and their structure change as they interact" (Holland 2012, 58). The agents' behavior is, according to Holland, "determined by a collection of rules,"[294] typically in the form of "stimulus-response rules"— "IF stimulus s occurs THEN give response r. IF the market goes down THEN sell" (1995, 7).[295] Characterizing his theoretical outlook as an "evolutionary approach to learning" (1996, 282), Holland argues that the behavior-guiding rules can be "viewed as hypotheses that are undergoing testing and confirmation" (ibid., 53), and which are adapted "as experience accumulates" (ibid., 10).[296] They provide agents with an "internal model," allowing them to "anticipate the consequences of certain responses" (1992, 20).[297] Furthermore, Holland emphasizes, because "many rules can be active simultaneously, a distributed rule-based system can handle perpetual novelty" (ibid., 22).

Even if Hayek neither used the term "complex adaptive systems" or worked out a general research program comparable to Holland's project, he significantly contributed to the project, both with his psychological arguments, presented in *TSO*, and with his social theoretical thoughts on the "twin ideas of

---

[293] For a more detailed account of Holland's theory and its relation to Hayek's approach, see Vanberg 2002, 12ff.; 2012, 522ff.

[294] Hayek's view of the brain as a classifying apparatus comes to mind when Holland (2012, 63) characterizes adaptive, rule-based agents as "classifier systems": "*Classifier systems* . . . provide a class of formally defined, rule-based signal-providing systems useful for defining agents. Individual rules in the system, called classifiers, are of the form IF (a required set of signals is present) THEN (send an outgoing signal based on these signals)."

[295] Holland (1995, 49): "A particular agent is described by setting down the cluster of rules . . . that generates its behavior. Rules so defined act much as instructions in a computer, the cluster serving as a program that determines the agent's behavior."

[296] Holland (2012, 20) emphasizes that, because experience shapes the collection of rules determining agents' behavior, "history and context play a critical role."

[297] Holland (2012, 60): "Clearly, anticipation *doesn't* require consciousness, even though anticipation is usually discussed in the context of consciousness. . . . In general, anticipation appears whenever an agent, conscious or otherwise, acquires an internal model of its environment. In a *cas*, the environment includes other agents, so the internal model usually includes models of other agents." That they "use internal models to *anticipate* the future" is, as Holland (1992, 24) notes, the "attribute that distinguishes complex adaptive systems from other kinds of complex systems."

spontaneous order and evolution," thoughts to which I shall turn below.[298] If Hayek has ever made an attempt at a general theory of complex adaptive systems, the most likely candidate would seem to be his "Within Systems and About Systems" paper, though, as noted before, he left it unfinished. While he abandoned this particular attempt, his social theoretical work from the late fifties onwards documents that he did not abandon his inquiry into the issue that the "Within Systems" paper was supposed to address:

> The particular kind of causal system which we will consider here will be systems capable of "classifying" external actions upon them and of responding to any one of the external events belonging to the same class . . . by the "appropriate" one among the class of responses to which the state of the system at the time disposes it. ("Within Systems," § 9; this volume, p. 365)

The aim that Hayek seems to have pursued with his abandoned paper is to generalize, as an explanatory scheme, what he had argued in *TSO* about the brain being a system within a larger system.[299] More explicitly than in the "Within Systems" paper itself, Hayek states this aim in retrospect, when he describes the paper as an attempt "to elaborate the crucial concept of 'systems within systems'" (this volume, p. 385). In the remainder of this introduction I shall seek to show that Hayek's social theory, revolving around the "twin ideas of evolution and spontaneous order," can be understood as an application of the "systems within systems" concept as a general explanatory scheme.

As noted above (p. 16), the "central problem" Hayek sought to address in *TSO* was to explain the relation between the "microcosm" in the brain and the "macrocosm" of the external world (*TSO*, 1.10), a problem of which he said:

> Our task is . . . to show in what sense it is possible that within parts of the macrocosm a microcosm may be formed which reproduces certain aspects of the macrocosm and through this will enable the substructure of which it

---

[298] In his assessment of Hayek's work, Fuster (2011, 10) states: "Thus, the brain dynamics between perception and action is more than a metaphor of market dynamics, not only because the former underlies the latter, but also because both serve the continuous regulation toward adaptive equilibrium that characterizes the dynamics of all open adaptive systems in biology as well as in human society. Feedback and self-correction are essential components of adaptive systems."

[299] In "Degrees of Explanation," an offshoot of the "Within Systems" paper (see above, fn. 210), Hayek ([1955] 2014, 212) notes in reference to the problems faced by sciences of complex phenomena: "Especially in those fields where . . . in discussing a system of events we must at the same time move within the system, there are probably definite limits to what we can know. These limits can be ascertained only by studying the *kind* of relations which exist between what can be said within a given system and what can be said about that system."

forms a part to behave in a manner which will assist its continued existence. (*TSO*, 5.78)[300]

Looking back after twenty-five years, he remarked on the subject:

> My conclusion at an early stage was . . . that mental events are a particular order of physical events within a subsystem of the physical world that relates the larger subsystem of the world that we call organism (and of which they are a part) with the whole system so as to enable that organism to survive. (this volume, p. 383)[301]

Apparently, after completing *TSO*, Hayek started to think about generalizing the idea of a system adapting to a more comprehensive system of which it is a part. One indication is that, as Bruce Caldwell (2004a, 298) reports, Hayek organized in the fall of 1952 a seminar entitled "Scientific Method and the Study of Society," the material for which included "a chart listing phenomena at different 'levels of organization' (gene, cell, individual, interbreeding population, society, biota)." One of his sources of inspiration for how to conceptualize the relations between such different levels of organization was apparently L. von Bertalanffy.[302] In the "Within Systems" paper, Hayek refers to Bertalanffy's *General Systems Theory*, noting that he follows roughly Bertalanffy's definition in using the "expression 'system' in the sense of a coherent structure of causally connected physical parts" (this volume, p. 364f.). Interestingly, Bertalanffy explicitly mentions, in support of his own theory, Warren Weaver's distinction between unorganized and organized complexity,[303]

---

[300] Ebenstein (2001, 244) reports that Hayek "inscribed in a copy of *The Sensory Order* that the volume was a 'contribution to the problem of how a part of the ordered universe can adapt its actions to the fact that the whole is ordered.'"

[301] Hayek ([1960] 2011, 74): "His mind is itself a system that constantly changes as a result of his endeavor to adapt himself to his surroundings."

[302] About Bertalanffy's influence on his own thinking about "the conception of higher level regularities," Hayek has said in retrospect: "I suspect it is really what Bertalanffy with his *General Systems Theory* was after and the conception itself was of course already implied in my 'Degrees of Explanation'" (Letter to Popper of February 27, 1960; quoted here from Caldwell 2014, 18). As Caldwell (2013, 28) notes, Hayek's continued interest in the issues he had sought to address in the "Within Systems" paper "is evident from his interactions with people like Bertalanffy and von Neumann in the 1950s." In "Within Systems" (§ 7, this volume, p. 363), Hayek refers to von Neumann's "logic of automata" as "a field to which indeed our particular problem belongs."

[303] Bertalanffy (1969, 34): "Classical physics, Weaver said, was highly successful in developing the theory of unorganized complexity. . . . In contrast, the fundamental problem today is that of organized complexity. Concepts like those of organization, wholeness, directiveness, teleology, and differentiation are alien to conventional physics. However, they pop up everywhere in the biological, behavioral and social sciences, and are, in fact, indispensable for dealing with living organisms or social groups." See also Bertalanffy 1969, 59f.: Where "we are confronted with *problems of*

the very distinction that had led Hayek to emphasize the contrast between sciences of simple and sciences of complex phenomena.[304]

At a 1968 symposium in Alpbach entitled "Beyond Reductionism: New Perspectives in the Life Sciences," at which both Hayek and Bertalanffy were present,[305] Arthur Koestler, the organizer of the symposium,[306] commented on Bertalanffy's system perspective in words that could easily be applied to Hayek's thoughts on "systems within systems":

> But wholes and parts in this absolute sense do not exist anywhere, either in the domain of living organisms or of social organizations. What we find are intermediary structures on a series of levels in ascending order of complexity, each of which has two faces looking in opposite directions: the face turned towards the lower levels is that of an autonomous whole, the one turned upward that of a dependent part. . . . It seems that life in all its manifestations . . . is governed by rules of the game which lend it order and stability but also allow for flexibility; and that these rules . . . are represented in coded form on various levels of the hierarchy. (Koestler 1969, 197ff.)

Koestler's image of the upward and downward looking faces is of particular interest because it points to a central feature of theories that deal with the relations among systems at different levels. It is a feature that Hayek ([1967c] 2014, 288) refers to when he says about societies as complex systems:

> Societies differ from simpler complex structures by the fact that their elements are themselves complex structures whose chance to persist depends on (or at least is improved by) their being part of the more comprehensive structure. We have to deal here with integration on at least two different levels, with on the one hand the more comprehensive order assisting the preservation of ordered structures on the lower level, and, on the other, the kind of order which on the lower level determines the regularities of individual conduct assisting the prospect of the survival of the individual only through its effect on the overall order of the society. . . . This implies a sort of inversion

---

organized complexity at all levels of the hierarchic structure of the universe . . . there is a need for the development of 'general systems theory' . . . concerned with properties and principles of 'wholes' or systems in general, irrespective of their particular nature and the nature of their components."

[304] In the context of his comments on Weaver's concept of organized complexity, Bertalanffy (1968, 36) notes: "Here we should consider that there are degrees in scientific explanation, and that in complex and theoretically little-developed fields we have to be satisfied with what the economist Hayek has justly termed 'explanations of the principle.'"

[305] Hayek presented his "The Primacy of the Abstract" at this symposium. Bertalanffy's statement quoted in the previous footnote is from his contribution to the same event.

[306] On the symposium and on Koestler, see Caldwell 2014, 28f.

of the relation between cause and effect in the sense that the structures possessing a kind of order will exist because the elements do what is necessary to secure the persistence of that order. The "final cause" or "purpose," i.e., the adaptation of the parts to the requirements of the whole, becomes a necessary part of the explanation of why structures of the kind exist. . . . A "teleological" explanation is thus entirely in order so long as it . . . merely [implies] the recognition that the kind of structure would not have perpetuated itself if it did not act in a manner likely to produce certain effects, and that it has evolved through those prevailing at each stage who did.

For what Hayek calls "a sort of inversion of the relation between cause and effect," Donald T. Campbell (1974b) has coined the term "downward causation," a term that has become a standard label for the causal relations between different levels of organization that Hayek describes in his above-quoted statement. Campbell's concept allows one to explicate more precisely what Hayek metaphorically refers to as "final cause," "purpose," and "teleological" explanation.[307] This is how Campbell (ibid., 180) specifies the principle of "downward causation":

> Where natural selection operates through life and death at a higher level of organization, the laws of the higher level selective system determine in part the distribution of lower-level events and substances. . . . All processes at the lower levels of a hierarchy are restrained by and act in conformity to the laws of the higher levels.
>
> "Downward causation" . . . is downward only if substantial extents of time, covering several reproductive generations, are lumped as one instant for purposes of analysis. (ibid., 180)[308]

While dissociating himself from two polar extremes—from "vitalists" who advocate "the autonomy of higher levels" (ibid., 182)[309] and from "a common class of reductionists who deny the existence of . . . emergent higher levels

---

[307] Hayek leaves no doubt that he uses these terms in a metaphorical sense only, and that by them he is circumscribing the working of evolutionary processes. See, for example, Hayek 1983a, 182: "Insight into the how processes of selective evolution work teaches us . . . that the persistence of orders or structures can depend on their effects or, in other words, that in evolutionary processes an effect can be the cause (causa finalis) of prevailing structures" (my translation—Ed.).

[308] Campbell (1974a, 142): "For . . . all problems of fit, there is available today only one explanatory paradigm: blind variation and selective retention. . . . Not only is it the sole explanatory conception for the achievement of fit between systems, it is also an essential explanatory component for all instances of purposiveness, of teleological achievements or teleonomy. It is also an essential part of processes producing and maintaining form and order."

[309] Campbell (1974b, 182): "I advocate not the autonomy of higher levels, but rather the additional restraints, aspects of selective systems that these higher levels encounter."

of organization" (1974a, 142)—Campbell (1974b, 179f.) identifies his own outlook of "hierarchical organization in biological systems" with a qualified reductionism characterized by two principles:

(1) All processes at the higher levels are restrained by and act in conformity to the laws of lower level, including the levels of subatomic physics.
(2) The teleonomic achievements at higher levels require for their implementation specific lower-level mechanisms and processes. Explanation is not complete until these micromechanisms have been specified.[310]

Campbell's qualified reductionism implies that the causal relations between different levels of organization involve "upward" as well as "downward" causation,[311] and that to account for these causal relations requires one to show how higher-level phenomena can be explained in terms of mechanism effective at the lower level as well as to show how lower-level phenomena are impacted by conditions prevailing at the higher level.[312]

Campbell's arguments can help to clarify the theoretical issue that Hayek seems to have struggled with in the "Within Systems" paper. They also provide important clues for the role that the concept of "systems within systems"

---

[310] In speaking of "teleonomic achievements," Campbell tacitly invokes the notion of stored information. H. C. Plotkin (1982, 6, 8, 9) indicates how stored information and downward causation are connected to each other when he argues: "Thus information or knowledge, in biological terms, describes a *relationship* between the order of the world, whatever this order is, and the answering and reciprocal organization of an organism. . . . Information is always gained *a posteriori* in biological systems. That is, it is established as the effects of selection on variant forms. . . . Biological systems are never prescient. They may, however, simulate prescience by feeding information that has been gained *a posteriori* at a more fundamental level of a hierarchy to another less fundamental level. . . . Any biological system, as 'knower,' acts upon the world that it knows and thus changes it. Knowledge . . . is a constant interplay between a changing world and a changing knower."

[311] Using Campbell's terminology, Popper (1978, 348) argues: "We may speak of downward causation whenever a higher structure operates causally upon its substructure. The difficulty of understanding downward causation is this. We think we can understand how the substructures of a system cooperate to affect the whole system; that is to say, we think that we understand upward causation. But the opposite is very difficult to envisage. . . . I suggest that downward causation can sometimes at least be explained as selection operating on the randomly fluctuating elementary particles." See also Popper's (Popper and Eccles 1977, 19f.) comment: "Downward causation is of course important in all tools and machines which are designed for some purpose. . . . The most interesting examples of downward causation are to be found in organisms and in their ecological systems, and in societies of organisms." Discussing the connection between "Reductionism and 'Downward Causation'" (ibid., 14), Popper speaks of "reduction in principle" (ibid., 19) as a variation on Hayek's concept of "explanation of the principle" (ibid., fn.).

[312] Hayek ([1967c] 2014, 282): "The relations which are essential for the existence of the whole cannot be accounted for wholly by the interaction of the parts but only by their interaction with an outside world both of the individual parts and the whole."

plays as a systematic link integrating the psychological and the social theoretical branch of Hayek's work. In fact, in the epilogue to *Law, Legislation and
Liberty*, Hayek explicitly recognized the affinity of Campbell's arguments to his
own research program when he said:

> We understand now that all enduring structures above the level of the
> simplest atoms, and up to the brain and society, are the result of, and can
> be explained only in terms of, processes of selective evolution, and that the
> more complex ones maintain themselves by constant adaptation of their
> internal states to changes in the environment. . . . These changes in structure
> are brought about by their elements possessing such regularities of conduct,
> or such capacities to follow rules, that the result of their individual actions
> will be to restore the order of the whole if it is disturbed by external influ-
> ences. Hence what on an earlier occasion I have called the twin concepts of
> evolution and spontaneous order enables us to account for the persistence of
> these complex structures, not by a simple conception of one-directional laws
> of cause and effect, but by a complex interaction of patterns which Professor
> Donald Campbell described as "downward causation." (1979, 158)[313]

12. "The Twin Ideas of Evolution and Spontaneous Order"

When, in his "reductionist principles," Campbell speaks of "teleonomic
achievements," he tacitly refers to the role that *stored information*, emphasized
by Ernst Mayr as the clue to a causal explanation of seeming teleology, plays
in cases of downward causation. He thereby invokes the core notion of evolutionary epistemology, namely that, as H. C. Plotkin (1982, 3) puts it, "biological systems in general are knowledge systems," and that "evolution itself is a
process of gaining knowledge."

The theory Hayek had sketched in his student days and more fully stated
in *TSO* focuses on, in Plotkin's terminology, *individuals* as knowledge systems.
With his "Economics and Knowledge" paper, Hayek embarked on a research
program that extends the analysis of the knowledge problem from the individual to the social level. What, as I submit, gives coherence to this social theoretical research program is the notion of social groups/societies as *knowledge
systems*, with the concept of "systems within systems" providing the critical
link between the psychological and the social theoretical branches of Hayek's

---

[313] Hayek ([1967c] 2014, 289): "It was indeed what I have elsewhere called the twin ideas of
evolution and spontaneous order . . . which have opened the way for an understanding, both in
biological and social theory, of that interaction between the regularity of the conduct of the elements and the regularity of the resulting structure."

work. The figure below indicates how Hayek's oeuvre can be understood as a coherent system of thought, the constituent parts of which address different aspects of the knowledge problem.

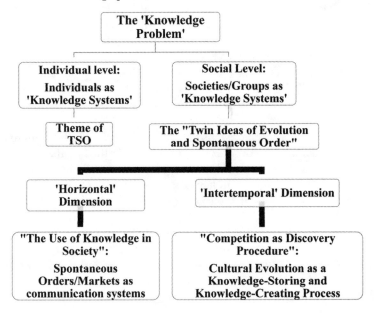

What, in the above figure, I refer to as the "horizontal dimension" of the social-level knowledge problem is the principal subject of Hayek's most often quoted paper, "The Use of Knowledge in Society." About "the problem of the utilization of knowledge dispersed among many people," Hayek ([1942–44] 2010, 161) said before in his *Scientism* essay to solve it "is precisely the function which the various 'markets' perform" (ibid., 163). Market and prices, he noted there, "help to utilize the knowledge of many people . . . and thereby make possible that combination of decentralization of the decisions and mutual adjustment of these decisions which we find in a competitive system" (ibid.).

As Hayek argues, spontaneous, polycentric orders, of which the market is a paradigm example, owe their superior—compared to centralized, command-based orders—capacity to utilize dispersed knowledge to the fact that they are *rule-based* orders. Because within the limits defined by general "rules of the game" individuals are free to choose, they can utilize their knowledge of particular circumstance of time and place,[314] knowledge that would not be avail-

---

[314] Hayek (Weimer-Hayek Discussion 1982, 325): "In the larger (say economic) order, knowledge is utilized that is not planned or centralized or even conscious. The essential knowledge

able to a central coordinating agent.[315] As much as he stresses that a spontaneous order can utilize more local knowledge than a command-based order, Hayek also points out that the framework of rules within which the spontaneous mutual adjustment of individual actions takes place is critically important for whether, and what kind of, overall order will result.[316]

> Some rules governing individual behavior might clearly make altogether impossible the formation of an overall order. Our problem is what kind of rules of conduct will produce an order of society and what kind of order particular rules will produce. (Hayek 1973b, 44)

The critical function that, as Hayek argues, the rules of the game have to perform in a spontaneous order is to compensate for the fact that the individuals, in pursuit of their interests, will take the particular circumstances known to them into account, but will not, and cannot, account for the more indirect and remote consequences of their actions.[317] Their function is to solve what, in "Individualism: True and False," Hayek had described as the problem the classical founders of economics had addressed. The question they had sought to answer was, as Hayek puts it, how the "limited concerns, which did in fact determine people's actions, could be made effective inducements to cause them voluntarily to contribute as much as possible to needs which lay outside the range of their vision" ([1946] 2010, 60).

---

is possessed by literally millions of people, largely utilizing their capacity of acquiring knowledge that, in their temporary position, seems to be useful. . . . In our whole system of actions, we are individually steered by local information—information about more particular facts than any other person or authority can possibly possess. And the price and market system is in that sense a system of communication, which passes on (in the form of prices, determined only on the competitive market) the available information that each individual needs to act, and to act rationally."

[315] Hayek ([1967c] 2014, 285): "Such a non-hierarchic order dispenses with the necessity of first communicating all the information on which its several elements act to a common center and conceivably may make the use of more information possible than could be transmitted to, and digested by, a center."—Hayek (1973b, 13f.): "This structure of human activity constantly adapts itself, and functions through adapting itself, to millions of facts which in their entirety are not known to anybody."

[316] Hayek (1973b, 14): "In a social order the particular circumstances to which each individual will react will be those known to him. But the individual responses to particular circumstances will result in an overall order only if the individuals obey such rules as will produce an order."

[317] Hayek ([1942–44] 2010, 154f.): "But the demand that every action should be judged after full consideration of all its consequences . . . is due to a failure to see that the submission to general rules . . . is the only way in which for man with his limited knowledge freedom can be combined with the essential minimum degree of order."—Hayek (1973b, 13): "The fact of our irremediable ignorance of most of the particular circumstances which determine the processes of society is, however, the reason why most social institutions have taken the form they actually have."

Hayek approaches this question by dividing the societal knowledge problem into two subquestions, namely

(1) how the individuals come to acquire, and to act upon, the knowledge that enables them to successfully navigate the problem environment within the horizon of their vision, and
(2) how the groups/societies they form "learn" to adopt rules of the game that account for the requirements of the overall order.

Hayek provides the answer to the first problem in *TSO* by explaining how in the "microcosm" of the brain a model of the "macrocosm" of the external world is formed, embodying knowledge of relevant contingencies in the external world. He answers the second problem with his theory of cultural evolution, a theory that, in the spirit of evolutionary epistemology, views "learning" at the group level as a process of variation and selective retention.

Hayek refers to both aspects of the societal knowledge problem when he says about the "law" as the framework of rules within which individuals act:

> If the law thus serves to enable the individual to act effectively on his own knowledge and for this purpose adds to his own knowledge, it also embodies knowledge, or the results of past experience. . . . In fact, the collaboration of individuals under common rules rests on a sort of division of knowledge, where the individuals must take account of particular circumstances but the law ensures that their actions will be adapted to certain general or permanent characteristics of their society. The experience, embodied in the law, that individuals utilize by observing rules . . . is ordinarily not known to them or any one person. Most of these rules have . . . grown through a gradual process of trial and error in which the experience of successive generations has helped to make them what they are. ([1960] 2011, 225)[318]

He further explains:

> This sort of "knowledge of the world" that is passed on from generation to generation will thus consist in a great measure not of knowledge of cause

---

[318] In the "Scientism" essay, Hayek ([1942–44] 2010, 153) notes on this subject: "The individualist approach, in awareness of the constitutional limitations of the individual mind, attempts to show how man in society is able, by the use of various resultants of the social process, to increase his powers with the help of the knowledge implicit in them and of which he is never aware; it makes us understand that the only 'reason' which can in any sense be regarded as superior to individual reason does not exist apart from the interindividual process in which, by means of impersonal media, the knowledge of successive generations and of millions of people living simultaneously is combined and mutually adjusted, and that this process is the only form in which the totality of human knowledge ever exists." On this see also Hayek 1973b, 11, 14f.

and effect, but of rules of conduct adapted to the environment and acting like information about the environment although they do not say anything about it. Like scientific theories, they are preserved by proving themselves useful, but, in contrast to scientific theories, by a proof which no one
needs to know, because the proof manifests itself in the resilience and progressive expansion of the order of society which it makes possible. ([1970]
2014, 345)[319]

Not only the rules of conduct but our entire cultural heritage can, as Hayek
suggests, be understood as an embodiment of the "knowledge of the world"
that accumulates over generations,[320] and much of which is implicit in "the
language which we learn in early childhood."[321]

Underlying Hayek's theory of cultural evolution is the notion that the
"macrocosm" to which the individuals must adapt is structured in multiple
levels of organization,[322] and that the social groups within which the individ-

[319] Hayek (1979, 157): "Thus a tradition of rules of conduct . . . began to govern human life.
It was when these learnt rules . . . began to include a sort of model of the environment that
enabled man to predict and anticipate external events, that what we call reason appeared. There
*was then probably much more 'intelligence' incorporated in the system of rules of conduct than in man's thoughts
about his surroundings*" (emphasis in the original).

[320] Hayek ([1960] 2011, 77): "The growth of knowledge and the growth of civilization are the
same if we interpret knowledge to include all the human adaptations to environment in which
past experience has been incorporated." For an early statement of this idea, see Hayek (1942–
44) 2010, 146f.: "Though our civilization is the result of a cumulation of individual knowledge,
it is not by the explicit or conscious combination of all this knowledge in any individual brain,
but by its embodiment in symbols which we use without understanding them, in habits and institutions, tools and concepts, that man in society is constantly able to profit from a body of knowledge neither he nor any other man completely possesses." See also Hayek (1945a) 2014, 101.

[321] Hayek ([1965] 2014, 44): "The extent to which the language which we learn in early childhood determines our whole manner of thinking and our view and interpretation of the world
is probably much greater than we are aware of. It is not merely that the knowledge of earlier
generations is communicated to us through the medium of language; the structure of the language itself implies certain views about the nature of the world; and by learning a particular
language we acquire a certain picture of the world, a framework within which we henceforth
move without being aware of it. . . . This phenomenon of implicit learning is clearly one of the
most important parts of cultural transmission, but one which we as yet only imperfectly understand." To the above-quoted passage (fn. 320), Hayek adds in a footnote: "The best illustration,
perhaps, of how we constantly make use of the experience or knowledge acquired by others is
in the way in which, by learning to speak, we learn to classify things in a certain manner without acquiring the actual experiences which have led successive generations to evolve this system
of classification" ([1942–44] 2010, 146, fn. 10). See also Hayek 1956/57 for a more detailed discussion of this issue.

[322] The notion of multiple levels of organization is implied when Hayek ([1967c] 2014, 286)
speaks of "such ordered structures as galaxies, solar systems, organisms, and social orders . . .
observing as wholes regularities which cannot be wholly reduced to the regularities of the parts,
because they also depend on the interaction of the whole with the environment."

uals interact are themselves complex systems that must adapt to an environment, an environment in which they compete with other, differently organized groups.[323]

In analogy to competition in the market arena, Hayek views competitive selection in cultural evolution as a *discovery procedure* (Hayek [1968b] 1978). Just as the independent problem-solving efforts of market participants can be seen as experiments that lead to the discovery of superior problem-solutions, the rules adopted by different groups can, as he suggests, be viewed as experiments in matters of social organization that generate knowledge about which rules allow groups to deal more successfully with the problems they face.

This introduction is not the place to go into details about Hayek's theory of cultural evolution. There is, however, one aspect that deserves a closer look because the above comments on the system-within-system notion and the concept of downward causation can help to clarify some of the issues it raises. I am referring to the ambiguities that surround Hayek's use of the concept of "group selection,"[324] ambiguities that have been, and continue to be, the subject of controversy.[325] The central issue in this controversy is whether Hayek assigns to group selection an explanatory role that is in conflict with the methodological individualism that he otherwise asserts.[326]

In order to locate the ambiguity in Hayek's arguments on group selection, it is useful to distinguish between two issues, namely (1) whether group selection is a relevant *fact* in cultural evolution, and (2) what this fact can *explain*. That at the level of groups competition and evolutionary selection take place can hardly be questioned and there is, accordingly, hardly any controversy about Hayek's claims "that the selection process of evolution will operate on the order as a whole" ([1967c] 2014, 283). Hardly controversial should also be Hayek's (1973b, 17) general claim that group selection works on "practices or rules of conduct" which make "a group of men successful,"[327] and that "it is the efficiency of the resulting order of actions which will determine whether groups whose members observe certain rules of conduct will prevail"

---

[323] Hayek ([1960] 2011, 226): "Thus the rules under which the citizens act constitute an adaptation of the whole of society to its environment and to the general characteristics of its members."

[324] Hayek (1984, 319) defines group selection as "a selection of groups for common attributes possessed by them."

[325] As Bruce Caldwell (2001, 539) notes, "Hayek's contributions on cultural evolution and group selection are among his most controversial," resulting in a "by now rather large secondary literature." See, for example, Beck 2011; D. R. Steele 1987; Stone 2010; Whitman 2004; Zywicki 2000.

[326] I have argued that such a conflict exists in Vanberg (1986) 1994, 82ff.

[327] Because they are not of immediate relevance in the present context, I disregard here problems of interpretation that are caused by ambiguities in Hayek's arguments on what constitutes "success." On this issue see Vanberg 2014.

(ibid., 74).[328] The ambiguities in Hayek's comments on group selection that have become the principal source of controversy have to do with the question of whether, and if so how, group success can serve to explain why individuals comply with the rules that make a group successful. Hayek ([1967c] 2014, 279), at least implicitly, recognizes that a distinction between the reasons for *group success* and the reasons for *individual rule compliance* must be drawn when he states:

> [The] *transmission* of rules takes place *from individual to individual*, while what may be called the natural *selection* of rules will operate on the basis of the greater or lesser efficiency of the resulting *order of the group*.[329]

Yet he passes over the difference between the explanatory problems that are thus posed at the group level and at the individual level when, for instance, he argues that rules "have come to govern the actions of the individuals because actions in accordance with them have proved more successful than those of competing individuals or groups" (1973b, 18). With statements such as "we are bound to explain the fact that the elements behave in a certain way by the circumstance that this sort of conduct is most likely to preserve the whole" ([1967c] 2014, 288),[330] Hayek tends to suggest that group success per se can explain why individuals follow group-beneficial rules, irrespective of what actually motivates their conduct.[331] And it is this claim that is the principal subject of controversy.

Where individual motives and group success are aligned (i.e., where following the rules that make for group success is in the *immediate* interest of the individual members of the group), one may ignore the fact that to explain why rules make groups successful is not the same as explaining why individuals follow rules. This is, however, definitely not so in cases where following group-advantageous rules is per se not advantageous but, on the contrary, costly for the individual group members. Such cases, in which a conflict between immediate individual interest and group advantage exists, pose a *collective good problem*, as Hayek ([1970] 2014, 342) recognizes when he notes:

[328] Hayek ([1967c] 2014, 280): "The evolutionary selection of different rules of individual conduct operates through the viability of the order it will produce."

[329] See also Hayek 1973b, 44: "It should be remembered that . . . selection will operate as between societies of different type, that is, be guided by the properties of their respective orders, but that the properties supporting this order will be properties of the individuals, namely their propensity to obey certain rules of conduct on which the order of action of the group as a whole rests."

[330] See also Hayek 1973b, 19:"Such rules come to be observed because in fact they give the group in which they are practiced superior strength."

[331] Hayek (1984, 324): "Group selection thus does not primarily choose what the individuals recognize as serving their own ends, or that they desire."

> The rules we are discussing are those that are not so much useful to the individuals who observe them, as those that (if they are *generally* observed) make all the members of the group more effective, because they give them opportunities to act within a social order.

The collective good problem that Hayek points to is, of course, this: While it is surely advantageous to be a member of a group in which group-beneficial rules are generally followed, it is even more advantageous to follow one's immediate interests while other group members bear the costs of rule compliance. In the apparent belief that it can help to answer the collective good problem, Hayek adopted the notion of group selection from V. C. Wynne-Edwards, who had proposed the concept as an explanation for how group-beneficial but self-sacrificial behavior can survive in biological evolution.[332] It was exactly because of its failure to account for the collective good problem[333] that Wynne-Edwards's theory had lost its appeal in biology, a fact that Hayek recognized (1973b, 202, fn. 37), but even so he still insists that "cultural evolution operates chiefly through group selection" (1984, 318). He does not specify, though, why the collective good problem should be less of a challenge for the group selection argument in the social than in the biological realm.[334]

Restating the issue that Hayek sought to address as a *systems-within-systems problem* can help to clarify the ambiguities that plague Hayek's use of the group-selection concept. Hayek's apparent ambition was to explain the interaction between two adaptive systems, between the individuals who, as member of a group, need to adapt to the environment they face, and the group, which, as a whole, needs to adapt to its own environment.[335] Accounting for

---

[332] Hayek ([1967c] 2014, 282, fn. 8) refers to V. C. Wynne-Edwards's *Animal Dispersion in Relation to Social Behavior* (Edinburg, 1966) as support for the claim that "all the individuals of the species which exist will behave in that manner because groups of individuals which have thus behaved have displaced those which did not do so." References to Wynne-Edwards appear in Hayek 1973b, 164, fn. 8; 1979, 2002, fn. 37.

[333] Campbell (1980, 73): "Any socially useful self-sacrificial behavior benefits both the 'altruists' and the nonaltruists in the group, the *net* benefit being greater to the nonaltruists because the gains to the altruists are reduced by the self-sacrificial risk costs they bear."

[334] For a more detailed discussion, see Vanberg (1986) 1994, 85ff.

[335] Hayek ([1967c] 2014, 282f.): "From any given set of rules of conduct of the elements will arise a steady structure (showing 'homeostatic' control) only in an environment in which there prevails a certain probability of encountering the sort of circumstances to which the rules of conduct are adapted. A change of environment may require, if the whole is to persist, a change in the order of the group and therefore in the rules of conduct of the individuals."—Hayek (1973b, 17): "The fact is, of course, that this mind is an adaptation to the natural and social environment in which man lives. . . . Mind is as much the product of the social environment in which it has grown up . . . as something that has in turn acted upon and altered these institutions. It is the result of man having developed in society and having acquired those habits and practices that increased the chances of persistence of the group in which he lived."

this interaction requires, in Campbell's terminology, an explanation of both the *upward causation* by which the interactions among the group members produce certain characteristics of the group as a whole, and the *downward causation* by which the characteristics of the group affect the conduct of its individual members. Hayek, it appears, assumes that by employing the concept of group selection, he can account for the downward causation that leads individuals to follow group-beneficial rules. Yet, by merely appealing to group selection, one can only provide a seeming answer to the issue that is at stake, as long as one does not specify the actual mechanisms by which group success is supposed to translate into individual rule compliance. In a letter to Hayek, dated December 14, 1983, Ernst Mayr commented on this issue:

> No truly social organism, however, can survive, and prosper without a certain amount of altruism and this, as you quite rightly say, can be established only through cultural tradition, which in turn is due to group selection. However, individual selection is not entirely excluded. . . . There must be a mechanism for the acquisition of the moral code of the group. . . . There has to be selection for an open program in which at an early age the learned moral code can be laid down. This is the importance of moral education of the child and young individual, something so glaringly neglected in our age.[336]

Mayr implicitly draws attention to his before-mentioned distinction between proximate and ultimate causes, a distinction that is of critical importance in specifying the causal link between group selection and individual rule following. The proximate causes of individuals' behavior can only be those that provide direct incentives for the conduct in question. Accordingly, one must identify such proximate causes in order to explain why individuals comply with rules that are group beneficial when compliance is per se costly. Of course, as Hayek stresses, ultimately only those groups that succeed in securing a viable group order (i.e., groups that find a way to solve the problem of providing the necessary proximate causes for individuals' compliance) will be able to prevail in evolutionary selection. In other words, proximate causes work under conditions that, in turn, are subject to the forces of evolutionary selection as the

---

[336] Letter, E. Mayr to F. A. Hayek, December 14, 1983, Hayek papers, box 37, folder 24, HIA. On the same issue, Campbell (1974b, 185) comments: "Social cooperation among men, as among wolves and among apes, coexists with genetic competition among the cooperators. This sets strict limits on genetically based complex social coordination, division of labor, and self-sacrificial altruism. In the social insects, this genetic competition among cooperators was eliminated as a prior step to their evolution of complex social systems. Because of the human genetic predicament, in achieving man's complex social coordination and *social* evolution has had to provide many of the relevant behavioral dispositions and has had to overcome some selfish biological dispositions in the process."

ultimate causes that determine what has a chance to persist. It is, so I submit, in the sense of such simultaneous working of proximate and ultimate causes that Hayek's reasoning about cultural group selection can be given its most fruitful interpretation.[337]

Explicitly distinguishing between proximate causes and ultimate causes in cultural evolution is not least important as a reminder of the fact that the problem of motivating individuals to honor the rules that make a group successful is a permanent task. Group success once achieved cannot guarantee its own persistence but may be lost again due to the group's failure to secure the necessary proximate causes.

Lastly, ending this introduction, I shall take a brief look at the conclusions that Hayek draws from his arguments on the knowledge problems we face in dealing with economy and society as complex adaptive systems for the scope and limits of policy.

The limits that the complexity of the social world sets to what we can explain and predict it equally sets—this is Hayek's principal claim—to what we can hope to achieve by deliberate policy. As he puts it:

> [The] irremediable ignorance on everyone's part of most of the particular facts which determine the actions of all the several members of human society . . . is a very inconvenient fact which makes both our attempts to explain and our attempts to influence intelligently the processes of society much more difficult, and which places severe limits on what we can say or do about them. (1973b, 12)

> It seems to me to be of the greatest importance that we fully recognize and come to terms with this limitation of our knowledge, because the pretence to more knowledge than we possess or can obtain has certain dangerous consequences. It creates a great temptation to create conditions under which we would be able to predict specific economic events and to assure that particular things will happen. But this is incompatible with the main benefit we derive from the market system, namely that it makes use of more knowledge of circumstances than any single mind can possess. ([1961] 2014, 385f.)

That in our ambition to explain and predict social events we have to be essentially content with explanations of the principle and pattern prediction requires from us, Hayek argues, a corresponding modesty on the policy side.

---

[337] Hayek ([1967c] 2014, 288f.): "The order which will form as a result of these actions is of course in no sense 'part of the purpose' or of the motives of the acting individuals. The immediate cause, the impulse which drives them to act, will be something affecting them only; and it is merely because in doing so they are restrained by rules that an overall order results."

I need hardly dwell on the significance for policy of the insight that all that science can tell us in this field are certain general characteristics of the order that will form itself in different sets of equally generally defined circumstances, but that the particular manifestations of that order will always remain unpredictable. The whole case in favor of a policy which confines itself to provide a general framework within which the market operates but leaves the continuous formation of an order to the operation of that market rests on this general insight. Once one understands this it also becomes clear why methodological and political differences so frequently go together: those who believe that it is in the power of science to predict particular individual events, or the position of individuals, naturally also want to use the power to produce the particular results they desire. ([1963b] 2014, 442)

As limited as the knowledge that an explanation of the principle offers may be, it can provide, Hayek notes, useful guidance for policy. By telling us what kinds of outcome patterns will tend to result under certain kinds of conditions, it "will enable us to make circumstances more favorable to the kinds of events we desire . . . even if it does not allow us to control the outcome" ([1955] 2014, 210).[338]

The appropriate aim for policy is, in this sense, to seek to improve the resulting order of actions *indirectly* by appropriately modifying the general conditions to which the individuals adapt their behavioral choices. Which means, as Hayek emphasizes, that the rules of law, the rules "we can deliberately alter . . . become the chief instrument whereby we can affect the resulting order" (1973b, 45).[339] In contrast to "government by order," Hayek ([1946] 2010, 62f.) has called this type of policy approach "government by rules."[340] It

---

[338] Hayek ([1964b] 2014, 271): "Predictions of a pattern are nevertheless both testable and valuable. Since the theory tells us under which general conditions a pattern . . . will form itself, it will enable us to create such conditions and to observe whether a pattern of the kind predicted will appear."—Hayek ([1961] 2014, 440): "But if certain kinds of patterns are for some reason preferable to others, it may be of the greatest importance to know what the general circumstances must be in order that the one kind of pattern rather than another will form itself."

In reference to the processes "to which the growth of mind is due," Hayek ([1942–44] 2010, 151) states: "Such knowledge of the mere principle (either a theory of knowledge or a theory of the social processes involved) will assist in creating conditions favorable to that growth, but could never provide a justification for the claim that it should be deliberately directed."

[339] Hayek ([1965] 2014, 50): "It turns out to be an instance of a general method of indirectly creating an order in situations where the phenomena are far too complex to allow us the creation of an order by separately putting each element in its appropriate place. . . . It is therefore an order which we cannot improve upon but only disturb by attempting to change by deliberate arrangement any one part of it. The only way we can effectively improve it is by improving the abstract rules which guide the individuals."

[340] It is worth noting that what Hayek describes as "government by rules" corresponds to what the Ordoliberals of the Freiburg School call *Ordnungspolitik*. On Hayek's connection with the Freiburg School, see Vanberg 2013.

is a kind of policy of which he says that "it should perhaps better be described by the term *cultivation* than by the familiar term 'control'—cultivation in the sense in which the farmer or gardener cultivates his plants, . . . and in which the wise legislator or statesman will probably attempt to cultivate rather than to control the forces of the social process" ([1955] 2014, 210).[341]

Yet, as much as Hayek acknowledges the role that "government by rules" can play as an instrument for improving the social condition, he also warns against a pretense of knowledge that may mislead overzealous reformers to disregard the knowledge embodied in evolved institutions and traditions.[342] About the improvements in the framework of rules that we may expect from such "government by rules," he says:

> This, however, is of necessity a slow and difficult task, because most of the rules which do govern existing society are not the result of our deliberate making, and in consequence we often understand only very imperfectly what depends on them. . . . They are the product of a slow process of evolution in the course of which much more experience and knowledge has been precipitated in them than any one person can fully know. This means that, before we can hope successfully to improve them, we must learn to comprehend much better than we do now in what manner the man-made rules and the spontaneous forces of society interact. This will require not only a much closer cooperation between the specialists in economics, law, and social philosophy than we have had in recent times; even after we have achieved this, all we can hope for will be a slow experimental process of gradual improvement rather than any opportunity for drastic change. ([1964b] 2014, 50)

13. Conclusion

As its title is meant to indicate, my purpose with this introduction has been to document that *TSO* is by no means an exotic outlier in the whole body of

[341] Hayek alludes here to Adam Smith's concept of political economy as "the science of a legislator" (A. Smith (1776) 1981, 486). See also Hayek (1961) 2014, 386: "In fields like ours it would probably be more appropriate if instead of speaking of prediction and control we described our aim as 'orientation and cultivation.' Though our knowledge is not sufficient to predict or produce specific events, it enables us . . . to create conditions which improve the prospects of a desirable outcome—or which are conducive to the formation and preservation of that orderliness of which success of our individual efforts so largely depends."

[342] Hayek (Weimer-Hayek Discussion 1982, 328f.): "There is a great deal of implicit knowledge involved in habits, rules, and in traditional customs. . . . It is obvious that it is not a reason for rejecting a pattern of behavior that we cannot explain why we do it unless we have, in theory, a way of showing that it is an ineffective procedure. In that sense, it is just an indication of respecting traditions."

Hayek's writings but is an integral part of the impressively coherent theoretical system that he systematically developed over the many decades of his active academic life.

Earlier I had quoted William Butos's observation that, even though in recent decades *TSO* has increasingly been paid attention to, "the relevance of Hayek's cognitive theory for social theory remains controversial and unsettled."[343] I hope I have succeeded in convincing the reader not only that, but also how, this controversy should be settled. As a comment on his quoted observation, Butos (2010b, 10f.) adds: "These doubts are not without foundation, after all, if economics concerns social interaction in the context of scarcity, delving into the working of the brain might be seen as pushing economics far beyond its legitimate disciplinary boundaries." This comment tends to hide the difference between two questions that should be carefully separated. One is whether *TSO* should be understood as an invitation to economists to expand their research domain and, by "delving into the workings of the brain," to take on, as a side job, the task on which neuroscientists specialize. In this regard doubts are surely justified, and I consider it quite unlikely that Hayek would have endorsed neuroeconomics as the research program most congenial to what he regarded as the significance of *TSO* for economics as a social science.[344] The other question is whether *TSO* should be understood as an invitation to economists to ground their social theoretical reasoning in more realistic, empirically contentful behavioral conjectures than their self-made rational choice model provides. Clearly this question should be answered in the affirmative.

In this introduction I have sought to show that the behavioral theory Hayek outlines in *TSO* cannot only serve this purpose but also, in important respects, informs the very core tenets of his social theory.

References[345]

Agnito, Rosemary. 1975. "Hayek Revisited: Mind as a Process of Classification." *Behaviorism* 3: 162–71.

Bartley, William W. 1987. "Philosophy of Biology versus Philosophy of Physics." In *Evolutionary Epistemology, Rationality, and the Sociology of Knowledge*, edited by G. Radnitzky and W. W. Bartley, 7–45. La Salle, IL: Open Court.

Basar, Erol. 2005. "What Is the Place of Psychophysiology in the Interdisciplinary Sciences? Welcoming Address of the Vice-President (Academic Affairs) at the Open-

[343] See above, p. 24.
[344] See above, fn. 25.
[345] Where applicable the year of original publication appears first in parentheses.

ing Ceremonies of the 12th World Congress of Psychophysiology, I.O.P. 2004." *International Journal of Psychophysiology* 58: 117–18.

Beck, Naomi. 2011. "Be Fruitful and Multiply: Growth, Reason, and Cultural Group Selection in Hayek and Darwin." *Biological Theory* 6: 413–23.

Bertalanffy, Ludwig von. 1968. *General System Theory—Foundations, Development, Application.* Rev. ed. New York: George Braziller.

———. 1969. "Chance or Law." In *Beyond Reductionism. New Perspectives in the Life Sciences (The Alpbach Symposium 1968),* edited by A. Koestler and J. R. Smythies, 56–84. London: Hutchinson.

Birner, Jack. 1994. "Introduction: Hayek's Grand Research Programme." In *Hayek, Co-Ordination and Evolution,* edited by J. Birner and R. von Zijp, 1–21. London and New York: Routledge.

———. 1999. "The Surprising Place of Cognitive Psychology in the Work of F. A. Hayek." *History of Economic Ideas* 7: 43–84.

———. 2009. "From Group Selection to Ecological Niches: Popper's Rethinking of Evolutionary Theory in the Light of Hayek's Theory of Culture." In *Rethinking Popper, Boston Studies in the Philosophy of Science,* edited by R. S. Cohen and Z. Parusniková, 185–202. Dordrecht: Springer.

Boettke, Peter J., and J. Robert Subrick. 2002. "From the Philosophy of Mind to the Philosophy of the Market." *Journal of Economic Methodology* 9: 53–64.

Boring, Edwin G. 1953. "Review of *The Sensory Order.*" *Scientific Monthly* 76: 182–83.

Bouillon, Hardy. 1991. *Ordnung, Evolution und Erkenntnis. Hayeks Sozialphilosophie und ihre erkenntnistheoretische Grundlage.* Tübingen: J.C.B. Mohr (Paul Siebeck).

Bühler, Karl. 1934. *Die Darstellungsfunktion der Sprache.* Jena: Gustav Fischer.

Butos, William N. 1997. "Hayek and Rational Expectations." In *Austrian Economics in Debate,* edited by W. Keizer, B. Tieben, and R. von Zijp, 220–42. London: Routledge.

———, ed. 2010a. *The Social Science of Hayek's 'Sensory Order'.* Vol. 13 of *Advances in Austrian Economics.* Bingley, UK: Emerald.

———. 2010b. "The Unexpected Fertility of Hayek's Cognitive Theory: An Introduction to The Social Science of Hayek's 'Sensory Order.'" In *The Social Science of Hayek's 'Sensory Order',* edited by W. N. Butos, 1–20. Vol. 13 of *Advances in Austrian Economics.* Bingley, UK: Emerald.

Butos, William N., and Roger G. Koppl. 1993. "Hayekian Expectations: Theory and Empirical Applications." *Constitutional Political Economy* 4: 303–29.

———. 2006. "Does *The Sensory Order* Have a Useful Economic Future?" In *Cognition and Economics,* edited by E. Krecke, C. Krecke, and R. Koppl, 19–50. Vol. 9 of *Advances in Austrian Economics.* Bingley, UK: Emerald.

Butos, William N., and Thomas J. McQuade. 2002. "Mind, Market and Institutions: The Knowledge Problem in Hayek's Thought." In *F.A. Hayek as a Political Economist,* edited by J. Birner, P. Garrouste, and T. Aimar, 113–33. London: Routledge.

———. 2009. "The Adaptive Systems Theory of Social Orders." *Studies in Emergent Orders* 2: 76–108.

Caldwell, Bruce. 1988. "Hayek's Transformation." *History of Political Economy* 20: 513–41.

———. 1992a. "Hayek the Falsificationist? A Refutation." *Research in the History of Economic Thought and Methodology* 10: 1–15.

———. 1992b. "Reply to Hutchison." *Research in the History of Economic Thought and Methodology* 10: 33–42.

———. 1997. "Hayek and Socialism." *Journal of Economic Literature* 35: 1856–90.

———. 2001. "Hodgson on Hayek: A Critique." *Cambridge Journal of Economics* 25: 539–53.

———. 2004a. *Hayek's Challenge: An Intellectual Biography of F. A. Hayek.* Chicago: University of Chicago Press.

———. 2004b. "Some Reflections on F. A. Hayek's *The Sensory Order.*" *Journal of Bioeconomics* 6: 239–54.

———. 2006. "Hayek and the Austrian Tradition." In *The Cambridge Companion to Hayek*, edited by E. Feser, 13–33. Cambridge, MA: Cambridge University Press.

———. 2010. Introduction to *Studies on the Abuse and Decline of Reason: Text and Documents*, by F. A. Hayek, edited by Bruce Caldwell, 1–45. Vol. XIII of *The Collected Works of F. A. Hayek.* Chicago: University of Chicago Press.

———. 2013. *F. A. Hayek and the "Economic Calculus": The Cambridge and Virginia Lectures.* Lecture held at the University of Richmond, April 13, 2013.

———. 2014. Introduction to *The Market and Other Orders*, by F. A. Hayek, edited by Bruce Caldwell, 1–35. Vol. XV of *The Collected Works of F.A. Hayek.* Chicago: University of Chicago Press.

Camerer, Colin. 2008. "The Case for Mindful Economics." In *The Foundations of Positive and Normative Economics*, edited by A. Caplin and A. Schotter, 43–69. London: Oxford University Press.

Campbell, Donald T. 1974a. "Unjustified Variation and Selective Retention in Scientific Discovery." In *Studies in the Philosophy of Biology*, edited by F. J. Ayala and T. Dobzhansky, 139–61. London: Macmillan.

———. 1974b. "Downward Causation in Hierarchically Organized Biological Systems." In *Studies in the Philosophy of Biology*, edited by F. J. Ayala and T. Dobzhansky, 179–84. London: Macmillan.

———. 1974c. "Evolutionary Epistemology." In *The Philosophy of Karl Popper*, edited by P. A. Schilpp, 413–63. La Salle, IL: Open Court.

———. 1975. "On the Conflicts between Biological and Social Evolution and between Psychology and Moral Tradition." *American Psychologist* 30: 1103–26.

———. 1980. "Social Morality Norms as Evidence of Conflict between Biological Human Nature and Social System Requirements." In *Morality as a Biological Phenomenon: The Presuppositions of Sociobiological Research*, edited by G. S. Stent, 67–82. Rev. ed. Berkeley: University of California Press.

———. 1987a. "Evolutionary Epistemology." In *Evolutionary Epistemology, Rationality, and the Sociology of Knowledge*, edited by G. Radnitzky and W. W. Bartley, 47–89. La Salle, IL: Open Court.

———. 1987b. "Blind Variation and Selective Retention in Creative Thought and in Other Knowledge Processes." In *Evolutionary Epistemology, Rationality, and the Sociology of Knowledge*, edited by G. Radnitzky and W. W. Bartley, 91–114. La Salle, IL: Open Court.

———. 1997. "From Evolutionary Epistemology via Selection Theory to a Sociology of Scientific Validity." Edited by C. Heyes and B. Frankel. *Evolution and Cognition* 3: 5–38.

Chisholm, Roderick M. 1954. *Review of The Sensory Order. Philosophical Review* 63: 135–36.

Cubeddu, Raimondo. 2002. "Uncertainty, Institutions and Order in Hayek." In *F. A. Hayek as a Political Economist*, edited by J. Birner, P. Garrouste, and T. Aimar, 134–52. London: Routledge.

D'Amico, Daniel, and Peter Boettke. 2010. "Making Sense of *The Sensory Order*." In *The Social Science of Hayek's 'Sensory Order'*, edited by W. N. Butos, 357–81. Vol. 13 of *Advances in Austrian Economics*. Bingley, UK: Emerald.

Darwin, Charles. 1974. *Metaphysics, Materialism and the Evolution of Mind—Early Writings of Charles Darwin*. Chicago: University of Chicago Press.

De Vecchi, Nicolò. 2003. "The Place of Gestalt Psychology in the Making of Hayek's Thought." *History of Political Economy* 35: 135–62.

de Vries, Robert P. 1994. "The Place of Hayek's Theory of Mind and Perception in the History of Philosophy and Psychology." In *Hayek, Co-Ordination and Evolution*, edited by J. Birner and R. von Zijp, 311–22. London: Routledge.

Ebenstein, Alan. 2001. *Friedrich Hayek: A Biography*. New York: Palgrave Macmillan.

———. 2003. *Hayek's Journey: The Mind of Friedrich Hayek*. New York: Palgrave Macmillan.

Edelman, Gerald M. 1982. "Through a Computer Darkly: Group Selection and Higher Brain Functions." *Bulletin of the American Academy of Arts and Sciences* 36: 18–49.

———. 1987. *Neural Darwinism: The Theory of Neuronal Group Selection*. New York: Basic Books.

———. 2004. *Wider Than the Sky: The Phenomenal Gift of Consciousness*. New Haven, CT: Yale University Press.

Falk, Raphael. 1993. "Evolutionary Epistemology: What Phenotype is Selected and which Genotype Evolves?" *Biology and Philosophy* 8: 153–72.

Feser, Edward. 2006. "Hayek the Cognitive Scientist and Philosopher of Mind." In *The Cambridge Companion to Hayek*, edited by E. Feser, 287–314. Cambridge, MA: Cambridge University Press.

———. 2011. "Hayek, Popper, and the Causal Theory of the Mind." In *Hayek in Mind: Hayek's Philosophical Psychology*, edited by L. Marsh, 73–102. Vol. 15 of *Advances in Austrian Economics*. Bingley, UK: Emerald.

Fuster, Joaquin M. 1995. *Memory in the Cerebral Cortex—An Empirical Approach to Neural Networks in the Human and Nonhuman Primate*. Cambridge, MA: MIT Press.

———. 1997. "Network Memory." *Trends in Neuroscience* 20: 451–59.

———. 2011. "Hayek in Today's Cognitive Neuroscience." In *Hayek in Mind: Hayek's Philosophical Psychology*, edited by L. Marsh, 3–11. Vol. 15 of *Advances in Austrian Economics*. Bingley, UK: Emerald.

Gaus, Gerald F. 2006. "Hayek on the Evolution of Society and Mind." In *The Cambridge Companion to Hayek*, edited by E. Feser, 232–58. Cambridge, MA: Cambridge University Press.

Gray, John. 1984. *Hayek on Liberty*. New York: Basil Blackwell.

Grenell, Robert G. 1954. "Review of *The Sensory Order*." *Quarterly Review of Biology* 29: 409–10.

Hacohen, Malachi Haim. 2000. *Karl Popper—The Formative Years, 1902–1945*. Cambridge, MA: Cambridge University Press.

Hamlyn, David W. 1954. "Review of *The Sensory Order*." *Mind* 63: 560–62.

Hayek, F. A. (1933) 1991. "The Trend of Economic Thinking." In *The Trend of Economic Thinking: Essays on Political Economists and Economic History*, edited by W. W. Bartley III and Stephen Kresge, 17–34. Vol. III of *The Collected Works of F. A. Hayek*. Chicago: University of Chicago Press.

———. (1937) 2014. "Economics and Knowledge." In *The Market and Other Orders*, edited by Bruce Caldwell, 57–77. Vol. XV of *The Collected Works of F. A. Hayek*. Chicago: University of Chicago Press.

———. (1939) 1997. *Freedom and the Economic System*. Public Policy Pamphlet No. 29. Chicago. Now in *Socialism and War*, edited by Bruce Caldwell, 189–211. Vol. X of *The Collected Works of F. A. Hayek*. Chicago: University of Chicago Press.

———. (1941) 2010. "The Counter-Revolution of Science." In *Studies on the Abuse and Decline of Reason: Text and Documents*, edited by Bruce Caldwell, 167–281. Vol. XIII of *The Collected Works of F. A. Hayek*. Chicago: University of Chicago Press.

———. (1942–44) 2010. "Scientism and the Study of Society." In *Studies on the Abuse and Decline of Reason: Text and Documents*, edited by Bruce Caldwell, 75–166. Vol. XIII of *The Collected Works of F. A. Hayek*. Chicago: University of Chicago Press.

———. (1943) 2014. "The Facts of the Social Sciences." In *The Market and Other Orders*, edited by Bruce Caldwell, 78–92. Vol. XV of *The Collected Works of F. A. Hayek*. Chicago: University of Chicago Press.

———. (1944) 2007. *The Road to Serfdom*. Edited by Bruce Caldwell. Vol. II of *The Collected Works of F. A. Hayek*. Chicago: University of Chicago Press.

———. (1945a) 2014. "The Use of Knowledge in Society." In *The Market and Other Orders*, edited by Bruce Caldwell, 93–104. Vol. XV of *The Collected Works of F. A. Hayek*. Chicago: University of Chicago Press.

———. 1945b. *What Is Mind? A Working Hypothesis on the Origin of Sensory Qualities and Abstract Concepts*. First draft, typescript. Hayek papers, box 128, folder 34. Hoover Institution Archives, Stanford University, Stanford, CA.

————. (1946) 2010. "Individualism: True and False." In *Studies on the Abuse and Decline of Reason: Text and Documents*, edited by Bruce Caldwell, 46–75. Vol. XIII of *The Collected Works of F. A. Hayek*. Chicago: University of Chicago Press.

————. 1947. *What Is Mind? An Essay in Theoretical Psychology*. Second draft, typescript. Hayek papers, box128, folder 35. Hoover Institution Archives, Stanford University, Stanford, CA.

————. 1948. *Individualism and Economic Order*. Chicago: University of Chicago Press.

————. (1952) 2006. *Die sensorische Ordnung—Eine Untersuchung der Grundlagen der theoretischen Psychologie*. Translated and with additional contributions edited by Manfred E. Streit, Friedrich A. von Hayek, *Gesammelte Schriften in deutscher Sprache*, Vol. B 5. Tübingen: Mohr Siebeck.

————. (1955) 2014. "Degrees of Explanation." In *The Market and Other Orders*, edited by Bruce Caldwell, 195–212. Vol. XV of *The Collected Works of F. A. Hayek*. Chicago: University of Chicago Press.

————. 1956/57. "Über den Sinn sozialer Institutionen." *Schweizer Monatshefte* 36: 512–24.

————. (1960) 2011. *The Constitution of Liberty*. Edited by Ronald Hamowy. Vol. XVII of *The Collected Works of F. A. Hayek*. Chicago: University of Chicago Press.

————. (1961) 2014. "A New Look at Economic Theory." Virginia Lectures. In *The Market and Other Orders*, edited by Bruce Caldwell, 373–426. Vol. XV of *The Collected Works of F. A. Hayek*. Chicago: University of Chicago Press.

————. (1962a) 1967. "The Moral Element in Free Enterprise." In *Studies in Philosophy, Politics and Economics*, 229–36. Chicago: University of Chicago Press.

————. (1962b) 2014. "Rules, Perception and Intelligibility." In *The Market and Other Orders*, edited by Bruce Caldwell, 232–53. Vol. XV of *The Collected Works of F. A. Hayek*. Chicago: University of Chicago Press.

————. (1963a) 1992. "The Economics of the 1920s as Seen from Vienna." In *The Fortunes of Liberalism: Essays on Austrian Economics and the Ideal of Freedom*, edited by P. G. Klein, 19–38. Vol. IV of *The Collected Works of F. A. Hayek*. Chicago: University of Chicago Press.

————. (1963b) 2014. "Economists and Philosophers." In *The Market and Other Orders*, edited by Bruce Caldwell, 427–43. Vol. XV of *The Collected Works of F. A. Hayek*. Chicago: University of Chicago Press.

————. (1964a) 1992. "Epistemological Problems of Economics." In *The Fortunes of Liberalism: Essays on Austrian Economics and the Ideal of Freedom*, edited by P. G. Klein, 147–49. Vol. IV of *The Collected Works of F. A. Hayek*. Chicago: University of Chicago Press.

————. (1964b) 2014. "The Theory of Complex Phenomena." In *The Market and Other Orders*, edited by Bruce Caldwell, 257–77. Vol. XV of *The Collected Works of F. A. Hayek*. Chicago: University of Chicago Press.

————. (1965) 2014. "Kinds of Rationalism." In *The Market and Other Orders*, edited by

Bruce Caldwell, 39–53. Vol. XV of *The Collected Works of F. A. Hayek*. Chicago: University of Chicago Press.

———. (1966) 1978. "Personal Recollections of Keynes and the 'Keynesian Revolution.'" In *New Studies in Philosophy, Politics, Economics and the History of Ideas*, 283–89. Chicago: University of Chicago Press.

———. (1967a) 1978. "Dr. Bernard Mandeville." In *New Studies in Philosophy, Politics, Economics and the History of Ideas*, 249–66. Chicago: University of Chicago Press.

———. (1967b) 1992. "Ernst Mach (1838–1916) and the Social Sciences in Vienna." In *The Fortunes of Liberalism: Essays on Austrian Economics and the Ideal of Freedom*, edited by P. G. Klein, 172–75. Vol. IV of *The Collected Works of F. A. Hayek*. Chicago: University of Chicago Press.

———. (1967c) 2014. "Notes on the Evolution of Rules of Conduct." In *The Market and Other Orders*, edited by Bruce Caldwell, 278–92. Vol. XV of *The Collected Works of F. A. Hayek*. Chicago: University of Chicago Press.

———. 1967d. *Studies in Philosophy, Politics and Economics*. Chicago: University of Chicago Press.

———. (1968a) 1992. "The Austrian School of Economics." In *The Fortunes of Liberalism: Essays on Austrian Economics and the Ideal of Freedom*, edited by P. G. Klein, 42–60. Vol. IV of *The Collected Works of F. A. Hayek*. Chicago: University of Chicago Press.

———. (1968b) 1978. "Competition as a Discover Procedure." In *New Studies in Philosophy, Politics, Economics and the History of Ideas*, 179–90. Chicago: University of Chicago Press.

———. (1968c) 1978. "The Confusion of Language in Political Thought." In *New Studies in Philosophy, Politics, Economics and the History of Ideas*, 71–97. Chicago: University of Chicago Press.

———. (1969) 2014. "The Primacy of the Abstract." In *The Market and Other Orders*, edited by Bruce Caldwell, 314–27. Vol. XV of *The Collected Works of F. A. Hayek*. Chicago: University of Chicago Press.

———. (1970) 2014. "The Errors of Constructivism." In *The Market and Other Orders*, edited by Bruce Caldwell, 338–56. Vol. XV of *The Collected Works of F. A. Hayek*. Chicago: University of Chicago Press.

———. (1973a) 1992. "The Place of Menger's *Grundsätze* in the History of Economic Thought." In *The Fortunes of Liberalism: Essays on Austrian Economics and the Ideal of Freedom*, edited by P. G. Klein, 96–107. Vol. IV of *The Collected Works of F. A. Hayek*. Chicago: University of Chicago Press.

———. 1973b. *Rules and Order, Law, Legislation and Liberty*. Vol. 1. London: Routledge & Kegan Paul.

———. (1975) 2014. "The Pretense of Knowledge." In *The Market and Other Orders*, edited by Bruce Caldwell, 362–72. Vol. XV of *The Collected Works of F. A. Hayek*. Chicago: University of Chicago Press.

———. 1976. *The Mirage of Social Justice, Law, Legislation and Liberty.* Vol. 2. London: Routledge & Kegan Paul.

———. 1978. *New Studies in Philosophy, Politics, Economics and the History of Ideas.* Chicago: University of Chicago Press.

———. 1979. *The Political Order of a Free People, Law, Legislation and Liberty.* Vol. 3. London: Routledge & Kegan Paul.

———. 1983a. "Die überschätzte Vernunft." In *Evolution und Menschenbild,* edited by R. J. Riedl and F. Kreuzer, 164–92, 225–41 (discussion). Hamburg: Hoffmann und Campe.

———. 1983b. Nobel prize–winning economist oral history transcript. Completed under the auspices of the Oral History Program, University of California, Los Angeles.

———. 1984. "The Origins and Effects of Our Morals: A Problem for Science." In *The Essence of Hayek,* edited by C. Nishiyama and K. R. Leube, 318–30. Stanford, CA: Hoover Institution Press.

———. 1986. "The Moral Imperative of the Market." In *The Unfinished Agenda,* edited by R. Harris et al., 143–49. London: Institute of Economic Affairs.

———. (1988) 1992. "Notes and Recollections." In *The Fortunes of Liberalism: Essays on Austrian Economics and the Ideal of Freedom,* edited by P. G. Klein, 153–59. Vol. IV of *The Collected Works of F. A. Hayek.* Chicago: University of Chicago Press.

———. 1992. *The Fortunes of Liberalism: Essays on Austrian Economics and the Ideal of Freedom.* Edited by P. G. Klein. Vol. IV of *The Collected Works of F. A. Hayek.* Chicago: University of Chicago Press.

———. 1994. *Hayek on Hayek—An Autobiographical Dialogue.* Edited by S. Kresge and L. Wenar. London: Routledge.

———. 2010. *Studies on the Abuse and Decline of Reason: Text and Documents.* Edited by Bruce Caldwell. Vol. XIII of *The Collected Works of F. A. Hayek.* Chicago: University of Chicago Press.

———. 2014. *The Market and Other Orders.* Edited by Bruce Caldwell. Vol. XV of *The Collected Works of F. A. Hayek.* Chicago: University of Chicago Press.

Hebb, Donald O. 1949. *The Organization of Behavior—A Neuropsychological Theory.* New York: John Wiley & Sons.

Hennecke, Hans Jörg. 2000. *Friedrich August von Hayek. Die Tradition der Freiheit.* Düsseldorf: Verlag Wirtschaft und Finanzen.

Herrmann-Pillath, Carsten. 1992. "The Brain, Its Sensory Order, and the Evolutionary Concept of Mind: On Hayek's Contribution to Evolutionary Epistemology." *Journal of Social and Evolutionary Systems* 15: 145–86.

Holland, John H. 1992. "Complex Adaptive Systems." *Daedalus—Journal of the American Academy of Arts and Sciences* 121: 17–30.

———. 1995. *Hidden Order: How Adaptation Builds Complexity.* Reading, MA: Helix Books.

———. 1996. "The Rationality of Adaptive Agents." In *The Rational Foundations of Economic Behavior—Proceedings of the IEA Conference held in Turin, Italy*, edited by K. J. Arrow, E. Colombatto, M. Perlman, and C. Schmidt, 281–301. New York: St. Martin's Press.

———. 1998. *Emergence: From Chaos to Order*. Reading, MA: Perseus Books.

———. 2012. *Signals and Boundaries: Building Blocks for Complex Adaptive Systems*. Cambridge, MA: MIT Press.

Horwitz, Steven. 2000. "From *The Sensory Order* to the Liberal Order." *Review of Austrian Economics* 13: 23–40.

———. 2010. "I Am Not a 'Neuro-Hayekian,' I'm a Subjectivist." In *The Social Science of Hayek's 'Sensory Order'*, edited by W. N. Butos, 383–89. Vol. 13 of *Advances in Austrian Economics*. Bingley, UK: Emerald.

Hutchison, Terence W. 1981. *The Politics and Philosophy of Economics: Marxians, Keynesians, and Austrians*. Oxford: Blackwell.

———. 1992. "Hayek and 'Modern Austrian' Methodology: Comments on a Non-Refuting Refutation." *Research in the History of Economic Thought and Methodology* 10: 17–32.

Kneale, Martha. 1954. "Review of *The Sensory Order*." *Philosophical Quarterly* 4: 189.

Koestler, Arthur. 1969. "Beyond Atomism and Holism—the Concept of the Holon." In *Beyond Reductionism: New Perspectives in the Life Sciences (The Alpbach Symposium 1968)*, edited by A. Koestler and J. R. Smythies, 192–232. London: Hutchinson.

Koestler, Arthur, and J. R. Smythies, eds. 1969. *Beyond Reductionism: New Perspectives in the Life Sciences (The Alpbach Symposium 1968)*. London: Hutchinson.

Kraft, Victor. 1968. *Der Wiener Kreis: Der Ursprung des Neopositivismus*. 2nd ed. New York: Springer.

Kreuzer, Franz. 1983. *Markt, Plan, Freiheit—Gespräch mit Friedrich von Hayek und Ralf Dahrendorf*. Wien: Franz Deuticke.

Leeson, Robert. 2013. Introduction to *Hayek: A Collaborative Biography, Part 1: Influences from Mises to Bartley*, edited by Robert Leeson, 1–42. New York: Palgrave Mcmillan.

Lindemans, Jan Willem. 2011. "Hayek's Post-Positivist Empiricism: Experience Beyond Sensation." In *Hayek in Mind: Hayek's Philosophical Psychology*, edited by L. Marsh, 143–70. Vol. 15 of *Advances in Austrian Economics*. Bingley, UK: Emerald.

Lorenz, Konrad. (1935) 1937. "The Companion in the Bird's World." *Auk* 54: 245–73. (English version of "Der Kumpan in der Umwelt des Vogels Der Artgenosse als auslösendes Moment sozialer Verhaltensweisen," *Journal für Ornithologie* 83: 137–213, 289–413).

———. (1941) 1982. "Kant's Doctrine of the A Priori in the Light of Contemporary Biology." In *Learning, Development, and Culture*, edited by H. C. Plotkin, 121–43. Chichester: John Wiley & Sons. (English version of "Kant's Lehre vom Apriorischen im Lichte gegenwärtiger Biologie," *Blätter für Deutsche Philosophie* 15 (1941): 94–125.)

———. 1942. "Die angeborenen Formen möglicher Erfahrung." *Zeitschrift für Tierpsychologie* 5: 235–409.

———. 1950. "The Comparative Method in Studying Innate Behavior Patterns." In *Symposia of the Society for Experimental Biology, Number IV: Physiological Mechanisms in Animal Behavior*, 221–68. Cambridge, MA: At the University Press.

———. 1985. "My Family and Other Animals." In *Leaders in the Study of Animal Behavior: Autobiographical Perspectives*, edited by D. A. Dewsbury, 258–87. Lewisburg, PA: Bucknell University Press.

Mach, Ernst. 1883. *Die Mechanik in ihrer Entwicklung*. Leipzig: F. A. Brockhaus.

———. 1885. *Die Analyse der Empfindungen und das Verhältnis des Physischen zum Psychischen*. Jena: Gustav Fischer.

———. 1896. *Populärwissenschaftliche Vorlesungen*. Leipzig: Barth.

Markose, Sheri M. 2005. "Computability and Evolutionary Complexity: Markets as Complex Adaptive Systems (CAS)." *Economic Journal* 115 (504): F159–92.

Marsh, Leslie. 2010. "Hayek: Cognitive Scientist Avant la Lettre." In *The Social Science of Hayek's 'Sensory Order'*, edited by W. N. Butos, 115–55. Vol. 13 of *Advances in Austrian Economics*. Bingley, UK: Emerald.

———, ed. 2011a. *Hayek in Mind: Hayek's Philosophical Psychology*. Vol. 15 of *Advances in Austrian Economics*. Bingley, UK: Emerald.

———. 2011b. "'Socializing' the Mind and 'Cognitivizing' Sociality." In *Hayek in Mind: Hayek's Philosophical Psychology*, edited by L. Marsh, xiii–xxiv. Vol. 15 of *Advances in Austrian Economics*. Bingley, UK: Emerald.

Mayr, Ernst. 1961. "Cause and Effect in Biology." *Science* 134: 1501–6.

———. 1982a. *The Growth of Biological Thought—Diversity, Evolution, and Inheritance*. Cambridge, MA: Harvard University Press.

———. 1982b. "Teleological and Teleonomic: A New Analysis." In *Learning, Development, and Culture*, edited by H. C. Plotkin, 17–38. Chichester: John Wiley & Sons.

———. 1988. *Toward a New Philosophy of Biology—Observations of an Evolutionist*. Cambridge, MA: Harvard University Press.

———. 1992. "The Idea of Teleology." *Journal of the History of Ideas* 53: 117–35.

McQuade, Thomas J. 2006. "Science and Market as Adaptive Classifying Systems." In *Cognition and Economics*, edited by E. Krecke, C. Krecke, and R. Koppl, 51–86. Vol. 9 of *Advances in Austrian Economics*. Bingley, UK: Emerald.

McQuade, Thomas J., and William N. Butos. 2005. "The Sensory Order and Other Natural Classifier Systems." *Journal of Bioeconomics* 7: 335–58.

Miller, Mark S. 1996. "Learning Curve: Review of John Holland, *Hidden Order*," *Reason Magazine* (December 1996): 59–64.

Mises, Ludwig von. 1949. *Human Action—A Treatise on Economics*. New Haven, CT: Yale University Press.

———. (1962) 2006. *The Ultimate Foundation of Economic Science—An Essay on Method*. Indianapolis: Liberty Fund.

———. 1990. *Money, Method, and the Market Process*. Essays by Ludwig von Mises, Selected by Margit von Mises, Edited with an Introduction by Richard M. Ebeling. Norwell, MA: Kluwer Academic Publishers.

North, Douglass C. 2005. *Understanding the Process of Economic Change*. Princeton: Princeton University Press.

Plotkin, Henry C. 1982. "Evolutionary Epistemology and Evolutionary Theory." In *Learning, Development, and Culture*, edited by H. C. Plotkin, 3–13. Chichester: John Wiley & Sons.

Popper, Karl R. (1948a) 1972. "The Bucket and the Searchlight: Two Theories of Knowledge." In *Objective Knowledge—An Evolutionary Approach*, 341–61. Oxford: At the Clarendon Press.

———. (1948b) 1989. "Prediction and Prophecy in the Social Sciences." In *Conjectures and Refutations: The Growth of Scientific Knowledge*, 336–46. 5th ed. London: Routledge.

———. (1953a) 1989. "Language and the Body-Mind Problem." In *Conjectures and Refutations: The Growth of Scientific Knowledge*, 293–98. 5th ed. London: Routledge.

———. (1953b) 1989. "A Note on Berkeley as Precursor of Mach and Einstein." In *Conjectures and Refutations: The Growth of Scientific Knowledge*, 166–74. 5th ed. London: Routledge.

———. (1957) 1994. *The Poverty of Historicism*. London: Routledge.

———. (1963a) 1994. "Models, Instruments, and Truth: The Status of the Rationality Principle in the Social Sciences." In *The Myth of the Framework: In Defence of Science and Rationality*, 154–84. London: Routledge.

———. (1963b) 1994. "Science: Problems, Aims, Responsibilities." In *The Myth of the Framework: In Defence of Science and Rationality*, 82–111. London: Routledge.

———. (1968) 1972. "On the Theory of the Objective Mind." In *Objective Knowledge—An Evolutionary Approach*, 153–90. Oxford: At the Clarendon Press.

———. 1972. *Objective Knowledge—An Evolutionary Approach*. Oxford: At the Clarendon Press.

———. 1974a. "Intellectual Autobiography." In *The Philosophy of Karl Popper*, edited by P. A. Schilpp, 3–181. La Salle, IL: Open Court.

———. 1974b. "Replies to My Critics." In *The Philosophy of Karl Popper*, edited by P. A. Schilpp, 961–1197. La Salle, IL: Open Court.

———. 1974c. "Scientific Reduction and the Essential Incompleteness of All Science." In *Studies in the Philosophy of Biology*, edited by F. J. Ayala and T. Dobzhansky, 259–84. London: Macmillan.

———. 1978. "Natural Selection and the Emergence of Mind." *Dialectica* 32: 339–55.

———. (1982) 1994. "Knowledge and the Shaping of Reality." In *In Search of a Better World: Lectures and Essays from Thirty Years*, 3–29. London: Routledge.

———. 1997. "Tribute to the Life and Work of Friedrich Hayek." In *Hayek: Economist and Social Philosopher—A Critical Retrospect*, edited by S. F. Frowen, 311–12. London: Macmillan.

Popper, Karl R., and John C. Eccles. 1977. *The Self and Its Brain: An Argument for Interactionism*. London: Routledge.

Radnitzky, Gerard, and W. W. Bartley III, eds. 1987. *Evolutionary Epistemology, Rationality, and the Sociology of Knowledge*. La Salle, IL: Open Court.

Rizello, Salvatore. 1999. *The Economics of the Mind*. Aldershot, NH: Edward Elgar.

Rust, Joshua. 2011. "Hayek, Connectionism, and Scientific Naturalism." In *Hayek in Mind: Hayek's Philosophical Psychology*, edited by L. Marsh, 29–50. Vol. 15 of *Advances in Austrian Economics*. Bingley, UK: Emerald.

Scheall, Scott. 2015. "Hayek the Apriorist?" *Journal of the History of Economic Thought* 37: 87–110.

Schütz, Alfred. 2010. "Kommentar zum Wiener Hayek-Vortrag über 'Wissen und Wirtschaft.'" In *Zur Methodologie der Sozialwissenschaften*, edited by T. S. Eberle, J. Dreher, and G. Sebald, 91–122. Konstanz: UVK Verlag.

Smith, Adam. (1776) 1981. *An Inquiry into the Nature and Causes of the Wealth of Nations*. Indianapolis: Liberty Classic. First published 1976 by Oxford University Press.

Smith, Barry. 1997. "The Connectionist Mind: A Study of Hayekian Psychology." In *Hayek: Economist and Social Philosopher—A Critical Retrospect*, edited by S. F. Frowen, 9–29. London: Macmillan.

Smith, Vernon L. 2003. "Experimental Methods in (Neuro)Economics." In *Encyclopedia of Cognitive Science*, edited by Lynn Nadel, 1070–79. Vol. 1. London: Nature Publishing Group.

Sprich, Christoph. 2008. *Hayeks Kritik an der Rationalitätsannahme und seine alternative Konzeption. Die Sensory Order im Lichte anderer Erkenntnistheorien*. Marburg: Metropolis.

Sprott, Walter John H. 1954. "Review of *The Sensory Order*." *Philosophy* 29: 183–85.

Steele, David R. 1987. "Hayek's Theory of Cultural Group Selection." *Journal of Libertarian Studies* 8: 171–95.

Steele, Gerald R. 2002. "Hayek's *Sensory Order*." *Theory & Psychology* 12: 387–409.

———. 2005. "Psychology, Social Evolution and Liberalism: A Hayekian Trinity." *Review of Political Economy* 17: 1–16.

———. 2007. *The Economics of Friedrich Hayek*. 2nd ed. New York: Palgrave Macmillan.

———. 2010. "Reflecting upon Knowledge: Hayek's Psychology and Social Science." In *The Social Science of Hayek's 'Sensory Order'*, edited by W. N. Butos, 57–81. Vol. 13 of *Advances in Austrian Economics*. Bingley, UK: Emerald.

Stone, Brad L. 2010. "The Current Evidence for Hayek's Cultural Group Selection Theory." *Libertarian Papers* 2, art. no. 45.

Streit, Manfred E. 1993. "Cognition, Competition, and Catallaxy: In Memory of Friedrich August von Hayek." *Constitutional Political Economy* 4: 223–62.

———. 2006. "Nachwort des Übersetzers und Herausgebers." In *Die sensorische Ordnung*, by F. A. von Hayek, 259–68. Vol. B 5 of *Gesammelte Schriften in deutscher Sprache*. Tübingen: Mohr Siebeck.

Tuerck, David G. 1995. "Economics as Mechanism: The Mind as Machine in Hayek's Sensory Order." *Constitutional Political Economy* 6: 281–92.

Vanberg, Viktor J. 1975. *Die zwei Soziologien. Individualismus und Kollektivismus in der Sozialtheorie*. Tübingen: J. C. B. Mohr (Paul Siebeck).

———. (1986) 1994. "Spontaneous Market Order and Social Rules: A Critical Examination of F. A. Hayek's Theory of Cultural Evolution." In *Rules and Choice in Economics*, 77–94, 252–60. London: Routledge.

———. 1993. "Rational Choice, Rule-Following and Institutions." In *Rationality, Institutions and Economic Methodology*, edited by U. Mäki, Bo Gustafsson, and C. Knudsen, 171–200. London: Routledge.

———. 2002. "Rational Choice vs. Program-Based Behavior." *Rationality and Society* 14: 7–53.

———. 2004a. "Austrian Economics, Evolutionary Psychology, and Methodological Dualism: Subjectivism Reconsidered." In *Evolutionary Psychology and Economic Theory*, edited by Roger Koppl, 155–99. Vol. 7 of *Advances in Austrian Economics*. Bingley, UK: Emerald.

———. 2004b. "The Rationality Postulate in Economics: Its Ambiguity, Its Deficiency and Its Evolutionary Alternative." *Journal of Economic Methodology* 11: 1–29.

———. 2011. "Freiheit und Verantwortung: Neurowissenschaftliche Erkenntnisse und ordnungsökonomische Folgerungen." In *Das Prinzip der Selbstverantwortung. Grundlagen und Bedeutung im heutigen Privatrecht*, edited by K. Riesenhuber, 45–72. Tübingen: Mohr Siebeck.

———. 2012. "Rational Choice, Preferences over Actions and Rule-Following Behavior." In *Handbook of the Philosophy of Science, Vol. 13: Philosophy of Economics*, edited by U. Mäki, 505–30.

———. 2013. "Hayek in Freiburg." In *Hayek: A Collaborative Biography, Part 1, Influences, from Mises to Bartley*, edited by R. Leeson, 93–122. New York: Palgrave Macmillan.

———. 2014. "Darwinian Paradigm, Cultural Evolution and Human Purposes: on F. A. Hayek's Evolutionary View." *Journal of Evolutionary Economics* 24: 35–57.

Vaughn, Karen I. 1999. "Hayek's Theory of the Market Order as an Instance of the Theory of Complex Adaptive Systems." *Journal des Économists et des Études Humaines* 9: 241–56.

Weaver, Warren. 1948. "Science and Complexity." *American Scientist* 36: 536–44.

Weimer, Walter B. 1982. "Hayek's Approach to the Problems of Complex Phenomena: An Introduction to the Theoretical Psychology of *The Sensory Order*." In *Cognition and the Symbolic Processes*, edited by W. B. Weimer and D. S. Palermo, 241–85. Vol. 2. Hillsdale, NJ: Lawrence Erlbaum.

———. 2011. "'Marginal Men': Weimer on Hayek." In *Hayek in Mind: Hayek's Philosophical Psychology*, edited by L. Marsh, xxv–xxviii. Vol. 15 of *Advances in Austrian Economics*.

Weimer, W. B., and D. S. Palermo, eds. 1982. *Cognition and the Symbolic Processes*. Vol. 2. Hillsdale, NJ: Lawrence Erlbaum.

Weimer-Hayek Discussion. 1982. "Weimer-Hayek Discussion." In *Cognition and the Symbolic Processes*, edited by W. B. Weimer and D. S. Palermo, 321–29. Vol. 2. Hillsdale, NJ: Lawrence Erlbaum.

Whitman, Douglas G. 2004. "Group Selection and Methodological Individualism: Compatible and Complementary." *Advances in Austrian Economics* 7: 221–49.

Yeager, Leland B. (1984) 2011. "Hayek on the Psychology of Socialism and Freedom." In *Is the Market a Test of Truth and Beauty? Essays in Political Economy*, 397–406. Auburn, AL: Ludwig von Mises Institute. First published by American Enterprise Institute.

Zywicki, Todd J. 2000. "'Was Hayek Right About Group Selection After All?' Review Essay of *Unto Others: The Evolution and Psychology of Unselfish Behavior*, by Elliot Sober and David Sloan Wilson." *Review of Austrian Economics* 13: 81–95.

THE SENSORY ORDER

AN INQUIRY INTO THE FOUNDATIONS

OF THEORETICAL PSYCHOLOGY

PREFACE

A great deal of explanation would be necessary were I to try and justify why an economist ventures to rush in where psychologists fear to tread. But this excursion into psychology has little connection[1] with whatever competence I may possess in another field. It is the outcome of an idea which suggested itself to me as a very young man, when I was still uncertain whether to become an economist or a psychologist. But though my work has led me away from psychology, the basic idea then conceived has continued to occupy me; its outlines have gradually developed, and it has often proved helpful in dealing with the problems of the methods of the social sciences. In the end it was concern with the logical character of social theory which forced me to re-examine systematically my ideas on theoretical psychology.

The paper in which as a student more than thirty years ago I first tried to sketch these ideas, and which lies before me as I write, I was certainly wise not to attempt to publish at the time even though it contains the whole principle of the theory I am now putting forward. My difficulty then was, as I had been aware even at the time, that though I felt that I had found the answer to an important problem, I could not explain precisely what the problem was. The few years for which I then thought to put the draft away have become a much longer period; and it is little likely that the time will still come when I can devote myself wholly to the working out of these ideas. Yet, rightly or wrongly, I feel that during those years I have learnt at least to state the nature of the problem I had been trying to answer. And as the solution at which I then arrived seems to me to be still new and worth consideration, I have now attempted this fuller exposition of what I had clumsily tried to say in my youthful effort.

The origins of this book, therefore, trace back to an approach to the problem that was current a full generation ago. The psychology which, without much guidance, I read in Vienna in 1919 and 1920, and which led me to

---

[1] [Hayek's spelling "connexion" has been changed throughout to the standard spelling "connection."—Ed.]

my problem, was indeed in all essentials still the psychology of before 1914. Most of the movements which in the interval have determined the direction of psychological research were then either unknown to me or still altogether unheard of: behaviorism (except for the work done in Russia by Pavlov[2] and Bechterew[3]), the Gestalt school,[4] or the physiological work of such

[2] [Ivan Petrovich Pavlov (1849–1936) was a Russian physiologist who became famous for his research on the conditioned reflex for which he was awarded the Nobel Prize in Physiology or Medicine in 1904. Pavlovian or classical conditioning has become a label for a form of associative learning where an originally neutral stimulus, by being paired with an unconditioned stimulus, comes to trigger, as a conditioned stimulus, the same kind of response that is originally triggered only by the unconditioned stimulus. Pavlov discovered this phenomenon by observing that dogs salivated not only when offered food but also in response to a bell ring after, in previous feeding episodes, the offering of food had been paired with a bell sound. Pavlov's work became a founding contribution to behaviorism as a school of thought that seeks to explain behavior exclusively in stimulus and response terms, omitting any references to internal mental states. As a second form of associative learning, different from classical conditioning, behaviorists emphasized operant conditioning as a mechanism by which the probability of a behavior being emitted is increased or decreased depending on whether or not it is followed by a reward.—Ed.]

[3] [Wladimir Michailovic Bechterew (1857–1927) was a Russian neurologist and psychiatrist who developed, independently of and in rivalry with Pavlov, a theory of conditioned reflexes which he called association reflexes. Foreshadowing, like Pavlov, the behaviorist program, he propagated an "objective psychology" that, eschewing introspection, seeks to explain behavior in terms of observable phenomena only.—Ed.]

[4] [The Gestalt school was founded by the German psychologists—all of whom eventually emigrated to the United States—Max Wertheimer (1880–1943), Kurt Koffka (1886–1941), and Wolfgang Köhler (1887–1967) in opposition to what they criticized as "atomistic" theories of perception. Its principal tenet is that organisms perceive external stimuli as wholes or configurations (Gestalt) rather than as the mere sum of their component parts. On the relation between his own "theory and the views of the Gestalt school," Hayek notes below, in 7.15, "that in some respect at least, our theory may be regarded as a consistent development of the approach of the Gestalt school." In reference to the insights gained in the "gradual emancipation" of human cognitive psychology "from the conception of simple elementary sensations . . . culminating in the Gestalt school," Hayek has argued that "they all stress in one way or another that our perception of the external world is made possible by the mind possessing an organizing capacity." See F. A. Hayek, "The Primacy of the Abstract" [1978], reprinted in *The Market and Other Orders*, ed. Bruce Caldwell, vol. 15 (2014) of *The Collected Works of F. A. Hayek* (Chicago: University of Chicago Press), 317. See also Hayek's comment that, in light of his own theory, "there would, however, seem to be no justification for the unwarranted ontological conclusion which many members of the Gestalt school draw from their interesting observations; there is no reason to assume that the 'wholes' which we perceive are properties of the external world and not merely ways in which our mind classifies complexes of stimuli like other abstractions, the relations between the parts than singled out may be significant or not" (F. A. Hayek, *Studies on the Abuse and Decline of Reason*, ed. Bruce Caldwell, vol. 13 (2010) of *The Collected Works of F. A. Hayek*, 111, fn. 4). For a detailed discussion on the relation between Hayek's theoretical outlook and Gestalt psychology, see Nicolò De Vecchi, "The Place of Gestalt Psychology in the Making of Hayek's Thought," *History of Political Economy* 35 (Spring 2003): 135–62.—Ed.]

men as Sherrington[5] or Lashley.[6] And although discussion in Vienna at that time was, of course, full of psychoanalysis, I have to admit that I have never been able to derive much profit from that school. The main authors from which I derived my knowledge were still H. von Helmholtz[7] and W. Wundt,[8]

[5] [Sir Charles Scott Sherrington (1857–1952) was an English neurophysiologist who was awarded the Nobel Prize in Physiology or Medicine in 1932 for his work on the functions of neurons. Sherrington, who had also studied in Germany with Hermann von Helmholtz, coined the now common terms "neuron" and "synapse" to designate the nerve cell and the point at which nervous impulses are transmitted from one cell to another. In his classic work *The Integrative Action of the Nervous System* (1906), he distinguished between *exteroceptive* sense organs that detect stimuli like light or sound, *interoceptive* sense organs such as taste receptors, and *proprioceptive* sense organs that detect stimuli internal to the organism.—Ed.]

[6] [Karl Spencer Lashley (1890–1958) was an American psychologist who was strongly influenced by the behaviorism of John B. Watson (1878–1958), but whose stimulus-response formula Lashley came to criticize for failing to recognize the function of the brain in mediating the causal connection between stimulus and response. Lashley coined the interrelated concepts "equipotentiality" and "mass action." The first concept refers to the fact that regions in the cerebral cortex are equipotential in the sense that, if parts of the cortex are destroyed, other parts can take over the functions of the destructed cells. The concept of mass action refers to the fact that, in learning, the whole cortex—not just a specific part—is involved such that memory traces are duplicated and dispersed in the brain. Lashley's contribution to a theory of neural functions was further developed by his most prominent student, Donald O. Hebb (1904–1985). See below, preface, fn. 12.—Ed.]

[7] [Hermann von Helmholtz (1821–1894) was a German physiologist and physicist. He was a true polymath, known for a variety of significant achievements across a broad range of scientific fields. Of particular relevance in the present context are his contributions to the physiology of hearing and vision, to the theory of perception, and to epistemology. Helmholtz, who was a student of the physiologist Johannes Müller (1801–1858; see below, *TSO* 1.34, fn. 18), rejected his teacher's vitalism, insisting that "no other forces than the common physical-chemical ones are active within the organism." He distinguished between *sensation* as the response of sense organs to stimuli and *perception* as the brain's interpretation of sensations, allowing for differences between physical reality and human perception. According to Helmholtz the senses do not transmit a mirror-image of physical reality to the brain, but the brain constructs from sensory impulses a meaningful interpretation, based on the organism's past experience. Because, Helmholtz asserts, meaningful perception results from a process of "unconscious inference," insights into the nature of the process cannot be gained by introspection but "can only be inferred from the physiological investigation of the sensory organs."—Ed.]

[8] [Wilhelm Wundt (1832–1920) was a German physiologist and psychologist who established in 1879 the first laboratory for psychological research and is widely recognized as the founder of experimental psychology. Wundt, who studied with Johannes Müller and worked from 1858–62 as an assistant with Hermann von Helmholtz, presumed a psycho-physical parallelism, categorically distinguishing between physiological and psychological processes. He considered the study of conscious experience to be the principal task of scientific psychology, requiring introspection as the appropriate research method. The introspection Wundt advocated was a controlled, experimental method of internal perception, involving experienced observers who were to report on their reactions—thoughts, feelings, emotions, etc.—to stimuli to which they were exposed in controlled experimental environments.—Ed.]

W. James[9] and G. E. Müller,[10] and particularly Ernst Mach.[11] I still vividly remember how in reading Mach, in an experience very similar to that which Mach himself describes with reference to Kant's concept of the *Ding an sich*, I suddenly realized how a consistent development of Mach's analysis of perceptual organization made his own concept of sensory elements superfluous and otiose, an idle construction in conflict with most of his acute psychological analysis.

It was with considerable surprise that, thirty years later, in examining the lit-

---

[9] [William James (1842–1910) was an American physician, psychologist, and philosopher who—jointly with Charles Sanders Peirce (1839–1914)—is considered the founder of pragmatism as a distinct philosophical tradition. When in 1867 to 1868 he stayed in Germany for health reasons, James attended lectures in Berlin and reported in a letter his assessment that psychology was emerging as a science concerned with the relation between "physical changes in the nerves" and the "occurrence of consciousness phenomena," referring to "Helmholtz and a man named Wundt in Heidelberg" as working on this issue. After commencing his teaching career at Harvard in 1873, James taught the first course in physiological psychology in 1875 and established the first laboratory of experimental psychology in America. His seminal work *Principles of Psychology* (1890)—including chapters such as "The Functions of the Brain" and "On Some General Conditions of Brain Activity"—emphasizes the study of consciousness phenomena through introspection as the method of "looking into our own minds and reporting what we there discover."—Ed.]

[10] [Georg Elias Müller (1850–1934) was a German psychologist and one of the cofounders of experimental psychology. He established a laboratory at the University of Göttingen in 1887, where as a student he had attended lectures by Hermann von Helmholtz. His major interests were in the relation between stimulus and sensation, memory and learning, and color vision.—Ed.]

[11] [Ernst Mach (1838–1916) was an Austrian polymath who is best known for his contributions to physics (his name is used as the unit measuring the speed of sound) but whose work has been of significant influence in philosophy and in psychology as well. His positivist-empiricist approach to epistemology influenced the Vienna Circle, which actually grew out of a group that called itself Ernst Mach Verein. Mach considered knowledge, including science, as the mind's adaptation to the environment. His view that our perception of the world is always in light of a preexisting cognitive structure that is conditioned by past experience and continuously adapted in response to new experiences inspired the founders of Gestalt psychology. In his short essay "Ernst Mach (1938–1916) and the Social Sciences in Vienna" (1967; reprinted in *The Fortunes of Liberalism: Essays on Austrian Economics and the Ideal of Freedom*, ed. Peter Klein, vol. 4 (1992) of *The Collected Works of F. A. Hayek*, 172–75), Hayek notes: "It so happens that in the three years between 1918 and 1921 I was studying at the university in my native Vienna and that during this time Mach's ideas were the main focus of philosophical discussions. . . . I no longer remember exactly how I happened to come across Mach almost immediately on my return from the battle lines in November 1918. . . . I know that I had been very engrossed in Mach's *Populärwissenschaftliche Vorlesungen, Die Mechanik in ihrer Entwicklung*, and particularly his *Analyse der Empfindungen* . . . . From a personal point of view, I was stimulated by Mach's work to study psychology and the physiology of the senses—I even wrote a study at that time about these questions, which finally, thirty years later, resulted in a book." With this last remark, Hayek is referring to his 1920 manuscript, *Beiträge zur Theorie der Entwicklung des Bewußtseins* (published for the first time in English translation in this volume, pp. 321–47), and, of course, to *The Sensory Order*.—Ed.]

erature of modern psychology I found that the particular problem with which I had been concerned had remained pretty much in the same state in which it had been when it first occupied me. It seems, if this is not too presumptuous for an outsider to suggest, as if this neglect of one of the basic problems of psychology were the result of the prevalence during this period of an all too exclusively empirical approach and of an excessive contempt for 'speculation'. It seems almost as if 'speculation' (which, be it remembered, is merely another word for thinking) had become so discredited among psychologists that it has to be done by outsiders who have no professional reputation to lose. But the fear of following out complex processes of thought, far from having made discussion more precise, appears to have created a situation in which all sorts of obscure concepts, such as 'representative processes', 'perceptual organization', or 'organized field', are used as if they described definite facts, while actually they stand for somewhat vague theories whose exact content requires to be made clear. Nor has the concentration on those facts which were most readily accessible to observation always meant that attention was directed to what is most important. Neither the earlier exclusive emphasis on peripheral responses, nor the more recent concentration on macroscopic or mass processes accessible to anatomical or electrical analysis, have been entirely beneficial to the understanding of the fundamental problems.

Since this book is concerned with some of the most general problems of psychology, I fear that to many contemporary psychologists it will appear to deal more with philosophical than with psychological problems; but I should be sorry if they should regard it for that reason as falling outside their province. It is true that it presents no new facts; but neither does it employ any hypotheses which are not common property of current psychological discussion. Its aim is to work out certain implications of generally accepted facts or assumptions in order to use them as an explanation of the central problem of the nature of mental phenomena. Indeed, if the views generally held on the subject are approximately true, it would seem as if something of the kind here described must happen, and the surprising fact would seem that so little attempt has been made to work out systematically these consequences of existing knowledge. Perhaps such an effort of effectively thinking through these implications requires a combination of qualifications which nobody possesses to a sufficient degree and which the specialist who feels sure in his own field therefore hesitates to undertake. To do it adequately one would indeed have to be equally competent as a psychologist and as a physiologist, as a logician and as a mathematician, and as a physicist and as a philosopher. I need scarcely say that I possess none of these qualifications. But since it is doubtful whether anybody does, and since at least nobody who possesses them as yet has tried his hand at this problem, it is perhaps inevitable that the first attempt should be made by somebody who had to try and acquire the necessary equipment as he went along. A satisfactory execution of the thesis which I have outlined would probably require the collaboration of several specialists in the different fields.

The parts of the problem on which I feel tolerably confident that I have something of importance to say are the statement of the problem, the general principles of its solution, and some of the consequences which follow from the latter for epistemology and the methodology of the sciences. The sections of the book with which I am therefore tolerably satisfied are the beginning and the end: Chapters I and II and chapters VII and VIII. Perhaps it would have been wiser if I had made no attempt to implement the programme outlined in the earlier chapters, since the central part of the book in which this is attempted is unavoidably both more technical and more amateurish than the rest. Yet it seemed important to illustrate the general principles stated in the earlier chapters by some attempt at elaboration, even at the risk of slipping at particular points. In some ways this would not greatly matter: I am much more concerned about what would constitute an explanation of mental phenomena than whether the details of this theory are entirely correct. Since we are still in a position where we are not certain what would constitute an explanation, any theory which, if it were correct, would provide one would be a gain, even if it should not be tenable in all respects.

Even the present version of this book has occupied me for several years, and though I have endeavoured to acquaint myself with the relevant literature, I am not sure that I have been able fully to keep up with current developments. It seems as if the problems discussed here were coming back into favour and some recent contributions have come to my knowledge too late to make full use of them. This applies particularly to Professor D. O. Hebb's *Organization of Behavior* which appeared when the final version of the present book was practically finished.[12] That work contains a theory of sensation which in many

---

[12] [Donald Olding Hebb (1904–85) was a Canadian psychologist whose seminal book, *The Organization of Behavior: A Neuropsychological Theory* (New York: Wiley, 1949), by proposing a "general theory of behavior that attempts to bridge the gap between neurophysiology and psychology" (p. vii), laid the foundation for neuropsychology. Critical of the behaviorist S-R formula, Hebb focused on what goes on *between* stimulus and response, emphasizing the role neural processes in the brain play in psychological processes such as learning and memory. The three central conjectures of Hebb's theory are known as "Hebb synapse" or "Hebb rule," "cell-assembly," and "phase sequence." The first of them postulates that the strength of connections (synapses) between neurons increases when both are activated simultaneously, a phenomenon referred to as "Hebbian learning." The second conjecture postulates that groups of neurons which are repeatedly active form a network, a cell assembly, such that nerve impulses can travel from any cell to any other cell within the assembly. Thirdly, the term "phase sequence" refers to the idea that neural activity in one cell assembly can stimulate neural activity in other assemblies, and that what we experience as a thought process is equivalent to a sequence of such activation from one cell assembly to another.—Ed.]

respects is similar to the one expounded here; and in view of the much greater technical competence of its author I doubted for a while whether publication of the present book was still justified. In the end I decided that the very full-ness with which Professor Hebb has worked out the physiological detail has prevented him from bringing out as clearly as might be wished the general principles of the theory; and as I am concerned more with the general signifi-cance of a theory of that kind than with its detail, the two books, I hope, are complementary rather than covering the same ground.

I owe a debt of deep gratitude to the London School of Economics and the Committee on Social Thought of the University of Chicago for giving me the leisure to devote so much time to problems which lie outside the field where my main duties lie. To my friends Karl R. Popper[13] and L. von Bertalanffy[14]

[13] [Karl Raimund Popper (1902–94) was an Austro-British philosopher who is best known as the name-giver and founder of "critical rationalism" as a distinct philosophical perspective. The son of a wealthy assimilated Jewish family, Popper, like Hayek, grew up in Vienna and was exposed to the intellectual-cultural environment that prevailed there in the post-WWI era. In critical distance to the Vienna Circle, he developed his falsificationist philosophy of science, first published in his 1934 *Logik der Forschung*, which was later translated and published as *The Logic of Scientific Discovery* (1959). The central tenet of his methodology is that in order to qualify as scien-tific, a theory must have implications that are potentially falsifiable in the sense of being incom-patible with facts that are logically possible. In 1935 through 1936, concerned about the growing anti-Semitism and seeking to explore his professional options as an émigré, Popper spent several months in England, where he met Hayek. Accepting an offer to teach at Canterbury University College in Christchurch, he emigrated in 1937 to New Zealand, where he wrote *The Poverty of Historicism* (1957; a book that was first published as a series of articles in 1944–45 in *Economica*, a journal that Hayek edited) as well as his influential treatise *The Open Society and its Enemies* (1945), two contributions to social philosophy that criticize historicism as an ingredient to totalitarian-ism and defend the open society. Upon Hayek's recommendation, Popper received an offer to join the faculty of the London School of Economics where he taught from 1946 to 1969.—Ed.]

[14] [Ludwig von Bertalanffy (1901–72) was an Austrian-born biologist who is generally recog-nized as the founder of the general systems theory, the subject matter of which he defines in his *General System Theory: Foundations, Development, Applications* (New York: George Braziller, 1968) as the formulation and derivation of universal principles which apply to systems in general, "irre-spective of their particular kind, the nature of their component elements and the relation or 'forces' between them" (32). In Vienna, Bertalanffy studied with Moritz Schlick (see above, edi-tor's introduction, pp. 12ff.), under whom he wrote his doctoral dissertation on the psychologist and philosopher Gustav Theodor Fechner, the founder of psychophysics. Bertalanffy was a pro-fessor at the University of Vienna from 1934 to 1948 before he left his native Austria to teach at various universities in England, Canada, and the United States. In 1969 he moved to the last sta-tion of his academic career, the State University of New York at Buffalo. Central to Bertalanffy's theoretical outlook is the claim that in the life sciences we typically deal with "open systems" by contrast to the "closed systems" that are the subject of conventional physics. While in closed sys-tems that are isolated from their environment the initial conditions determine the system's final state, living organisms as open systems are in exchange with their environment and exhibit a self-organizational dynamics, maintaining a so-called "steady state" (*Fließgleichgewicht*), a concept to which Hayek refers below (*TSO*, 4.14).—Ed.]

and to Professor J. C. Eccles[15] I am much indebted for reading and commenting upon earlier drafts of this book. And without the acute criticism of the manuscript by my wife the book would contain even more obscurities and so slovenly expressions than it undoubtedly still does.

F. A. HAYEK

[15] [John Carew Eccles (1903–97) was an Australian neurophysiologist who began his academic career with C. S. Sherrington (see preface, fn. 5). Together with his British colleagues A. L. Hodgkin and A. F. Huxley, he was awarded in 1963 the Nobel Prize in Physiology or Medicine for his research in the nature of synaptic transmission. Jointly with K. R. Popper, Eccles published *The Self and Its Brain—An Argument for Interactionism* (1977), in which the authors address in separate parts the mind-body problem, and especially the mind-brain problem, describing themselves as "dualists or even pluralists, and interactionists." Eccles explicitly endorsed Popper's three-world concept (i.e., the distinction between the world of physical objects, of states of consciousness, and of objective knowledge).—Ed.]

CONTENTS

INTRODUCTION

by Heinrich Klüver

It has been said that a philosopher is a man who has a bad conscience whenever he hears the word philosophy. Nowadays psychologists no longer seem to develop feelings of guilt when encountering the word psychology. This state of affairs can certainly not be accounted for by assuming that the whole field of psychology has suddenly acquired the status of a 'science'. In fact, scientific progress in psychology within the last generation according to some critics has been deplorable. A turn for the better, however, would not necessarily be achieved by eliminating all psychologists. There is no doubt that physiologists, neurologists, psychiatrists, anatomists, sociologists, biologists, and workers in other fields would keep psychology alive in one form or another if psychologists were to disappear from the contemporary scene. Investigators in various non-psychological fields are, in the pursuit of their inquiries, again and again forced to deal with psychological problems and even driven to consider problems of theoretical psychology. For example, about ten years or so ago, Sherrington[1] felt compelled to consider the interrelations of neuro-physiological and psychological phenomena and to devote several hundred pages in his *Man: On His Nature* to an examination of problems of the 'mind'.

Dr. Hayek's book, which represents an analysis of the sensory order in relation to problems of theoretical psychology, raises the question whether the time has not again come for psychologists to develop, at least occasionally, a bad conscience when hearing the word psychology. On the one hand, there seems to have been a decline in the quality and quantity of systematic endeav-

[Heinrich Klüver (1897–1979) was a German-American experimental psychologist and neuroscientist whose *Behavior Mechanisms in Monkeys* (Oxford: University of Chicago Press, 1933) had a major influence in behavioral and neurological research. After his military service in WWI, Klüver studied psychology first at the University of Berlin and then at the University of Hamburg, where he worked with Max Wertheimer, one of the founders of Gestalt psychology. Klüver moved to the United States in 1923 and earned his PhD in psychology at Stanford University in 1924. Following appointments at the University of Minnesota and Columbia University, he joined the University of Chicago in 1933, where he taught until his retirement in 1963. In Chicago he became a member of the "Neurology Club," a group of neuroscientists that included Karl Spencer Lashley (see above, preface, fn. 6), his lifelong colleague.—Ed.]

[1] [See above, preface, fn. 5.—Ed.]

ours in the field of theoretical psychology during the last decades; on the other hand, the multifarious activities of psychologists seem to make it more than ever necessary to find a common point of reference. As long as it is assumed, or as long as the illusion is to be kept alive, that the diverse activities of psychologists involve a common factor referred to by the word psychology, the general conceptual framework of such a psychology must remain of fundamental interest. There is, of course, no lack of theorizing in modern psychology. It is one thing, however, to develop a theory based on the detailed experimental analysis of a particular problem; it is another thing to examine the conceptual tools of theoretical psychology itself. Even particular theories do not always escape the complexity of matters psychological. When G. E. Müller[2] summarized his fifty years of efforts in the field of color vision, it took him about 650 pages to present his theory of color vision and he insisted that any simpler theory could be formulated only at the price of ignoring relevant facts. When it comes to systematic efforts, in the field of theoretical psychology, it has become increasingly obvious in recent years that psychologists find their particular tasks (ranging from an analysis of ocular to an analysis of political movements and from investigations of the sexual behavior of male army ants to that of human females) so all-absorbing, time-consuming and exacting that they rarely seem to do anything but increase the number of hastily conceived and irresponsible theories. In fact, nowadays, only a man like Dr. Hayek who is sufficiently removed from the noisy market places of present-day psychology appears to have the necessary detachment and peace of mind for a systematic inquiry into the foundations of theoretical psychology.

It is fortunate indeed that Dr. Hayek has chosen the sensory order as a basis for discussing problems of theoretical psychology. More than a century ago, in 1824, Flourens[3] insisted that *une anatomie sans physiologie serait une anatomie sans but*. There is no doubt that an 'anatomy without physiology' as well as a 'physiology without anatomy' are still with us. Even at the present time, it is not difficult to find books on the 'physiology' of the nervous system which are in effect nothing but books on 'anatomy' containing elaborate physiological footnotes. The relations between physiology and anatomy acquire particular significance and complexity when it comes to the field of sensory physiology. If not the last, at least the last monumental attempt to cope with problems of the sensory order is to be found in J. von Kries's[4] *General Sensory Physi-*

---

[2] [See above, preface, fn. 10.—Ed.]

[3] [Marie Jean Pierre Flourens (1794–1867) was a French physiologist who pioneered experimental brain research and demonstrated that different parts of the brain are responsible for different functions.—Ed.]

[4] [Johannes Adolf von Kries (1853–1928) was a German physiological psychologist who is best known for his theory of color-vision which integrated vision theories by Hermann von Helmholtz, with whom he had worked in Berlin, and by Ewald Hering (see below, 1.34, fn. 18).—Ed.]

ology[5] published in 1923. It was von Kries who explicitly stated what has been recognized by practically all investigators in this field, namely, that sensory physiology is different from all other fields of physiology and, in fact, from all other natural sciences in that its problems are intimately related to, if not identical with, certain problems of psychology, epistemology, and logic. In fact, sensory physiology and sensory psychology are to a great extent indistinguishable. The psychologist will remember that the duplicity theory of vision formulated by von Kries has stood the test of time longer than is generally the case with scientific theories and that Selig Hecht,[6] only a few years ago, when performing energy measurements to determine the minimum energy necessary for vision, found values of the same order of magnitude as were found by von Kries more than forty years ago although von Kries did not even make energy measurements. Since Hecht considered it 'astonishing to see the admirable way' in which von Kries accomplished this task, he felt called upon to pay tribute to von Kries's skill and care in the evaluation of absorptions, reflections, lens factors, and the like, which are necessary in determining the minimum energy. It cannot be said, therefore, that the man who insisted that problems of sensory physiology cannot be adequately treated without recourse to psychology, epistemology, and logic did not have the necessary 'hard-boiled' attitude in scientific matters; the converse is obviously true. Just why the sustained and disciplined thinking of a 'hard-boiled' professor of physiology in matters of sensory physiology should be dismissed as 'mere' philosophy by psychologists is a problem which clearly requires an analysis by a competent historian unless one assumes that the inability of most psychologists to handle logical and epistemological tools explains such a phenomenon. Such phenomena, unfortunately, have not been rare in the history of psychology. Ziehen, the neuro-anatomist, psychiatrist, psychologist, and logician, who wrote a textbook of physiological psychology that went through numerous editions, also wrote an 'epistemology on psychophysiological and physical basis' in 1913.[7] It is true that this book has a forbidding title and about 600 pages; but it is probably also true that no psychologist alive ever read all of its pages in the period between World War I and World War II. There is no doubt that a critical examination of the concepts of general sensory physiology in relation to psy-

[5] [The reference here is to the German edition, *Allgemeine Sinnesphysiologie* (Leipzig: F. C. W. Vogel, 1923). An English edition does not exist.—Ed.]

[6] [Selig Hecht (1892–1947) was an American biophysicist who, born in Austria, came to the United States in 1898 and earned his PhD at Harvard University in 1917. From 1926 he was professor of biophysics at Columbia University, where he headed the newly founded laboratory of biophysics.—Ed.]

[7] [Theodor Ziehen (1862–1950). The references are to his textbook, *Introduction to Physiological Psychology* (London: Swan Sonnenschein, 1892), and to *Erkenntnistheorie auf psychophysiologischer und physikalischer Grundlage* (Jena: Fischer, 1913).—Ed.]

chology and other fields is a prerequisite for further progress in many physiological and psychological areas of investigation. Dr. Hayek, who appears to be
far too modest in evaluating his own competence in handling and elucidating
sensory physiological and psychological concepts, is, therefore, performing a
task urgently needed for further scientific progress.

Problems of the sensory order and the relations between physical and sensory phenomena have been of perennial interest not only to psychologists and
physiologists, but also to mathematicians, logicians, and physicists. Recently
they have even become of interest to communication engineers. As P. du Bois-
Reymond once pointed out, all of us are enclosed 'in the box of our perceptions'.[8] There have always been some who think that it is possible to escape
from this box, and there have always been others who think that this is not
possible. Ziehen, for instance, was of the opinion that we find everywhere
identities, similarities, and differences in examining the 'given', i.e., the raw
data furnished by experience or, to use his expression, the 'gignomene'. A fundamental classificatory principle is thus part and parcel of the 'gignomene'
themselves and constitutes an ultimate 'unexplainable and indefinable fact'. It
is of interest that von Kries, too, believed that the existence of similarities is
an ultimate fact neither requiring nor permitting of an explanation. The view,
however, that the real content of experience resisting any further analysis is to
be found in sensory phenomena has always clashed with the view that the persistence of fixed functional relations between these phenomena constitutes the
content of true reality.

In a brief space, it is impossible to outline even the essentials of Dr. Hayek's
theory, but from a broad point of view his theory may be said to substantiate Goethe's famous maxim 'all that is factual is already theory'[9] for the field
of sensory and other psychological phenomena. According to Dr. Hayek, sensory perception must be regarded as an act of classification. What we perceive are never unique properties of individual objects, but always only properties which the objects have in common with other objects. Perception is thus
always an interpretation, the placing of something into one or several classes
of objects. The characteristic attributes of sensory qualities, or the classes

---

[8] [David Paul Gustave du Bois-Reymond (1831–89) was a German mathematician. The quotation "We are enclosed in the box of our perceptions and for what is beyond them born blind"
is from his work *Über die Grundlagen der Erkenntnis in den exacten Wissenschaften* (Tübingen: H. Laupp,
1890), chapter 8. His brother, Emil du Bois-Reymond (1818–96), was a student of Johannes
Müller (see below, 1.32, fn. 17), whom he succeeded as professor of physiology at the University of Berlin.—Ed.]

[9] [The German original reads: "Das Höchste wäre, zu begreifen, dass alles Faktische schon
Theorie ist." See Johann Wolfgang von Goethe, *Sprüche in Prosa* (Frankfurt: Insel Verlag, 2005),
57, no. 1.308.—Ed.]

into which different events are placed in the process of perception, are not attributes which are possessed by these events and which are in some manner 'communicated' to the mind; they consist entirely in the 'differentiating' responses of the organism by which the qualitative classification or order of these events is created; and it is contended that this classification is based on the connections created in the nervous system by past 'linkages'. The qualities which we attribute to the experienced objects are, strictly speaking, not properties of objects at all, but a set of relations by which our nervous system classifies them. To put it differently, all we know about the world is of the nature of theories and all 'experience' can do is to change these theories. All sensory perception is necessarily 'abstract' in that it always selects certain aspects or features of a given situation. Every sensation, even the 'purest', must therefore be regarded as an interpretation of an event in the light of the past experience of the individual or the species. Experience operates on physiological events and arranges them into a structure or order which becomes the basis of their 'mental' significance. In the course of ontogenetic or phylogenetic development, a system of connections is formed which records the relative frequency with which different groups of internal and external stimuli have acted together on the organism. Each individual impulse or group of impulses on its occurrence evokes other impulses which correspond to stimuli which in the past have usually accompanied its occurrence. The primary impulse through its acquired connections will set up a bundle of secondary impulses, a 'following' of the primary impulse. It is the total or partial identity of this 'following' which determines different forms of classification. The essential characteristic of the order of sensory qualities is that, within that order, each stimulus or group of stimuli does not possess a unique significance represented by particular responses, but that the stimuli are given different significance if they occur in combination with, or are evaluated in the light of, an infinite number of other stimuli which may originate from the external world or from the organism itself. A wide range of mental phenomena, such as discrimination, equivalence of stimuli, generalization, transfer, abstraction, and conceptual thought, may all be interpreted as different forms of the same process of classification which is operative in creating the sensory order. The fact that this classification is determined by the position (in a topological, not a spatial, sense) of the individual impulse or group of impulses in a complex structure of connections, extending through a hierarchy of levels, has important consequences when it comes to considering the effects of physiological or anatomical changes.

These formulations of the author must suffice to characterize at least some aspects of the theory presented in his book. Investigators concerned with an analysis of the logical structure of natural sciences have insisted that the transition from concepts of 'substance' to concepts of 'function' is characteristic of the historical development of science. 'Thing-concepts' have gradually and often painfully yielded to 'relational concepts'. Even Freud, some critics have insisted, is still a 'substance' thinker. In this connection Dr. Hayek's theory appears very modern indeed since not even traces of 'thing-concepts' are left in his theory. 'Mind' for him has turned into a complex of relations; it is simply 'a particular order of a set of events taking place in some organism and in some manner related to, but not identical with, the physical order of events in the environment'. In addition, his theory, perhaps more than any other, emphasizes the far-reaching importance of 'experience' and 'learning'. Certain theories have always stressed the factor of 'experience' while others have stressed the importance of the conditions, structures, or pre-suppositions which make experience possible. The *relations* between these two sets of factors, however, present peculiar difficulties. In elucidating the complexity of these relations, Dr. Hayek probably makes his most important and original contributions. It has been said that there are no permanent or fixed 'objects', but only ways of knowing 'objectively'. The implication of the theory presented here is that even the ways of knowing 'objectively' are not stable, or only relatively stable, and that the ordering principles themselves are subject to change. Dr. Hayek, therefore, does not take a static view of either the 'elements' or the 'relational' structure involved in the sensory or any other kind of order. Conceptual thinking, as he rightly emphasizes, has long been recognized as a process of continuous reorganization of the (supposedly constant) elements of the phenomenal world. In his opinion, however, there is no justification for the sharp distinction between the more abstract processes of thought and direct sensory perception since the qualitative elements, of which the phenomenal world is built up, and the whole order of the sensory qualities are themselves subject to continuous change. The fact that there can be nothing in our mind which is not the result of ontogenetically or phylogenetically established 'linkages' is not meant to exclude processes of reclassification. At the same time it is to be clearly understood that at least a certain part of what we know at any moment about the external world is not learned by sensory experience, but is rather implicit in the means through which we can obtain such experience; that is, it is determined by the order of the previously established apparatus of classification. To express it differently, there is, on every level, a part of our knowledge which, although it is the result of experience, cannot be controlled by experience because it constitutes the ordering principle. In considering the implications of Dr. Hayek's theory, the impression is gained that not only the characteristics and properties of the organism involved in 'classifying' activities but also the characteristics of the 'environment' appear in a new light. Man occupies only a small corner of the terrestrial biosphere, including the recently developed, chemically highly active, and man-made anthroposphere of A. P. Pavlov.[10] If pre-sensory and sensory 'linkages' are formed not only during the life of the individual, but also in the course of phylogenetic development, the characteristics of the environment, in which the building-up of the apparatus of classification or orientation occurs, assume special importance. If the apparatus of classification is shaped by the conditions in the environment in which we live and if it represents a kind of map or reproduction of relations between elements of this environment, the question arises as to the extent to which environmental factors 'color' or 'condition' principles of ordering. Perhaps Vernadsky's[11] biogeochemistry has, in the light of Dr. Hayek's theory, unexpected psychological implications. In the meantime, the striking results on 'conditioned sensations' recently obtained by Ivo Kohler[12] have demonstrated how strongly environmental factors and conditions may influence sensory phenomena during the life of an individual.

It is not possible to comment in detail on the skill and knowledge with which Dr. Hayek has utilized psychological, physiological, and other data to support his thesis and to enumerate the many problems and theories upon which his penetrating analysis has significant bearing. His concepts of the 'map', the 'model', and related concepts appear to be promising tools in analyzing brain mechanisms and behavior. What is perhaps most pertinent is that his theory suggests definite lines of experimentation. For instance, it should be possible not only to change sensory qualities experimentally, but to create altogether new sensory qualities which have never been experienced before. The psychologist is likely to find this theory helpful in devising new experiments even beyond the scope indicated by the author himself. In considering the consequences and implications of his own theory and in trying to define its content

[10] [Aleksei Petrovich Pavlov (1854–1929), not to be confused with I. P. Pavlov (see above, preface, fn. 2), was a Russian geologist and paleontologist.—Ed.]

[11] [Vladimir Vernadsky (1863–1945) was a Russian-Ukrainian mineralogist and geochemist.—Ed.]

[12] [Ivo Kohler (1915–85) was an Austrian experimental psychologist who had worked as a student and assistant with Theodor Erismann (see below, 7.24, fn. 31) and later occupied his teacher's chair at the University of Innsbruck. Erismann and Kohler studied how subjects wearing glasses with various types of vision-distorting lenses managed to adapt their perception. They were able to show that, over an adaptation period, the subjects learn to correct the distorted visual stimuli and restore the undistorted pattern. In his 1969 essay, "The Primacy of the Abstract," Hayek refers to Ivo Kohler's article "Experiments with Goggles" (in *Scientific American*, May 1962) and notes that Kohler speaks there "of the 'general rules' by which the visual system learns to correct exceedingly complex and variable distortions produced by prismatic spectacles." See F. A. Hayek, "The Primacy of the Abstract," in *The Market and Other Orders*, ed. Bruce Caldwell, vol. 15 (2014) of *The Collected Works of F. A. Hayek* (Chicago: University of Chicago Press), 317, fn. 9. See also Hayek's note on Kohler appended to the bibliography of *TSO*.—Ed.]

as unambiguously as possible, the author does not hesitate to point out that an experimental confirmation of theories, such as Richard Semon's[13] 'engram' theory or Paul A. Weiss's[14] 'resonance' theory, would disprove his own theory.

A great historian once expressed the view that 'no man, and no product of all a man's labour either, is like a perfectly thought-out book, and merely to point out lacunae in some pages and deficiencies in others must seem much more an envious job of rival contemporaries than a historian's true duty . . .'.[15] When viewing the complex structure of a psychological theory, envious 'rival contemporaries' undoubtedly will always try, no matter how difficult the job may be, to establish that certain *petits faits significatifs* or even merely 'little facts' have not been built into the edifice. About twenty years ago, Lashley, in commenting on an experimental investigation concerned with analysing the interdependence of relations and relata and establishing forms of invariance in behavior, spoke of 'the tracing of relations through the intricate web of dependent processes which is "mind"'. Dr. Hayek has done more than his share in tracing relations through the intricate web of 'mind'. His is one of the most interesting and significant books on theoretical psychology that has appeared in this country during the last decades.

[13] [Richard Wolfgang Semon (1859–1918) was a German biologist who developed a theory of memory storage and retrieval. He coined the term "mneme" (derived from the Greek muse of memory, Mneme) for a unit of memory and conjectured that memories are stored as "mnemic traces" or "engrams" in the brain and are retrieved when reminiscent stimuli are encountered.—Ed.]

[14] [Paul Alfred Weiss (1898–1989) was an Austrian neurobiologist who graduated from the University of Vienna in 1922 and moved to the United States in 1930 where he taught at Yale University, the University of Chicago, and Rockefeller University.—Ed.]

[15] [The quotation is from Ernst Cassirer, *The Problem of Knowledge: Philosophy, Science, and History since Hegel* (New Haven: Yale University Press, 1950), 283.—Ed.]

CHAPTER I

THE NATURE OF THE PROBLEM

1. What Is Mind?

1.1. The nature of the subject of this study makes its first task the most important and the most difficult: clearly to state the problem to which it will attempt an answer. We shall have moved a considerable distance towards the solution of our problem when we have made its meaning precise and have shown what kind of statement could be regarded as a solution.

1.2. The traditional heading under which our problem has been discussed in the past is that of the 'relation' between mind and body, or between mental and physical events. It can also be described by the questions of 'What is mind?' or 'What is the place of mind in the realm of nature?' But while these expressions indicate a general field of inquiry, they do not really make it clear what it is that we want to know. Before we can successfully ask how two kinds of events are related to each other (or connected with each other), we must have a clear conception of the distinct attributes by which they can be distinguished. The difficulty of any fruitful discussion of the mind-body problem consists largely in deciding what part of our knowledge can properly be described as knowledge of mental events as distinguished from our knowledge of physical events.

1.3. We shall attempt to avoid at first at least some of the difficulties of this general problem by concentrating on a more definite and specific question. We shall inquire how the physiological impulses proceeding in the different parts of the central nervous system can become in such a manner differentiated from each other in their functional significance that their effects will differ from each other in the same way in which we know the effects of the different sensory qualities to differ from each other. We shall have established a 'correspondence' between particular physiological events and particular mental events if we succeed in showing that there can exist a system of relations between these physiological events and other physiological events which is identical with the system of relations existing between the corresponding mental events and other mental events.

1.4. We select here for examination the problem of the determination of the order of sensory qualities because it seems to raise in the clearest form the peculiar problem posed by all kinds of mental events. It will be contended that an answer to the question of what determines the order of sensory qualities constitutes an answer to all questions which can be meaningfully asked about the 'nature' or 'origin' of these qualities; and further, that the same general principle which can be used to account for the differentiation of the different sensory qualities serves also as an explanation of the peculiar attributes of such other mental events as images, emotions, and abstract concepts.

1.5. For the purposes of this discussion we shall employ the term sensory 'qualities' to refer to all the different attributes or dimensions with regard to which we differentiate in our responses to different stimuli. We shall thus use this term in a wide sense in which it includes not only quality in the sense in which it is contrasted with intensity, extensity, clearness, etc., but in a sense in which it includes all these other attributes of a sensation.[1] We shall speak of sensory qualities and the sensory order to distinguish these from the affective qualities and the other mental 'values' which make up the more comprehensive order of 'mental qualities'.

2. The Phenomenal World and the Physical World

1.6. A precise statement of the problem raised by the existence of sensory qualities must start from the fact that the progress of the physical sciences has all but eliminated these qualities from our scientific picture of the external world.[2] In order to be able to give a satisfactory account of the regularities

---

[1] See E. G. Boring, 1933, pp. 22–23, and 1942, p. 42. [Edwin Garrigues Boring (1886–1968) was an American experimental psychologist who served as laboratory director at Harvard University from 1924 to 1949 where he also taught as full professor from 1928 to 1956. He was known in particular for his treatise *A History of Experimental Psychology* (1929). He took early notice of *The Sensory Order*, publishing a review in *Scientific Monthly*, vol. 76, 1953, pp. 182–83.—Ed.]

[2] Cf., e.g., M. Planck, 1925, p. 5: 'The sense perceptions have been definitely eliminated from physical acoustics, optics and heat. The physical definitions of sound, color, and temperature are today in no way associated with the immediate perception of the respective senses, but sound and color are defined respectively by the frequency and wavelength of oscillations, and temperature is measured theoretically on the absolute temperature scale corresponding to the second law of thermodynamics.' See also M. Planck, 1949, p. 108. [Max Karl Ernst Planck (1858–1947), a German theoretical physicist and Nobel Laureate in Physics (1918), is known in particular for originating quantum theory. Planck, offspring of a prominent academic family, had studied under Herrmann von Helmholtz in Berlin and held professorships at the universities of Munich (1880–85), Kiel (1885–89), and Berlin (1889–1928). In 1930 he was appointed president of the Kaiser Wilhelm Society for the Advancement of Science, which after World War II was renamed after him as the Max Planck Society.—Ed.] On the fact that this applies not only to the 'secondary' qualities see H. Margenau, 1950, pp. 7 and 49. [Henry Margenau (1901–97) was a German-born physicist who earned his PhD and later taught at Yale University. His pub-

existing in the physical world the physical sciences have been forced to define the objects of which this world exists increasingly in terms of the observed relations between these objects, and at the same time more and more to disregard the way in which these objects appear to us.

1.7. There exist now, in fact, at least two[3] different orders in which we arrange or classify the objects of the world around us: one is the order of our sense experiences in which events are classified according to their sensory properties such as colors, sounds, odours, feeling of touch, etc.; the other is an order which includes both these same and other events but which treats them as similar or different according as, in conjunction with other events, they produce similar or different other external events.

1.8. Although the older branches of physics, particularly optics and acoustics, started from the study of sensory qualities, they are now no longer directly concerned with the perceptible properties of the events with which they are dealing. Nothing is more characteristic of this than the fact that we find it now necessary to speak of 'visible light' and 'audible sound' when we want to refer to the objects of sense perception. To the physicist 'light' and 'sound' now are defined in terms of wave motions, and in addition to those physical events, which, as is true of certain ranges of 'light' and 'sound' waves, cause definite sense experiences, he deals with imperceptible events like electricity, magnetism, etc., which do not directly produce specific sensory qualities.[4]

1.9. Between the elements of these two orders there exists no simple one-to-one correspondence in the sense that several objects or events which in the one order belong to the same kind or class will also belong to the same kind or class in the other order. They constitute different orders precisely because events which to our senses may appear to be of the same kind may have to be treated as different in the physical order, while events which physically may be of the same or at least a similar kind may appear as altogether different to our senses.

1.10. These two orders have been variously described by different authors as the subjective, sensory, sensible, perceptual, familiar, behavioral, or phenomenal[5] world on the one hand, and as the objective, scientific, 'geographical', physical, or sometimes 'constructional' on the other. In what follows

---

lications include works on the philosophical foundations of physics, such as *The Nature of Physical Reality*, to which Hayek here refers.—Ed.]

[3] Since, as we shall see, the movement from the sensory to the physical order is a gradual one, there is, strictly speaking, an infinite range of such orders of which the naive picture of the sensory world and the latest scientific knowledge are merely the most significant types.

[4] Cf., J. von Kries, 1923, p. 67; and E. G. Boring, 1942, p. 97. As late as 1935 the latter author could still write that 'it is the traditional view of psychology that the attributes of sensation show a one-to-one correspondence to the dimensions of the stimulus' (Boring, 1935, p. 236).

[5] In German often by the not fully translatable word '*anschaulich*'.

we shall regularly employ the pair of terms 'phenomenal' and 'physical'[6] to describe the order of events perceived in terms of sensory qualities and the order of events defined exclusively in terms of their relations respectively, although we shall occasionally employ the term 'sensory' as equivalent to phenomenal, especially (as in the title of this book) in the phrase 'sensory order'. We shall later (chapters V and VIII) also describe these two orders as the 'macrocosm' and the 'microcosm' respectively. Their relation is the central problem of this book.

1.11. It is important not to identify the distinction between the phenomenal and the physical order with the distinction between either of these and what in ordinary language is described as the 'real' world. The contrast with which we are concerned is not between 'appearance' and 'reality' but between the differences of events in their effects upon each other and the differences in their effects on us. It is indeed doubtful whether on the plane on which we must examine these problems the term 'real' still has any clear meaning.[7] For the purposes of our discussion, at any rate, we shall not be interested in what a thing 'is' or 'really is' (whatever that may mean), but solely in how a particular object or event differs from other objects or events belonging to the same order or universe of discourse. It seems that a question like 'what is x?' has meaning only within a given order, and that within this limit it must always refer to the relation of one particular event to other events belonging to the same order. We shall see that the mental and the physical world are in this sense two different orders in which the same elements can be arranged; though ultimately we shall recognize the mental order as part of the physical order, a part, however, whose *precise* position in that larger order we shall never be able to determine.

1.12. Historically the concept of the 'real' has been formed in contradistinction to mere 'illusions' based on sense deceptions or on other experiences of purely mental origin. There is, however, no fundamental difference between such corrections of one sense experience by others, as we employ, e.g., to discover an optical illusion, and the procedure employed by the physical sciences when they ascertain that two objects which may to all our senses appear to be

[6] To prevent confusion it should perhaps be pointed out that the 'physical language' of the logical positivists refers to the phenomenal and not to the physical order.

[7] These doubts have not been dispelled by the careful distinction of various kinds and degrees of 'reality' (*Wirklichkeit*) by W. Metzger, 1941, chapter 2. [Wolfgang Metzger (1899–1979) studied with the founders of the Berlin Gestalt school (see above, preface, fn. 4) and is considered one of the main representatives of Gestalt psychology in Germany. In the early 1930s he worked as assistant, and did his habilitation, with Max Wertheimer at the University of Frankfurt. In 1939 he took the chair in psychology that Wertheimer had vacated in 1933 when the National Socialist regime forced him into exile. From 1942 until his retirement, Metzger taught at the University of Münster.—Ed.]

alike do not behave in the same way in relation to others. To accept this latter test as the criterion of 'reality' would force us to regard the various constructs of physics as more 'real' than the things we can touch and see, or even to reserve the term 'reality' to something which by definition we can never fully know. Such a use of the term 'real' would clearly pervert its original meaning and the conclusion to be drawn from this is probably that it should be altogether avoided in scientific discussion.[8]

1.13. The relation between the physical and the phenomenal order raises two distinct but related problems. The first of these problems presents the task of the physical sciences while the second creates the central problem of theoretical psychology. The task of the physical sciences is to replace that classification of events which our senses perform but which proves inadequate to describe the regularities in these events, by a classification which will put us in a better position to do so. The task of theoretical psychology is the converse one of explaining why these events, which on the basis of their relations to each other can be arranged in a certain (physical) order, manifest a different order in their effect on our senses.

1.14. The problems of the physical sciences arise thus from the fact that objects which appear alike to us do not always prove to behave in the same way towards other objects; or that objects which phenomenally resemble each other need not be physically similar to each other, and that sometimes objects which appear to us to be altogether different may prove to be physically very similar.

1.15. It is this fact which has made it necessary, in order to build up a science capable of predicting events, to replace the classification of objects or events which our senses effect by a new classification which corresponds more perfectly to the manner in which those objects or events resemble or differ from each other in the effects which they have upon each other. But this progressive substitution of a purely relational for a qualitative or sensory order of events provides the answer to only one part of the problem which is raised by the existence of the two orders. Even if we had fully answered this problem we should still not know why the different physical objects appear to us as they do.

1.16. It is because the physical sciences have shown that the objects of the external world do not regularly differ in their effects upon each other in the same way in which they differ in their effects upon our senses that the question why they appear to us as they do becomes a legitimate problem and indeed the central problem of theoretical psychology. In so far as the similarities or differences of the phenomena as perceived by us do not correspond with the similarities or differences which the perceived events manifest in their rela-

---

[8] On the gradual evolution of the scientific world picture from the efforts of the child, and on the use of the term 'real', see M. Planck, 1949, especially pp. 90, and 95–105.

tions to each other, we are not entitled to assume that the world appears to us as it does because it is like that; the question why it appears to us as it does becomes a genuine problem.[9]

1.17. It is, perhaps, still true that psychologists in general have not yet become fully aware of the fact that, as a result of the development of the physical sciences, the explanation of the qualitative order of the phenomenal world has become the exclusive task of psychology. What psychology has to explain is not something known solely through that special technique known as 'introspection', but something which we experience whenever we learn anything about the external world and through which indeed we know about the external world; and which yet has no place in our scientific picture of the external world and is in no way explained by the sciences dealing with the external world: qualities. Whenever we study qualitative differences between experiences we are studying mental and not physical events, and much that we believe to know about the external world is, in fact, knowledge about ourselves.[10]

1.18. It is thus the existence of an order of sensory qualities and not a reproduction of qualities existing outside the perceiving mind which is the basic problem, raised by all mental events. Psychology must concern itself, in other words, with those aspects of what we naively regard as the external world which find no place in the account of that world which the physical sciences give us.

1.19. This reformulation of the central problem of psychology has thus been made necessary by the fact that the physical sciences, even in their ideal perfect development, give us only a partial explanation of the world as we know it through our senses and must always leave an unexplained residue. After we have learnt to distinguish events in the external world according to the different effects they have upon each other, and irrespective of whether they appear to us as alike or different, the question of what makes them appear alike or different to us still remains to be solved. The empirical establishment of correspondences between certain phenomenal and certain physical constellations of events is no sufficient answer to this question. We want to know the kind of process by which a given physical situation is transformed into a certain phenomenal picture.

[9] Cf., K. Koffka, 1935, pp. 75ff. [Kurt Koffka (1886–1941) is known as one of the founders of the Gestalt school of psychology (see above, preface, fn. 4). He taught at the University of Gießen from 1911 to 1924. His article "Perception: An Introduction to Gestalt Theory," published in 1922 in the *Psychological Bulletin*, as well as his *Growth of the Mind: An Introduction to Child Psychology*—the 1924 English edition of *Die Grundlagen der psychischen Entwicklung: Eine Einführung in die Kinderpsychologie* (1921)—helped to make Gestalt theory known in the United States. From 1924 to 1925 Koffka taught as visiting professor at Cornell University and later at the University of Wisconsin–Madison before he took a permanent position at Smith College in Northampton, Massachusetts, in 1927, where he stayed until the end of his life.—Ed.]

[10] Cf., F. A. Hayek, 1942, p. 279.

1.20. Since the peculiar order of events which we have called the phenomenal order manifests itself only in the responses of certain kinds of organisms to these events, and not in the relation of those events to each other, it is natural to search for an explanation of this order in some feature of the structure of these organisms. We shall eventually find it in the fact that these organisms are able within themselves to reproduce (or 'build models of') some of the relations which exist between the events in their environment.

1.21. The fact that the problem of psychology is the converse of the problem of the physical sciences means that, while for the latter the facts of the phenomenal world are the data and the order of the physical world the *quaesitum*, psychology must take the physical world as represented by modern physics as given and try to reconstruct the process by which the organism classifies the physical events in the manner which is familiar to us as the order of sensory qualities. In other words: psychology must start from stimuli defined in physical terms and proceed to show why and how the senses classify similar physical stimuli sometimes as alike and sometimes as different, and why different physical stimuli will sometimes appear as similar and sometimes as different.[11]

3. Stimulus, Impulse, and the Theory of the Specific Energy of Nerves

1.22. Before we proceed farther it is necessary to define more precisely some of the terms we shall have constantly to employ. This applies especially to the terms 'stimulus' and 'nervous impulse' and more particularly to the sense in which we shall speak of particular 'kinds' of stimuli or of the same and of different nervous impulses. It will be convenient also to consider already at this stage the meaning and significance of the famous principle of the 'specific energy of nerves'.[12]

1.23. The term *stimulus* will be used throughout this discussion to describe an event external to the nervous system which causes (through or without the mediation of special receptor organs) processes in some nerve fibers[13] which by these fibers are conducted from the point at which the stimulus acts to some other point of the nervous system. It appears that at least some receptor organs are sensitive not to the continuous action of any one given stimulus but

---

[11] Cf., E. G. Boring, 1942, p. 120: 'Nowadays we consider first the dimensions of the stimulus, and then seek to discover what phenomenal consequences they yield. We used to inquire about the physical causes of hue: now we ask about the effects of monochromatic light.'

[12] [The law of specific nerve energies states that differences in sensory experiences (e.g., between hearing, seeing, and touch) are not due to differences in the eliciting stimuli themselves but depend on which nerves are excited and on the part of the brain to which they transmit the impulses. The law was first proposed by Johannes Peter Müller. See below, 1.32, fn. 17.—Ed.]

[13] [Hayek's spelling "fibre" has been changed throughout to the standard spelling "fiber."—Ed.]

only to changes in that stimulus. Whatever it is that is produced in the nerve fiber and propagated through it we shall call the *impulse*.

1.24. The physical event acting as a stimulus is described as such only with regard to its action on the receptors.[14] This leads sometimes to a rather confusing distinction between the stimulus and its 'source', sometimes described as the stimulus object. What will here be described as stimulus will always be the proximal stimulus,[15] i.e., the last known physical event in the chain which leads to the production of the impulse. In some instances (particularly in the case of odours) this proximal physical stimulus, however, is not certainly known, and we must be satisfied with reference to some more remote event which has then to be regarded as the source of an unknown proximal stimulus.

1.25. It is necessary from the outset carefully to avoid the assumption that to each kind of sensation there will always correspond *one* stimulus of a particular kind. Not only can several different stimuli produce the same sensation, but it appears that in many instances, and perhaps as a rule, several different stimuli, acting on different receptors, may be required to produce a particular sensation.[16]

1.26. Since our central problem is the manner in which different stimuli affect our nervous system, or how they are classified by it, we clearly cannot make our starting point that classification of the stimuli which our senses perform. The distinction between different stimuli, or between different kinds of stimuli, must be independent of the different effects they have on the organism. This independence can never be complete, since all our knowledge of the external events is derived from our sensory experience. But it can be independent in the sense that we can classify the stimuli not according to their direct effects on our senses, but according to the effects which they exercise on other external events, which in turn act as stimuli on our senses. This classification of the events which act as stimuli, according to their effects on other events which in turn are classified according to their effects on still others, is, of course, the classification of the stimuli developed by the physical sciences; and it is this which we must adopt.

[14] R. S. Woodworth, 1938, p. 451. [Robert S. Woodworth (1869–1962) studied at Harvard University with William James and taught as professor of psychology at Columbia University from 1903 to 1942. His textbook *Psychology: A Study of Mental Life* (1921) and his handbook *Experimental Psychology* (1938) became standard references in teaching and research. His ambition was to reconcile different perspectives in psychology as reflected in particular in his book *Contemporary Schools in Psychology* (1932).—Ed.]

[15] K. Koffka, 1935, p. 80.

[16] C. T. Morgan, 1943, pp. 297–98. [Clifford T. Morgan (1915–76) graduated from the University of Rochester in 1939, where he was introduced to physiological psychology. He then worked in Karl Lashley's laboratory at Harvard University and later taught at several universities before he settled at the University of Texas. His book *Physiological Psychology* (1943), a fruit of his studies and experiments at Rochester and Harvard, established him as *the* authority in this field. His textbook *Introduction to Psychology* (1956) was a best seller.—Ed.]

1.27. We shall, e.g., have to regard as the same physical stimulus not all light which appears to us to have the same color, or all substances which smell alike, but only light waves which in various combinations with other physical objects (usually apparatus designed for the purpose) produce the same effects, or substances which in their chemical composition are identical.

1.28. For our purpose it will also be necessary to regard as different any stimuli which are physically identical but which act on different parts of the body, since it is by no means obvious (or always true) that such stimuli should produce the same sensory qualities. The question why as a rule stimulation of different individual receptors by physically identical stimuli should produce similar sensations is in fact the simplest form in which our problem arises.

1.29. The production of a nervous impulse by a stimulus is usually mediated by the selective action of specific receptor organs, which respond to certain kinds of stimuli but not to others. This selectivity of the receptor organs is, however, not perfect. Even the so-called 'adequate stimuli' to which a given receptor normally responds, consist as a rule not only of one precisely defined physical stimulus (such as, e.g., waves of a particular frequency) but to a more or less wide range of such stimuli extending, e.g., over a certain band of frequencies. In addition to this, some events other than the adequate stimuli can often set up impulses in a given nerve fiber. An impulse in the visual nerves and the consequent sensation of light may, for instance, be caused by a blow on the eyeball.

1.30. The receptor organs thus already perform a certain sorting out, or classification, of the stimuli, and there will be no strict correspondence between the different stimuli and the different impulses. Moreover, only a small part of the physical events in our environment are capable of acting as stimuli or are recorded by impulses in the nerve fibers. Of the continuous range of electromagnetic waves only a very small band acts on our organs of vision while by far the greater part of this range does not act as a stimulus on our nerves.

1.31. Impulses in a particular sensory nerve fiber may thus be set up by any one of a group of stimuli which physically may be similar or altogether different. But if a given fiber responds to any of these stimuli, the character of the impulse transmitted will always be the same, irrespective of the nature of the stimulus. The effect of the impulse is independent of the nature of the particular kind of stimulus which evokes it, and any characteristic effects which this particular impulse brings about must therefore be due to something connected with that impulse and not to any attributes of the stimulus.

1.32. This is the main contention of the so-called principle of the specific energy of nerves. When it was first announced by Johannes Müller,[17]

[17] [Johannes Peter Müller (1801–58) was a German physiologist who became known for proposing the "law of specific nerve energies." He conjectured that sense-perception is not defined by its objects per se but by the pathways over which nerves carry sensory information. His two-

it was aimed against the conception that the nervous impulses transmitted some attribute of the stimulus to the brain; and it was intended to empha-size that the sensation produced depended solely on the fiber which carried the impulse and not on what had caused that impulse. The form, in which it was stated, however, was not free from ambiguity and soon gave rise to a new misconception.

1.33. The fact that the theory was called the theory of the specific energy of nerves led to its being connected with one particular alternative explana-tion of the determination of sensory qualities which is no less questionable than the theory which it was intended to displace. On this interpretation it was understood to mean that, if it was not the physical properties of the stim-uli which determined the quality of the resulting sensations, it must be some property of the individual impulses proceeding in the different fibers, which in some sense 'corresponds' to the differences of the sensory qualities.

1.34. Although this is by no means a necessary consequence of the prop-osition which Johannes Müller had been anxious to establish, it was widely assumed, in fact, that the sensory qualities produced by impulses in different fibers would be different, similar or equal according as the physical properties of the corresponding impulses differed from or resembled each other. This interpretation was to some extent suggested by Müller's own formulation of the theory in which he asserted more than was necessary to establish his con-clusions. In his summary of his theory he stated that 'the sensation is not the conduction of a quality or state of an external body to the consciousness, but the conduction to the consciousness *of a quality or state of our sensory nerves* induced by an external cause';[18] and he went on to emphasize that these quali-ties are different with the different senses.

---

volume *Handbuch der Physiologie des Menschen* (1833–40) was translated into English and became world famous. There he states: "The same cause, such as electricity, can simultaneously affect all sensory organs, since they are all sensitive to it; and yet, every sensory nerve reacts to it differ-ently; one nerve perceives it as light, another hears its sound, another one smells it; another tastes the electricity, and another one feels it as pain and shock. . . . Sensation is not the conduc-tion of a quality or state of external bodies to consciousness, but the conduction of a quality or state of our nerves to consciousness, excited by an external cause . . ." (as quoted in E. Clarke and C. D. O'Malley, *The Human Brain and Spinal Cord—A Historical Study by Writings from Antiquity to the Twentieth Century*, 2nd ed. [San Francisco: Norman Publishing, 1996], 205f.). Müller's students include Emil du Bois-Reymond and Hermann von Helmholtz.—Ed.]

[18] Johannes Müller, 1838, I., p. 780, and II., p. 262. What we regard as the illegitimate inter-pretation of the theory of the specific energy of nerves was later explicitly formulated by G. E. Müller (1896) in the second of his five 'psychophysical axioms' (see E. G. Boring, 1942, p. 89), and became widely known mainly in the form in which it was expounded by E. Hering, 1884 (1913). [Karl Ewald Konstantin Hering (1834–1918) was a German physiologist who is known for his research on color vision.—Ed.] The basic idea has recently been revived by P. A. Weiss, 1941 [see introduction, fn. 14.—Ed.] and R. W. Sperry, 1945. [Robert Wolcott Sperry (1913–94) was a neuropsychologist and neurobiologist who won the Nobel Prize in Medicine in 1981

1.35. The recognition, however, that the difference of the sensory qualities is not due to the communication of a difference in the stimuli does by no means make the conclusion inevitable that it must then be a difference in the properties of the impulses taking place in the different fibers, which accounts for them. To interpret the theory of the specific energy of nerves in this sense is merely to accept at this stage an explanation similar to that rejected at the earlier stage: the specific character of the effect of a particular impulse need be neither due to the attributes of the stimulus which caused it, nor to the attributes of the impulse, but may be determined by the position in the structure of the nervous system of the fiber which carries the impulse.[19]

1.36. We do not only possess no information which would entitle us to assume that the impulses carried by the different fibers differ qualitatively, but, what is more important, it also seems impossible to conceive of such differences between the physical attributes of the individual impulses that they could be said in any sense to 'correspond' to the differences of the sensory qualities. Even if qualitative differences between the impulses were discovered, this would not yet provide an answer to our problem. It would still be necessary to show how these differences in quality determined the different effects which the different impulses exercise upon each other; and while it is conceivable that these latter differences may be connected with differences in their individual physical attributes, this need not be so. The important point here is that no differences of the individual impulses as such would provide an explanation of the differences between their mental equivalents, and that any differences of their causal connections with each other seem at least as likely to be due to structural connections as to qualitative affinities. This is important especially because the hope of thereby providing an explanation of the differences in mental qualities appears to have been the prime motive for the persistent and unsuccessful search for 'specific energies', and because the same conception seems also largely responsible for the persistence of the belief in a 'pure core' of sensation.[20]

1.37. The evidence which we possess suggests, in fact, that the impulses carried by the different fibers, at least within any one sense modality, are qualitatively identical, so that, if we were to cut two sensory fibers and to re-connect the lower part of each with the upper part of the other, they would still function but exchange the results which an impulse in either would cause. It seems,

---

for his split-brain research. He received his PhD with Paul A. Weiss at the University of Chicago and did post-doctoral research with Karl Lashley at Harvard University. Hayek refers to Sperry (1945) without listing a corresponding title in his original bibliography. There exist two publications by Sperry from 1945, both of which are relevant and may have been consulted by Hayek. They are now included in the bibliography as Sperry 1945a and 1945b.—Ed.]

[19] C. T. Morgan, 1943, p. 298; R. S. Woodworth, 1938, p. 465.

[20] E. G. Boring, 1942, p. 84.

therefore, that the cause of the specific effects of the impulses in different fibers must be sought not in the attributes of the individual impulses but in the position of the fiber in the central organization of the nervous system.

4. Differences in Quality Are Differences in the Effects

1.38. That the similarities and differences between the experienced sensory qualities do not correspond strictly to the differences and similarities between the physical attributes of the stimuli has become most familiar in connection with the perception of configurations or Gestalts. We all readily recognize as the same tune two different series of tones, or as the same shape or figure structures of different size and color. In all these instances groups of stimuli which individually may be altogether different do yet as groups evoke the same sensory quality or are classified by our senses as the same Gestalt.

1.39. But, though the fact that physically different stimuli produce similar sensory qualities is perhaps most conspicuous in connection with the perception of 'wholes', it is no less present or less important where more simple or 'elementary' sensations are concerned. The fact that physically similar stimuli which act on different individual receptors and therefore set up impulses in different fibers evoke the same sensory quality raises a real problem. And the question why different physical stimuli for which different receptor organs are sensitive, and even physically similar stimuli acting on different kinds of receptor organs, should produce different sensations raises a problem of the same character.

1.40. While as a rule the same kind of physical stimuli acting on different receptor organs produce the same sensory quality, this is generally true only if they act on receptors of the same kind and even then not in all instances. The same vibration which, if perceived through the ear, will be experienced as a sound, may be experienced as a vibration by the sense of touch. In other instances 'the same external agent in one case produces light, in another warmth'.[21] The same temperature may be experienced as hot, cold, or pain according as it affects different end organs.[22] The same chemical stimulus may produce different sensory qualities according as it affects the mucous membranes of the eye or of the mouth.[23] And an electrical stimulation seems to be capable of evoking an even greater variety of different sensations. Moreover, even the same stimulus affecting the same receptors may produce different

[21] E. Hering, 1884 (1913), p. 26.

[22] H. Head, 1920, II, p. 807. [Henry Head (1861–1940) was an English neurologist whose research focused on the physiological bases of sensation. After he had completed his degree in Cambridge he studied for two years with Ewald Hering in Prague.—Ed.]

[23] R. W. Moncrieff, 1944 (1946), p. 32.

sensations according as different other stimuli operate at the same time on other parts of the nervous system.

1.41. The same sensory quality, on the other hand, may be evoked by different physical stimuli. This happens not only where a particular receptor organ is excited by several different stimuli. In such a case any one of the different stimuli will, of course, evoke the same impulse. But impulses or groups of impulses set up in different fibers by different stimuli also often produce the same sensory quality. The classical instance is the case of color vision and particularly the sensation of 'white' which can be produced by an infinite variety of different mixtures of light rays. But this same fact that physically different stimuli acting on different kinds of receptors produce the same sensory qualities seems to be of very frequent occurrence.

1.42. There exists, therefore, no one-to-one correspondence between the kinds (or the physical properties) of the different physical stimuli and the dimensions in which they can vary, on the one hand, and the different kinds of sensory qualities which they produce and their various dimensions, on the other. The manner in which the different physical stimuli can vary and the different physical dimensions in which they can be arranged have no exact counterpart in the manner in which the sensory qualities caused by them will differ from each other, or in the dimensions in which these sensory qualities can be arranged. This is the central fact to which we have referred when we insisted that the two orders, the physical order of the stimuli and the phenomenal or mental order of the sensory qualities, are different.

1.43. It has long been believed that, e.g., in the field of vision the three dimensions of the stimulus, wave-length, homogeneity and intensity correspond to the three phenomenal dimensions of visual experience, hue, saturation and brightness, and that similarly in the field of hearing frequency and intensity as physical dimensions of the stimulus correspond to pitch and loudness respectively as the phenomenal dimensions of sensation. Recent work, however, has amply shown that within any given modality a change in one dimension of the stimulus may affect almost any dimension of the sensation. Hue depends not only on wave-length but also on intensity; pitch not only on frequency but also on intensity.[24]

1.44. The orders or dimensions of the stimuli and of the sensations, moreover, not only show no one-to-one correspondence; they also differ in their general character. Any one of the physical dimensions of light and partic-

---

[24] See, e.g., S. S. Stevens, 1934; [Stanley Smith Stevens (1906–73) was an American experimental psychologist. He had studied with E. G. Boring at Harvard and later founded Harvard's Psycho-Acoustic Laboratory. He developed techniques for the study of the neural aspects of sensory events. His *Handbook of Experimental Psychology* (1951) became a standard reference in the 1950s.—Ed.]; S. S. Stevens and H. Davis, 1938, p. 160; E. G. Boring, 1942, pp. 89, 376; F. L. Dimmick in: Boring, Langfeld and Weld, 1948, pp. 270–80.

ularly wave-length which is mainly (though not exclusively) the cause of variation in color, varies on a linear scale, while phenomenal colors can be arranged in a continuous circle in which the order of the wavelength is preserved, but the gap between the two extremes of the spectrum, yellowish red and violet, is closed by pure (or 'unique') red and purple which correspond to no distinct wave-length but can be produced only by various mixtures of different wave-lengths. Moreover, continuous variations of the stimuli often produce discontinuous variations in the sensory qualities[25], while in at least one case a continuous variation in the sensory qualities, namely from cold to hot, is brought about by what we must regard as a discontinuous variation of the stimuli, since the objectively continuous variation of temperature acts on the organism through different receptor organs.

1.45. It may be generally said that the organization of the sensory order, as represented by the various geometrical figures (such as the color octahedron,[26] Titchener's touch pyramid,[27] Henning's smell prism[28] and taste tetrahedron[29]) by which psychologists have described the dimensions in which the sensory qualities vary, are by no means identical with the order of the corresponding physical stimuli and often differ very substantially from them. The fact that the two orders resemble each other in some degree must not obscure the fact that they are distinct and different orders.

1.46. When we speak of the physical order we mean by similarity of two events that they will produce the same effects in certain circumstances but

[25] V. v. Weizsäcker, 1940 (1947), pp. 15–16. [Viktor von Weizsäcker (1886–1957) was a German physiologist who is considered the founder of psychosomatic medicine and medical anthropology. In the spirit of Gestalt psychology, he coined the concept of *Gestaltkreis*, which emphasizes the "unity of perception and movement," the functional interdependence of the mental and the physical.—Ed.]

[26] [The color octahedron—a double pyramid with differently colored surfaces—was introduced by the Austrian philosopher Alois Höfler (1853–1922) and used, among others, by E. Hering to illustrate the relationship between color vision and the psychological effects of colors.—Ed.]

[27] [Born in England, Edward Bradford Titchener (1867–1927) did his doctoral studies with Wilhelm Wundt in Leipzig. After receiving his PhD in 1892, he moved to the United States, where he became prominent as an experimental psychologist. He taught as professor of psychology at Cornell University from 1895 to 1927. The Titchener touch pyramid is a pyramid-shaped graphic representation of differently structured surfaces meant to illustrate the sensational resemblance of different touch qualities, similar to the study of color sensations with the help of the color octahedron.—Ed.]

[28] [Hans Henning (1885–1946) was a German philosopher and psychologist who is known for his research on olfactory qualities. Henning's smell prism or odor prism is a prism-shaped graphic representation of six primary odors (such as foul, flowery, burnt, etc.) intended to illustrate the interaction of different odorous stimuli.—Ed.]

[29] [Henning's taste tetrahedron is a three-sided pyramid, the four corners of which represent the primary tastes (sweet, salty, sour, bitter), intended to illustrate the relationships between them.—Ed.]

not in others. Different physical events can evidently be similar to each other both in different degrees and also in different respects: two events may each be similar to a third but not be similar to each other. In other words, similarity is a non-transitive relation.

1.47. The same is true with regard to mental events. Two sensory qualities will be equal if their effects on other mental events or on behavior will be the same in all respects. They may be similar in varying degrees and in different respects according as they will evoke the same or other mental events or the same behavior in certain circumstances but not in others.

1.48. It will now be clearer what we mean when we speak of the two orders of events, the physical[30] and the phenomenal or mental order. Some events will occupy definite positions in both orders, but the relations between several such events in each of the two orders may be different. Some events in the physical order, such as electrical currents which we can only infer, will have no corresponding events in the phenomenal order; and some events in the phenomenal order, such as images or illusions which are not produced by external stimuli, will have no counterpart in the physical order. While there will thus be some degree of correspondence between the individual events which occur in the two orders, it will be but a very imperfect correspondence.

1.49. *What we call 'mind' is thus a particular order of a set of events taking place in some organism and in some manner related to but not identical with the physical order of events in the environment.*[31] The problem which the existence of mental phenomena raises is therefore how in a part of the physical order (namely an organism) a sub-system can be formed which in some sense (yet to be more fully defined) may be said to reflect some features of the physical order as a whole, and which thereby enables the organism which contains such a partial reproduction of the environmental order to behave appropriately towards its surroundings. The problem arises as much from the fact that the order of this sub-system is in some respects similar to, as from the fact that it is in other respects different from the corresponding more comprehensive physical order. The meaning of the conception of an 'order' will be further explained in the next chapter (2.28–2.30).

[30] It is, perhaps, not inappropriate at this point explicitly to remind the reader, that in this context 'physical order' refers exclusively to the order of the external stimuli and not to the order of the physiological impulses which, of course, also form part of the physical order in a wider sense. The nature of this order of the impulses will be considered in the next chapter.

[31] Cf., G. Ryle, 1949, p. 167: 'When we speak of a person's mind . . . [we are speaking of] . . . certain ways in which some of the incidents of his life are ordered.' [Gilbert Ryle (1900–1976) was a British philosopher who challenged the Cartesian mind-body dualism as the doctrine of "the ghost-in-the-machine." He advocated a philosophical behaviorism that insists on the unity of the workings of the mind and the actions of the body, looking at mental states as disposition to act. Ryle is also famous for his distinction between "Knowing How" and "Knowing That."—Ed.]

1.50. In recent physiological psychology these problems have received attention, mainly owing to the work of H. Klüver, under the headings of *equivalence of stimuli* and of *sensory generalization*. Klüver's original statement of the problem is probably still the clearest exposition of it to be found in the literature.[32] Merely another aspect of the same problem is the phenomenon of *transfer* of acquired responses from a given stimulus to others, which is of course the process through which phenomenal similarity manifests itself in behavior. Yet, though the central character of this problem is now fairly generally recognized, it is usually mentioned merely to point out that it is 'one of the most perplexing problems to be faced'[33] or 'the recognized stumbling block to all simple mechanical hypotheses of habit formation'.[34]

1.51. Equivalence, generalization and transfer are all instances of identity of the effects of different stimuli, while discrimination means a difference in the effect of individual stimuli or groups of stimuli. The qualitative order of the sensations which manifests itself in these phenomena is thus a difference in the order in which the stimuli in various combinations produce different effects; and sensory qualities can be regarded as groups or classes of events which, with respect to the responses of the organism, are identical, similar or different in their effects. The order of sensory qualities thus is identical with the totality of the differences of the effects which the different nervous impulses will produce in different circumstances. If we can explain the process which determines the differential responses of the organism to the various physical stimuli, we have at the same time also explained the qualitative order which is the peculiar characteristic of mental phenomena.

1.52. The significance of this statement, which in its bare form may sound more 'behavioristic' than it is intended, will become clearer when we examine the kinds of different 'effects' which have to be considered in this connection (2.23–2.26). At this point it need only be pointed out that by the term 'effects' we do not mean only, or even mainly, overt behavior or peripheral responses, but shall include all the central nervous processes caused by the initial impulses, even though we may be able only indirectly to infer their existence.

[32] H. Klüver, 1933, especially pp. 330–32; 1936, p. 109; and 1949, p. 404. A clear statement is also to be found in E. R. Hilgard and D. G. Marquis, 1940, p. 176: 'The basic facts of stimulus equivalence and response equivalence are not limited in application to conditioned responses, but are true of reflexes and of complex voluntary responses. Every response is elicitable not just by one stimulus but by a *class* of stimuli. Correspondingly, every stimulus elicits, not just one response, but one of a *class* of responses.' (Italics ours.)

[33] C. T. Morgan, 1943, p. 514.

[34] E. D. Adrian, 1947, p. 82. [Edgar Douglas Adrian (1889–1977) was a British physiologist who became known for his studies of electrical activity of nerve fibers and in the human brain. In 1932 he won, jointly with Sir Charles Sherrington, the Nobel Prize in Physiology or Medicine for his work on the function of neurons.—Ed.]

1.53. Our problem is then to show how it is possible to build from the known elements of the nervous processes a structure of intermediate links between the physical stimuli and the overt responses which can account for the fact that the responses to different stimuli differ from each other in precisely that fashion in which we know the responses to the experienced sensory qualities to differ from each other. We must show that from the known physiological elements a structure can be formed which can differentiate between different impulses passing through it in exactly the same manner in which our sensory experience differentiates between the different stimuli.

1.54. Our problem must therefore be *stated* in terms of the relationships (of equality, similarity, difference, etc.) existing between the sensory qualities. It can be *answered* only by showing that a strictly equivalent system of relationships can exist between physiological events so that the effects of any event or any group of events in that system will produce a set of effects strictly corresponding to the effects the corresponding sensory qualities will produce. (The reader should observe already at this stage that this does not imply that any given physiological event will always produce the same effects irrespective of the other physiological events occurring at the same time. On this and on the general danger of a too narrow interpretation of the conception of a one-to-one correspondence between the sensory and the neural order, see below 2.10–2.13.)

1.55. This contention implies that if we can explain how all the different sensory qualities differ from each other in the effects which they will produce whenever they occur, we have explained all there is to explain; or that the whole order of sensory qualities can be exhaustively described in terms of (or 'consists of nothing but') all the relationships existing between them.[35] There is no problem of sensory qualities beyond the problem of how the different qualities differ from each other—and these differences can only consist of differences in the effects which they exercise in evoking other qualities, or in determining behavior.

5. The Unitary Character of the Sensory Order

1.56. The conclusion to which we have been led means that the order of sensory qualities no less than the order of physical events is a relational order—

---

[35] That this is the consistent development of the approach started by John Locke was clearly seen by T. H. Green who argued (1884, p. 23) that 'if we take him [Locke] at his word and exclude from what we have considered real all qualities constituted by relation, we find that none are left. Without relation any simple idea would be undistinguished from other simple ideas, undermined by its surroundings in the cosmos of existence.' See also ibid., p. 31. [Thomas Hill Green (1832–82) was a British philosopher and member of the British idealism movement.—Ed.]

even though to us, whose mind is the totality of the relations constituting that order, it may not appear as such. The difference between the physical order of events and the phenomenal order in which we perceive the same events is thus not that only the former is purely relational, but that the relations existing between corresponding events and groups of events in the two orders will be different.

1.57. The order of the sensory qualities is difficult to describe, not only because we are not explicitly aware of the relations between the different qualities but merely manifest these relations in the discriminations which we perform,[36] and because the number and complexity of these relations is probably greater than anything which we could ever explicitly state or exhaustively describe, but also because, as we shall see, it is not a stable but a variable order. Yet we must attempt here to describe at least certain general characteristics of that order, because our problem is whether we can account for at least the kind of properties which it possesses, even if we cannot explain its detailed arrangement.

1.58. One main point about this order is that, in spite of its division into the different modalities, it is still a unitary order, in the sense that any two events belonging to it may in certain definite ways resemble each other, or differ from each other. Any color and any smell, any tone and any temperature, or any tactual sensation such as smoothness or wetness, and any experience of shape or rhythm may yet have something in common, or be at least in some sense akin to or in contrast with one another. Experiments have shown that these experienced similarities extend much further than we are usually aware of and that, e.g., even a person who at first thinks such an attempt nonsense, has no difficulty, once he can bring himself to try, to find a tone whose brightness is the same as that of the smell of lilac.[37]

1.59. Some qualities, especially those which, like colors or tones, are connected into qualitative continua and which, since Helmholtz, we describe as forming distinct modalities, probably always seem to belong more closely together than others such as, e.g., the sensations of pressure, pain, and temperature, which used to be regarded as belonging to the one sense of touch but do not form one modality in the sense just defined. But when we try to describe the differences between different qualities belonging to the same modality, such as different colors, we find that in order to do so we usually resort to expressions borrowed from other modalities. One color may be warmer or heavier or louder than another, one tone brighter or rougher or

[36] This distinction is probably the same as, or closely related to, that between 'Knowing-How' and 'Knowing-That' so well brought out by G. Ryle, 1945–46, and 1949.

[37] E. M. von Hornbostel, 1925, p. 290. [Erich Moritz von Hornbostel (1877–1935) was an Austrian-born ethnomusicologist who conducted research on psychoacoustics in Berlin. In 1933 he was forced to emigrate and eventually settled in Cambridge, England.—Ed.]

thicker than another. This indicates that, though in some respects one particular color or one particular tone may be most closely related to other colors or other tones respectively, yet in other respects they may be closer to qualities belonging to different modalities.

1.60. Although within any given modality qualities vary continuously[38] they need not vary in a constant direction or dimension. While it is true of tones that if one tone is higher than a second, and a third higher than the first, the third will also be higher than the second, we cannot similarly say that, because orange is yellower than red and green bluer than orange, green is therefore either more yellow or more blue than red. While, with regard to pitch, tones can be arranged in one linear scale, colors do not, in this sense, vary in a single direction.

1.61. It makes sense, on the other hand, to say that two different colors differ in the same manner in which two different temperatures or weights do, or that two tones differ similarly as do two sensations of color or touch. This means that qualities of different modalities may vary along similar or parallel directions or dimensions, or that the same kind of differences can occur in different modalities. It is, e.g., part of the difference between blue and red that blue is associated with coolness and red with warmth. There exist apparently certain intermodal or inter-sensory attributes, and with regard to some of the terms which we use for them, such as strong or weak, mild or mellow, tingling or sharp, we are often not immediately aware to which sense modality they originally belong.[39]

1.62. In our highly developed conscious picture of the sensory order these inter-sensory and intermodal relations are not very prominent and with the development of conceptual thought and particularly, as a result of the great influence which sensualism has had on it, in scientific thought, they are more and more driven back until they are almost completely disregarded.[40] We may

---

[38] Some doubt has recently been thrown even on the complete continuity of the qualities within one modality and the existence of sensory 'quanta' suggested by S. S. Stevens and J. Volkman, 1940a and 1940b, and S. S. Stevens, C. T. Morgan, and J. Volkman, 1941.

[39] See especially P. v. Schiller, 1932, and the instances of terms borrowed from other modalities to describe smells given by F. W. Hazzard, 1930, p. 318. It is also interesting to note that the meaning of the German word *hell* (bright) has shifted from its original reference to auditory experience to the visual field.

[40] Very characteristic in this connection is the categorical statement by M. Planck, 1949, p. 87, that the experiences of the different sensory fields 'are totally different from each other, and have initially nothing in common. There is no immediate, direct bridge between the perception of colors and the perception of sounds. An affinity, such as may be assumed by many art lovers to exist between a certain shade of color and a certain musical pitch, is not directly given but is the creation, stimulated by personal experiences, of our reflective powers of imagination.' The fact seems to be the other way round that sophistication makes us overlook what is obvious to naive experience.

become aware of their existence only when we attempt to describe a particular sensory quality and in doing so find ourselves driven to describe a color as soft or sweet, a tone as thin or dark, a taste as hot or sharp, or a smell as dry and sweet. There can be little doubt that these seemingly metaphorical expressions refer to truly inter-sensory attributes; and experimental tests have at least in some instances shown that different people tend to equate the same pairs or groups of different qualities.[41]

1.63. These facts may also be described by saying that relations between different qualities may in turn also possess distinct qualities and that the relations between different pairs or groups of qualities belonging to different modalities may possess the same qualities. These qualities attaching to the relations between different qualities may in turn be similar to individual sensory qualities. The successive musical intervals from the second to the octave, e.g., have been described as 'gritty', 'mellow', 'coarse', 'hollow', 'luscious', 'astringent', and 'smooth' respectively.[42]

1.64. These intermodal relations may occasionally be so strong that different sensations belonging to one modality may regularly be accompanied by the experience of qualities belonging to another modality, as in the case of color-hearing and other instances of synaesthesia.[43] There is some evidence that these synaesthetic modes of perception are particularly strong in relatively early stages of mental development, and that our habit of thinking of particular colors as primarily belonging to the range of colors, or of a tone primarily as being one of a range of tones, is the produce of a comparatively late and abstract attitude.[44]

1.65. More familiar than the facts of synaesthesia is the fact that most sensory qualities are closely associated with certain affective tones and that there exists thus a close connection between the order of sensory qualities and that of affective qualities. The emotional values attaching to various sensory qualities are well known, and there are indeed few sensory qualities which we do not regard at least as either pleasant or unpleasant, or as simply good or bad. The general relation between sensations and emotions or drives will, however, have to be considered later and cannot be further examined at this point.

1.66. The relations or connections between different sensory (and affective) qualities find expression in the expectations which their occurrence arouses. A

[41] On this and the following see G. W. Hartmann, 1935, pp. 141–51.

[42] E. M. Edmonds and M. E. Smith, 1923.

[43] [Synesthesia is a perceptual condition that occurs when a stimulus in one sensory modality (e.g., hearing) automatically triggers a sensation in a second modality (e.g., vision), such as in color hearing. Persons who experience such conditions are called synesthetes.—Ed.]

[44] H. Werner, 1948, p. 86. On synaesthesia see also H. Kleint, 1940, pp. 56–61; K. Goldstein, 1939, p. 267; and for bibliographies of the extensive literature on the subject, F. Mahling, 1926; A. Argelander, 1927; and A. Wellek, 1931.

red color does not merely evoke the image of warmth but we shall be rather surprised if a red object turns out to be very cold; and a certain smell will not only conjure up certain tastes but we shall be shocked if a deliciously smelling fruit turns out to have a vile taste. In this way certain groups of qualities tend to 'belong' together, and particular qualities come to 'mean' to us certain other qualities.

1.67. Whether the facts briefly summarized in this section do or do not justify the assertion of a 'Unity of the Senses' in such a manner that 'all senses are alike in respect to their attributive dimensions',[45] they probably entitle us to say that, directly or indirectly, all mental qualities are so related to each other that any attempt to give an exhaustive description of any one of them would make it necessary to describe the relations existing between all.

6. The Order of Sensory Qualities Not Confined to Conscious Experience

1.68. We have so far assumed that the reader is familiar with the system of sensory qualities from his own conscious experience of these qualities. This, however, is not to be understood to mean that this particular classification of events appears only in our subjective experience. Of course we know this system of qualities from this source. But just as experience tells us that in their relations to each other things do not always resemble each other or differ from each other in the same manner as they seem to be alike or different to us, so we also learn that what appears alike or different to us usually also appears alike or different to other men. Beyond this, it seems clear that not only other men in their conscious action, but both we and others in unconscious action, and also animals, treat as alike or different not what is so in the physical sense, but more or less what in our own conscious experience appears to us to be so. In other words, the order of sensory qualities, once it is known, can be recognized as present in actions which are not directed by consciousness or by a human mind.

1.69. It would, of course, not be possible to discuss the phenomenal world with other people if they did not perceive this world in terms of the same, or at least of a very similar order of qualities as we do. This means that the conscious mind of other people classifies stimuli in a manner similar to that in which our own mind does so, and that the different sensory qualities are for them related to each other in a manner which is similar to that which we know. In other words, although the system of sensory qualities is 'subjective' in the sense of belonging to the perceiving subject as distinguished from 'objec-

---

[45] This is the interpretation given to E. M. von Hornbostel's conception of the *Unity of the Senses* by E. G. Boring, 1942, p. 27.

tive' (belonging to the perceived objects)—a distinction which is the same as that between the phenomenal and the physical order—it is yet interpersonal and not (or at least not entirely) peculiar to the individual.

1.70. Nor is the classification of stimuli in terms of sensory qualities confined to conscious experience. We know that both we and other people classify stimuli in our unconscious responses (or in responses to stimuli of which we do not become conscious) according to roughly the same principles as we do in our conscious action.[46] The order of sensory qualities exists therefore also outside the realm of consciousness. If, as we shall suggest, we identify with the realm of mental phenomena the range of events within which a classification in terms of sensory (and similar mental) qualities occurs, this realm extends far beyond the sphere of conscious events which merely constitute a special group within the more comprehensive class of mental events.

1.71. It is possible, finally, to ascertain by various experimental methods that not only other men but also most higher animals classify stimuli according to an order which is similar to that of our own sensory experiences. It has even been shown that some animals, e.g., chicks in the famous Révész experiment,[47] are subject to the same optical illusions as men. We must therefore conclude that the general principles according to which the neural system of the higher animals classifies stimuli are, at least in their general outline, similar to those on which our own mind operates.

1.72. While it has been inevitable that in introducing our problem we started from the conscious experience of sensory qualities, this proves now to be only one particular aspect of a wider problem. In the further discussion we shall treat conscious experience as merely a special instance of a more general phenomenon, and speak of mental phenomena whenever we deal with any events which are ordered on principles analogous to those revealed by conscious experience. All further consideration of the peculiar additional attri-

---

[46] For the fact that this applies even to responses to configurations see K. Lorenz, 1942, p. 323; and on sub-conscious discrimination ('subception') R. A. McCleary and R. S. Lazarus, 1949, p. 178. [Konrad Lorenz (1903–89) was an Austrian zoologist and one of the founders of modern ethology. In 1973 he was awarded, jointly with Nikolaas Tinbergen and Karl von Frisch, the Nobel Prize in Physiology or Medicine for his "discoveries concerning organization and elicitation of individual and social behavior patterns." Hayek recollects that Lorenz, when a five-year-old boy, had been pointed out to him observing geese. See Franz Kreuzer, *Markt, Plan, Freiheit—Gespräch mit Friedrich von Hayek und Ralf Dahrendorf* (Wien: Franz Deuticke, 1983), 9. In his autobiographical essay, "My family and other animals," in D. A. Dewsbury, ed., *Leaders in the Study of Animal Behavior: Autobiographical Perspectives* (Lewisburg, PA: Bucknell University Press, 1985), 258–87, Lorenz reports on his childhood passion for studying the behavior of ducks. See also above, editor's introduction, pp. 42f.—Ed.]

[47] G. Révész, 1924, and C. N. Winslow, 1933. [Géza Révész (1878–1955) was a Hungarian psychologist who studied with Georg Elias Müller (see above, preface, fn. 10). He moved to the Netherlands in 1921, where he taught as professor of psychology at the University of Amsterdam.—Ed.]

156

butes which a mental event in this sense must possess in order to be described as 'conscious' will be postponed to a later stage (chapter VI).

1.73. It has undoubtedly been unfortunate for the development of psychology that the distinguishing attribute of its object was so long considered to be the 'conscious' character of experience, and that no definition of mental events was available which was independent of this conscious character.[48] The sphere of mental events evidently transcends the sphere of conscious events and there is no justification for the attitude frequently met that either identifies the two or even maintains that to speak of unconscious mental events is a contradiction in terms.[49]

1.74. But although we can agree with the Behaviorists in deploring the exclusive concentration of the older psychology on conscious events, they themselves, in their endeavour to get rid of consciousness, have gone to the opposite extreme and with the problem of consciousness have tried to eliminate the problem of the existence of the qualitative order which is peculiar to mental phenomena. This problem, as we shall see, cannot be disregarded even if we want merely to account for observed behavior.

7. The Denial or Disregard of Our Problem by Behaviorism

1.75. It will help to bring out more clearly the precise meaning of our problem if we contrast our approach with that of two other points of view which require either less or more of any explanation of sensory perception than our

---

[48] Cf., E. B. Holt, 1937, p. 41: 'Every school of psychology since certainly before the time of Herbart has found that by far the greater portion of the sensations, ideas and processes which must be called 'mental' never become explicitly conscious: they are not perceived and cannot by any known process of introspection be perceived.' Also the passage quoted by Holt from S. Freud, 1918, p. 9, where the latter says that 'mental processes in and of themselves are unconscious, and the conscious are merely isolated acts and passages in the total life of the mind.' [Holt's reference is to Sigmund Freud, *Vorlesungen zur Einführung in die Psychoanalyse*, 2nd unaltered ed. (Leipzig: Heller, 1918). Edwin Holt (1873–1946) taught as professor of philosophy and psychology at Harvard and Princeton. He advocated a "teleological behaviorism" that, building on Watson's behaviorism, seeks to account for the purposefulness and goal-directedness of behavior. Edward C. Tolman (see below, 1.76, fn. 50) was his student.—Ed.] Cf., also E. G. Boring et al., 1948, on the use of the term 'unconscious mind'.

[49] Several examples of the identification of 'mental' and 'conscious' are given by J. G. Miller, 1942, pp. 24ff. [James Grier Miller (1916–2002) was an American biologist who, along with L. v. Bertalanffy and N. Wiener, is counted among the founders of systems science. He coined the term "behavioral science" and served for decades as editor of the journal by the same name.—Ed.] C. J. Herrick, 1926, p. 280 says that 'the dynamic view of consciousness here adopted makes such expressions as "the unconscious mind" impossible contradictions.' H. Head, 1920, II, p. 747, states that 'sensation, in the strict sense of the term, demands the existence of consciousness.' M. Planck, 1949, p. 66 also describes a 'science of the unconscious or subconscious mind' as 'a contradiction in terms, a self-contradiction.'

statement of the problem demands. This and the next section will accordingly be devoted to an examination, firstly, of the views of a school of thought which either explicitly denied the existence of our problem, or at least proceeded as if it did not exist; and, secondly, to the consideration of an opposite point of view which would probably maintain that even if a complete answer to our problem were achieved, there would still remain unsolved a significant problem concerning the 'absolute' or 'intrinsic' nature of sensory qualities.

1.76. The point of view which denies, at least by implication, that ours is a genuine problem is (or was?) represented mainly by the classical behaviorists[50] and by similar schools aiming at a strictly 'objective' psychology. These schools maintained that psychology can entirely dispense with any knowledge of the subjectively experienced mental qualities, and that it ought to confine itself to the study of bodily responses to physical stimuli.

1.77. All the schools of psychology which thus claim to confine themselves to observed physical facts are, however, in fact always and inevitably inconsistent in their procedure: they never really avoid using knowledge which according to their professed principles they have no right to use. They almost invariably describe the external stimuli which elicit behavior not in terms of their physical properties but in terms of their sensory attributes. They naively accept as a fact not requiring explanation that different minds treat as equal, similar, or different, groups of stimuli which physically are not such but merely appear so to our senses.

1.78. The adherents of these schools, in other words, treat as something not requiring explanation the fact that stimuli which to their senses appear similar will also appear so to others; and they do this in spite of our knowledge that physically these stimuli may be very different events and in fact may have nothing in common except that very circumstance that whenever they act on us or other people they will evoke the same sensations (and/or responses).

[50] By 'Behaviorism' we shall mean throughout this discussion not only the original doctrines of J. Watson [John Broadus Watson's (1878–1958) 1913 article "Psychology as the Behaviorist Views It" is considered the founding document of behaviorism. For Watson psychology is a purely objective, natural science that, instead of seeking to study the "mind," focuses exclusively on external behavior and eschews introspection.—Ed.] but also the views represented in the nineteen-twenties and early 'thirties by men like E. B. Holt, A. P. Weiss, E. C. Tolman [Edward C. Tolman (1886–1959) was an American behavioral psychologist who, influenced by William James and the Gestalt psychology of K. Koffka, advocated a "mollified" behaviorism that includes the study of mental processes, accounting for variables "intervening" between stimulus and response.—Ed.], W. S. Hunter, and particularly K. S. Lashley, who in 1923, p.241 defined the position by the statement that 'the behaviorist denies sensations, images, and all other phenomena which the subjectivist claims to find by introspection.' More recently this radically objectivist attitude has been greatly modified and one may doubt whether the Lashley who (1942, p. 304) has 'come to doubt that any progress will be made towards a genuine understanding of nervous integration until the problem of equivalent nervous connections, as it is more generally termed, of stimulus equivalence, is solved,' can still be described as a behaviorist. See also K. W. Spence, 1948, p. 67.

They disregard, in other words, the very phenomenon which raises the problem of the existence of a peculiar mental order.

1.79. It might therefore be said that behaviorism, from its own point of view, was not radical and consistent enough, since it took for its starting point a picture of the external world which was derived from our naive sense experience, instead of taking, as it ought to have done, one obtained from the physical sciences which describe the objective properties of this world. If the behaviorists had been consistent in their desire to take no notice of the qualitative order of their own sense experience, they ought to have started by studying the effects on the organism of physical events of a certain kind, e.g., of light waves of a certain frequency, and then have proceeded to establish experimentally to which of these different physical stimuli the individual responded in the same, and to which he responded in a different manner. Before going any further they ought, in other words, to have built up experimentally that classification of the different stimuli which our senses effect.[51]

1.80. Behaviorists, however, did not seriously try doing anything of the kind. They uncritically accepted the fact that things which are physically different appear alike to our senses, and that things which are physically the same sometimes appear different, or that different things may appear to differ from each other in a manner which is in no way commensurable with the physical differences which objectively exist between them; and they appeared to see no problem in the fact that other organisms classify stimuli in the same manner as we do ourselves, or in a manner different from it.

1.81. This curious blindness to an important problem does not always show itself as blatantly as in the instance reported by W. Köhler[52] in which a behaviorist insisted on referring to a 'female' as 'a stimulus' to a male bird.[53] The error in this instance does not lie merely, as Köhler suggests, in the fact that

---

[51] Cf., F. A. Hayek, 1943, pp. 34–39.

[52] [Wolfgang Köhler (1887–1967), along with Kurt Koffka and Max Wertheimer (see above, preface, fn. 4), is considered one of the principal founders of Gestalt psychology. In Berlin, he studied with Max Planck, whose quantum field physics shaped his ideas about the relation between conscious experience and brain processes. As director of the Prussian Academy of Sciences Anthropoid Station at Tenerife (1913–20), he conducted his famous experiments on problem solving by chimpanzees. His findings made him a life-long critic of simple Watsonian behaviorism. From 1921 to 1935 he was the head of the Psychological Institute and professor of philosophy at the University of Berlin. As an outspoken opponent of the Nazi regime—he was the only one of Berlin University's professors who publicly criticized the dismissal of his Jewish colleagues—he left Germany in 1935 and took a position at Swarthmore College, Pennsylvania, where he remained until 1955. His book *Gestalt Psychology* (1929), based on lectures he had given in the United States, circulated widely. His hopes, though, to establish with his fellow emigrants from Germany—Wertheimer, Koffka, and Kurt Lewin (1890–1947)—a Gestalt School in America did not materialize, not least due to their early death.—Ed.]

[53] W. Köhler, 1929 p. 180: 66. Cf., also E. G. Boring, 1930, p. 121: 'Green light of 505 millimicrons wave-length may be a stimulus but my grandmother is not a stimulus', and W. Metzger, 1941, p. 283.

it involves 'closing one's eye to the problem of Gestalt and organization.' It appears already in the disregard of the fact that physically different stimuli affecting different receptors produce the same or similar sensory qualities and therefore are treated as being the same, and in pretending at the same time that sensory qualities do not enter at all into their considerations. (The language of the behaviorist in this instance could be justified only if he meant to imply that the female was always recognized through the same physical stimulus such as a certain smell, or rather by the stimulation of certain organs of olfaction by definite chemical substances.)

1.82. It would involve the same disregard of the central problem if, e.g., two red spots reflected on different parts of the retina, or the same temperature affecting different parts of the body, were treated as representing the same stimulus. In treating as the same kind of event all events which appear to us to possess the same sensory qualities, behaviorism tacitly assumes the existence of the whole order of such qualities which at the same time it pretends to ignore.

1.83. This acceptance as data of the sensory qualities as they are known to most men from their subjective experience is indeed inevitable in the study of any complex behavior. But it is only because, while thus accepting them, the behaviorists at the same time deceived themselves about the true character of their procedure, that they avoided the main problem which psychology has to face. If they had been more radical and more consistent in their efforts to link up psychology with the world of physical science, they would have discovered[54] that their attempt to explain behavior without reference to subjective sensory qualities could not be consistently carried through unless it was first shown what determined that system of sensory qualities.

1.84. Like many of the traditional schools of psychology, behaviorism thus treated the problem of mind as if it were a problem of the responses of the individual to an independently or objectively given phenomenal world, while, in fact, it is the existence of a phenomenal world which is different from the physical world which constitutes the main problem. Behaviorism merely appeared to avoid the problem of mind by confining itself to the study of man's behavior in the phenomenal world and by thus treating the main manifestation of mind as a datum rather than as something requiring explanation.

1.85. Although no behaviorist ever consistently adhered to what are the professed principles of his school, and although, if he had, he would never, in the present state of knowledge, have got on to the phenomena in which he was interested, it will be instructive briefly to consider what a consistently

---

[54] As they ultimately did—see the passage from Lashley quoted to 1.76 above. One might indeed date the end of behaviorism at the time of a general recognition of the central importance of the problem of equivalence of stimuli, i.e., soon after the appearance of H. Klüver, 1933.

'objectivist' study of behavior would have to be like. It will then be seen that even if the behaviorists had succeeded in carrying out their programme, there would still remain a problem of mind requiring an answer.

1.86. In the first instance, much knowledge that we undoubtedly possess but which is not derived from experimental evidence—such as the knowledge that we are likely to respond in the same manner to different physical stimuli which produce the same sensation—would have to be strictly excluded from such a study of human behavior. The first task of such a consistently objectivist approach would therefore have to be to ascertain experimentally what to us is the starting point of all knowledge, namely the phenomenal order in which the different stimuli appear in our mind.

1.87. It is at least not inconceivable, although not likely, that by proceeding thus we might in the course of time succeed in reconstructing approximately that grouping of the stimuli which our senses perform. We might then be able to list all the different physical stimuli which, acting on particular receptors and under particular conditions, produce the same sensations (or have always the same influence on the response), and also to reconstruct all the different conditions under which (and all the different respects with regard to which) the several stimuli produce different effects. In other words, we might, starting from the physical order of events, experimentally reconstruct the phenomenal order in which these events are reproduced by our senses.[55]

1.88. This would be merely the first task which a psychology would have to undertake which took the basic idea of behaviorism literally. Only after completing this task could it at least undertake to link directly observable behavior and physical stimuli. And in order to be quite consistent it would have to define not only the stimuli but also behavior in strictly physical terms. We need not inquire at this stage whether it is conceivable that this task should ever be fully completed. (We shall later give reasons why we think that this is impossible.) At this point we are concerned with the question whether, even if this task were achieved, there would still remain a problem of the kind with which we are here concerned.

1.89. A solution of that problem would show us what the apparatus of perception does in response to particular stimuli, but not how it does it. Even if we had established a correspondence between all the observed combinations of stimuli and the resulting sensations, we should still be ignorant of the mechanism by which the one kind of order is translated into the other. Our knowledge would be purely descriptive in the sense that it would be confined to a knowledge of the correspondence between observed stimuli and observed

[55] This would require more than that coordination of the dimensions of individual stimuli and the dimensions of the various 'elementary' sensory qualities which recently has been successfully attempted, especially with regard to hearing, by S. S. Stevens, 1934. It would require a similar co-ordination also for the instances where the same stimulus in different combinations with others produces different sensations.

responses. We should not possess a theory from which we could derive new conclusions which could be empirically tested.

8. The 'Absolute' Qualities of Sensations a Phantom-Problem

1.90. A different type of objection to our manner of stating the problem must be expected from a school of thought which, though not formally organized, is fairly widespread and which in some respects might be regarded as the extreme opposite of behaviorism. It would probably be contended by representatives of this point of view that, even if we succeeded in accounting for all the differences between the effects of the different stimuli or impulses, there would still remain an unexplained factor, the 'absolute' or 'intrinsic' qualities of the sensations which are not exhausted by all the differences in their effects but which must be experienced to be known.

1.91. This conception of the absolute character of sensory qualities derives probably from John Locke's conception of 'simple' ideas.[56] It has found an explicit defender in no less a student than William James.[57] It is a contention which raises what to us seems clearly a phantom-problem which cannot even be clearly stated and with regard to which it is impossible to say what kind of statement would provide an answer. It is nevertheless important, not only because of the pervasive influence of this conception, but also because it is probably one of the main roots of the belief in a peculiar mental substance.

1.92. The first point to note is that it is clearly possible that a sense discrimination of which some other person is capable can raise a problem for us though we ourselves may not be capable of it. The problem of color vision, e.g., can clearly become a problem to the totally color-blind person as much as it can to us. What we shall have to show is that there are no questions which we can intelligibly ask about sensory qualities which could not also conceivably become a problem to a person who has not himself experienced the particular qualities but knows of them only from the descriptions given to him by others. In other words, that nothing can become a problem about sensory qualities which cannot in principle also be described in words; and such a description in words will always have to be a description in terms of the relation of the quality in question to other sensory qualities.

---

[56] [In his *An Essay Concerning Human Understanding* (1690), John Locke (1634–1704) distinguishes between simple and complex ideas. The human mind—which Locke supposes to be at birth a tabula rasa—passively gains simple ideas through sensual experience (sight, hearing, touch, smell, and taste) and actively produces complex ideas from simple ideas through its powers of distinguishing, comparing, combining, and abstracting.—Ed.]

[57] W. James, 1890, vol. 2, p.12.

1.93. Most people will agree that the question of whether the sensory qualities which one person experiences are exactly the same as those which another person experiences is, in the absolute sense in which it is sometimes asked, an unanswerable and strictly meaningless question. All we can ever discuss is whether for different persons different sensory qualities differ in the same way. To establish whether a person is color-blind we have to find out, not how 'red' looks to him in any absolute sense, but whether and how it differs from various other shades of 'red' and from 'green'. In all such instances we can find out and know only whether, compared with other people, a person discriminates between given stimuli in the same or in a different manner.

1.94. In other words, all that can be communicated are the differences between sensory qualities, and only what can be communicated can be discussed. Such communication does not imply that the qualities perceived by different people are similar in any absolute sense. The problem which is raised, for instance, by the much greater capacity for pitch discrimination possessed by the experienced musician but not by ordinary persons is not fundamentally different from the problem created by the distinctions between the qualities which most of us experience.

1.95. It is instructive briefly to consider how we should proceed if we were to try to give a congenitally blind person an idea of sight and color. We should probably base our account in the first instance on the fact that the blind is familiar with three-dimensional space, with shape and movement, and attempt to explain to him that, as he can feel radiant heat or sound emitted by a distant source, so the eye enables us to perceive other qualities at a distance. We should then try to explain that these qualities with which he is unfamiliar will vary not only along a single dimension, as temperature does from cold to hot, but that it can also vary like tones from bright to dark, from loud to soft, from sharp to blunt, and from pleasant to unpleasant. We shall point out to him that in groups these qualities can form harmonies or may clash as tones do, and so on.

1.96. How far we could get in thus teaching a congenitally blind the relative values of the different colors has never been systematically tested, largely because the required description of the order of those sense qualities in terms of their common dimensions (1.62–1.67) has not been systematically developed and because we therefore lack the necessary words. That blind persons can at least learn to use the names of colors, so that a person who does not know that they are blind may remain unaware of it in hearing their descriptions, is shown by the writings of Miss Helen Keller[58] and others. Today, with

[58] [Helen Keller (1880–1968) was an American author and political activist who had, at the age of 19 months, contracted an illness that left her deaf and blind. Due to the support of her teacher and companion, Anne Sullivan, who had been trained at the Perkins Institute for the

our greater familiarity of the phenomenon of synaesthesia, it also no longer seems so absurd, as it seemed to John Locke, that the 'studious blind man' who thought that he had discovered what scarlet looked like, described it as 'like the sound of a trumpet.'[59]

1.97. An illustration given in a recent book may be quoted at length, as its concluding passage raises our problem in a particularly clear manner:

> 'The approach of a scientist to the phenomena which he observes may be realized perhaps by means of an analogy. Suppose you enter a room and see a man playing the violin. You say at once that this is a musical instrument and is producing sound. But suppose that the observer were absolutely deaf from birth, had no idea of hearing, and had never been told anything of sound or musical instruments, his whole knowledge of the world having been acquired through senses other than hearing. This deaf observer entering the room where a violinist was playing would be entirely unable to account for the phenomenon. He would see the movements of the player, the operation of the bow on the strings, the peculiarly shaped instrument, but the whole thing would appear to him irrational. But if he were a scientist interested in phenomena and their classification, he would presently find that the movements of the bow on the violin produced vibrations, and these vibrations could be detected by means of physical instruments, and their wave form could be observed. After some time, it might occur to him that the vibrations of the strings and violin must be communicated to the air and could be observed as changes of pressure. Then he could record the changes of pressure produced in the air in the playing of a piece of music, and by analysing the record could observe that the same groups of pressure changes were repeated periodically. Eventually he would attain to a knowledge of the whole phenomenon of music—the form of musical composition and the nature of different musical forms—but none of this would give him any approach to the absolute truth in that he would still be unaware of the existence of sound as sense and of the part that music could play in the mental life of those who could hear.'[60]

1.98. Except for the last sentence this passage provides an excellent illustration of the distinction we have drawn between the physical and the phenomenal order of events. The last sentence, however, raises two difficulties (apart

---

Blind, Keller learned, based on touch and smell, to experience her environment and to communicate. She learned not only her mother tongue English but also French and German, earned a BA, and became a prominent author and lecturer.—Ed.]

[59] John Locke, 1690, bk. III, chap. IV, sec. xi.

[60] C. E. K. Mees, 1946, p. 59.

from the fact that the author speaks of the 'phenomenon' of music where he refers to what we would describe as its physical equivalent). In the first instance the impression which this sentence conveys, that a 'knowledge of the whole phenomenon of music' can be attained without at the same time attaining some knowledge not only of the physical but also of the sensory attributes of these events, is somewhat misleading. A reconstruction of the theory of music in the manner suggested could involve a study not only of the 'objective' attributes of sound but also a study of the manner in which the people producing the music deal with it. It would, e.g., have to include the discovery that for the musicians the continuum of sound waves of different frequencies was divided into discrete steps, so that all the waves belonging to certain narrow intervals were treated as alike or indistinguishable, while wave-lengths of intermediate intervals would not be employed at all; further, that of the distinct musical notes thus determined some were treated as resembling each other and some as being related in other ways, that certain combinations of notes were preferred to others, and that certain successions of notes were in some respects treated as equivalents of other such successions, etc., etc.

1.99. The theory of music thus constructed would therefore not really refer to the relations between physical events or to relations between them defined according to the similarity or difference of their action on other physical events, but to elements defined in terms of their similarity or dissimilarity to the persons who wrote, played, or heard the music. It would be a theory, not about the objective (experimentally tested) relations between the different physical events, but about what these events meant to the persons concerned with music.

1.100. The second problem arising from the concluding sentence of the passage quoted is contained in the suggestion that there is an 'absolute truth', an absolute quality of sound as a sensory experience which must forever remain inaccessible to the deaf from birth. The term 'absolute' used in this connection unquestionably refers to some significant aspects of sensory experience. What we are denying is not that sensory qualities may possess attributes which those who cannot hear cannot learn about, but that whatever incommunicable attributes sensory qualities may possess can ever raise a scientific problem.

1.101. One fact which is probably referred to by the use of the term 'absolute' in this connection is that, however far we may go in describing or explaining differences between sensory qualities, there will always remain some further differences which have not yet been enumerated. This is closely connected with a circumstance which we shall have to consider later, namely that, because of constitutional limitations of our mind, we shall never be able to achieve more than an explanation of the principle on which mind operates, and shall never succeed in fully explaining any particular mental act. But the fact that the differences between the different sensory qualities are too numerous and varied for us ever to be able to state them all does not mean that any one of these differences should not be capable of becoming a problem to which, at least in principle, we may provide an answer.

1.102. It is merely another aspect of the same problem if it is pointed out that the immediate experience of a group of sensory qualities (say a number of sounds and colors) will always convey more to us (will involve a large number of implied distinctions among themselves and from other possible experiences) than any possible description can convey. In other words: the congenitally blind or deaf can never learn *all* that which the seeing or hearing person owes to the direct experience of the sensory qualities in question, because no description can exhaust all the distinctions which are experienced. This, however, does not mean that there is more than differences from other qualities, and still less that any such 'absolute' character of the qualities can raise a genuine problem.

1.103. It seems thus impossible that any question about the nature or character of particular sensory qualities should ever arise which is not a question about the differences from (or the relations to) other sensory qualities; and the extent to which the effects of its occurrence differ from the effects of the occurrence of any other qualities determines the whole of its character.

1.104. To ask beyond this for the explanation of some absolute attribute of sensory qualities seems to be to ask for something which by definition cannot manifest itself in any differences in the consequences which will follow because this rather than any other quality has occurred. Such a factor, however, could by definition not be of relevance to any scientific problem. The 'absolute' quality seems to be unexplainable because there is nothing to explain, because absolute, if it has any meaning at all, can only mean that the attribute which is so described has no scientific significance.

1.105. The contention that all the attributes of sensory qualities (and of other mental qualities) are relations to other such qualities, and that the totality of all these relations between mental qualities exhausts all there is to be said about the mental order, corresponds, of course, (perhaps we should say follows from) to the conception of mind itself as an order of events. And with the recognition that mind itself and all the attributes of mental events are a complex of relations, there disappears of course the need for any peculiar kind of things which by themselves have attributes which constitute them a peculiar 'substance'.

1.106. The abandonment of the phantom-problem of the absolute character of mental qualities, and the recognition of the relative significance of these attributes, is of fundamental importance, because it opens, as we shall see, the way for a general application of a principle which has long been used to explain those attributes of sensory experience which had been recognized to be relative, such as spatial position.

1.107. It also follows from the relative character of all mental qualities that any discussion of these qualities in terms of their relations to each other must necessarily remain within the realm of mental events: it can never provide a bridge which leads from them to physical events. In the next chapter we shall attempt to show how this circle can be broken.

CHAPTER II

AN OUTLINE OF THE THEORY

1. The Principle of the Explanation

2.1. The first chapter led to the conclusion that the sensory qualities known to us from our subjective experience form a self-contained system so that we can describe any one of these qualities only in terms of its relations to other such qualities, and that many of these relations themselves also belong to the qualitative order. This means that, if in our attempt toward an explanation we are to move in a circle but are to succeed in explaining the relation of this system of qualities to the world of physics, the object of our explanation must be the whole complex of relations which determine the order of the system of sensory (or rather of mental) qualities. In order to provide such an explanation, it will be necessary to show how in a physical system known forces can produce such differentiating relationships between its elements that an order will appear which strictly corresponds to the order of the sensory qualities.

2.2. The only way in which we can break the circle in which we move so long as we discuss sensory qualities in terms of each other, and can hope to arrive at an explanation of the processes of which the occurrence of sensory qualities forms a part, therefore, is to construct a system of physical elements which is 'topologically equivalent' or 'isomorphous' with the system of sensory qualities; this means that the relations of the former must strictly reproduce the relations prevailing in the latter so that the effect of any group of events in the former will correspond to the effects of the corresponding group of events in the latter.

2.3. The mathematical concept of isomorphism has been used by the members of the Gestalt school[1] in a sense somewhat similar to that in which it is employed here. The use made of it by that school is, however, somewhat ambiguous and imprecise and I am not certain whether it is the same as that employed here. It is therefore important to remember that, whenever the term isomorphism is used in the following discussion, it will be used in its strict

---

[1] W. Köhler, 1929, p. 61f.; K. Koffka, 1935, p. 62. For the different sense in which this concept is used by E. G. Boring, see below, 2.10.

mathematical meaning of a structural correspondence between systems of related elements in which the relations connecting these elements possess the same formal properties, rather than in any sense borrowed directly from the Gestalt school.

2.4. It is especially important to realize that the isomorphism of two structures does not, as some of the discussions by the Gestalt school suggest, imply similarity of their arrangement in space. Although two three-dimensional structures which are similar in the geometrical meaning of this term will also be isomorphous, such spatial similarity is not necessary. If the relevant relationship is, e.g., connectedness, and we conceive of a three-dimensional net or lattice of rubber threads in which the knots represent the elements and the threads the connections, isomorphism will be preserved however much we stretch, twist or crumple up the net: Since in this process of spatial distortion the relevant relations between the elements are preserved so long as no thread is broken and no new knots formed, all these various states of the net or lattice would be isomorphous. It will have to be remembered throughout this book that whenever we speak, e.g., of a 'pattern within the brain', the term pattern and similar terms will have to be understood in this topological and not in a spatial meaning.

2.5. The importance of not interpreting isomorphism as spatial similarity will be seen from the fact, for instance, that in a system in which the position of one element is determined by the connections with other elements, two distinct elements may occupy identical positions, which is clearly impossible in a spatial sense: Two distinct points in space cannot have identical spatial relations to every one of a group of other points, but each of two distinct elements of a merely 'connectional' order can be connected with the identical set of other elements. This in fact applies not only to individual elements but also to sub-groups of connected elements within the larger structure which, without being isomorphous with each other, may yet, considered as groups, occupy identical places in the larger structure, i.e., may as a group of elements have connections with the same other elements.

2.6. Isomorphism thus describes only a similarity of structures as wholes and of the position of corresponding elements within the structure, but says nothing about any other properties of the corresponding elements apart from their position in the structure. Such individual properties of the elements from which the structure is built are totally irrelevant for the question of whether the two structures are isomorphous; and isomorphism may not only exist between structures made of different materials but even between material and immaterial structures so long as there exist any common formal attributes of the relations which connect the elements.

2.7. In the application of the concept of isomorphism to psychological problems there has been a good deal of confusion with regard to the terms or structures which might be said to be isomorphous. There are three such different structures, any pair of which might be and has been represented as the terms between which isomorphism prevails. There are:

1. The physical order of the external world, or of the physical stimuli, which for the present purpose we must assume to be known, although our knowledge of it is, of course, imperfect.
2. The neural order of the fibers, and of the impulses proceeding in these fibers, which, though undoubtedly part of the complete physical order, is yet a part of it which is not directly known but can only be reconstructed.
3. The mental or phenomenal order of sensations (and other mental qualities) directly known although our knowledge of it is largely only a 'knowing how' and not a 'knowing that',[2] and although we may never be able to bring out by analysis all the relations which determine that order.

2.8. Our problem is determined partly by the fact that the first and third of these orders are not isomorphous, i.e., that the physical order differs from the phenomenal order. Although the problem would also exist if these two orders were isomorphous (if that is conceivable), we might never, or at least not for a long time, have become aware of its character if it were not for the fact of the difference of these two orders. While they are in some measure similar, and while we owe it to this similarity that we can find our way about the physical world, they are, as we have seen, far from being identical.

2.9. The isomorphism which we have suggested to exist refers to the relation between the second and the third of these orders, i.e., to the relation between the neural and the phenomenal order. If this is correct, and if the first and the third of these orders are not isomorphous, it also follows that the first and the second cannot be isomorphous. (That the second cannot be strictly isomorphous with the first also follows from the fact that strictly speaking it is a part of the first.)

2.10. Isomorphism between two structures or orders does not imply isomorphism between any properties their elements may possess apart from their place in the structure. This needs special emphasis as the term isomorphism has been used by Boring[3] to describe a correspondence between individual mental events (i.e., parts of our third order) and individual physical and neural events. He speaks of 'isomorphic transmission' of some constant structural feature from the stimulus through the impulse to the sensation, and in this sense the concept of isomorphism would indeed, as he points out, be merely a form of the naïve conception against which Johannes Müller's theory of the

[2] G. Ryle, 1945–46.
[3] E. G. Boring, 1935, p. 244; 1936, pp. 574–75; and 1942, pp. 83–90.

specific energy of nerves was directed. It is possible that in the vague use made of the concept by the Gestalt school this meaning has been mixed up with the other one, but it need hardly be stressed that it has nothing to do with the sense in which the concept is employed here.

2.11. It should be pointed out at once, however, that our use of the term isomorphism, though useful for the purposes of exposition at this stage, will in the end also prove somewhat inappropriate. We are at present concerned with the relations of an inferred order, the terms of which are unknown (since they are left without attributes if we regard all mental attributes as determined by relations), with an order which might be established between the known neural elements. We shall, in fact, come to the conclusion that the two orders are not merely isomorphous but identical and that to postulate a separate set of terms for the mental order would be redundant. But at this step in the exposition we shall content ourselves to ask whether a topological equivalent of the mental order can be reconstructed from physical elements.

2.12. Another misunderstanding to which the use of the conception of a one-to-one correspondence in the discussion of isomorphism could give rise should at once be met. It is the old idea that individual stimuli and individual nervous impulses are invariably and uniquely related with particular individual sensory qualities. This cardinal error which, it will soon be seen, has been the main obstacle to the understanding of our problem, follows by no means from the conception of isomorphism as used here. On the contrary, if the action of an impulse depends on the position of the fiber that carries it, in the whole system of connected fibers, it would seem at once probable that its effects will depend on what other impulses are proceeding at the same time. Although at any given time (or within any given structure) any particular group of impulses occurring at the same time will have the same significance, there is no reason to expect that the effects of a single impulse will be the same whether it appears in company with one group or with another group of other impulses.

2.13. This particular misunderstanding of the idea of a one-to-one correspondence between impulse and sensation has been persistently and successfully criticized by the members of the Gestalt school[4] under the name of the 'constancy hypothesis'. Their experimental work has amply confirmed that

---

[4] W. Köhler, 1913, p. 52; K. Koffka, 1935, pp. 85ff.; and D. Katz, 1944 for a clear distinction between this 'constancy hypothesis' and the 'constancy phenomenon', i.e. the fact that different stimuli and different combinations of stimuli can produce the same sensory qualities. [David Katz (1884–1953) was a German experimental psychologist who had worked as an assistant with G. E. Müller in Göttingen. He was a professor of psychology at the University of Rostock from 1919 to 1933 when the National Socialists expelled him from his position. After an interim stay in England he moved to Sweden in 1937, where he taught at the University of Stockholm.—Ed.]

such an invariable connection between individual impulse and elementary sensations does not exist.

2.14. Closely connected with this 'constancy hypothesis' is the conception of an 'invariable core of pure sensation' which is supposed to be in some manner originally attached to the nervous impulse and to continue to exist independently of all the modifications of, and additions to, this basic quality which may be effected by experience or acquired relations. Bertrand Russell, e.g., explicitly states with reference to this that 'the essence of sensation . . . is its independence of past experience.'[5]

2.15. It has, of course, long been a common place in psychology that a large part of the experienced content of the sensory qualities is the result of interpretation based on experience. But these relational determinants of sensory qualities have invariably been represented as mere modifications of, or additions to, an original core of pure sensation.[6] It will be the central thesis of the theory to be outlined that it is not merely a part but the whole of sensory qualities which is in this sense an 'interpretation' based on the experience of the individual or the race. The conception of an original pure core of sensation which is merely modified by experience is an entirely unnecessary fiction, and the same processes which are known to modify and alter the qualitative attributes of sensations can also account for the initial differentiation.

2.16. With this contention we do not mean to assert that the 'learning' process which can account for the determination of the order of sensory qualities takes place entirely or pre-dominantly in the course of the development of the individual. In this sense our contention does not take side in the dispute between the 'nativists' and the 'empiricists'. But this dispute seems usually to involve also the distinct question whether the order of sensory qualities can be understood as having been formed by the combined experience of the race and the individual, or whether it must be regarded as something unaccountably and unexplainably existing apart from the effects which the environment exercises on the development of the organism. In this second sense our thesis belongs to the 'empiricist' position (see 5.15).

2.17. It might indeed be said that the whole theory of the formation of sensory qualities to be developed in the following pages is no more than an extension and systematic development of the widely held view that every sensation contains elements of interpretation based on learning, an extension by

[5] B. Russell, 1921, p. 144. Cf., also ibid., p. 139. [In the preface to his *Analysis of the Mind* (1921)—in which he thanks John B. Watson for "many valuable suggestions" on an earlier draft—Bertrand Russell (1872–1970) notes that his book is an attempt to reconcile the "materialistic tendency" of behaviorist psychology with the "anti-materialistic tendency" of Einstein's physics, building on the "view of William James and the American new realists" (see 8.38 below).—Ed.]

[6] For an account of these historical antecedents see chapter VI.

which the *whole* of the sensory qualities is accounted for as such an interpretation. It will be contended that in the course of its phylogenetic and ontogenetic development the organism learns to build up a system of differentiations between stimuli in which each stimulus is given a definite place in an order, a place which represents the significance which the occurrence of that stimulus in different combinations with other stimuli has for the organism. We shall see later in what sense and to what extent this 'classification' (as we shall call it) of the stimuli by the organism can be said to 'reproduce' the relations between those stimuli in the physical world.

2.18. It should, however, at once be noted, although a fuller discussion of this must be postponed to a later point,[7] that when we claim to provide an 'explanation' this will never mean more than an 'explanation of the principle' by which phenomena of the kind in question can be produced. By such an 'explanation of the principle' we shall provisionally understand an explanation which not only confines itself to showing 'that such and such actions lie within the range of known physical actions, or that known physical phenomena produce effects similar to them',[8] but also that, though we may be able to explain the general character of the processes at work, their operation may be so complicated in detail as to place their full description forever beyond the power of the human mind.

2.19. The reason for confining ourselves to such an 'explanation of the principle' is, therefore, not only that in the present state of psychology and neuro-physiology the main need seems to be for a hypothesis suggesting a possible way in which the phenomena in question may be produced, but also that there appear to exist reasons which should make for man a *full* explanation of his own processes of thought absolutely impossible, because this conception involves, as we hope to show, a contradiction.

2. The Order of Sensory Qualities in Its Static and Its Dynamic Aspects

2.20. It is necessary now to examine a little more carefully than we have yet done the character of the various 'relations' existing between the sensory qualities. It would seem at first as if the fact which we have pointed out (1.56–1.61), that these 'relations' possess themselves different qualitative attributes, would constitute an absolute obstacle to any attempt to reproduce an equivalent or isomorphous physical system built up from the known physiological

---

[7] See chapter VIII below.

[8] D. W. Thompson, 1942, p. 309. Cf., also E. G. Boring, 1946, p. 178, where he argues that 'it is enough for our purpose if we can produce the function *in kind*' and 'if we could *get the principle* of [the suggested synthetic professor of psychology] without actually producing him.' (Italics ours.)

173

processes, since in the latter case the different elements can be ordered solely by the one relation of cause and effect. We have provisionally met this difficulty by pointing out that differences in quality can also be reduced to differences in the effects, but it clearly needs yet more explicit consideration.

2.21. This problem is closely connected with what may be called the difference between the 'static' and the 'dynamic' aspect of the system of sensory qualities. We usually think of all the different sensory qualities as (at least potentially) existing at the same time, and it is this imagined simultaneous existence to which we refer when we speak of the 'static' aspect of the whole order. But as we have tried to show (1.38–1.55), all the questions which we can meaningfully ask about the differences between these qualities must necessarily refer to the different effects which in different combinations they will exercise on succeeding events: on how their appearance in a given situation affects our estimation of the other elements of the situation and so on. This is the system of qualities seen in its dynamic aspect. We shall later (2.44, 3.51, 5.42) see that the neural counterpart of the system of sensory qualities can similarly be regarded under the static aspect of an apparatus capable of performing the various discriminations, or dynamically by describing the various processes which it can perform.

2.22. Even when we imagine the system of sensory qualities as existing as a whole at a given moment, we do not mean that we ever have images of all the possible sensory qualities. What we mean when we think of that system as complete at any moment is, that we could, as it were, run through it proceeding from one quality to similar qualities, and by thus moving along all the possible dimensions, ultimately exhaust all possibilities. Even the 'static' system is thus in fact a sequence of images causally connected in complex ways.

2.23. The validity of the contention that all that can become a problem are the different effects which the different qualities produce will depend on what in this connection we include under 'effects'. If, with the strict behaviorists, we were to confine the term 'effects' to externally observable behavior (overt action or other peripheral responses) the contention could certainly not be defended. There is no justification, however, for that exclusive concentration on overt action which, under the influence of behaviorism, has been the fashion in psychology during the last thirty years. Physiological research during the same period has rather made it clearer than ever that we cannot hope to account for observed behavior without reconstructing the 'intervening processes in the brain'.[9]

2.24. It would indeed be absurd to recognize differences in the responses only in so far as they manifest themselves in overt behavior and to disregard our subjective knowledge of discrimination: not only because such an attempt

[9] C. T. Morgan, 1943, p. 476.

could not be carried through consistently (1.84–1.88), but also because we know that the central nervous system provides an apparatus for just the kind of processes which, although they elude direct observation, can be shown to be necessary to bring about the observable results.[10] Any attempt to explain the distinction between sensory qualities in terms of peripheral responses was bound to fail, because there are no unique responses attached to particular stimuli. As we shall presently see, there is a process of multiple classification inserted between stimulus and response which makes it possible for the response to take account of the significance which the stimulus has in the context of other (external and internal) stimuli.

2.25. We shall have to show later (4.35–4.41) how this exclusive emphasis on peripheral responses is also misleading because, even in so far as peripheral responses contribute to the discrimination between stimuli, they can affect the further course of the mental processes only through the proprioceptive impulses[11] (the 'feedback') by which they in turn are centrally recorded; even in these instances the decisive factors are therefore not the motor responses themselves, but the sensory impulses which they send back to the higher centers. We shall then see that it is also at least highly probable that, once a direct connection has been established between the initial sensory impulse and the impulse recording the motor response evoked by it, the actual motor response becomes unnecessary for the continued functioning of this particular mechanism.

2.26. Once we include among the 'effects' of a stimulus all the intermediate links which may intervene between the stimulus causing a sensation and the overt response to it, the difficulty of defining sensory qualities in terms of their effects largely disappears. Whether we speak in terms of the physiological processes or in terms of the sensory qualities which they evoke, we shall find that the relevant differences between the individual events consist in the different immediate effects which they produce in different combinations. Each event or group of events will be distinguished from most others by the fact that it will evoke a particular set of other events. The ultimate overt response may thus be brought about *via* a long series of intermediate links which in the neural process cannot be directly observed but can only be reconstructed from what we know of the mental counterparts of these processes and of those marginal overt responses to which the latter lead.

2.27. The apparent paradox that certain relations between non-mental events should turn them into mental events resolves itself as soon as we accept the definition of mind as a peculiar order. Any individual neural event may have physical properties which are similar or different from other such events

---

[10] C. C. Pratt, 1939, p. 147.

[11] [Below in 4.8, Hayek defines proprioceptive impulses as "those impulses which record not external stimuli but various states of different parts of the organism."—Ed.]

if investigated in isolation. But, irrespective of the properties which those events will possess by themselves, they will possess others solely as a result of their position in the order of inter-connected neural events. As an isolated event, tested for its effects on all sorts of other such events, it will show one set of properties and therefore have to be assigned a particular place in the order or classification of such single events; as an element of the complete neural structure it may show quite different properties.

2.28. That an order of events is something different from the properties of the individual events, and that the same order of events can be formed from elements of a very different individual character, can be illustrated from a great number of different fields. The same pattern of movements may be performed by a swarm of fireflies, a flock of birds, a number of toy balloons or perhaps a flight of aeroplanes; the same machine, a bicycle or a cotton gin, a lathe, a telephone exchange or an adding machine, can be constructed from a large variety of materials and yet remains the same kind of machine within which elements of different individual properties will perform the same functions. So long as the elements, whatever other properties they may possess, are capable of acting upon each other in the manner determining the structure of the machine, their other properties are irrelevant for our understanding of the machine.[12]

2.29. In the same sense the peculiar properties of the elementary neural events which are the terms of the mental order[13] have nothing to do with that order itself. What we have called physical properties of those events are those properties which will appear if they are placed in a variety of experimental relations to different other kinds of events. The mental properties are those which they possess only as a part of the particular structure and which may be largely independent of the former. It is at least conceivable that the particular kind of order which we call mind might be built up from any one of several kinds of different elements—electrical, chemical, or what not; all that is required is that by the simple relationship of being able to evoke each other in a certain order they correspond to the structure which we call mind.

2.30. That a particular order of events or objects is something different from all the individual events taken separately is the significant fact behind the endless and unprofitable talk about 'the whole being greater than the mere sum of its parts'. Of course, an order does not arise from the parts being thrown together in a heap, and one arrangement of a given set of parts may constitute something different from another arrangement of the same set of

[12] We are deliberately not using here the even greater number of examples of an order existing irrespective of the character of the elements of which it consists, in which in any way mental factors are involved, such as, e.g., in the relation between a poem in its printed and in its spoken form, etc.

[13] E. G. Boring, 1933, p. 233.

parts. An order involves elements *plus* certain relations between them, and the same order or structure may be formed by any elements capable of entering into the same relations to each other. The capacity of entering into such a relation is, of course, a property of the elements as much as any of those other properties which are irrelevant so far as the particular order is concerned. A particular order can exist as little without elements possessing that capacity, as the elements without the order in which they are related to each other would possess the particular significance which they have in that order. But it is only when we understand how the elements are related to each other that the talk about the whole being more than the parts becomes more than an empty phrase. All that theoretical biology has in this respect to say on the significance of structural properties as distinct from the properties of the elements, and about the significance of 'organization'[14], is directly applicable to our problem.

2.31. The question which thus arises for us is how it is possible to construct from the known elements of the neural system a structure which would be capable of performing such discrimination in its responses to stimuli as we know our mind in fact to perform.

3. The Principle of Classification

2.32. The phenomena with which we are here concerned are commonly discussed in psychology under the heading of 'discrimination'. This term is somewhat misleading because it suggests a sort of 'recognition' of physical differences between the events which it discriminates, while we are concerned with a process which *creates* the distinctions in question. The same is true of most of the other available words which might be used, such as 'to sort out', 'to differentiate', or 'to classify'. The only appropriate term which is tolerably free from misleading connotations would appear to be 'grouping'.[15]

---

[14]J. H. Woodger, 1929, p. 291 and *passim*. [Joseph Henry Woodger (1894–1981) was a British theoretical biologist and philosopher of biology. In 1926, Woodger had paid a research visit to the Institute of Biology in Vienna. He became a close colleague and friend of Ludwig von Bertalanffy (see above, preface, fn. 14). He prepared an English translation and adaptation of Bertalanffy's 1928 book, *Kritische Theorie der Formbildung* (Berlin: Borntraeger), published as *Modern Theories of Development: An Introduction to Theoretical Biology* (London: Oxford University Press, 1933).—Ed.]; L. von Bertalanffy, 1942 and 1949.

[15]'Grouping' was used somewhat in this same sense by G. H. Lewes, 1879, Problem III, chapter 3, §§ 33 and 34 [George Henry Lewes (1817–78) was an English philosopher who, while being influenced by the positivism of Auguste Comte, stressed the need to combine objective methods with introspection in psychological research.—Ed.], and more recently by J. Piaget, 1947. [Jean Piaget (1896–1980) was a Swiss development psychologist who is known for his studies on the cognitive development of children, establishing the field of *genetic epistemology*. He

2.33. For the purposes of the following discussion it will nevertheless be convenient to adopt the term 'to classify' with its corresponding nouns 'classes' and 'classification' in a special technical meaning. The next few paragraphs will serve solely to make precise the exact meaning in which we propose to use this term. We shall at first consider extremely simple processes of classification which will have little resemblance to the more complex kinds which are relevant to our main task. Our present purpose will be more to make clear what the principle of classification as such involves, than to show how it operates in the nervous system.

2.34. By 'classification' we shall mean a process in which on each occasion on which a certain recurring event happens it produces the same specific effect, and where the effects produced by any one kind of such events may be either the same or different from those which any other kind of event produces in a similar manner. All the different events which whenever they occur produce the same effect will be said to be events of the same class, and the fact that every one of them produces the same effect will be the *sole* criterion which makes them members of the same class.

2.35. We may conceive of a machine constructed for the purpose of performing simple processes of classification of this kind. We can, for instance, imagine a machine which 'sorts out' balls of various size which are placed into it by distributing them between different receptacles. We will assume that no two balls have the same size so that size is merely a means of identifying the individual balls. Indeed we shall even assume that no two balls have any property in common which they do not share with every other ball in the set, so that there are not 'objective' similarities peculiar to the different members of any sub-group or class of these balls; any grouping of different balls by the machine which places them into the same receptacle will create a class which is based exclusively on the action of the machine and not on any similarity which those balls possess apart from the action of the machine.[16]

2.36. We may find, for instance, that the machine will always place the balls with a diameter of 16, 18, 28, 31, 32, and 40 mm in a receptacle marked *A*, the balls with a diameter of 17, 22, 30, and 35 in a receptacle marked *B*, and so forth. The balls placed by the machine into the same receptacle will then

---

distinguished four stages of intellectual development—"sensori-motor (up to 2 years), pre-operational (2–7 years), concrete operational (7–11 years), formal operational (11 years and up)"—using the child's ability of "classification" (i.e., the ability to group objects on the basis of common features) as an essential defining category.—Ed.]

[16] J. Piaget, 1947, p. 45: 'Un concept de classe n'est psychologiquement que l'expression de l'identité de réaction du sujet vis-à-vis des objets qu'il réunit en une classe.' [In the English edition, *The Psychology of Intelligence* (London: Routledge & Kegan, 1950), 34, this sentence is translated as: "Psychologically, a class-concept is only the expression of the identity of the subject's reaction to objects which he combines in one class."—Ed.]

be said to belong to the same class, and the balls placed by it into different receptacles to belong to so many different classes. The fact that a ball is placed by the machine into a particular receptacle thus forms the sole criterion for assigning it to a particular class.

2.37. Another kind of machine performing this simplest kind of classification might be conceived as in a similar fashion sorting out individual signals arriving through any one of a large number of wires or tubes. We shall regard here any signal arriving through one particular wire or tube as the same recurring event which will always lead to the same action of the machine. The machine would respond similarly also to signals arriving through some different tubes or wires, and any such group to which the machine responded in the same manner would be regarded as events of the same class. Such a machine would act like a simplified telephone exchange in which each of a number of incoming wires was permanently connected with, say, a particular bell, so that any signal coming in on any one of these wires would ring that bell. All the wires connected with any one bell would then carry signals belonging to the same class.

2.38. An actual instance of a machine of this kind is provided by certain statistical machines for sorting cards on which punched holes represent statistical data. If we regard the appearance of any card with the same data punched on it as the recurrence of the same event, and assume that the machine is so arranged that various groups of different data are placed into the same receptacle, we should have a machine which performs a classification in the sense in which we use this term.

4. Multiple Classification

2.39. In the kind of simple classification which we have just considered, any one of the individual recurrent events is always grouped with the same group of other events and with them only. But the same principle can effect what may be called multiple classification: at any moment a given event may be treated as a member of more than one class, each of these classes containing also different other events; and a given event may also on different occasions be assigned to different classes according to the accompanying events with which it occurs. The classification may thus be 'multiple' in more than one respect. Not only may each individual event belong to more than one class, but it may also contribute to produce different responses of the machine if and only if it occurs in combination with certain other events. Different groups consisting of different individual events may in this manner evoke the same response and the machine would then classify not only individual events but also groups consisting of a number of (simultaneous or successive) events. In this latter case the groups (or sequences) of individual events would as groups constitute the elements of the different classes.

2.40. The first kind of multiple classifications could be performed, for instance, by a machine similar to the first we have imagined if, instead of placing the balls into different receptacles, it were to show different signs, say lights of different colors, every time a ball is placed into it. A ball to which the machine responded by showing a red and a green light would then belong to two classes of balls, that of all balls evoking a red light and that of all balls evoking a green light. Or, in the case of the second kind of machine described before, which performs the classification by establishing connections with different bells, each incoming signal might be passed on to more than one bell and belong accordingly to a corresponding number of different classes.

2.41. The second type of multiple classification would be represented by a machine whose responses depended not only on the individual events to be classified but also on the combinations in which they occurred. The classification of the groups of events by such a machine might be either additional to the classification of the individual events, or occur in the place of it, so that the individual event which if it occurred in isolation evoked, say, a green light, would not do so, but contribute to produce a blue light if it occurred at the same time with, or within a short interval of certain other events.

2.42. We shall later (3.52–3.57) have to consider yet a third type of multiple classification: namely one in which successive acts of classification follow upon each other in relays, or on different 'levels'; in this type the distinct responses which effect the grouping at a first level become in turn subject to a further classification (which also may be multiple in both the former senses). This is probably the most important characteristic of the particular kind of classificatory mechanism which the nervous system represents; but while we are merely concerned to bring out certain general principles, we shall disregard this aspect until the next chapter.

2.43. In the system of classification in which we shall be interested the different individual events will be the recurrent impulses arriving through afferent fibers at the various centers of the nervous system. For the purposes of this discussion we shall have to assume that these individual impulses possess no significant individual properties which distinguish them from one another. They must be regarded initially as what the logician describes an 'uninterpreted set of marks'. Our task will be to show how the kind of mechanism which the central nervous system provides may arrange this set of undifferentiated events in an order which possesses the same formal structure as the order of sensory qualities.[17]

---

[17] For a somewhat similar statement of the problems of the order of sensory qualities see R. Carnap, 1928. [Rudolf Carnap (1891–1970) was a German-born philosopher and leading

2.44. Throughout the discussion of that neural apparatus of classification it will be important to keep in mind the distinction between the structural and the functional (or the static and the dynamic) aspect of that mechanism (2.20–2.31). The elements of the (anatomical) structure will be the different fibers; the elements of the (physiological) process will be the impulses conducted by these fibers. It will be the impulses which (as individuals or groups) will be the object of the classificatory process.

2.45. Our task will thus be to show how these undifferentiated individual impulses or groups of impulses may obtain such a position in a system of relations to each other that in their functional significance they will resemble one another or differ from another in a manner which corresponds strictly to the relations between the sensory qualities which are evoked by them.

5. The Central Thesis

2.46. We shall maintain that a classification of the sensory impulses which produces an order strictly analogous to the order of sensory qualities can be effected by a system of connections through which the impulses can be transmitted from fiber to fiber; and that such a system of connections which is structurally equivalent to the order of sensory qualities will be built up if, in the course of the development of the species or the individual, connections are established between fibers in which impulses occur at the same time.

2.47. That such connections through which impulses are transmitted are created as a result of the simultaneous occurrence of sensory impulses is an almost universally accepted hypothesis which seems indeed indispensable if we are to account for such well-established facts as conditioned reflexes,[18] even though we do not yet know exactly how they are established or maintained. For the purposes of our argument it is irrelevant whether the establishment of such connections involves, as used to be generally assumed, a change in the anatomical structure of the central nervous system (such as the 'formation of new paths'), or whether, as some more recent investigations suggest, they are

---

exponent of logical positivism. He insisted on the logical analysis of language as the principal instrument in philosophy, rejecting metaphysical statements as meaningless because they cannot be proved or disproved by experience. He submitted his first major work, *Der logische Aufbau der Welt*, in 1926 as habilitation thesis at the University of Vienna, where he became a prominent figure in the Vienna Circle. In Vienna he taught as Privatdozent until 1931 when he took an appointment at the German University in Prague. In 1936 he immigrated to the United States, where he first taught at the University of Chicago and later at Princeton University (1952–54) and the University of California, Los Angeles (until 1961).—Ed.]

[18] More recently the occurrence of such connections between sensory impulses has also been established by psychological experiments by W. J. Brogden, 1939, 1942, 1947, and 1950.

based on physiological or functional changes, such as the setting up of some continuous circular flow of impulses in certain pre-existing channels.[19]

2.48. The transmission of impulses from neuron to neuron within the central nervous system, which is thus conceived as constituting the apparatus of classification, may either take place between different neurons carrying primary impulses, or between such neurons and other ('internuncial') neurons which are not directly connected with receptor organs. In the former instance the same event, an impulse in an afferent neuron, may occur either as the primary object of classification or as a 'symbol' classifying some other primary impulse. But since, as we shall see, all impulses, whether primary or secondary in this sense, are likely to be subject to further acts of classification, and therefore to appear both as instruments and as objects of classification, this merely complicates the picture but does not alter the general character of the process.

2.49. The point on which the theory of the determination of mental qualities, which will be more fully developed in the next chapter, differs from the position taken by practically all current psychological theories[20] is thus the contention that the sensory (or other mental) qualities are not in some manner originally attached to, or an original attribute of, the individual physiological impulses, but that the whole of these qualities is determined by the system of connections by which the impulses can be transmitted from neuron to neuron; that it is thus the position of the individual impulse or group of impulses in the whole system of such connections which gives it its distinctive quality; that this system of connections is acquired in the course of the development of the species and the individual by a kind of 'experience' or 'learning'; and that it reproduces therefore at every stage of its development certain relationships existing in the physical environment between the stimuli evoking the impulses. (We shall see in chapter IV that this 'physical environment' within which the central nervous system operates includes the *milieu intérieur*, i.e., the organism itself in so far as it acts independently of the higher nervous centers; and in chapter V how this 'experience' differs from experience in the ordinary meaning of the word.)

2.50. This central contention may also be expressed more briefly by saying that 'we do not first have sensations which are then preserved by memory, but it is as a result of physiological memory that the physiological impulses are converted into sensations. The connections between the physiological elements are thus the primary phenomenon which creates the mental phenomena.'[21]

---

[19] For an account of these newer views see E. R. Hilgard and D. G. Marquis, 1940, p. 330.

[20] The closest approximation to the theory developed here seems to have been reached by D. O. Hebb, 1949, a work which came to my knowledge only after the present book was completed in all essentials.

[21] The quotation is a translation from the early German draft of the present work (1920) referred to in the Preface. [See "Contributions," this volume, p. 327.—Ed.]

2.51. Although suggestions of a theory of mental phenomena on these lines are implicit in much of the current discussion of those problems by physiological psychologists, the consequences of a systematic application of this basic idea appear never to have been worked out consistently. What follows is little more than an attempt to elaborate the main implications of this thesis. It will be seen that its consistent development leads to rather important conclusions and assists in the clearing up of several old puzzles.

CHAPTER III

THE NERVOUS SYSTEM AS AN INSTRUMENT OF CLASSIFICATION

1. An Inventory of the Physiological Data

3.1. Before we can attempt to state in greater detail the theory sketched in the preceding chapter, it will be necessary to take stock of the essential anatomical and physiological facts which we shall have to use as bricks from which to construct an apparatus of the kind we are seeking. For our purpose it will not be necessary to concern ourselves with the structure and the functioning of the central nervous system in any great detail. It will suffice if we briefly note certain general characteristics of its parts and of the processes taking place in them. The simplifications which we shall employ must be justified by the fact that our aim is not so much to elaborate a theory which is correct in every detail, as to show how any theory of this kind can account for the mental events with which we are concerned.

3.2. According to an almost universally held view the nervous system is built up, like the rest of the organism, from a large number of separate cells. These cells, called neurons, consist of a cell body and two kinds of attaching processes, the axon and the dendrites. Although some doubt has recently been expressed concerning this 'neuron theory', and the alternative theory of an essential continuity of the system of nervous fibers has been put forward,[1] we shall state the main facts in terms of the pre-dominant view, since confirmation of the alternative theory would not significantly affect the conclusions at which we arrive from the former. The main facts which we shall have to take into account may then be stated as follows:

3.3. The cerebral cortex is the highest and most complex of several 'bridges' which connect the afferent fibers conducting impulses from the peripheral receptors, and the efferent fibers conducting impulses to the motor organs. We must thus conceive of the central nervous system (and probably also of the cortex itself) as a hierarchy consisting of many superimposed levels of connections, all of which may be concerned in the transmission of impulses

[1] For a brief summary of the recent German work on the alleged 'continuity of the nervous system' see W. Bargmann, 1947, and for a criticism, N.-A. Hillarp, 1946.

from the afferent (sensory) to the efferent (motor) fibers. This conception of a hierarchy of centers or levels does, of course, not imply that these levels can always be sharply separated, either structurally or functionally, or that they are superimposed upon each other in a simple linear order.

3.4. The number of separate nerve cells within these centers by far exceeds the number of afferent fibers conducting impulses to them and of the efferent fibers conducting impulses from them. The cerebral cortex alone has been estimated to contain about ten thousand million separate cells while the number of afferent and efferent fibers is of the order of magnitude of a few millions only. The number of distinct afferent fibers reaching the cortex is also considerably lower than the number of distinct sensory receptors which are the source of the impulses reaching the brain through these fibers.

3.5. While the peripheral receptor organs in which the impulses are set up by stimuli are in general sensitive only to a limited range of stimuli, the impulses themselves which are conducted to the nervous centers are of uniform character and do not differ from each other in quality. There is no known correspondence between any attributes of the individual impulse and either the attributes of the stimulus which caused it or the attributes of the sensory quality which it evokes (1.31–1.37).

3.6. The impulse or state of excitation conducted by any nervous fiber is not a continuous flow but rather a succession of shocks following each other at very short intervals and usually described as a 'train' (or incorrectly as a 'volley') of impulses.

3.7. Each fiber will normally conduct impulses only in one direction, although it seems probable that the fiber itself is capable of transmitting impulses in either direction and that it is its position with respect to the body of the cell, and the position of the whole neuron in the chain of neurons, which determines in which direction the impulses will normally travel through a fiber.

3.8. The impulses conducted by the nerve fibers obey the 'all-or-nothing principle' which states that any given fiber may only either transmit or not transmit a given impulse, but that, if it does transmit it, the impulse will always be of the same strength. This means that we have throughout to deal with a kind of 'trigger phenomenon' where what is loosely called a 'transmission' of impulses does not really mean a conduction of energy but rather that one impulse releases energy stored up in the next cell in the chain.

3.9. The 'strength' of the impulse, which shows itself in its capacity to cause excitation in other neurons, however, will differ not only between different fibers but also between different segments and branches of the same fiber roughly in proportion to their thickness. But while the impulse conducted by a given fiber cannot vary in strength, it may vary in duration (or rather in the number of successive shocks of which the train of impulses is made up), and this variation in duration will in some respects operate similarly to a variation in strength (see 3.13 below).

3.10. In addition to the impulses transmitting excitation some nerve fibers appear to conduct another kind of impulses which quell or inhibit excitation.

3.11. At certain points called 'synapses' nervous impulses are transmitted from one neuron to another. Any theory that is to account for the known action of the central nervous system must assume that these 'synapses' are not permanent or invariable features of the nervous system but can be created and modified in the course of its operation, probably as a result of the simultaneous occurrence of impulses in two or more adjoining neurons. As has already been pointed out (2.47), we possess practically no knowledge about the nature of these synapses or the mechanism by which they are created. It is not even clear whether we ought to conceive of the creation of a new synapse as a change in the anatomical structure, which is the interpretation commonly given to the 'formation of a new path',[2] or whether it is brought about by a functional change, such as the establishment of the kind of permanent circular flow of impulses mentioned before. In so far as connections of this kind must be assumed to transmit not excitation but inhibition, there does not appear to exist even a plausible hypothesis about the conditions under which such new connections would be established, comparable to the role attributed to the simultaneity of the impulses for the formation of connections between excitatory impulses.

3.12. The assumption that connections or synapses between neurons are created as the result of the simultaneous excitation of these neurons implies the further assumption that these connections will be two-way connections, i.e., that if an impulse in a given neuron is regularly transmitted to a certain other neuron an impulse in this second neuron will also be regularly transmitted to the first. This assumption is independent of the question whether the transmission in the two opposite directions is effected by the same channel or whether separate channels capable of transmitting impulses in opposite directions are created by the same circumstances.

3.13. The operation of the 'all-or-nothing principle' is partly modified by the phenomenon of 'summation' which appears to operate in two ways, spatially and temporally: either impulses arriving simultaneously at a given cell through different fibers, although each of them individually may be too weak to cause excitation of that cell, may yet together produce that result; or the succession of shocks contained in a train of impulses in a single fiber may

---

[2] Cf. E. D. Adrian, 1947, p. 92: 'The notion that memories might be related to structural changes of this kind has often been rejected on the ground that no one has been able to detect them with the microscope, but the chance of doing so would be so remote that the objection need not be taken very seriously.'

build up sufficient strength to cause excitation to the cell to which they are conducted, although a single shock or a few shocks would not have been sufficient to do so.

3.14. It seems that in many instances the stimulation of more than one individual receptor organ and sometimes perhaps the stimulation of receptor organs of several different kinds, and consequently the arrival of impulses through a number of different afferent fibers, are required in order that a sensation of a particular quality should be produced.[3]

2. Simplifying Assumptions on which the Operation of the Principle Will Be Discussed

3.15. In the preceding enumeration of some of the main features of the functioning of the central nervous system certain facts have been deliberately left out which are not required for the very amplified account of its functioning as an instrument of classification which will be attempted here. In particular, we have left out much that would be important if we were to attempt to sketch the temporal pattern of the order of impulses. But although there can be no doubt that this time structure is very important, any attempt to describe it would have to make use of a great deal more of physiological detail than would be compatible with a clear presentation of the outline, or would be justified by the present state of our knowledge of these matters.[4]

3.16. Even when we leave out this problem of the temporal order of the neural events, the possibilities of classification of impulses which the structure of the neural system provides are of such a manifold character that, in order to obtain a clear picture of how the principle operates, it will be advisable to approach the actual situation by gradual steps. We shall therefore at first employ a number of simplifying assumptions which will later be gradually dropped. The simple models which we shall discuss in the present chapter serve merely to bring out certain salient features of the complex process of classification.

3.17. The first simplifying assumption of this kind which we shall employ provisionally is that we shall consider how a single afferent impulse arriving at the higher centers may here be classified or be discriminated from other similar impulses. This is, of course, a very artificial case, since it is most unlikely that at any moment only one such impulse will arrive, and even doubtful whether, if this ever happened, such an isolated impulse would give rise to a sensation.

3.18. The second simplifying assumption we shall adopt for the present is perhaps even more drastic and unrealistic. We shall concentrate entirely on

[3] C. T. Morgan, 1943, pp. 297–98.
[4] See, however, now D. O. Hebb, 1949.

the order created by connections formed between sensory neurons and for the time being entirely neglect the connections established between sensory and motor neurons. The whole problem of the relation between sensation and motor action or behavior will be taken up only in the next chapter.

3.19. Closely connected with this second simplification is a third which we also shall adopt for the time being, namely the disregard of the hierarchal structure of the central nervous system. We shall, in other words, begin by considering how connections between sensory neurons might create an order if they were all formed in a single center or on one and the same level.

3.20. The two last-mentioned simplifications mean, of course, that as a first approximation we shall neglect two facts which are of crucial and decisive importance for the actual functioning of the nervous system. It has rightly become a commonplace in neuro-physiology that we must not think in terms of separate sensory and motor mechanisms but rather in terms of a single sensori-motor system. If, nevertheless, at first we treat in isolation that part of the sensory order which might be produced by connections between the sensory impulses only, and postpone to the next chapter the questions of the interaction between sensory and motor impulses, this is in deliberate contrast to current practice. Our procedure is based on the belief that in recent times the direct connections between sensory and motor impulses have been rather overstressed at the expense of an adequate recognition of the order which may be determined by connections within the sensory sphere only.

3.21. When in the course of this chapter we speak of the 'effects' of particular sensory impulses we shall therefore refer to their effects on other central processes. These effects may consist in the evocation of other impulses either in neurons which can also be excited by primary impulses, or of impulses in 'internuncial' neurons in which an impulse acts, as it were, merely as a symbol or sign for a class of afferent impulses.

3.22. We shall also, for the purposes of the present discussion, continue to disregard one of the main difficulties which a fuller examination of our problem would have to face: the distinction between the phylogenetic and the ontogenetic aspects of the process of the formation of the order of sensory qualities. As we have already mentioned (2.49), it is probable that some of the connections formed in the development of the species become embedded in the structure of the central nervous system while others will be formed during the life of the individual. For the purposes of the present schematic sketch we shall neglect this distinction and proceed as if the formation of the system of connections commenced in an individual organism endowed with an apparatus capable of forming such connections but in which at the outset no such connections existed.

3.23. Another important question, which for lack of sufficient knowledge we must leave undecided, is whether the connections formed between neurons which simultaneously receive afferent impulses will be direct connections between these neurons or whether we ought to conceive of them as mediated by other cells which are not directly linked with receptor organs but serve merely as connecting links between other neurons. Such third-cell connections certainly occur, and from the proportion between the total number of neurons in the cortex and the much smaller number of afferent and efferent fibers (3.4) it would appear that the greater part of the neurons forming the cerebral cortex can have no direct connections with receptor or effector organs and are likely to perform some such mediating function.

3.24. Finally, it should be remembered throughout the following discussion that when we speak of connections this will include what we may call 'potential' as well as effective connections, i.e., connections which transmit impulses which by themselves would not be strong enough to cause excitation of the neurons to which they are conducted, unless they are reinforced (through summation) by other impulses arriving there more or less at the same time, as well as connections carrying impulses sufficiently strong by themselves to transmit excitation.

3. Elementary Forms of Classification

3.25. If we now turn to consider the significance of the fact that the different sensory neurons in the cortex will have acquired various sets of connections with other neurons, it will at once be evident that if each of two or more neurons should be connected with exactly the same other neurons, so that an impulse occurring in any one of the former will be transmitted to the same group of other neurons, the effects of an impulse in any one of the former will be the same. Their position in the whole structure of connections would be identical and their functional significance would be the same (Cf., 2.5).

3.26. With this extreme instance of complete identity of all connections possessed by a number of neurons we may at once contrast the opposite instance where a number of neurons possess no common connections with the same other neurons. Between these two limiting cases there may exist any number of intermediate positions: groups of neurons which have a larger or smaller part of their connections in common. We can thus speak of greater or smaller degrees of similarity of the position of the different neurons in the whole system of such connections.

3.27. This similarity of the positions of the individual neurons in the whole system of connections can vary not only in degree but also in kind. Of three neurons, a, b, and c, possessing the same number of connections with other neurons, a may have the same number of connections in common with b as it has with c, which would mean (at least if all these connections were also of the same strength) that the similarities between the positions of a and b and between the positions of a and c were of the same degree. Yet these similarities might be of different kinds, because some or all of the connections which a had in common with b might be different from those which a had in common with c. This means, of course, that although the position of a in the whole system of connections would be similar to that of b and to that of c, there might be much less similarity or no similarity at all between the positions of b and c. This merely expresses the fact that the relation of similarity is non-transitive (1.46).

3.28. A very high degree of similarity in the position of the different neurons in the system of connections is likely to exist where ever the neurons are served by receptors sensitive to stimuli which always or almost always occur together. This is most likely where these receptors are not only sensitive to the same kind of physical stimuli but also situated in close proximity.

3.29. If we can show how all the afferent impulses which give rise to sensations of the same quality are likely to be transmitted to the same group of further neurons, and by this fact will be distinguished from impulses producing different sensory qualities, we shall have provided an answer to our problem in the simplest form in which it occurs: we shall have explained the equivalence of the impulses occurring in different fibers. There are several obvious reasons which lead us to expect that such a classification of certain impulses as equivalent in all or some respects will be brought about as a result of the relative frequency with which different impulses occur together.

3.30. In the first instance, it is on the whole more likely that receptor organs sensitive to physically similar stimuli will be excited at the same time, and it is therefore to be expected that especially close connections will be formed between the central neurons to which the corresponding impulses are transmitted. Where the physical stimuli can vary continuously in one or more dimensions, as in the case of light or sound, mixtures or bands of various frequencies of light or sound waves usually occur together, and those which are more closely similar in a physical sense probably also occur more frequently together. It is thus to be expected that, e.g., not only all impulses set up by light waves (or by sound waves) will acquire some common connections but also that there will be more such common connections according as these stimuli are more or less closely akin physically.

3.31. These connections are likely to be closest where the receptors are situated near to each other, but we shall also expect all the receptors of a given organism which are sensitive to the same kind of physical stimuli to be frequently excited at the same time, so that a fairly dense net of connections will be formed between the corresponding central neurons. Similarly we shall expect fairly close connections to be formed between the neurons served by neighbouring receptors which are sensitive to stimuli which occur frequently together because they emanate from the same physical objects, such as pressure and temperature, certain chemical agents acting simultaneously on mouth and nose, etc., etc.

3.32. Secondly, any particular kind of stimulus will usually occur more frequently in the company of some other stimuli than in that of others, and the connections between the central neurons corresponding to physically different stimuli will thus come to reflect the relative frequency in which these different stimuli occur together. What has been said before about the specially close connections between impulses caused by physical stimuli of the same kind will also apply to impulses caused by stimuli which, although they are not, like all light waves, physically closely similar, at least, like movement and sound, usually occur together.

3.33. Thirdly, in many instances it is likely that certain kinds of stimuli will usually act together on the organism when the organism itself is in a particular state of balance or of activity, either because the stimulus regularly occurs under conditions producing that state, or because it occurs periodically so as to coincide with some rhythm of the body. The impulses which register such external stimuli will then become connected with impulses received from the proprioceptors which register the different states of the organism itself.

3.34. The result of all this will be that a system of connections will be formed which will record the relative frequency with which in the history of the organism the different groups of internal and external stimuli have acted together. Each individual impulse or group of impulses will on its occurrence evoke other impulses which correspond to the other stimuli which in the past have usually accompanied its occurrence. We shall call this bundle of secondary impulses which each primary impulse will set up through these acquired connections the *following* of the primary impulse. It will be the total or partial identity of this following of the primary impulse which makes them members of the same class.[5]

4. Complex Forms of Classification

3.35. Even as a result of the comparatively simple processes discussed in the last section each impulse would become the member not merely of one class but of as many distinct classes as will correspond, not only to the number

---

[5] We cannot, without going more deeply into the physiological problems involved than seems expedient, examine the question whether the group of connected impulses which thus form the following of any particular primary impulses may not come to form relatively stable aggregations in the sense that, by the individual impulses mutually evoking each other, they may maintain themselves for some time beyond the duration of the stimulus. Such a conception appears to underlie the construction of a 'cell assembly' used by D. O. Hebb, 1949.

of other impulses which constitute its following, but in addition also to the number of possible combinations (pairs, triples, quadruples, etc.) of such other impulses; it might have any such part of its following in common with different groups of other impulses and therefore form a distinct class with them. We obtain thus already a somewhat complex form of 'multiple' classification in the first of the senses distinguished before (2.39–2.40).

3.36. Attention should be directed already at this stage to a circumstance which will have to be further considered at a later point (3.52ff.), namely, the fact that the kind of classificatory processes which we are now considering differ from those performed by the machines discussed earlier in one important respect. In the instances which we are now considering, the classificatory responses are not different in kind from, but are events of the same sort as, those which are the object of classification. In consequence, it is possible that one and the same event may appear both as an object of classification and as an act of classification. The impulse produced by a peripheral stimulus is 'classified' by evoking other impulses which might also be produced by peripheral stimuli. We shall see that it is a consequence of this relationship between the classifying and the classified impulses that a process of classification can produce 'models' of extremely complex relationships between stimuli, and indeed can reproduce the order of any conceivable structure.

3.37. In accordance with the distinction we have drawn between 'effective' and 'potential' connections between neurons (3.24) we shall also have to distinguish between that part of the following of an impulse which will always occur whenever that impulse occurs, and that part which is merely 'potential' and which will appear only if the tendency towards an excitation of the neurons constituting the 'potential' following is supported by other impulses operating towards the same effect.

3.38. In the extreme case where the following acquired by any one neuron of a given class is completely identical with that of the other members of the class, their individual position in the whole system of connections and therefore their functional significance would also be identical. This result is possible but not likely to occur frequently. When I was first working on these problems I thought I had found an instance of such undistinguishable sensations caused by stimuli operating on different receptors in the case of pressure on teeth standing opposite each other; I am no longer in a position to verify this. Such pressure seemed to me indistinguishable so far as immediate experience was concerned, and I was able to decide which tooth was concerned only by calling in further sensory experience, such as touching the teeth individually with my fingers. This case would, of course, satisfy the condition that the two stimuli almost always occur together.

3.39. There are undoubtedly other instances where stimuli, although they set up impulses in distinct fibers, remain indistinguishable. As a rule, however, we find that even very similar sensations caused by the stimulation of different receptors differ from each other, if in no other way, at least by an awareness of the different points at which they occur, or by what used to be called their 'local sign'. If we are to account for these differences between the effects of impulses which produce sensation otherwise of the same quality, we shall, in addition to the common following which accounts for their similar quality, have to find differences which account for their assignment to different points in space.

3.40. If we examine this problem at first in connection with vision we enter a field where the kind of explanation which we are attempting to apply generally was first used to account for a special problem: ever since Bishop Berkeley[6] the connections between the impulses registering the visual stimuli on the retina and the kinesthetic impulses[7] recording the tension of the muscles used for focusing the eye have been employed for explaining the spatial order of sensations. A particular visual impulse may have acquired exactly the same connections with other visual impulses and thus be classified as differing qualitatively in the same manner from all other visual stimuli, and yet it may differ from the former by being connected with a different set of kinesthetic impulses.

3.41. The use we shall make of this fact, however, will in two respects differ from that made of it in the Berkeley-Helmholtz-Mach theory of spatial vision.[8] Firstly, the impulses registering the state of muscular tension will not be conceived as producing distinct sensations but will be considered merely as physiological events which are associated with, and evoked by, the visual stimuli, and which contribute to the peculiar effects which the latter are capable of producing.

3.42. Secondly, what we shall regard as connected with the visual impulses will not be the actual movements of the eye muscles but merely the sensory impulses which normally record such movements in the central nervous system but which may also occur, if they are associatively evoked by the visual impulses, without the eye movements actually occurring. It would, therefore,

---

[6] [Bishop George Berkeley (1685–1753) advanced the theory that—other than argued by Locke—not only secondary qualities of objects (such as their color, taste, or smell) but also their primary qualities (such as their weight, size, or motion) can only be subjectively perceived, exist only as ideas in the mind ("esse est percipi"). In his *An Essay Towards a New Theory of Vision* (1709) he argued that vision is about the perception of light and color rather than of material objects per se. Concerning spatial vision he posited that we perceive the distance from an object not through our senses per se but based on our experience of relations between magnitude and distance.—Ed.]

[7] [The term "kinesthetic sense" refers to a person's awareness of her bodily motions. From kinesthetic receptors—located in muscles, tendons, joints, and the inner ear—nervous impulses transmit information to the brain on the relative positions of the parts of the body.—Ed.]

[8] [See Hayek's reference to Helmholtz in 7.13 below.—Ed.]

not be a valid objection against this interpretation if it were pointed out that the movements of the eye postulated by the traditional theory do not, in fact, take place.

3.43. The theory of spatial vision serves here merely as an example of the manner in which the spatial order of sensations can in general be accounted for. And even this in turn is significant for us mainly as an illustration of the even more general way in which most specific acts of sensation require particular postures or attitudes of the body in order that the characteristic quality of the sensation should be produced. This fact will have to be considered further in the next chapter (4.35–4.44).

3.44. At this point the artificial separation of the connections existing between different sensory impulses from those between them and motor impulses becomes difficult to maintain. We have already been forced to take into account the motor responses usually accompanying the acts of perception—motor responses which are probably directed from some lower level of the central nervous system, and which in turn will give rise to kinesthetic and other proprioceptive impulses which will become part of the following of the initial sensory impulse. These matters, however, can only be considered further at a later stage.

3.45. The common spatial order,[9] which is part of the common order of all sensations, serves here merely as an instance of the great variety of relations between different sensory impulses which will help to build up that order. The bundles of connections or the following which any one of several sensory neurons may acquire can differ from those of others in an almost infinite variety of ways, ranging from complete identity of their following to complete absence of any common connections; and every difference in the connections which the individual neurons possess will have its peculiar functional significance.

3.46. To the possibilities of functional differentiation of the different impulses by connections transmitting excitation, we have to add the effects of the second kind of connections mentioned earlier, namely those transmitting inhibition (3.10). In whatever manner such inhibitory connections may be acquired in the first instance and later transferred, their existence extends the range of possible differences in the position which any one impulse may occupy in the whole system of connections: it adds the possibility of different impulses having effects which are directly opposed to each other. In such instances the evocation of certain other impulses normally following upon

---

[9] It is significant for our purposes that this common spatial order extends only as far as the same physical events give rise to the stimulation of different senses and that, e.g., as William James has pointed out, our perception of size within the cavity of the mouth, which in the nature of the case is not co-ordinated with visual stimuli, does not fully form part of the same spatial order as our visual experiences.

the occurrence of a given impulse would be prevented if still other impulses occurred at the same time. The range of functional differentiation of the impulses which may be determined by the differences in their following is thus extended, from equality through various degrees of similarity and difference, to contrariness and complete opposition.

3.47. The significance of the differences in the following which different neurons will have acquired will show itself in the differences between the effects which the impulses occurring in them will produce in different circumstances. The manner in which any newly arriving impulse will modify the existing excitatory state of the whole nervous system, and in which it will combine its effects with those of all other simultaneously arriving impulses, will depend on the different followings of all those impulses. The further course through which any one bundle of impulse-chains will run will be determined by the following of each successive impulse and by the manner in which the impulses of this following will combine with (i.e., reinforce or inhibit) other impulses proceeding at the same time (see 5.53).

3.48. In the complex interplay of many chains of impulses proceeding at the same time, the identity of the greater part of the followings which two or more neurons possess will bring it about that the occurrence of any one of them will in most situations produce the same or similar results, and that their simultaneous occurrence will tend to reinforce those parts of their followings which they have in common.

3.49. Such a system, in which each of a set of events is connected with many others in such a way that the occurrence of any one of any group of them causes (or contributes to bring about) the occurrence of certain others, evidently performs classifications in the sense in which we have defined this term. All the impulses or groups of impulses which evoke the same other impulses will belong to the same 'class' because they have this particular effect in common. Individual impulses or groups of impulses will of course almost always belong to a great many different classes, that is, multiple classification in the first of the different senses we have distinguished (2.40) will be the rule.

3.50. Since the different individual impulses will become members of a class through the fact that each of them evokes the same other impulses, it seems permissible to say that the latter *represent* the common attribute of the members of the class—though it would be more correct to say that they *constitute* that attribute. The classification is effected by the evocation of certain other impulses, and the latter serve, as it were, as the 'signs' or 'symbols' representing the class; the expression 'representative processes in the brain', which has been much used in recent physiological psychology,[10] can therefore appropriately be applied to them.

[10] See C. T. Morgan, 1943, pp. 467, 476.

3.51. It has been suggested above (2.20–2.31, 2.44) that the mechanism which we are considering can be conceived either 'statically' as an apparatus capable of performing classifications, or 'dynamically', as a process of classification. In the preceding discussion we have sometimes spoken in terms of the former, e.g., when we spoke of connections between neurons through which impulses are transmitted, and sometimes in terms of the latter, when we spoke of the impulses evoking each other. These two aspects of the same phenomenon correspond to the two aspects of the system of sensory qualities which we discussed then. It should now be clear that it is the dynamic aspect which is the really relevant one and that the static view is merely a method which is sometimes convenient to use for describing the potential operations of the system.

5. The Classification of the Relations between Classes

3.52. There is no reason why such connections as we have been considering should be formed only between primary sensory pulses, i.e., between impulses arriving through afferent fibers at the higher centers; they can evidently be formed in a similar manner between the further impulses which are evoked by the former and which represent classes of them. Any impulse which occurs as part of the following of one or more other impulses will, on each occasion when it thus occurs, acquire or strengthen connections with other impulses which form part of the same following. Connections of this kind will therefore also be formed between impulses which as primary impulses rarely if ever occur at the same time, but which on different occasions have become connected with the same third impulse, in the following of which they have in consequence become included.

3.53. This acquisition of connections between impulses in consequence of their simultaneous occurrence in a secondary or derived character is specially important in so far as those neurons in the cerebral cortex are concerned which are not directly served by sensory receptors but which appear to act solely as intermediaries between other sensory neurons or between sensory and motor neurons. Impulses in such neurons will occur, and in turn themselves acquire connections, only in so far as they are part of the following of other impulses; but once they have acquired such a position in the system of connections, they will in turn be able to acquire their own following, and this will include impulses belonging to the following of all the different other primary impulses of which they form a part.

3.54. In the higher centers there occur undoubtedly a great many impulses which do not uniquely correspond to particular stimulations of sensory receptors but which represent merely common qualities attributed to the primary impulses; these representatives of classes of primary impulses will in turn become the objects of further processes of classification; the classes for which they stand will be further grouped into classes of classes, and this process can be repeated on many successive levels. We need, of course, not assume that these 'levels' are clearly separated or that the same impulse may not form part of the following of several other impulses which belong to different 'levels'.

3.55. The process of classification which we are considering is therefore 'multiple' not only in the two senses which we have discussed before (2.39–2.43), but also in a third sense: it can take place on many successive levels or stages, and any one of the various classes in which an impulse may be included may in turn become the object of further classification. This third sense in which this process of classification may be multiple must not be confused with the second (2.41); the latter refers to the case where groups of simultaneously occurring impulses (a, b, c), (e, f, g), (i, k, l), which, when they occur as groups, are as groups treated as members of the same class of groups. In the third sense multiple classification refers to the class A (of which individual impulses a, b, c, or groups of impulses (a, b, c), (e, f, g), etc. may be members) and the class B (of which the impulses m, n, o, or the groups of impulses (m, b, o), (p, q, r), etc. are members) and the similar class C, or rather to the 'symbols' representing the classes A, B, and C, which, by the common following they acquire, become members of a class of a higher order.

3.56. These different forms of multiple classification which it is necessary to distinguish conceptually, will, of course, occur in various combinations, and we obtain thus possibilities of classification of (or discrimination between) the different individual impulses and groups of impulses which are practically unlimited. The consequent differences in the influence which different impulses will exercise on the whole course of the nervous processes, varying from identity through various degrees of similarity to complete difference, would be adequate for building up an extremely complex system of relations among the millions of impulses.

3.57. The word classification scarcely conveys an adequate idea of the almost infinite wealth of variety and gradation of the discriminations which can be performed by such an apparatus. Since it is not merely a question of a particular impulse either belonging or not belonging to a particular class, but also of its belonging to it more or less 'strongly' (according as the connections with the classifying impulses are 'effective' or merely 'potential', and therefore in the latter case requiring more or less support in order to become 'effective'— 3.24 and 3.37), it would be more appropriate to describe these complex processes by some such term as 'evaluation'. We shall occasionally employ this latter term in the place of 'classification' in order to stress that the process is capable of making distinctions of degree as well as distinctions of kind.

3.58. The combination of the different kinds of multiple classification opens up the possibility of a still further organization of the order of the impulses, because through it the differences of the positions occupied in the whole system of classification by the impulses belonging to different classes may themselves become the object of classification and thereby acquire distinct qualities of their own.

3.59. It has been pointed out before (3.17) that it is a somewhat misleading and artificial approach to trace the effects of a single afferent impulse as if it ever occurred in isolation and as if its position were to be determined in an otherwise quiescent system; and that it is doubtful whether such a single isolated impulse, even if it ever occurred, could produce a sensory quality. It is probable that only groups of impulses as such can acquire that distinct position in the whole system which we call its quality. There exists, moreover, a good deal of physiological evidence which makes it probable that it is the so-called 'gradients' between different impulses rather than the individual impulses which are the significant features.[11] We must, therefore, consider more fully this case where not a single impulse but only certain groups of impulses as groups acquire a distinct following of their own (the second kind of multiple classification) and where in consequence the specific following determining a class of groups of impulses will be evoked only if the whole of a group belonging to this class occurs.

3.60. The constituents of a following that will appear only if certain impulses forming a group occur together must be connected with the individual impulses forming the group by what we have called 'potential' connections. The simplest instance of such a position would be provided by several primary impulses which possess potential connections with the same other secondary impulse which will be called forth only if all the primary impulses forming the group occur at the same time (or in rapid succession). Several different groups of such individual impulses may evidently thus become connected with the same symbolic impulse (or following of impulses) which will then stand for a class of such groups of impulses. And the symbolic or secondary impulses (or following of such impulse) which stands for any one of this class of groups of impulses (performing thus the second kind of multiple classification) may then (by the third, or relay type, of multiple classification) become itself a member of some new and higher class of impulses representing classes of groups of impulses. This higher class will then be represented by impulses which are symbols of classes of symbols, and so on.

3.61. As a result of such combinations of the different kinds of multiple classification it is evidently possible that the simultaneous occurrence of members of several different pairs (or groups) of different classes of impulses, will be classed as similar events or, we might say, as different events related

[11] Cf. E. D. Adrian, 1947, p. 82; and especially V. von Weizsäcker, 1947 *passim*.

similarly to each other. Since in such a case the same classifying impulse or impulses will be evoked by different pairs (or groups) of impulses which separately do not belong to the same class, it is legitimate to speak here of a classification of the difference (or relations) between classes of the first kind.

3.62. In order to bring out distinctly the meaning of such a classification of the difference (or relation) between different classes, it will be useful to consider the different meanings of the expressions 'respond differently to different impulses', 'show the same difference in the response to different pairs of impulses', and 'respond to a difference between impulses'. In these expressions 'respond', of course, does not necessarily refer to any peripheral response of the organism but to the symbolic or classifying responses in the central nervous system. 'To respond differently to different impulses' then corresponds to what we have called simple classification. 'To show the same difference in the response to impulses of different pairs which in other respects are classified as equal' means that although, e.g., the impulses a and b in most respects belong to the same classes and similarly the impulses e and f also belong in most respects to the same other classes, there is at least one reaction which a and e, and another which b and f have in common. 'To react to a difference', finally, means that any member of the class A occurring with any member of class B will produce the same response. If this same classifying response is also evoked by the occurrence of any member of class E together with any member of class F, and by the occurrence of any member of class K together with any member of class L, we can say that the differences or relations between the classes (or qualities) A and B, E and F, and K and L are the same.

3.63. The impulses which in this manner come to stand for, or to represent, particular classes of relations between other impulses will in turn also acquire their own following and thereby obtain their own distinct functional significance: the qualities represented by their common following would attach to the relations between the primary impulses rather than to those impulses themselves. Or, to express the same idea differently, the various kinds of relations between different impulses may themselves become differentiated from each other and thus become capable of forming the starting points of distinct chains of further impulses.

3.64. The relations between impulses or classes of impulses may thus be ordered as a system, or be classified, in the same way and by the same kind of process by which the individual impulses or groups of impulses are arranged in an order. It is in fact only at this point that, strictly speaking, we are entitled to speak of different relations between the impulses (see 1.56–1.61 and 2.20). It will now be seen how, as a result of the hierarchical organization of the connections between different impulses, the one kind of 'relation' from which we started (namely the causal connection between the impulses) can be used to build up complex structures with regard to which it is legitimate to speak of different kinds of relations existing between the various elements.

3.65. This process, by which the relations on which the classification of the primary impulses is based become in turn the object of classificatory processes, can evidently be repeated on many levels. Not only relations between impulses, but relations between relations between impulses, and so forth, may all acquire their distinct following and in consequence become capable of forming the starting point for distinct further processes.

3.66. The complexity of the order which can be built up by means of this variety of relations is for all practical purposes unlimited. Given the number of separate neurons in the higher nervous centers and the number of the possible connections between them, the problem is not one of the limitation of the number of possible differences between their respective positions in the whole system, but rather the inadequacy of our mind to follow out the full degree of complexity of the order which can thus be determined. It seems indeed that any conceivable order or structure of relationships could be reproduced within such a system.

3.67. The differences in the functional significance or in the 'quality' which different groups of impulses may acquire as groups, and which may be independent of the functional significance which the individual impulses forming these groups possess if they occur singly, is thus a problem of the same character as that of the functional differentiation of the individual impulses, and can be answered by recourse to the same principle. But although the processes which bring about these differentiations are in principle independent of each other, and while it is even possible that only the classification of the groups and never that of individual impulses is the significant phenomenon, these classifications on different levels will, of course, interact with each other.

3.68. There will, thus, exist as much justification for saying that the capacity of the individual impulses to combine with others into groups possessing distinct functional significance will contribute to the distinct character which these impulses possess individually as there is for saying that the latter will contribute to the distinctive following possessed by the group as group. Neither of these two aspects of what is a single process can in any sense be regarded as more fundamental. Both contribute in the same way to the organization of the whole system of sensory qualities; and it is the whole complex order thus produced which determines the characteristic position within this order of individual impulses as well as of groups of impulses.

3.69. The fact that chains of further processes ('associations') can be evoked not only by the 'elementary' sensory qualities (which were supposed to correspond to the occurrence of particular primary impulses), but also by certain 'abstract' attributes of different groups of sensations (such as figures, tunes, rhythms, or abstract concepts), has usually been regarded as an insurmountable obstacle to any physiological explanation of mental processes.[12] For the approach followed here no such difficulty arises: the problem of the equivalence of 'similar' complexes of stimuli is not different in principle from the problem why the same associations should become attached to different impulses which correspond to the same 'elementary' qualities. The problem of equivalence in both these instances is basically the same and can be solved by the application of the same general principle of explanation.

3.70. Once a given impulse has acquired a definite following in common with other impulses, any new connection which it acquires will become attached also to the impulses of its following and will be evoked, therefore, also by the other primary impulses with which it shares part of its following, although those other primary impulses may never have occurred at the same time with those others with which they become in this indirect manner associated. If all the different qualities which different impulses have in common are represented by certain symbolic impulses standing for these qualities and included in the following of all the impulses possessing that quality, there is no difficulty about the manner in which associations will become attached to such common qualities of different impulses rather than to the individual impulses. The phenomena of transfer and generalization of learning (1.50) are a direct consequence of the fact that identical mental attributes are represented by identical physiological impulses.

6. The Universal Character of the Process of Classification: Gestalt Phenomena and Abstract Concepts

3.71. The fact that relations between the parts of the total sensor situation, which individually may be quite unlike each other, may yet be recognized as similar, of course, is the most general aspect of the problem of Gestalt. But while the significance of the phenomenon has come to be generally appreciated, mainly as the result of the work of the Gestalt school, it is by now recognized by practically all schools of psychology. That in perception we do not merely add together given sensory elements, and that complex perceptions possess attributes which cannot be derived from the discernible attributes of the separate parts, is one of the conclusions most strongly emphasized by practically all recent developments in psychology.

---

[12] Cf., e.g., G. F. Stout, 1915, p. 88; and E. D. Adrian, 1947, p. 82: 'The nervous system reacts to relations between stimuli and performs the appropriate task with any part of the motor system that is available. We cannot represent it as a series of machines for operating upon the map of events unless we add a number of devices to make good this fundamental difference. On the sensory side there must be something to abstract the significant element of a pattern and on the motor side something to do just the reverse, to convert the abstraction into concrete movement.'

3.72. As we have seen, it is, in fact, no more difficult to explain why different impulses caused by different combinations of stimuli, which singly would occupy altogether different positions in the whole system of relations, should as combinations occupy similar positions in that system, than why different single impulses produced by different physical stimuli should acquire the same or a similar functional significance. That the problem of Gestalt perception was singled out as a special problem was largely due to the fact that it was still widely believed that the 'elementary' sensory qualities were somehow originally, and in a manner either not requiring or not capable of explanation, attached to the elementary nervous impulses. The fight which even before the rise of the Gestalt school some psychologists had conducted against the 'mosaic psychology', which conceived the more complex phenomena as built up from mental elements corresponding to the physiological elements,[13] was, however, bound to be unsuccessful so long as the purely relative character of *all* sensory qualities was not recognized.

3.73. With regard to the more complex sensory phenomena our theory leads indeed to conclusions very similar to those of the Gestalt school. This, however, is so because our approach leads us to raise with regard to *all* sensory qualities, even those presumed to be the most 'elementary', the same question which the Gestalt school raised with regard to configurations. Once we are led to account even for what used to be regarded as 'simple' or 'elementary' sensory qualities by the principles outlined here, Gestalt phenomena and 'abstractions' do not raise any fundamentally new or different problem.

3.74. As a result of the work of the Gestalt school the view has now become widely accepted that sensory qualities must not be regarded as atomic fact but should be conceived as determined by the 'organization of the field'. It may be suggested that the theory of the determination of sensory qualities here developed gives this somewhat vague conception of the 'organization of the field' a precise meaning; and, at the same time, that it takes this whole approach some steps further by making it clear, firstly, that the 'organization of the field' is based on, and is in principle capable of explanation in terms of, causal connections between physiological impulses; and, secondly, that this organization of the field is not additional to the qualities of any kind of atomic sensations (as most of the discussion of 'perceptual organization' still implies), but that it is the structure of that field which determines the peculiar functional significance of the individual impulse, or groups of impulses, which we know as their sensory qualities.

3.75. The conception of the 'organized field' is usually applied to the system

[13] See W. McDougall, 1923, p. x, where James Ward, F. H. Bradley, Dawes Hicks and G. F. Stout are mentioned as protagonists of the fight against the 'mosaic psychology'. A similar list of German writers of that period could be given.

of qualities belonging to one particular sense or modality. For our purposes it will be necessary to interpret its meaning more widely and to include in the conception not only the relations between the different qualities belonging to the same modality, but also the relations which exist between the qualities belonging to different modalities (1.56–1.67). The fact that the whole system of sensory qualities must in this sense be regarded as one organized field need not prevent us, however, from occasionally speaking of different fields as sub-systems of the more comprehensive systems—sub-systems within which the elements are differentiated by a more dense and complex system of relations.

3.76. In treating the so-called elementary sensations and the more complex sensory phenomena as instances of the same process, and, therefore, as being capable of being explained by recourse to the same principle, we arrive (again in agreement with the views of the Gestalt school) at the conclusion that there is no substantial difference between the acts of 'sensation' and of 'perception': both appear as essentially similar and, as we shall see later, they constitute merely different stages in an even more comprehensive range of processes, all of which can be interpreted as acts of classification (or evaluation) performed by the central nervous system. We shall therefore henceforth use the terms 'perception' and 'perceiving' in their popular meaning in which they include the experiencing of 'elementary' sensory qualities as well as the perception of shapes, objects, etc.[14]

3.77. It will be shown later (6.44–6.50) that the principle used to explain these phenomena applies also to the so-called 'higher' mental processes such as the formation of abstract concepts and conceptual thought. With regard to those we are, of course, more familiar with the interpretation as processes of classification in which classes of events, or classes of such classes, inter-act in a complex manner. It should be noted, however, that if what are called abstractions are most easily accounted for as classes of classes, etc., this does not mean that they must always be secondary, in the sense of being derived from previous conscious experience. The perception of an abstract feature of a situation may in some measure be independent of the perception of the 'concrete' elements of which that situation may seem to be made up (6.40).

3.78. The processes of classification and re-classification on successive levels, and the 'higher' mental processes corresponding to them, will have to be considered further (chapters V and VI) in connection with the whole pro-cess of the building up of the system of connections as a whole. Before we can turn to this, however, we must consider another source of classification which, in consequence of the simplifying assumptions made, we have so far disregarded.

---

[14] On the apparent conflict with the views of the Gestalt school in which we have been led by explaining the formations of Gestalt qualities by a sort of experience, see 5.16 below.

CHAPTER IV

SENSATION AND BEHAVIOR

1. Sensation and the Organism

4.1. In the preceding chapters the apparatus for the classification of impulses has been represented as if it were a neutral, self-contained and completely centralized system which passively registered the simultaneous occurrence of impulses set up by external stimuli and thus came to reflect the significance which the stimuli possessed in the environment of this system. Such a passive apparatus of registration is conceivable, and to consider it served to bring out the general principle of our theory. But it would be something very different from the sort of apparatus which the nervous system constitutes. While it would register the significance of the stimuli in the environment, it would not indicate the special significance which they possess for the living organism of which that apparatus forms a part.

4.2. The exclusive concentration on the order that might be created by the establishment of the connections between sensory impulses only has been adopted quite deliberately (3.18). It was intended to emphasize one aspect of the more complete picture which, under the influence of behaviorism, has been somewhat neglected during the last generation. The emphasis which was placed during that period on the observable peripheral responses brought it about that the role played by the higher nervous centers has been largely disregarded, and that the whole relation between stimulus and response has often been treated as if the higher centers did not exist. In the preceding chapters we have gone to the other extreme and practically disregarded everything except the central effects of any sensory impulse. This temporary disregard of the fact that the nervous system operates within a living and acting organism which in some measure is capable of adaptive and regulative behavior apart from control by the higher nervous centers must now be corrected by an explicit consideration of these facts.

4.3. In the present chapter, therefore, we shall have to examine not only the effects of the sensory on the motor processes, but also have to give much greater attention than we have yet done to the sensory impulses set up by the various processes in the body, that is, to the registration of stimuli which originate in what has appropriately been called the *milieu intérieur*, the internal environment, within which the central nervous system functions. Of the latter we shall have to conceive as a sort of apparatus of control super-imposed upon a living whole rather than as a self-contained and fully centralized structure of its own.

4.4. In turning to these problems we are entering a field in which the very attitudes which during the past generation have led to a comparative neglect of our main problem have led to great progress and the accumulation of a wealth of new knowledge. We have nothing to add to this and cannot even hope to give the barest outline of all the relevant facts which a more systematic survey of the field would have to take into account. The sole purpose of this chapter is to show how our theory of the determination of sensory qualities fits into the picture of the 'integrated action of the nervous system' which is gradually emerging.

4.5. At the same time it should be pointed out, however, that in one respect in which the task which we are undertaking is most in need of a solid foundation, theoretical biology is only just beginning to provide the needed theoretical tools and concepts. An adequate account of the highly purposive character of the action of the central nervous system would require as its foundation a more generally accepted biological theory of the nature of adaptive and purposive processes than is yet available.

4.6. The consideration of the inter-relations between sensory and motor processes will also make it necessary to take more explicit notice of the hierarchical order of the central nervous system. We shall see that the organization of all connections between sensory and motor processes on many super-imposed levels, and the corresponding existence of a hierarchy of centers of increasing comprehensiveness, is of the greatest importance for the understanding of the sensory order.

4.7. In some measure connected with this hierarchical order of the nervous system is the distinction between the phylogenetic and the ontogenetic aspects of the processes in question, or between those connections which are inherited and those which are acquired by the individual. There is, however, not a great deal which, in the present state of our knowledge, can be said on this question; we shall on the whole have to continue to disregard this distinction and to represent the process of the building up of the sensory order as if it took place in the course of the life of the individual.

4.8. The relation between sensory and motor processes which we shall have to consider is a double one: we shall have to consider both, how various complexes of sensory impulses will influence behavior, and how in turn the motor responses will influence sensory discrimination. The latter question will make necessary some consideration of the interoceptive and proprioceptive impulses, i.e., those impulses which record not external stimuli but various states of different parts of the organism.

4.9. A more systematic discussion of the connection between the sensory and the motor apparatus would also have to include an examination of the manner in which the efferent (or motor) impulses are themselves ordered so as to produce certain co-ordinated patterns of movement, and of how the bundles of efferent impulses interact with the proprioceptive afferent impulses by which the resulting movements are recorded at the centers. In this respect we can, however, attempt no more than the barest sketch which must serve as an indication of the sort of problems which a fuller elaboration of our theory would have to answer.

4.10. In examining the significance of the proprioceptive impulses we shall have briefly to consider not only the effects which the impulses recording postures and movements accompanying perceptions have on sensory discrimination, and the role played in this connection by the back-reports of responses which are produced by the stimuli at various sub-cortical levels; but in particular also to examine the significance of the various 'biogenic' impulses which are caused by the vegetative processes of the organism and are closely connected with the various 'urges', 'drives', or 'wants'. The latter are, of course, essential for any explanation of purposive behavior.

2. Evolution and the Hierarchical Order of the Central Nervous System

4.11. The continued existence of those complex structures which we call organisms is made possible by their capacity of responding to certain external influences by such changes in their structure or activity as are required to maintain or restore the balance necessary for their persistence. This involves, even in the most primitive organisms, some capacity of discriminating responses to different physical stimuli and perhaps even some capacity of 'learning',[1] although we know very little about the nature of such individual learning (as distinguished from the process of hereditary selection of such individuals as show appropriate adjustments).

4.12. The fact that an organism will respond differently to different external forces acting upon it is, of course, not peculiar to organisms. It would be merely an instance of different causes producing different effects. The pecu-

---

[1] See H. S. Jennings, 1906. [Herbert Spencer Jennings (1868–1947) was an American microbiologist, zoologist, and geneticist who is known for his experimental research on primitive animals, on their behavior and their responses to stimuli, as well as for his studies on the genetics and evolution of single-celled organisms.—Ed.]

liar problems presented by organisms appear only where they respond to particular stimuli in the manner which will secure their continued existence, and in so far as they develop specific organs which enable them not only to discriminate between different stimuli, but to react differently to the same stimuli if they appear in different combinations with other stimuli or when the organism itself is in different states.

4.13. It is perhaps worth stressing that the problem of purposive adjustment of organisms to changes arises long before the problem of its purposive behavior with regard to external objects. The question of what determines (or what is meant by) purposiveness is in the last instance really the same question as that of what ensures the continued existence of the organism. It arises as much in connection with the normal functioning and growth of the organism, the processes of metabolism and the replacement of damaged parts, as in connection with those movements of the organism which we commonly describe as behavior.

4.14. It has already been suggested that in a certain sense any attempt to explain the highly complex kind of purposive action made possible by a developed central nervous system may be premature so long as we do not possess a fully adequate biological theory of the comparatively simpler kind of purposive functioning. Many of the problems often regarded as peculiar to mental phenomena in fact arise already at a much earlier stage, where there can be no question yet of that complex order that is shown in the response to external stimuli which we have described as mind. It cannot be our task here to restate the present position of biological theory with regard to these problems, and we must content ourselves to refer in this connection to W. B. Cannon's concept of homeostasis[2] and its development by other authors, and especially to the more recent and most promising work of L. von Bertalanffy. His theory of 'open systems' in a steady state (*Fliessgleichgewicht*) in which 'equifinality' prevails because the equilibrium that will be reached will in some measure be independent of the initial conditions seems to provide the most helpful contribution to the problem.[3] Any further comments we shall have to make with particular reference to the problem of purposiveness will be reserved to the next chapter (5.63–5.76).

4.15. Here we are not directly concerned with the regulative functions of the organism other than those which are effected through the central nervous system. It is merely necessary to remain aware throughout that this system functions within an organism which independently of the former is capable

[2] [Walter Bradford Cannon (1871–1945) coined the term "homeostasis" to describe the ability of an open system, such as a living organism, to maintain its equilibrium by self-regulating mechanisms.—Ed.]

[3] W. B. Cannon, 1932; L. v. Bertalanffy, 1942, 1949. [On Bertalanffy see above, preface, fn. 14.—Ed.] See also J. H. Woodger, 1929.

of some adaptive and purposive responses to external causes, responses which are brought about through a system of neuro-chemical regulation. Our task begins essentially where the somatic nervous system makes possible discriminatory responses to a great variety of combinations of stimuli, and particularly where learning becomes the dominant factor.

4.16. The mere fact that the organisms in the course of their evolution develop specific receptor organs which are sensitive only to fairly narrow ranges of stimuli must not be confused with the development of a sensory order and of distinct sensory qualities. It is to be assumed that this development goes hand in hand with the acquisition of different motor responses to the different stimuli. But even an organism which had developed distinct receptors sensitive to all those various stimuli which in a highly developed central nervous system produce different sensory qualities, for that reason could not yet be said to discriminate in terms of a system of sensory qualities similar to that familiar to us.

4.17. While such an organism would perform the simplest kind of classification we have discussed (2.35–2.38), it would still be unable to perform the multiple classifications which alone give rise to the system of sensory qualities. The different stimuli which evoke the different sensory qualities would, if occurring in isolation, all produce different effects, but these different effects would not differ from each other in the specific manner in which the sensory qualities differ from each other.

4.18. The essential characteristic of the order of sensory qualities is that, within that order, each stimulus or group of stimuli does not possess a unique significance represented by the particular response, but that they are given different significance if they occur in combination with, or are evaluated in the light of, an infinite variety of other stimuli which may originate from the external world or from the organism itself.

4.19. Such an order implies that any impulse recording a particular stimulus is connected not merely with one particular motor response, but that some apparatus exists by which the effects of any impulse are adjusted to, and integrated with, the effects of other impulses proceeding within the central nervous system at the same time. In other words, the various sensory impulses, whose effects are thus to be adjusted to each other, must in some manner be brought together before the effect of their joint action is decided.

4.20. This does not mean that individual afferent impulses, or groups of such impulses, might not also be uniquely connected at low levels with certain efferent impulses so that, as soon as the former occur, a particular movement is produced. Such a relation would correspond to the ideal simple reflex arc of traditional theory. In the present context such reflex responses are important mainly because of the proprioceptive impulses by which they in turn will be recorded in the higher centers. The original exteroceptive impulse which sets up such a reflex will in consequence arrive at the centers to which it is conducted already accompanied (or rapidly followed) by a report of the spontaneous response of the organism to the external stimulus. The impulse recording the external stimulus is thus already 'marked' as meaning (involving) a certain kind of response.

4.21. This sort of relationship we must suppose to recur in relays, or at many successive stages: the initial sensory impulse at the first stage, the spinal cord, setting up both a motor response and a further afferent impulse proceeding on to the higher centers. At the next level it will arrive together with the report of the motor responses it has produced at the lower level, and with other sensory impulses recording other peripheral stimuli, which may be similarly accompanied by the reports of the reflex responses which they have set up at lower levels. At this stage this particular combination of signals may again produce a distinct motor response, so that at the next higher level the bundle of impulses arriving there will include reports of responses which take already a wider range of exteroceptive impulses into account. And as we ascend to higher and higher levels, both the comprehensiveness of the range of external stimuli which are taken into account in any response, and the number of responses effected at lower levels and reported back to these higher levels will constantly increase.

4.22. It is not difficult to see how such an arrangement for the mutual adjustment of the responses to different simultaneously occurring stimuli is made necessary by the development of specific receptors for different kinds of stimuli. So long as the whole organism was merely susceptible to irritation by a wide range of stimuli, and was capable only of a few simple responses, such as contraction and expansion, no special apparatus for co-ordinating the responses to different stimuli was required. But as soon as specific responses became attached to particular classes of stimuli, the mutual adjustment of these responses according to the significance of the particular combination of stimuli became necessary.

4.23. Between the case where specific responses are uniquely attached to particular stimuli, and the case where all responses are decided in view of all the stimuli, there is, of course, an enormous range of intermediate possibilities. Nor need in a given organism only either the one or the other type of arrangement exist. Some other stimuli will be more likely to affect the appropriateness of a given response to one particular stimulus than will be true of others, and there will be more need—or it may be easier for the organism to provide—for the mutual adjustment between those than between others. We must probably assume that, in the course of evolution, the original direct connections between particular stimuli and particular responses are being preserved, but that control mechanisms are being super-imposed capable of inhibiting or modifying these direct responses when they are inappropriate in view of other simultaneously acting stimuli.

4.24. Parallel with this progressively more complex evaluation of the stimuli in the light of an ever more comprehensive collection of other stimuli, a similar organization will operate on the motor side: instead of simple movements of particular muscles, more and more complex patterns of behavior will be evoked as a whole; and the groups of impulses which evoke this pattern of movements are probably evoked as groups by a few central impulses which 'stand for' the whole pattern (4.48–4.51).

4.25. The sketchy manner in which these questions must be treated here ought not to give the impression that these relations are simple. It is neither to be assumed that comparatively simple patterns of stimulation will normally produce comparatively simple responses, and that the integrative action of the higher centers will operate only when more complicated stimulation patterns are involved; nor that the motor responses are built up in a simple additive manner from the effects of individual impulses producing the movement of individual muscles. It is very likely that, just as more than one afferent impulse will generally be required to produce anything like a 'simple' (or sharply discriminated) sensation, so a single efferent impulse will as a rule produce somewhat diffuse movements and only the overlapping of many such impulses will produce a clearly differentiated movement of the separate muscles.[4]

4.26. The increasing differentiation of the different stimuli from each other, and the accompanying increased variability and complexity of the responses to any sub-groups of stimuli, involves, as we have seen, that impulses representative of these stimuli are brought together so that they can act upon each other in a manner which reproduces their significant relations. The more comprehensive this adjustment is, the more elaborate must be the centers set aside from, and capable of overruling the effects of, the more direct connections between stimulus and response.

3. From Specific Reflex to Generalized Evaluation

4.27. It is doubtful whether the ideal simple reflex arc, where the impulse from a single afferent fiber is transmitted to a single efferent fiber, is of any importance, and even whether it occurs at all. But between it as the one extreme ideal type and the other extreme or the voluntary or 'conscious' responses there exists probably a continuous range of connections between stimuli and responses of intermediate types in which processes of classification take place

[4] V. von Weizsäcker, 1947, p. 48.

which are more or less analogous to those which determine the system of sensory qualities. The simplest of these intermediate cases which is of interest is that in which a particular motor response becomes attached to every one of a group of sensory impulses, so that any one of the latter will be transmitted to the motor fiber and produce the response in question. This represents the simplest possible instance where we can speak of a classification of the stimuli.

4.28. The operation of this simple kind of classification is familiar from the experiments with conditioned reflexes and from the phenomenon known as generalization. It has been found that after a conditioned response has been developed to one stimulus, other 'similar' stimuli may also elicit the same response.[5] In these instances the grouping of certain impulses as similar has the effect that further impulses which become connected to some of these impulses become also attached to the other impulses forming the group.

4.29. A higher degree of selection or classification is reached when several responses are alternatively connected with each of a given group of sensory impulses, so that which of these responses will be elicited by a particular stimulus depends on which of a number of other sensory impulses occur at the same time with the former. Which response will be produced in this case by any sensory stimulus will depend on what other stimuli accompany it, and any particular sensory impulse may in some context produce results which are similar to those produced by others, and in other contexts produce results which are different.

4.30. On the lower levels on which connections of this still relatively simple or quasi-reflex type prevail, there will thus already exist some sort of qualitative ordering or discrimination. But it will be greatly limited in two respects: it will involve selective responses to the stimulation of particular sensory receptors for only a very few kinds of responses; and it will select between this limited number of possible responses only with regard to a limited number of simultaneously occurring other stimuli.

4.31. While on these lower levels the discrimination may thus be fairly detailed in so far as it refers to particular responses or functions, it will be specific in the sense that it will be effective only with regard to a particular group of responses, and take into account only a comparatively small range of stimuli. In the famous case of the decapitated frog which is still capable of wiping

---

[5] E. R. Hilgard and D. G. Marquis, 1940, p. 46.—The conditioned reflex is usually represented as a comparatively recent discovery, but the bare facts have been known for a very long time and were already described by M. de Montaigne in the chapter on "The Force of Imagination" of his *Essais* (1580, book I, chapter 20). He there describes the case of a man who, after he had for a long time regularly tested with his hand the temperature of the water prepared for an enema, found that the actual injection had become unnecessary because his taking up the appropriate posture together with his placing the hand in the water already produced the desired effect.

a drop of acid from its back, the signal evoked by the drop of acid will be sufficiently discriminated as regards location to guide the movement of the leg. But the localization of the stimulus which this proves will probably be specific in the sense of being effective only with respect to this particular response.

4.32. Such limited classification may be effected in sub-centers which offer the opportunity for connections among a limited number of sensory and motor fibers. As the impulse is transmitted to higher and more comprehensive centers, there will arise opportunities for more extensive connections, and with them will appear the possibility of a more complex discrimination both with regard to the range of different responses and to the variety of stimuli which will contribute to the decision which of the potential responses will take place.

4.33. The increasing opportunities for connections between fibers carrying sensory impulses from different parts of the body, and the correspondingly increased comprehensiveness of the net of connections which can be formed on the higher levels, does mean neither that at these higher centers the individual stimuli must always be represented by individual impulses as they are on the lower levels, nor that the lower level connections are confined to impulses belonging to the same sense modality.[6] It means merely that at the lower levels only such other sensory impulses will generally be able to modify the response to a particular impulse as are most immediately relevant to the interpretation of (or most frequently associated with) the particular stimulus; while at the higher levels a wider range of less immediately significant other factors will have an opportunity of modifying the result. Similarly, the increasing comprehensiveness of the connections possible at the higher levels *need* not mean the possibility of connections with a larger *number* of individual impulses, but may mean merely the possibility of connections with impulses representing a greater variety of stimuli.

4.34. The responses to any given stimulus thus become at the higher levels more and more liable to be modified by the influence of impulses from other sources. The continuous range of connections between the simple reflex and conscious action thus becomes one in which an ever-increasing number of different stimuli contribute jointly in determining the response. Even though we are directly familiar only with the classification of stimuli which lead to

---

[6] V. von Weizsäcker, 1947, p. 55, points out that, e.g., to the more than four million points on the skin below the neck which produce distinct sensations correspond at most one half million fibers conducting the impulses set up by these stimuli beyond the spinal level. That in spite of this these individual stimuli can be distinguished is presumably due to the fact that with the report of any stimulus acting on the skin there will also arrive reports of the low level reflexes caused by them, reflexes which may be different for stimuli whose direct report arrives in the brain through the same last common path.

behavior that is conscious, and in which this comprehensiveness of the stimuli taken into account has presumably reached the highest degree, at least a great part of observable behavior is probably guided by processes which are intermediate between this and reflex action.

4. Proprioception of Low-Level Responses

4.35. The fact that the sensory impulses may evoke responses on many successive levels has great influence on the manner in which they will be discriminated at the higher levels. In so far as sensory impulses evoke such responses at lower levels, they will arrive at the higher levels accompanied by the proprioceptive impulses recording those responses. The higher centers will in consequence at any one time receive reports not only of given external stimuli but also of the body's spontaneous reaction to those stimuli. The effect of a bright light will not be only a visual impulse but also an impulse reporting the contraction of the pupil, etc. So far as the higher centers are concerned, the self-moving organism must indeed be regarded as part of the environment in which they live.

4.36. Since as a result of the excessive stress placed by the behaviorists on the peripheral responses, certain misconceptions about their significance are still prevalent, it will be necessary to consider with some care the role which such peripheral movements can play in the structure of nervous action. The first point which requires emphasis is that peripheral events, in order to influence further central nervous processes, must be reported back to the centers in which these processes take place. It will therefore be neither the resulting movements as such, nor the efferent motor impulses, but the proprioceptive impulses recording these movements which affect the further neural processes. (The theoretical possibility that part of every efferent neural impulse may, as it were, be branched off before it leaves the center from which it originates, so as to represent there the resulting movement, can be disregarded because there appears to exist no evidence for this.)

4.37. This means not only that, even where distinct motor responses to the individual stimulus take place, it will still be the (proprioceptive) sensory impulses and not the motor impulses themselves which are important for our purposes, but also that, once a certain peripheral response has become the regular effect of any group of stimuli, it will no longer need actually to occur, since the reports of its occurrence will be associatively evoked by the original stimulus. The emphasis placed by the behaviorists on actual movements, and their efforts to discover at least traces of such movements in the form of 'implicit speech' and the like, were thus misplaced. They are not required and the establishment of their existence would not help to answer the problem of what, for instance, constitutes thought.[7]

4.38. Nevertheless, it is true that the sensory order with which we are concerned is both a result and a cause of the motor activities of the body. Behavior has to be seen in a double role: it is both input and output of the activities of the higher nervous centers. The actions which take place independently of the higher centers help to create the order of the sensory impulses arriving at that center, while the actions directed from that center are determined by that order.

4.39. The evaluations of sensory impulses arriving at the highest centers may be compared to the appreciation of the events on the road observed by a person who is being driven in a car, or to the judgements of the pilot of an aeroplane which is being steered by an automatic pilot. In these instances different observed events will lead the passenger of the car, or the pilot of the plane, to expect certain responses of the car or the plane, and those events will come to 'mean' for the person particular kinds of responses of the vehicle, just as certain kinds of stimuli mean certain spontaneous responses of the body. The sight of an oncoming car will come to mean the sensation of the car in which the person rides drawing to the right, and the sight of a red traffic light will mean the feeling of the car slowing down. Very soon what will actually be noticed will no longer be that normal response, but only its absence if it fails to occur.

4.40. The position of the highest centers in this respect is somewhat like that of the commander of an army (or of the head of any other hierarchical organization), who knows that his subordinates will respond to various events in a particular manner, and who will often recognize the character of what has happened as much from the response of his subordinates as from direct observation. It will also be similar in the sense that, so long as the decision taken by his subordinates in the light of their limited but perhaps more detailed observation seems appropriate in view of his more comprehensive knowledge, he will not need to interfere; and that only if something known only to him but not to his subordinates makes those normal responses inappropriate will he have to overrule their decisions by issuing special orders.

4.41. In the same manner as, for instance, the captain of a battleship may sometimes recognize the nature of an observed object less from his direct perception of it than from the responses of his ship, so the brain often may get a direct report merely about the action of one of a large class of stimuli and yet be able to recognize its character from the almost simultaneous reports of the responses of the body directed by lower levels. At the same time these responses of the lower centers to particular stimuli, of which the higher cen-

[7] See C. T. Morgan, 1943, p. 476.

ters have no reports, may be governed by general 'directives' issued by the higher centers. (We shall see presently that this 'set' of the whole organism which determines what the response to a particular stimulus shall be, may in turn be determined either by processes in the highest center or be the result of sub-cortical regulation.)

4.42. So far as the higher centers are concerned, a given combination of external stimuli will not merely mean that such and such other external events are to be expected, but also that certain adjustments of the organism are taking place. The significance of the effect of cold on the skin will not only be that certain action is indicated, but also that certain responses of the body will automatically come about—not merely a report of a single external stimulus but at the same time also of a change in the state of a great part of the body.

4.43. While it is on the whole more likely that responses *via* the lowest centers will be innate for the individual, that is, acquired by the race in the course of evolution, while the responses effected by the higher centers will be largely based on individual experience, this cannot be regarded as a universal rule. Probably some inherited responses are effected on fairly high levels, while some learned responses may, after sufficient repetition, become almost completely automatic and be effected at low levels.

4.44. It should also be noted that the degree of modifiability of the response to a particular stimulus by other simultaneous stimuli need not vary in strict correspondence with the extent to which these responses can be altered by individual experience: an acquired response to a given stimulus may be uniquely determined by that one stimulus, while an inherited response may be capable of considerable variation according to the accompanying circumstance.

5. Postures and Movements Connected with Perception

4.45. The first group of motor responses to sensory stimuli which we must consider further are those which assist perception directly and which might almost be described as part of the act of perception. We have already mentioned the classical instance of the kinesthetic sensations connected with the focusing of the eye. The familiar effects of displacing the eyeball or of crossing the fingers on the localization of the sensations affected belong to the same category. It is becoming increasingly clear that these are merely special instances of a very general phenomenon, and that the proprioceptive reports of the body postures and movements designed to help perception serve always as a sort of indispensable background for the proper evaluation of the stimulus.

4.46. Recent investigations of the relation between sensation and movement show that this connection is even closer than had been commonly supposed and that practically all sensory impulses are evaluated in the light of, or corrected for, simultaneous muscular activities. V. von Weizsäcker, to whom we owe a great deal of knowledge on this question, speaks with considerable justification of a complete 'entwinement' (*Verflechtung*) of sensation and movement.[8] This seems to apply as much to the evaluation of external stimuli in the light of the simultaneous proprioceptive impulses as reciprocally to the evaluation of the latter in the light of the usually accompanying exteroceptive impulses. Stretching my leg downwards means for me that I expect to feel the ground, and stretching my whole body means that I expect it to cool more rapidly than in a crouched position, etc., etc. The proprioceptive impulses thus receive their significance as much from the exteroceptive ones which are associated with them, as the reverse is true.

4.47. Every sensory situation thus means, among other things, that various movements will have such and such effects, and the totality of the simultaneous exteroceptive and proprioceptive impulses forms the background, as it were, against which the individual impulse is evaluated. It might even be said that every single sensory impulse is probably multivalent, capable of producing various different sensations, and that which sensation it will produce will depend on what other impulses occur at the same time.

6. Patterns of Motor Responses

4.48. The manner in which the separate motor impulses are co-ordinated so as to produce complex patterns of behavior consisting of many simultaneous and successive movements can be considered here only very briefly. We must probably assume that these patterns can be elicited as wholes by a few signals sent out from the higher centers, and that we have thus on the motor side to deal with a phenomenon of 'bundling' which in some respects is the converse of the process of classification on the sensory side. As in the latter case, different complexes of sensory impulses will be represented at the higher centers by a few 'representative' impulses, so that a few central impulses may suffice to evoke bundles of motor impulses producing complex patterns of behavior. The particular manner in which this behavior is executed may then be determined by the interplay of motor and sensory impulses at lower levels.

4.49. These behavior patterns, however, must not be conceived as fixed but as highly variable. Just as at the higher centers it will not be only one particular sensory impulse, but any one of a class of many different combinations

[8] V. von Weizsäcker, 1947. See also K. Goldstein, 1939; and E. G. Boring, 1942, p. 563: 'In the twentieth century it eventually became apparent that the organism behaves first and feels afterwards, just as James, speaking of emotions, said it does.'

of impulses, which will give rise to a particular response, so the motor signal sent out from the higher centers will be for the execution not of one particular pattern of co-ordinated movements but for any one of a class of such patterns. Such a class of patterns will consist of those different combinations of movements which under different conditions will produce a particular result. Which of these patterns will be put into effect will be decided in the light of the whole sensory position.

4.50. At the higher centers the connections will thus increasingly exist, not between particular stimuli and particular responses, but between classes of stimuli and classes of responses, and between classes of classes of stimuli and classes of classes of responses, etc. The order given by the highest center in response to a particular situation may thus be of the kind which we have called a general 'directive' for an action of a certain class, and it may be only at lower levels that the appropriate response is selected from the class of behavior patterns which in different situations may produce the desired result.

4.51. The extent to which behavior patterns can be adjusted to the sensory situation probably varies with the level which is in control. There is reason to believe that some highly stereotyped, or 'mechanical' patterns, such as those of the movements of flying and running, are co-ordinated on a fairly low level, and that even at these low levels the execution is constantly controlled and modified by sensory signals from the kinesthetic receptors and the semi-circular canals. At higher levels the pattern of movement will be variable to a higher degree.

4.52. We can again not concern ourselves here with the question to what extent behavior patterns are innate to the individual and how the innate and the learned behavior pattern interact.[9] There can be little doubt that even fairly complex behavior patterns, or rather classes of behavior patterns from which a selection will be made in the light of the whole sensory situation, are innate and can be elicited by fairly simple stimuli. A well-known instance is the evocation of the maternal behavior in the rat by definite chemical stimuli.[10]

4.53. The selection of the particular behavior pattern from the class of such patterns appropriate to the result aimed at must not be conceived as taking place in one act. The choice of a kind of behavior pattern and its continued control, modification, and adjustment while it takes place, will be a process in which the various factors act successively to produce the final outcome. It is not as if the whole behavior pattern were determined upon before any movement takes place, but rather that during the process of execution further adjustments are constantly made to secure the result.

4.54. In connection with these continuous adjustments, made while the

[9] K. Lorenz, 1942, *passim.*
[10] C. T. Morgan, 1943, p. 411.

movement proceeds, the interaction between the exteroceptive and the proprioceptive impulses and the operation of the 'feed-back' principle[11] become of special significance. In the first instance, the sensory representation of the environment, and of the possible goal to be achieved in that environment, will evoke a movement pattern generally aimed at the achievement of the goal. But at first the pattern of movement initiated will not be fully successful. The current sensory reports about what is happening will be checked against expectations, and the difference between the two will act as a further stimulus indicating the required corrections. The result of every step in the course of the actions will, as it were, be evaluated against the expected results, and any difference will serve as an indicator of the corrections required.

4.55. In this process the intervention of the highest centers is probably needed only to give the general directions, while the execution and current adjustment is left to the guidance of the lower centers. Once the 'course is set', the deviations will be automatically corrected by the differences between the expected and the effective stimuli acting as the signs which produce the correction. Such responses to a difference between expectations and outcome are merely a special case, on the one hand, of the general principle that a response to any new stimulus is determined by the pre-existing sensory state, and, on the other, of the capacity of the nervous system to respond in a particular manner to certain kinds of relations between impulses rather than merely to particular impulses. Both these characteristics of the higher centers, the pre-dominant importance of the pre-existing excitatory state, and the tendency to respond to differences between expected and realized impulses, will have to be considered further in the next chapter.

7. Biogenic Needs and Drives

4.56. We still have not yet noticed the prime sources of activity of the organism, namely those changes in its constitution or balance which occur periodically as a result of its normal vegetative processes and which make action by the organism necessary if it is to survive. In consequence of our stress on the

---

[11] N. Wiener, 1948a and 1948b [Norbert Wiener (1894–1964) was an American mathematician who is known as the founder of cybernetics, the study of feed-back controlled systems, or, in Wiener's (1948a) words, "the scientific study of control and communication in the animal and the machine."—Ed.]; W. S. McCulloch, 1948 [Warren Sturgis McCulloch (1898–1969) was an American neuropsychologist who is known for his work in neural network modeling and cybernetics.—Ed.]; W. R. Ashby, 1947a and 1947b, 1948, and 1949. [William Ross Ashby (1903–72) was an English psychiatrist whose work was influential in the development of cybernetics.—Ed.]

sensory organization we have so far treated the whole problem as if it were mainly one of adaptation of the organism to changes originating in the environment. But even more important than the question why the organism will behave differently in different environments is the question why it will at different times behave differently in the same environment.

4.57. Even more than before our discussion must here pre-suppose a great deal which belongs to theoretical biology and physiology. As has already been pointed out (4.13), there is really no other difference between the problem of the purposive internal functioning of the organism and that of its purposive behavior towards its environment, than that the latter raises the problem of a comprehensive order of the various external stimuli which determines how in different combinations they will modify each other's effects. This includes the problem of why internal stimuli may bring it about that a given organism will at different times respond differently to the same set of external stimuli.

4.58. What is significant here for our purposes is not so much the precise nature of the physiological processes which determine such states as hunger, thirst, and the like, but what the 'attitudes', 'dispositions', or 'sets' corresponding to these physiological states mean for the responses of the organism towards its environment. Since these various 'needs' or 'drives' may be produced by visceral, glandular or general metabolic processes, it is convenient to refer to them by the generic term 'biogenic needs'.[12]

4.59. It may be mentioned at once that these 'needs' resulting from the spontaneous vegetative processes of the body are, of course, closely related to, and sometimes practically indistinguishable from, another kind of attitudes or sets such as fear or rage, which, though usually caused by some sensory perception, also consist of a disposition for a certain range or type of actions. The problems which these 'emotions' or 'feelings' raise are thus very similar to those raised by the needs in the narrower sense. It would be difficult to decide whether the sexual urge provoked by a sensory impression is in this sense a 'need' or an 'emotion'. Similarly, appetite may be stimulated by the smell of some delectable food without hunger being present, or a sense of fear caused by bodily processes without any sensory (i.e., exteroceptive) experience inspiring the fear.

4.60. While we shall in the first instance consider the significance of needs and wants proper, and leave to the next sections any more specific comments on emotions, most of what is to be said about needs applies equally to emotions. Both involve not only a disposition of the organism towards a certain class of actions, but also a special receptivity for certain classes of stimuli. As a result of a peculiar state of balance the whole organism comes to 'like' or

[12] C. T. Morgan, 1943.

'dislike' particular kinds of stimuli. We shall later in connection with 'attention', (6.26–6.27) have to consider more fully the nature of this state of excitatory preparedness.

4.61. It is perhaps useful to distinguish between the term 'set'[13] as the name for the preparedness of the organism for certain kinds of actions, and the term 'expectancy' for the increased receptivity for certain kinds of stimuli which will elicit the corresponding responses. But such a distinction between the sensory and the motor aspect of what is essentially a relation between a class of stimuli and a class of responses must not lead us to treat them as if they were really separate. The important point is their close connection, the fact that the organism will be disposed to respond in a particular manner to any one of a class of stimuli.

4.62. At this stage of the exposition it is yet too early to try to show even in outline how such a state of need, which at first may produce merely an aimless increase of motor activity, may become directed towards the purposive search for certain kinds of stimuli, so that the animal searches for food or for a sex partner, which, when found, will produce the consuming activity. This will have to be attempted in the next chapter.

4.63. Our present purpose was merely to show that in addition to the 'objective' significance which the different stimuli will acquire for the organism as the result of their regular association with other stimuli, they will also acquire a special 'subjective' or 'pragmatic' significance through their capacity of satisfying certain needs. The connections which will give them this significance will operate not only through certain stimuli producing certain actions if the need is present, but also through the need of making the organism search for stimuli of the appropriate kind. This evaluation of stimuli with respect to goals which are determined by the momentary needs will have to be considered further when we examine the general problem of how a representation of the environment enables the organism to act 'purposively' (5.64ff.).

8. Emotions and the James-Lange Theory

4.64. The second kind of dispositions, emotions, are dispositions for a type of actions which in the first instance are not made necessary by a primary change in the state of the organism, but which are complexes of responses appropriate to a variety of environmental conditions. Fear and anger, sorrow and joy, are attitudes towards the environment, and particularly towards fellow members of the same species, which may become attached to, and then regularly evoked by, a great many different classes of stimuli.

[13] See J. J. Gibson, 1941.

4.65. This means that a great variety of external events, and also some conditions of the organism itself, may evoke one of several patterns of attitudes or dispositions which, while they last, will affect or 'color' the perception of, and the responses to, any external event. In the mental order of events, that is in the influence which external stimuli can exercise on further mental processes and on behavior, these states will occupy positions which in many ways will be similar to those of the sensory qualities: the occurrence of any one of them will be capable of modifying the result of a given sensory situation in the same kind of way in which the appearance of a new sensory experience could do so.

4.66. Emotions may thus be described as 'affective qualities' similar to the sensory qualities and forming part of the same comprehensive order of mental qualities. But they differ, of course, in some respects from the sensory qualities and must be regarded as forming a distinct sub-system of the more comprehensive mental order. The relation between the order of affective qualities and the order of sensory qualities must be conceived as somewhat similar to the relations between the orders of the different sensory modalities which also form sub-systems of the more comprehensive order of all sensory qualities (3.75).

4.67. The most conspicuous difference between the order of the sensory qualities and the order of the affective qualities is that, while the former is organized with spatial relationships as one of its main ordering principles, the affective qualities do not refer to particular points in space. They represent not qualities of particular things but rather a condition of an interval of time as a whole. They will refer not to what is to be expected of an external position but are rather a temporary bias or preference for certain types of responses towards any external situation.

4.68. These important differences between sensory and affective qualities, however, do not alter the fact that the general principle by which they are determined is the same. The similarity of the response to different stimuli will in both instances be determined by the fact that the corresponding different nervous impulses will evoke the same following of other impulses. Similar emotions, as similar sensations, are nervous impulses which evoke the same following and which are therefore functionally equivalent and classified as the same kind of event. The main difference is that within the sensory sub-system of the mental order the classifying connections will be mainly with other impulses representing sensory stimuli, while in the affective sub-system the classifying connections will be mainly with impulses representing certain types of behavior.

4.69. But although the order of affective qualities will constitute a sub-system in the more comprehensive system of qualities (in the sense that the impulses belonging to it will be less closely connected with impulses in other parts of the larger system than they are connected among themselves), this does not prevent this sub-system from contributing to the differences between sensory qualities, and vice versa. By becoming connected with sensory qualities those differently organized qualities can add, as it were, an additional dimension to the order of sensory qualities; and similarly the differences between the different sensory qualities associated to different groups of the latter may assist in enriching the variety of differentiations between the former.

4.70. This account of the determination of the affective qualities of course corresponds very closely to the familiar James-Lange theory of emotions.[14] As we said before of the Berkeleyan theory of spatial vision (3.40–3.42), the James-Lange theory also may be regarded as a special case of the theory of mental qualities here outlined. The modifications which are required to make the James-Lange theory fit into our scheme are practically the same as those which we had to make with regard to the role which proprioceptive impulses play in determining the perception of space. We shall not regard the actual sensations produced by the various bodily accompaniments of a given stimulus as determining its affective values, but merely the following of physiological impulses which record the states of the body and which, in the same manner in which such a following can determine the peculiar functional significance which we know as sensory qualities, can also determine affective qualities.

4.71. We do, therefore, not propose to say, with William James, that emotions are 'a set of kinesthetic and organic sensations'. We shall merely contend that the connections with impulses recording certain connected sets of changes in the general state of the body can give certain central impulses that peculiar position in the whole system of mental events which we know as the different affective qualities.

4.72. The James-Lange theory of emotions (like Berkeley's theory of spatial vision) would thus appear to be justified in its endeavour to reduce the qualitative attributes of those mental events to relations between different impulses which, if fully evaluated, might evoke certain other sensations. Both theories, however, fall short of a real answer to their problem, and in fact merely shift

[14] [William James and the Danish psychologist Carl Lange (1834–1900) independently developed a theory of emotions, the basic thrust of which James (*The Principles of Psychology*, 1890, vol. 2, pp. 449–50) summarized as follows: "My theory . . . is that the bodily changes follow directly the perception of the existing fact, and that our feeling of the same changes as they occur is the emotion. Common sense says, we lose our fortune, are sorry and weep; we meet a bear, are frightened and run; we are insulted by a rival, are angry and strike. The hypothesis here is that this order of sequence is incorrect . . . and that the more rational statement is that we feel sorry because we cry, angry because we strike, afraid because we tremble." An early critic of the James-Lange theory was the above (4.14) mentioned Walter B. Cannon ("The James-Lange Theory of Emotions: A Critical Examination and an Alternative Theory," *American Journal of Psychology* 29 [1927]: 106–24).—Ed.]

the problem to a different point, because they attempt to explain the quality of one kind of experience by reference to qualities occurring in another kind of experience, which latter they take as not requiring explanation. In so far as they were concerned with only that one kind of mental quality, this procedure was inevitable. But if we consistently follow up and generalize the principle underlying those theories, there remain of course no given mental qualities; we are forced to replace the whole system of qualities by a system of relations between initially undifferentiated elements which can be conceived to be isomorphic with the system of qualities which we have to explain.

CHAPTER V

THE STRUCTURE OF THE MENTAL ORDER

1. Pre-Sensory Experience or 'Linkages'

5.1. In the preceding chapters we have given the general outline of the principle by which a set of neural impulses in principle may become organized in a manner analogous to the familiar order of the mental qualities. We shall now have to try and fill in this outline by a sketch of the process by which this order is formed, and of the general character of that order itself.

5.2. This account of the formation of the mental order will still have to be extremely schematic, in the sense that we shall not attempt more than a general indication of a possible way in which such an order may be built up, without attempting to show in what manner this will happen in any particular organism. We shall also still have largely to disregard the distinction between the part of this process which takes place in the course of the development of the single individual, and the part which takes place in the course of the development of the species and the results of which will be embedded in the structure of the individual organism when it commences its independent life (or when it reaches maturity).

5.3. There is at present still very little knowledge available which would enable us to draw such a distinction between the part of the mental order which for the individual is determined by its inherited constitution and the part which for it may be regarded as being of experiential origin.[1] But as we are concerned with the genesis of mind as such, it is comparatively unimportant what for the individual are constitutional and what are experiential factors; indeed, it is at least likely that what for one species or at one developmental stage may be of experiential origin, may in other instances be constitutionally determined. What is important for our purposes is that it would appear that the principle which determines the formation of the mental order may operate either in the ontogenetic or in the phylogenetic process. Such an assumption of a general similarity between the kind of processes which take place in the evolution of the species and in that of the individual does,

---

[1] See, however, the very important contributions to this problem by K. Lorenz, 1942.

of course, in no way pre-judge the issues of the great controversies on the mechanism of evolution.

5.4. For the purposes of the following schematic exposition we shall, therefore, proceed as if at the commencement of the life of the individual the structure of the central nervous system were fully completed before any connections between neurons corresponding to the simultaneous occurrence of stimuli had been established. This means in effect that we shall disregard the possibility of the transmission from generation to generation of connections in the higher nervous centers which constitute adaptations to the environment; and that we shall treat a process as if it took place in the development of the single individual which in fact probably occurs to a large extent in the course of the development of the species. This assumption perhaps may be justified in some measure in so far as the highest centers are concerned, but it certainly does not apply to the connections existing at the lower levels, which form an essential part in the complete process of classification.

5.5. An afferent impulse arriving for the first time at the higher centers of such a system would thus not yet possess any connections with other such impulses and therefore not yet occupy a definite position in the order of such impulses, or have a distinct functional significance. But since every occurrence of a combination of such impulses will contribute to the gradual formation of a network of connections of ever-increasing density, every neuron will gradually acquire a more and more clearly defined place in the comprehensive system of such connections, and with it a distinct functional significance which in a great many ways will differ from that of other impulses.

5.6. In a certain sense it might be said that the qualitative distinctions which will thus be built up between the significance of the different impulses are created by 'experience'. In doing so, however, we should have to be aware that we are using the term 'experience' in a somewhat special sense. Since the impulses between which these first connections are formed would not yet occupy a place in an order of sensory qualities, and no such order would yet exist, their occurrence could not yet be described as experience in the ordinary meaning of this term. It would not yet represent a mental event but would be a purely physiological event because it would possess none of the attributes which give it a place in a mental or qualitative order.

5.7. The term 'experience' in this connection is thus somewhat ambiguous and misleading, because it suggests the occurrence of sensory qualities, while the phenomenon with which we are concerned is a kind of pre-sensory[2] expe-

---

[2] This concept of pre-sensory experience must not be confused with the conception of 'pre-sensation' as used by F. R. Bichowsky, 1925, and R. B. Cattel, 1930, to describe the 'first conscious effect that can be traced to a stimulus . . . which does not yet possess spatial or temporal quality, that is to say, is not felt to be located in space or time, or to have the definite qualities and relations usually associated with sensations' (Bichowsky, 1925, p. 589).

rience which only creates the apparatus which later makes qualitative distinctions possible. To avoid the misleading connotations which attach to the term experience it will therefore be expedient to employ a more neutral term to describe the formation of new connections by the simultaneous occurrence of several afferent impulses. We shall for that purpose adopt as the technical term the word 'linkage'.

5.8. By a *linkage* we shall thus understand the most general lasting effect which groups of stimuli can impress upon the organization of the central nervous system. It implies a physiological effect of external events on that organization, but not necessarily that when these external events occur they already possess any distinct significance for the organism. It is a sort of learning to discriminate which may occur before any discriminations are yet possible, an 'experience' which, though it will later, when the same stimuli occur again, give them special significance for the organism, need at the time as yet have no meaning for the individual.

5.9. When we stress that events producing these linkages need not be in any sense mental or sensory events, we of course do not merely mean that they need not be conscious. It must be remembered that we employ here the term 'mental' in a sense which is wider than, and includes, the conscious (1.67–1.73). The events between which linkages occur need not possess even such a place in the mental order which would make them mental events in this wider sense.

5.10. In some respects it might have been preferable instead of introducing the clumsy new term 'linkage', to revive in the same technical sense the old term 'impression'. But this term not only is so much charged with the meaning of a mental experience that it seemed better to avoid it, but it also seemed desirable to choose a term which expressly stressed that all such experience which can give rise to memory must always consist in the creation of connections between several physiological events. And since all memory consists in the linking of two or more such events it seemed better to describe the effect which produces memory by a term referring to the creation of such links.

5.11. Although it may sound commonplace that all experience, in the widest sense of the term, causes, and that all memory is based on, the creation of connections between physiological events representing stimuli, this still requires emphasis, since there exists another view which, just because it is rarely explicitly stated, yet exercises considerable influence and is one of the main supports of the idea of a special mental substance. This view is what might be called the 'storage' theory of memory, the conception that with every experience some new mental entity representing sensations or images enters the mind or the brain and is there retained until it is returned at the appropriate moment.

5.12. This conception is, of course, part and parcel of the theory of the absolute character of sensory qualities, and connected with the erroneous interpretation of the theory of the specific energy of the nerves, according to which the nature of the process in the different fibers determines the quality of the resulting sensation. Against it we should remember that we know of no physiological mechanism which can retain anything except connections between different events, and that, therefore, any theory of mind which is to be expressed in physiological terms must use 'experience' and 'memory' in the sense which we stress by employing the term 'linkage'.

5.13. The theory here developed then assumes that every sensory quality which occurs pre-supposes the previous occurrence of linkages between impulses which may not yet have been classified as belonging to a particular qualitative group. Even after relatively simple systems of connections, effecting some measure of classification, have been formed, this system will be constantly modified by new linkages. But as the existing system of connections becomes more and more complex and more firmly embedded, any new linkage will be less likely to alter its general character.

5.14. One important consequence of this relation between physiological linkages and sensory experience is that there will be implicit in all sensory experience certain relations determined by earlier linkages (i.e., by the influence of the external world on the organism) which have never been the object of sensory experience in the ordinary meaning of this term; and that the order of sensory qualities will be subject to continuous modification by new linkages between impulses which may not lead to sense experience. The epistemological significance of this fact will be examined in the last chapter (8.1–8.27).

5.15. The terminological point discussed in this section has some bearing on the question whether our theory of the determination of sensory qualities can be properly described as 'empiricist'. It seems that in the dispute between the 'empiricists' and the 'nativists' there were really two different issues involved. The first is whether, so far as the individual is concerned, the order of sensory qualities is congenital or acquired by individual experience. On this probably no general answer is possible. The second is whether the whole sensory order can be conceived as having been built up by the experience of the race or the individual, i.e., whether it is based on the retention of connections between effects exercised upon them by the external world. With regard to this second question our answer is definitely empiricist (2.16).

5.16. It might at first seem as if this empiricist character of our theory would stand in irreconcilable contrast to the strongly anti-empiricist attitude of the Gestalt school with whose arguments our theory is in other respects in close agreement. I am not certain, however, that the opposition of the Gestalt school to an empiricist explanation of Gestalt qualities as being 'built up' by experience from sensory 'elements' need apply to a theory which, as the theory developed here, traces *all* sensory qualities, 'elementary' as well as

Gestalt qualities, to the pre-sensory formation of a network of connections based on linkages between non-mental elements.

2. The Gradual Formation of a 'Map' Reproducing Relations between Classes of Events in the Environment

5.17. The connections formed by the linkages between different impulses will evidently reproduce certain regularities in the occurrence of the external stimuli acting on the organism. The network of these connections will reproduce not any attributes of the individual stimuli (whose identity is determined solely by their capacity of setting up impulses in a particular sensory fiber, or group of fibers), but a sort of record of past associations of any particular stimulus with other stimuli which have acted upon the organism at the same time. While such a record, dependent upon the frequency with which in the course of the development of an individual (or possibly species) certain stimuli have occurred together, will reproduce certain relationships between these stimuli determined by the physical differences between them, it will clearly not give a full or correct reproduction of all the relations which can be said 'objectively' to exist between these stimuli.

5.18. We have seen in the first chapter (1.14–1.19) that a description of the stimuli in physical terms involves a classification of these stimuli based solely on their observed relations towards each other and neglecting any difference or similarity of the response of the organism on which they act. It seems to be in conformity with general scientific procedure to treat only those differences between stimuli which manifest themselves in their relations to other stimuli as differences belonging to the physical world (or as differences constituting the physical order of the universe), and to regard differences and similarities between groups of stimuli which show themselves solely in their effects on certain types of organisms as due to the organization of these organisms. Our present task is to show the kind of classification, or of ordering of the stimuli, which, through the process we have sketched, such an organism is likely to develop.

5.19. The gradual evolution of the mental order involves thus a gradual approximation to the order which in the external world exists between the stimuli evoking the impulses which 'represent' them in the central nervous system. But while conceptual thinking has long been recognized as a process of continuous reorganization of the (supposedly constant) elements of the phenomenal world, a reorganization which makes their arrangement correspond more perfectly with experience, we have been led to the conclusion that the qualitative elements of which the phenomenal world is built up, and the whole order of the sensory qualities, are themselves subject to continuous

228

change. There remains, in consequence, no justification for the sharp distinction between the direct sensory perception of qualities and the more abstract processes of thought;[3] we shall have to assume that the operations of both the senses and the intellect are equally based on acts of classification (or reclassification) performed by the central nervous system, and that they are both part of the same continuous process by which the microcosm in the brain progressively approximates to a reproduction of the macrocosm of the external world.

5.20. The order which the linkages will gradually create in the central nervous system will, for several reasons, constitute not only a very imperfect but in some respect even a definitely erroneous reproduction of the relations which exist between the corresponding physical stimuli. In the first instance, the receptor organs through which the physical stimuli set up nervous impulses are imperfectly selective in several respects: the organism possesses receptor organs which are sensitive for only certain kinds of external events but not for others; and these receptor organs which it does possess also do not sharply distinguish between stimuli which are physically different. Physically different events may stimulate the same receptor organs and set up impulses in the same sensory fiber, and physical stimuli of the same kind but acting on different receptors may be recorded as different sensory modalities (1.39). Which external events are recorded at all, and how they will be recorded, will thus depend on the given structure of the organism as it has been shaped by the process of evolution.

5.21. Secondly, the kinds of physical stimuli which will act on a particular organism, and the relative frequency of the simultaneous occurrence of the different stimuli, will correspond not to conditions in the world at large, but to conditions in the particular environment in which the organism has existed. The partial reproduction of the relations between the stimuli acting on the organism will therefore be a reproduction of those relations only which appear in a certain sector of the external world, and will not necessarily be representative of those existing in the whole of it.

5.22. Thirdly, as we have seen already (chapter IV), one of the most important parts of the 'environment' from which the central nervous system will receive signals producing linkages will be the *milieu intérieur*, the internal en-

---

[3] Cf., H. Margenau, 1950, p. 54, and H. Werner, 1948, pp. 222-25, 234–36. [Henry Margenau (1901–97), born in Germany, was Professor of Physics and Natural Philosophy at Yale University from 1950 until his formal retirement in 1986. Heinz Werner (1890–1964) was a development psychologist who, being dismissed as a Jew from the University of Hamburg, was forced to leave Germany in 1933. He found refuge in the United States, where he taught at a number of universities, eventually at Clark University, Worcester, Massachusetts, whose Institute of Developmental Psychology has been renamed Heinz Werner Institute of Developmental Psychological Research.—Ed.]

vironment, or the rest of the organism in which the central nervous system exists. Since the events in the organism will in some degree be co-ordinated with each other and with the events in the external world proper, independently of the functioning of the higher nervous centers, it is inevitable that the relations existing between them should play a large part in shaping the order that will be formed in the higher centers.

5.23. Fourthly, there is no reason to assume that the capacity of the higher centers to form connections between the neurons in which impulses occur at the same time is uniform throughout those centers. It is probable that the given anatomical structure will facilitate the formation of certain connections and make the formation of others more difficult (or impossible). The resulting structure of connections would by this be further distorted or prevented from giving a true reproduction of the relations between even those impulses which unequivocally represent specific physical stimuli.

5.24. Fifthly, as a result of the successive classification of the impulses on several different levels (4.33), the signals reaching the higher and more comprehensive centers will often not represent individual stimuli, but may stand for classes or groups of such stimuli formed at lower levels for particular functional purposes. Any further classification effected at the higher centers will therefore be subject to all the distortions which, for reasons similar to those already mentioned, have occurred on lower levels.

5.25. In discussing the relationships between the network of connections which will thus be formed, and the structure of external events which it can be said to reproduce, it will be useful sometimes to employ the simile of the *map* which in a somewhat analogous manner reproduces some of the relations which exist in certain parts of the physical world. The picture of the geographical map in this connection comes so readily to one's mind[4] because of its similarity with the simple arrow diagram which is the most obvious method of schematically depicting the structure of a complex dynamic system whose elements are connected as cause and effect.

5.26. This 'map' of the relationships between various kinds of events in the external world, which the linkages will gradually produce in the higher nervous centers, will not only be a very imperfect map, but also a map which is subject to continuous although very gradual change. It will not only give merely some of the relations existing in the external world, and give in addition some which are different from those which exist objectively, but it will also not give a constant but a variable picture of the structures which it reproduces.

5.27. The different maps which will thus be formed in different brains will

---

[4] For similar uses of the concept of the map, see, e.g., E. D. Adrian, 1947, p. 16–18, and E. C. Tolman, 1948.

be determined by factors which are sufficiently similar to make those maps also similar to each other. But they will not be identical. Complete identity of the maps would pre-suppose not only an identical history of the different individuals but also complete identity of their anatomical structure. The mere fact that for each individual the map will be subject to constant changes practically precludes the possibility that at any moment the maps of two individuals should be completely identical.

5.28. The conception of 'similarity' between several different systems of relationships which are not completely identical, such as would exist between two maps of this kind, and still more so the conception of varying degrees of similarity, and that of similar positions in similar systems of relationships, present considerable conceptual difficulties. It is the same difficulty which we encounter when we consider the degrees of similarities between various qualities or Gestalts. The simile of the map, however, will show what is meant: we can recognize without great difficulty not only the similarity of different maps of the same region, although they may be drawn in different projections, contain different details and refer to different dates, but we shall in general also be able to identify corresponding points on two such maps as referring to the same point in the real world. Two persons discussing the same walk, with different maps of the region before them, will in general encounter no difficulty in understanding each other, although particular points on their route may have different significance for them.

5.29. In the 'map' with which we are concerned, the relevant relations between the individual points are not their spatial relations, however, but solely the paths through which impulses can be transmitted. It is a topological and not a topographical map. It will resemble rather one of those schematic railway maps in which connections are indicated by straight lines without representing accurate distances. It will resemble a topographical map only in the sense that it will also show where any given movement will lead us.

5.30. For a description of the process by which linkages will gradually produce a map of the relations between the stimuli acting on the organism, the simile of the map, however, soon becomes inadequate, because the classification with which we are concerned will, as we have seen, occur on many successive levels. We should have to think of the whole system of connections as consisting of many vertically super-imposed sub-systems which in some respects may operate independently of each other. Every sub-system of this kind will constitute a partial map of the environment, and the maps formed at the lower levels will serve for the guidance of merely a limited range of responses, and at the same time act as filters or pre-selectors for the impulses sent on to the higher centers, for which, in turn, the maps of the lower levels constitute a part of the environment.

5.31. While the full and detailed classification of sensory impulses, corresponding to the order of sensory qualities which we know from conscious experience, is effected mainly at the highest centers, we must assume a more limited classification on somewhat similar principles to take place already at the lower levels, where certainly no conscious experience is associated with it. The qualitative order which is familiar to us in its most developed form from our conscious experience will exist in a more rudimentary form on lower levels where we have no direct knowledge of it, but can only attempt to reconstruct it as part of our endeavour to understand the whole hierarchy of the apparatus of classification which culminates in conscious mind. There can be little doubt that we must assume the existence on lower levels of such an order of the sensory impulses somewhat analogous to that revealed by our conscious experience, an order which we can ascertain only from the character of the discriminatory responses of which we are not conscious.

5.32. We have already discussed the significance of this hierarchical order of the central nervous system and the significance which the classification of impulses will have for the operation of the whole (4.11–4.26), and we shall leave aside until the next chapter the question of the 'conscious' character of some of the processes which take place at the highest levels. It will also be seen now, although a fuller discussion of this must wait until later in this chapter, that the difference between what are commonly regarded as merely 'mechanical' and as mental processes respectively is not one of kind but merely one of degree; and that the extent to which a process partakes of the character of the mental will depend on the complexity of the ordering processes which intervene between the stimulus and the response; or rather, since the stimulus-response terminology becomes somewhat inappropriate at this stage, between the excitatory state of the sensory apparatus and the resulting behavior.

3. The 'Map' and the 'Model'

5.33. We must now consider the manner in which, within a given structure of connections, the many impulses proceeding at any one moment can mutually influence each other. Up to this point we have examined only the mutual effects which new afferent impulses arriving more or less at the same time will exercise upon each other. The centers at which such impulses arrive will, however, never be found in an inactive state. As we ascend to higher and higher levels, the function of new impulses arriving there will be less and less to evoke specific responses but increasingly merely to modify and control behavior in the light of the whole situation, represented not only by simultaneously arriving other impulses but also by the retained picture of the environment. This involves that a sort of record of recently received stimuli is kept at these higher centers.

5.34. As any afferent impulse is passed on to higher levels, it will send out more and more branches which will potentially be capable of reinforcing or inhibiting an ever-increasing range of other impulses. This increasing ramification of every chain of impulses, as it ascends through successive relays to higher levels, will mean that at any moment the general excitatory state of the whole nervous system will depend less and less on the new stimuli currently received, and more and more on the continued course of chains of impulses set up by stimuli which were received during some period of the past. In consequence, an ever-increasing part of the forces determining the response will consist of the pre-existing distribution of impulses throughout the whole system of connected fibers, while the newly arriving impulses will play a correspondingly smaller part.

5.35. It is a corollary of this steadily increasing influence of the pre-existing excitatory state that the main significance of any new stimulus will be that it will alter the general disposition for responding in particular ways to further stimuli, and that less and less of its effect will consist in producing a specific response. In other words, a greater and greater part of the effects of impulses set up by any new stimuli will go to create a 'set' controlling future responses, and a smaller part directly to influence current responses. As we reach higher levels, the classification of the impulses becomes thus less specific to a particular function, and more general in the sense that it will help to create a disposition to a certain range of responses to an ever-growing variety of stimuli.

5.36. As the classification becomes thus more 'general' and less 'specific', the classifying event also becomes more and more definitely a central process while the relations to any particular peripheral response become at the same time more remote and round-about. As higher and more embracing centers are reached the effect of any newly arriving afferent impulse on the central process will become more and more important compared with its direct effect on peripheral responses. We must think increasingly in terms of a continuous central process which at any moment will merely be somewhat modified by the newly arriving afferent impulses and only part of which will, as it were, continuously spill over into efferent signals producing peripheral responses.

5.37. It thus will be the totality of all the different impulses proceeding at any given moment in the higher centers which determines what is to be the response to any newly arriving impulse. Since all these impulses thus act as a sort of representation or picture of the momentary environment, to which the response to any new impulse is adjusted, it is not fanciful to describe the whole as an apparatus of orientation.[5] By providing a reproduction of the environment in which the organism moves at the moment, it adjusts the responses to those elements in the environment which are represented in it.

[5] H. Kleint, 1940, p. 40.

5.38. It seems probable that at these higher centers some of the impulses representing external stimuli continue for a time to circulate in some manner through the same fibers after the stimulus has ceased to operate, and to indicate the presence of an external object although it no longer acts as a stimulus. This may be brought about by the impulses which represent the total sensory situation of a moment becoming associated with each other and mutually evoking each other, until this representation of a given object is wiped out by some new stimulus indicating that a different object now occupies the same point in the spatial order. (See 3.15 and 3.34 above.)[6]

5.39. It is indeed a difficult problem why and in what circumstances a given set of representative impulses will ever lead to the expectation of a more or less constant environment, or produce the persistence of a given picture of the particular environment in which the organism exists. The explanation probably is that, as suggested, certain constellations of impulses mutually support each other, or that by a sort of circular process they will tend to re-evoke themselves rather than a different constellation corresponding to a different environment. The interaction of the chains of associations attached to the different impulses and groups of impulses will effect some kind of selection from the infinite range of possibilities which the several elements of the complex picture would tend to evoke.

5.40. Whether this actually is the case or not, we must certainly distinguish between two different kinds of physiological 'memory' or traces left behind by the action of any stimulus: one is the semi-permanent change in the structure of connections or paths which we have already discussed and which determines the courses through which any chain of impulses can run; the other is the pattern of active impulses proceeding at any moment as a result of the stimuli received in the recent past, and perhaps also merely as part of a continuous flow of impulses of central origin which never altogether ceases even if no external stimuli are received.

5.41. The pattern of impulses which is traced at any moment within the given network of semi-permanent channels may be regarded as a kind of model of the particular environment in which the organism finds itself at the moment and which will enable it to take account of that environment in all its movements. This 'model', which is formed at any moment by the active impulses, must not be confused with what we have called the 'map', the semi-permanent connections representing not the environment of the moment but the kind of events which the organism has met during its whole past. This distinction between what for lack of better terms we shall continue to describe

---

[6] This important point can here only just be touched upon since a fuller discussion would require a more detailed consideration of physiological detail than would be appropriate here. For an important attempt at elaboration in this direction see now D. O. Hebb, 1949.

as the 'map' and the 'model' respectively, both of which are reproductions of relations between events in the outside world, is so important that it requires some further elucidation.

5.42. The semi-permanent map, which is formed by connections capable of transmitting impulses from neuron to neuron, is merely an apparatus for classification or orientation, capable of being called into operation by any new impulse, but existing independently of the particular impulses proceeding in it at a given moment.[7] It represents the kind of world in which the organism has existed in the past, or the different *kinds* of stimuli which have acquired significance for it, but it provides by itself no information about the particular environment in which the organism is placed at the moment. It is the apparatus of classification in what we have called its static aspect (2.21) and would continue to exist (if this were possible) if at any moment the central nervous system were completely at rest.

5.43. This semi-permanent structure provides the framework within which (or the categories in terms of which) the impulses proceeding at any time are evaluated. It determines what further impulses any given constellation of impulses will set up, and represents the kinds of classes or 'qualities' which the system can record, but not what particular events will be recorded at any moment. This structure itself in turn is liable to change as a result of the impulses proceeding in it, but relatively to the constantly changing pattern of impulses it can be regarded as semi-permanent.

5.44. Within this structural framework of paths the flow of impulses will at any moment trace a further pattern which will have significance only by its position in that structural framework within which it moves. This 'model' formed by the moving impulses or by a particular operation of the apparatus of classification manifests the latter in its dynamic aspect. Its nature is, of course, limited by the possibilities which the structural 'map' provides, by the connections or channels which exist; but within these limits its character will be determined by the combined effects of the active impulses.

5.45. The response to any newly arriving sensory impulses will thus depend not only on the semi-permanent map formed by the network of connections; it will also depend on the pattern of the impulses already proceeding at that movement within the pattern of channels; and it will be the position of the former within the latter pattern which will determine the significance of the new impulses. The complete apparatus of orientation thus consists of a struc-

---

[7] This manner of stating the difference is correct only on the assumption that the connections involve structural changes and are not merely 'functional', i.e., produced by something like a continuous circuit of impulses (2.47). If the connections should prove to be based not on structural changes but on some functional change of the latter kind, this would probably not affect the principle of the distinction made above but would make the description of the mechanism much more difficult.

ture of which a certain part will be activated, or of a sort of model within a model which has significance only by its position within that model, and which adjusts the responses to any new stimulus not only to the general significance which stimuli of that sort will possess in any circumstances, but to the particular significance which they will possess in the situation existing at the moment.

5.46. This relationship between our 'model' and our 'map' is the same as that which, in a game of war (*Kriegsspiel*) played with symbolic figures on a map, exists between the patterns traced on the map by the figures and the map itself. Or we may think of a game of Nine Men's Morris[8] where similarly the relative position of the men to each other is significant only with respect to the pattern on the board on which the game is played. To make the comparison closer we would have to imagine that the 'men' in either instance are individually undistinguishable from one another apart from their position on the map or the board, and that at any moment, in addition to the men present as the result of the preceding moves, new men may appear at certain points and, finally, that in moving the men leave traces which gradually alter the pattern on the map or the board. The important point, with respect to which these illustrations correspond with our case, is that the pattern traced by the movement of the men is significant *not* by its shape in space but solely by its relation to the other pattern within which those movements take place (cf. 2.5).

5.47. A closer parallel to our case would in some respects be provided by a system of pipes or tubes through which move columns of a pliable substance. If we assume that at many points of interconnection these tubes are joined by 'afferent' tubes which can bring in from the outside new columns of the substance, and by 'efferent' tubes which may drain such columns from the system, that at any junction the columns may divide, and that the direction of the pressure of the columns meeting at such junctions[9] will decide in which further direction they will jointly move on, we get an approximate representation of the situation with which we have to deal. We might even complete the picture by assuming that, e.g., because the system of tubes is bored into some yielding material, pressure from adjoining tubes may lead to some new channels being formed through which the moving substance first seeps and then moves freely. It will then be the pattern which the moving columns trace within (and relative to) the pattern formed by the system of tubes, which will

[8] [Nine Men's Morris is a strategy game for two persons. It is also called *Mill* (*Mühle* in German; *Jeu de Moulin* in French; *Mulino* in Italian; and so forth).—Ed.]

[9] Any mechanical model of this kind is misleading in suggesting a transmission of substance or energy, while in the transmission of nervous impulses we have, of course, to deal with a case of 'trigger action' where the connections between the neurons merely effect a release of energy stored up in the individual neuron (3.8).

correspond to the pattern traced by the nervous impulses within (and relative to) the structure of connected fibers.

5.48. The relation which exists between our 'model' and the 'map' may also be compared in some respects to the relation existing between some complex geometrical structure and the system of co-ordinates with reference to which it can be defined. The essential characteristics of the structure will be described in terms of an equation which can be interpreted with reference to many possible systems of co-ordinates, and the actual structure will appear different according as we represent it within different (say Cartesian or polar) co-ordinates. What is significant about the structure of our 'model' is not the actual relations in space between the impulses, but solely their relations to the structure of connections, relations which correspond to those expressed by the equation by which a given structure is defined in analytical geometry.

5.49. Once such a continuous reproduction of the environment is maintained in the highest centers, it becomes the main function of the sensory impulses to keep this apparatus of orientation up to date and capable of determining the responses to particular stimuli in the light of the whole situation. The classification of these impulses is then no longer specific to particular functions, but has become general in the sense that any one of them may, by its position in the comprehensive pattern, exercise some influence on practically any response. The classified impulses proceeding at any moment operate as symbols representing the significance of the stimuli which have evoked them for any behavior which a newly arriving stimulus will tend to evoke, or which would be determined by the joint effect of the multiplicity of processes set in train by stimuli recorded earlier.

4. Associative Processes

5.50. The pattern of nervous impulses which at any moment will be traced within the structure of connected fibers is, of course, a constantly changing pattern. The representations of the different part of the environment which the impulses produce will derive their significance exclusively from the fact that they tend to evoke certain other impulses. Each impulse representing an event in the environment will be the starting point of many chains of associative processes; in these the various further impulses set up will represent events which in the past have become connected for the individual with those which are represented by the impulses which evoke them. If each of these several chains of associative processes were allowed to run its course, unaffected by other similar chains which have been set up by other impulses (which were either part of the same initial position or which are produced by new stimuli), they would tend to produce representations of a variety of consequences which would follow from the initial environment, rather than present a definite picture of that environment.

5.51. The pattern of impulses formed within the structure of connections will thus function as an apparatus of orientation by representing both the actual state of the environment and the changes to be expected in that environment. This, of course, must not be understood to mean that representations of several different states of affairs can exist simultaneously. It means that each part and the whole of the representation of the existing environment derive their significance from the penumbra of possible consequences attaching to them: what gives every element or group of elements of which the total situation exists their sensory value is their following representing their various potential effects.

5.52. It is particularly important in this connection not to fall back upon the traditional conception of the individual impulses as such corresponding to particular mental qualities, or to conceive of associative processes as simple chains of impulses where physiological elements correspond to mental units. The physiological impulse owes its mental quality to its capacity of evoking other impulses, and what produces the succession of different mental qualities is the same kind of process as that which determines the position of the impulses in the order of mental qualities: it possesses such a quality only because it can evoke a great variety of associated impulses. Association, in other words, is not something additional to the appearance of mental qualities, nor something which acts upon given qualities; it is rather the factor which determines the qualities.

5.53. The mental qualities which succeed each other in the course of associative processes do therefore not correspond to the units between which physiological connections exist. The sequence of individual mental images (or reproductions) is rather the resultant of the interaction of a multiplicity of streams of impulses, and every new mental quality which is thus evoked will be the effect not only of those physiological impulses preceding it which have themselves been fully evaluated, but also of those which have merely contributed to the evaluation of the former, and of others which have not received sufficient support to obtain a distinct following. Even the simplest succession of mental qualities which appear directly to evoke each other must probably be conceived as the resultant of a complex process of convergence of many impulses.

5.54. We must probably assume that in order that an impulse should be able to produce its own distinctive following and thus obtain a distinct place in the qualitative order, it will, as a rule, require the support from other impulses whose followings closely overlap with its own. But while those to which this applies will occupy, as it were, the center of the stage, those which are not sufficiently supported to produce their complete following will nevertheless exercise some influence on the further course of the associative processes. Even though only the concentrated stream of impulses which forms the 'foreground' will be fully evaluated, its effects will also depend on the less distinct background.

5.55. So far as the appearance in consciousness of successive images is concerned, of which we think in the first instance when we mention 'associations', this means, of course, that what further images will be evoked by a conscious event will depend not only on it but also on much which is not conscious. But, as we shall see more fully in the next chapter, the difference between conscious and non-conscious events is a difference of the same kind as that which appears on the highest level as the difference between more or less fully evaluated events. In all these instances the effect which on a given level will be produced by an event occupying a distinct position in the order of that level will depend not only on itself but also on the sub-structure of less fully discriminated events on which it rests and which forms its background.

5.56. The different associations attaching to individual impulses, and still more those attaching to any one of a group of simultaneous impulses, will often not only not be convergent but even conflicting; and not all the representations which will form part of the following of the elements of the complete situation will be capable of simultaneous realization, or would produce a significant new pattern if they did. Since from each element of the structure of connected fibers impulses can pass in a great variety of directions, the initial stream of impulses would merely diffuse and dissipate itself if the overlapping of the following of the many different impulses did not determine a selection of some among the many potential paths on which they might travel.

5.57. This selection will be brought about by the fact that, where the followings of the representations of the different parts of the environment overlap, the corresponding impulses will reinforce each other by summation (3.13) and by their joint effects evoke sequences of representations which otherwise would have remained merely 'potential'; while, in so far as the various elements set up divergent or even conflicting (mutually inhibiting) tendencies, these flows of impulses will mutually neutralize each other.

5.58. The representation or model of the environment will thus constantly tend to run ahead of the actual situation. This representation of the possible results following from the existing position will, of course, be constantly checked and corrected by the newly arriving sensory signals which record the actual developments in the environment. The newly arriving impulses, on the other hand, in turn will always be evalued against the background of the expectations set up by the previously existing pattern of impulses.

5.59. The representations of the external environment which will guide behavior will thus be not only representations of the actually existing environment; but also representations of the changes to be expected in that environment. We must therefore conceive of the model as constantly trying out possible developments and determining action in the light of the consequences which from the representations of such actions would appear to follow from it.

5.60. We shall have further to consider the character of these associative processes in the next chapter when we consider conscious thought, and again in the last chapter when we shall have to examine the nature of explanation. At this stage our concern is merely to emphasize that processes essentially analogous to the processes of association which are familiar to us from conscious thought must be assumed to play a similar role already on preconscious levels. The processes of classification with which we are concerned, and which will determine conscious as well as unconscious responses, constitute classifications of complex situations by the joint results to be expected from the simultaneous occurrence of the elements; and this in turn involves the representation of the range of expected results by a pattern of impulses essentially in the same manner in which the actual environment is represented by such a pattern.

5.61. The representation of the existing situation in fact cannot be separated from, and has no significance apart from, the representation of the consequences to which it is likely to lead. Even on a pre-conscious level the organism must live as much in a world of expectation as in a world of 'fact', and most responses to a given stimulus are probably determined only *via* fairly complex processes of 'trying out' on the model the effects to be expected from alternative courses of action. The reaction to a stimulus thus frequently implies an anticipation of the consequences to be expected from it.[10]

5.62. It is these chains of symbolic representations of the consequences to be expected from a given representation of events which we must conceive as constituting those 'symbolic processes in the brain' which physiological psychology has been led to postulate[11] in order to account for the complex adaptive responses, and to explain the delays involved between stimulus and response even on levels where there is no ground for assuming the presence of consciousness, or where we know that the responses take place without our being aware of the stimulus which has evoked them.

[10] Cf., R. Dodge, 1931 [Raymond Dodge (1871–1942) was an American experimental psychologist who taught at Wesleyan University and Yale University. He had studied with, and did his doctoral dissertation with, Benno Erdmann (see 7.14, fn. 12) at the University of Halle-Wittenberg, Germany. Together with Erdmann he published an acclaimed book on the experimental psychology of reading (*Psychologische Untersuchungen über das Lesen auf experimenteller Grundlage*, 1898).—Ed.]; V. von Weizsäcker 1947 [1940], p. 136.

[11] Cf., C. T. Morgan, 1943, p. 112.

5. Mechanical and Purposive Behavior

5.63. The principles by which the transmission of the individual impulses in the central nervous system is determined are of a kind which might well be described as 'mechanical' in the most general meaning of the word; yet the result of the interplay of these transmissions in the integrated nervous system will clearly show characteristics which are not only very different from, but in some respects even the opposite of those which we commonly associate with that term. It will therefore be useful explicitly to enumerate the points on which the multiple process of classification will act in a manner different from what we ordinarily regard as mechanical.

5.64. By a 'mechanism' or a 'mechanical process' we usually understand a complex of moving parts possessing a constant structure which uniquely determines its operations, so that it will always respond in the same manner to a given external influence, repeat under the same external conditions the same movements, and which is capable only of a limited number of operations. Such a mechanism cannot 'purposively' adapt its operations to produce different results in the same external conditions; and it is essentially 'passive' in the sense that which of the different operations of which it is capable it will perform will depend exclusively on the external circumstances.

5.65. In all these respects the operation of a system organized on the principles here described will show opposite characteristics. It will, as a result of its own operations, continuously change its structure and alter the range of operation of which it is capable. It will scarcely ever respond twice in exactly the same manner to the same external conditions. And it will as a result of 'experience' acquire the capacity of performing entirely new actions. Its actions will appear self-adaptive and purposive, and it will in general be 'active' in the sense that what at any given moment will determine the character of its operation will be the pre-existing state of its internal processes as much as the external influences acting on it.

5.66. Since the structure of connections in the nervous system is modified by every new action exercised upon it by the external world, and since the stimuli acting on it do not operate by themselves but always in conjunction with the processes called forth by the pre-existing excitatory state, it is obvious that the response to a given combination of stimuli on two different occasions is not likely to be exactly the same. Because it is the whole history of the organism which will determine its action, new factors will contribute to this determination on the later occasion which were not present on the first. We shall find not only that the same set of external stimuli will not always produce the same responses, but also that altogether new responses will occur, if we regard as one response not the movement of an individual muscle but the whole complex of co-ordinated movement of the organism.

5.67. The appearance of such new forms of behavior is the effect of the circumstance already noted (4.25, 4.49) that the individual motor impulses sent out by the higher centers will be signals not for particular movements but for classes or kinds of actions, and that the particular movement that will occur will be determined by the joint effect of many such general 'directives'. The signal for a particular succession of movements of various muscles may for instance be modified by other signals indicating that it is to take place fast and with the avoidance of noise, or that other types of modification of the basic pattern are required. Any one particular movement will thus be determined by the higher centers signaling the different 'qualities' required from the action, and these different 'qualities' of behavior will be closely interwoven (4.46) with the qualities ascribed to events in the external world.

5.68. The adaptive and purposive behavior of the organism is accounted for by the existence of the 'model' of the environment formed by the pattern of impulses in the nervous system. In so far as this model represents situations which might come about as the result of the existing external situation, this means that behavior will be guided by representations of the consequences to be expected from different kinds of behavior. If the model can pre-form or predict the effects of different courses of action, and pre-select among the effects of alternative courses those which in the existing state of the organism are 'desirable', there is no reason why it should not also be capable of directing the organism towards the particular course of action which has thus been 'mapped out' for it.[12]

5.69. In order that the 'desired result' should operate as a cause determining behavior, it must be evoked by, or form part of the following of, the reproduction of the actual environment and of the governing state of drive or urge. It must be a representation of the innumerable combinations of possible outcomes of the existing situation which the convergent associations tend to evoke—associations which are attached to the elements of the representation of that environment, and which give these representations their significance or meaning. The 'desired' result will be singled out from the many possible outcomes of the existing situation because it will form part of the following not only of the environment but also of the 'urge' or 'drive' for a certain class of results. That representation of the results which seem both possible in the existing external situation and 'desirable' in view of the state of the organism will thus be strengthened by the summation of two different streams of nervous impulses. This result will be represented with greater strength and distinctness and will thereby come to exercise the determining influence on further behavior.

[12] On this and the following see K. J. W. Craik, 1943, pp. 51ff. [Kenneth James William Craik (1914–45) was a British philosopher and psychologist whose promising career was prematurely ended by a road accident. In his book *The Nature of Explanation*, he developed the concept of "mental models" as explanatory and predictive "tools."—Ed.]

5.70. Such a representation of certain possible outcomes of the existing situation, which are strengthened because they appear desirable, constitute, however, only a first step towards purposive behavior. In most situations there will exist many possible courses of action which, in the sense that they have in the past become associated with the achievement of that goal, will appear to be 'directed' towards a desirable goal; but only some of these courses of action will be appropriate in the particular situation. There will, in general, also exist more than one possible goal of the desired kind, and more than one way of achieving any one goal. The determination of purposive action involves, therefore, a further process of selection among the various different courses of action which might satisfy the initiating urge.

5.71. The interpretation of the pattern of moving impulses as a model of the environment, which can try out possible developments in that environment, suggests answers to both these problems. We shall first consider the mechanism by which will be eliminated inappropriate moves which, though they would produce the desired result if those features of the environment which evoke that response were alone present, yet cannot in fact produce that result because other elements in the environment constitute an obstacle to the completion of this course of action.

5.72. Such a situation would have its neural counterpart in the impulses representing different parts of the environment tending to set up contradictory or incompatible chains of associations which will mutually blot each other out. Because representations of possible developments in the environment will have significance or meaning only as parts of an ordered picture of that environment, the various chains of associations set up by the elements of the representation of a complex situation will produce meaningful results only if they fit into the general order of such representations. The general spatial and temporal order of that representation will, e.g., require that either one thing or another must be in a given place, or that a thing must be either at rest or in motion, etc., etc. In so far as the chains of associations, set up by different parts of the representation of the environment, lead in this sense to conflicting results, e.g., to the representation of two different things as being in the same place at the same moment, or of two incompatible attributes being attached to a particular thing, these tendencies will neutralize each other: no distinct representation will result which could become the starting point for further associations.[13]

5.73. Of the many sequences of representations which different parts of the representation of the existing environment tend to evoke, only some will thus

[13] Cf., K. J. W. Craik, 1943, p. 57: 'As a result of such interactive or associative processes we might have, for example, $A=B$, $B=C$, $A=C$, where A, B, and C are neural patterns claiming to represent external things or processes. These patterns clearly cannot remain simultaneously excited; inconsistency means a clash in the interaction patterns.'

in fact lead to representations of meaningful results. The mechanism which in this manner eliminates abortive courses of action must also prevent, however, that at any moment more than one of the possible alternative courses of actions should be fully represented, although the model might successively try out different courses of action. How will it be determined which of the various courses promising to produce a desirable result will in fact be selected?

5.74. The first point to be noticed is that the desirability of one particular result will not be the only factor of an affective character which will be operative in such a situation. Most of the different courses of action between which the organism will have to choose, and most of the intermediate stages through which these different courses of action will lead it, will also possess affective qualities—they will themselves be either attractive or repellant in various degrees. In particular, the representation of the effort involved in the different courses of action will normally be charged with the representation of pain, or operate as something to be avoided, unless compensated for by the greater attraction of the result. The interaction of all these forces in the end will bring it about that from the possible courses the 'path of least resistance' will be chosen; while all the unduly painful courses will be avoided which might produce the same result, as well as courses leading to alternative results but requiring greater effort.

5.75. That such guidance by a model which reproduces, and experimentally tries out, the possibilities offered by a given situation, can produce action which is purposive to any desired degree, is shown by the fact that machines could be produced on this principle (and that some, such as the predictor for anti-aircraft guns, or the automatic pilots for aircraft, have actually been produced) which show all the characteristics of purposive behavior.[14] Such machines, however, are still comparatively primitive and restricted in the range of their operations compared with the central nervous system. They would be able to take account of only a minute fraction of the number of different facts of which the central nervous system takes account, and they would lack the capacity of learning from experience. But although for this reason such machines cannot yet be described as brains,[15] with regard to purposiveness they differ from a brain merely in degree and not in kind.[16]

5.76. It is notoriously difficult to discuss purposive behavior without employ-

[14] See also W. G. Walter, 1950. [William Grey Walter (1910–77) was an American-born British neurophysiologist who is famous for constructing some of the first autonomous robots. His article "An Imitation of Life" is about electromechanical tortoises, about which the author notes: "Although they possess only two sensory organs and two electronic nerve cells, they exhibit 'free will'" (Walter 1950, 42).—Ed.]

[15] C. Sherrington, 1949.

[16] K. J. W. Craik, 1943, p. 51. See also N. Wiener, 1948a and 1948b, and W. S. McCulloch, 1948.

ing terms which suggest the presence of conscious mental states. The phenomenon of purposive action, however, does not pre-suppose the existence of an elaborate mental order like the one which we know from conscious experience, and still less the presence of consciousness itself. Some degree of purposiveness can be attained by structures infinitely more simple than those which constitute the mental order, and once we have reached the degree of complexity in the ordering of stimuli and responses characteristic of the latter, it does not present a new or separate problem.

6. The Model-Object Relationship

5.77. It will be useful further to elucidate the character of the relationship between the 'model' and its object, and to illustrate the possibilities of 'reproducing' certain features of a complex structure within certain parts of the same structure, by constructing an imaginary and greatly simplified model of the model-object relationship itself. To be quite satisfactory for our purposes this super-model should be conceived in strictly physical terms, that is, it should be built up from elements whose properties are all defined in terms of explicit relations to the other elements of the system, and which possessed no phenomenal or sensory properties whatever. But as such a purely abstract model would give little help to the imagination, it will be necessary to resort in some measure to visual imagery.

5.78. While using the conception of a model for this purpose, we must, of course, avoid the suggestion, originally connected with the word model, that it must be the creation of a thinking mind. Since the purpose of introducing the conception is to show how the human mind itself may in a certain sense be conceived as a model of the macrocosm within which it exists, there must be no such three terms as object, model, and the modeler. Our task is rather to show in what sense it is possible that within parts of the macrocosm a microcosm may be formed which reproduces certain aspects of the macrocosm and through this will enable the sub-structure of which it forms part to behave in a manner which will assist its continued existence.

5.79. We shall conceive for this purpose of a self-contained system or universe consisting of a cloud of particles which individually differ from each other solely by the different effects which in different combinations or constellations they will exercise upon each other. With regard to this universe we shall assume that we possess the capacity of the Laplacean 'demon'[17] of knowing

---

[17] [The term "Laplace's demon" refers to the hypothetical "intellect" of whom the French mathematician and astronomer Pierre-Simon Laplace (1749–1827) speaks in the following quotation from the introduction to his 1814 *Essai philosophique sur les probabilités*: "We may regard

of every particle all its relations to other particles, and therefore of being able to identify each individual particle by the different effects it will have in all conceivable circumstances. Particles of the same kind would mean particles which in all conceivable circumstances could be substituted for one another without thereby altering the course of events.

5.80. Strictly speaking we ought, of course, not even conceive of what we have described as a 'cloud' of particles as being arranged in perceptual space, but should describe the relations of these particles to each other in terms of their acting upon each other in particular ways. But since we must resort to representation in perceptual terms, we cannot dispense with the familiar spatial order, and for the purposes of visualizing the order of our universe it will even be useful to imagine that the individual particles possess perceptible identifying marks, such as different colors, indicating the class to which they belong.

5.81. Among the different properties which the different kinds of particles will possess, one of the most important will be their different capacities of combining with other particles of the same or of different kinds into more or less stable structures, which, as structures, will show their own peculiar relations to other particles or structures of particles. By stability of such structures we mean the probability of their persistence in the face of the action upon them by the environment. All the possible structures which groups of particles may form within our universe will in this sense require for their persistence certain environmental conditions, which in the case of some kinds of such structures may almost always be satisfied, while for others they may be of rare occurrence. On the whole, the more complex the structure, the greater will be the number of external influences capable of destroying it, and the more special the circumstances required for its continued existence.

5.82. Some such structures may persist, not because their coherence resists most external circumstances, but because they will move away from such agents before they are destroyed. In the familiar world a drop of mercury is likely to preserve its cohesion because it is apt to 'get out of the way' of any mass which might squash it, and a leaf avoids being torn to shreds by a high wind by taking up a position of least resistance. There is, of course, nothing 'teleological' in these movements which assist the persistence of such struc-

---

the present state of the universe as the effect of its past and the cause of its future. An intellect which at a certain moment would know all forces that set nature in motion, and all positions of all items of which nature is composed, if this intellect were also vast enough to submit these data to analysis, it would embrace in a single formula the movements of the greatest bodies of the universe and those of the tiniest atom; for such an intellect nothing would be uncertain and the future just like the past would be present before its eyes." This quotation has become famous as the classic definition of a strict physical determinism.—Ed.]

tures; but the cause which would destroy them if it acted in its full force or for any length of time at the same time removes them from its influence.

5.83. In general, if the conditions required for the persistence of any more complex structure are not likely always to prevail at the place where it happens to be, it will continue to exist only if (and we shall encounter such substructures, except as temporary phenomena only in so far as) it can respond appropriately to certain events, and even in some measure anticipate their occurrence, i.e. perform the appropriate response as soon as certain other events occur which indicate the imminence of the harmful one. It is conceivable, though not very likely, that such structures may persist because they just happen thus to respond to all or most of the events which usually precede those which would destroy them.

5.84. The chance of persistence of any given structure will evidently be increased if it not only happens to respond appropriately to harmful or beneficial influences and to some symptoms of such factors, but if it also possesses the capacity of retaining a 'memory' of the connections between events which frequently precede such influences and these influences themselves, and thereby becomes capable of 'learning' to perform the appropriate response whenever those signals appear. Relative complex structures which, without this capacity could not exist long, may through it acquire a considerable degree of stability.

5.85. Correct anticipation of future events in the environment can rarely be based on a single present event but will as a rule have to take into account a combination of many present events. It involves thus different responses not only to different individual events but also to different combinations of such events according as they are likely to produce one result or another. Any mechanism which makes the structure respond to different combinations of external events according to the different further events they are likely to produce implies that there exists inside the structure a system of relationships between events caused by the external circumstances, which is in some measure structurally equivalent to the system of relationships which exists between those external events. Such an internal structure which reproduces some of the relations between the outside events we have called a model.

5.86. It is conceivable that a structure endowed with the capacity of retaining experienced connections might learn separately the appropriate responses to most of the possible combinations of events. But if it had to cope with the complexity of its environment solely by classifying individual events and learning separately for every combination of such events how to respond, both the complexity of the model required and the time needed for building it up would be so great that the extent to which any given structure could learn to adapt itself to varying circumstances would be very limited.

5.87. It is in this connection that the various processes of multiple classification which we have described, and the phenomena of 'transfer' and 'generalization' which they make possible, greatly extend the predicting capacity of any models that can be formed from a limited number of elements. Whenever the classifying mechanism treats as alike, or as alike in certain circumstances, any group of events, it will be able to transfer any experience with any one of them to all of them. The process of learning is thereby greatly abbreviated and the complexity of the apparatus required to cope with a given variety of situations is greatly reduced.

5.88. If, for instance, the combinations of any one of the events $(a_1, a_2, a_3, \ldots a_k)$ with any one of the group of events $(b_1, b_2, b_3, \ldots b_m)$ and any one of the group of events $(c_1, c_2, c_3, \ldots c_n)$ produce X, there will be $k \cdot m \cdot n$ (or if $k=m=n=10$, one thousand) possible different combinations of events for each of which it would have to be learnt separately that they produce X. But once it has already been learnt that in all other respects all members of class A (i.e., $a_1, a_2, a_3, \ldots a_k$) are equivalent, and the symbol o substituted for them, and similarly for all members of the class B the symbol p, and for all members of the class C the symbol q, then the experience that $o+p+q$ produces X will be sufficient to predict the outcome of the $m.n.k$ different combinations of individual events.

5.89. It is thus the process of multiple classification which builds the model. What we have before called the 'map', the semi-permanent apparatus of classification, provides the different generic elements from which the models of particular situations are built. The term 'map', which suggests a sort of schematic picture of the environment, is thus really somewhat misleading. What the apparatus of classification provides is more a sort of inventory of the kind of things of which the world is built up, a theory of how the world works rather than a picture of it. It would be better described as a construction set which supplies the parts from which the models of particular situations can be built.

5.90. The model-building by such an apparatus of classification simplifies the task and extends the scope of successful adaptation in two ways: it selects some elements from a complex environment as relevant for the prediction of events which are important for the persistence of the structure, and it treats them as instances of classes of events. But while in this way a model-building apparatus (and particularly one which can be constantly improved by learning) is of much greater efficiency than could be any more mechanical apparatus which contained, as it were, a few fixed models of typical situations, there will clearly still exist definite limits to the extent to which such a microcosm can contain an adequate reproduction of the significant factors in the macrocosm.

5.91. It is, from this angle, no more than a fortunate accident that the different events in the macrocosm are not all fully interdependent to any significant degree, but that as a rule it is possible to base predictions of certain kinds of events on a mere selection from the totality of all events. If it were not possible for practical purposes to isolate quasi-self-contained sub-structures, containing no more parts which significantly affect the relevant result than can be reproduced or matched point by point by 'representative' elements within our organism, prediction and purposive adaptation would be impossible. But while it seems that the complexity of the relations which must be taken into account for most purposes is sufficiently limited to make it possible for some structures to 'contain' adequate reproductions of them, this can evidently not be universally true. We shall have to concern ourselves in the last chapter with the significance of the fact that any coherent structure of this kind, which within itself contains a model guiding its actions, must be of a degree of complexity greater than that of any model that it can contain, and therefore than that of any object it can reproduce.

CHAPTER VI

CONSCIOUSNESS AND CONCEPTUAL THOUGHT

1. Conscious and Unconscious Mental Processes

6.1. We have used the term 'mental' to describe all processes which involve a classification of events in terms of a qualitative order, similar to that which we know from our subjective sensory experience, and differing from the physical order of these events. The sphere of 'mental phenomena' in this sense is far more extensive than that of conscious phenomena and includes many events which are undoubtedly not conscious. This definition of the mental raises the problem of the determination of this mental order in a form in which it would also arise from a consistently pursued behaviorist approach. We know that an order which is at least similar to that which we know from our conscious experience manifests itself not only in the behavior of lower animals, with regard to whom we have no ground for assuming that the events so ordered are accompanied by anything which could be described as conscious experience, but also in many responses of our own body where we know that the initiating stimuli do not give rise to any conscious experience.

6.2. Up to this point we have only incidentally referred to the conscious character which distinguishes some of those mental events, and have concentrated on the general character of the qualitative order of all mental events, whether they are conscious or not. What has already been said on this point should justify such a use of the term 'mental' as including both unconscious and conscious events, even though in the past such a use of the term has been often explicitly condemned by psychologists (1.73). We must now, however, attempt at least some indication of the additional characteristics or attributes which distinguish conscious from unconscious mental events.

6.3. While all qualitative discriminations thus imply the presence of a mental order in the sense in which we have used this term, it does not necessarily involve that the individual is 'conscious' or 'aware' of these processes. Consciousness, in the sense in which this term is synonymous with awareness,[1]

---

[1] J. G. Miller, 1942, p. 43, treats 'awareness of discrimination' as a definition of consciousness (or rather, unawareness of discrimination as a definition of unconsciousness). It is the last of six-

is an attribute which attaches only to some but not to all mental events. But although we all know what we mean when we say that we are 'conscious' or 'aware' of certain experiences, it is exceedingly difficult to state precisely of what the peculiar attribute of such conscious mental events consists.

6.4. It may be that it is impossible to give a satisfactory definition of what consciousness 'is', or rather that this is a phantom-problem of the same kind as the 'problem' of the 'absolute' character of the sensory qualities. We shall endeavour to avoid this difficulty by not asking what consciousness 'is' but by merely inquiring what consciousness does. In other words, we shall be concerned solely with the differences which exist between behavior which we know to result from conscious mental processes and behavior produced by unconscious mental processes. Before examining this question in any detail, three propositions may be stated which will probably command fairly general assent.

6.5. It seems clear, in the first instance, that, although the distinction between conscious and non-conscious processes refers originally to different kinds of processes occurring in ourselves, we also employ it to describe the differences which we observe in the behavior of other people. We know from our subjective experience that there are differences between those actions of our body which we 'deliberately' control and those which take place without our control, and we use this knowledge to distinguish similarly between correspondingly different actions of other people. Although we possess no certain criterion on which we can base this distinction, we are sufficiently familiar with the two kinds of actions to be able to attribute consciousness with fair assurance to persons whom we observe acting in certain ways.

6.6. There can, secondly, be little question, although in extreme instances the difference between conscious and unconscious mental events appears to be so complete as to make the difference appear to be one of kind, that there exist many forms intermediate between fully conscious and fully unconscious mental events which make this difference one of degree. Consciousness is evidently capable of many different degrees of intensity, and between the clearly conscious and the clearly unconscious states there exist many forms of semiconscious events with regard to which it is difficult to decide whether they ought to be described as conscious or not.[2]

6.7. Thirdly, it will probably be readily conceded that all conscious events possess in the highest degree the attributes characteristic of all mental pro-

teen definitions of consciousness which he lists, and he describes it as 'the golden meaning of the word for those who admit the validity of introspective testimony,' and later (p. 294) as 'the fundamental meaning of conscious' to most behaviorists. But while this distinguishes this meaning from others, it hardly defines the concept, since 'aware' seems merely a synonym for 'conscious' in this sense.

[2] J. G. Miller, 1942, p. 166.

cesses: conscious responses are to an especially high degree modifiable and purposive, different conscious events are very closely related to each other and very fully discriminated from each other; furthermore, this discrimination is even less 'specific' and more 'general', in the sense in which we have used these terms (5.36, 5.49) than is true of other mental phenomena; and they are even more likely to produce completely new complexes of behavior than is true of unconscious mental processes.

2. Criteria of Consciousness

6.8. What, then, are those special attributes of conscious behavior by which we distinguish it from behavior which also appears to be co-ordinated and purposive but of which the acting person is not 'aware'? Such unconscious behavior may occur either because the person's attention is at the particular moment otherwise engaged, or because he is altogether unconscious as is the case in some somnambulic states and hypnotic trances. There appear to exist three *prima facie* differences between such unconscious and conscious behavior which we may provisionally describe by saying that in conscious behavior a person will, (*a*) be able to 'give an account' of what he is or has been doing, (*b*) be able 'to take account' in his actions of other simultaneous experiences of which he is also conscious, and (*c*) be guided to a large extent not only by his current perceptions but also by images and reproduction of circumstances which might be evoked by the existing situation.

6.9. When we say that a person is able to 'give an account' of his mental processes we mean by this that he is able to communicate them to other people by means of 'symbols', that is by actions which, when perceived by other people, will occupy in their mental order a position analogous to that which they occupy in his own; and which, in consequence, will have for those other persons a meaning similar to that which it possesses for him.

6.10. The possibility of such communication between different persons is not only indicative of the presence of consciousness but the symbolisms employed for that purpose may also be an important factor which helps to raise the discrimination to that higher degree of clarity and precision which distinguishes conscious experience. The connections between sensory impulses and the highly developed apparatus of expression which man possesses undoubtedly greatly extend the means of classification available to him, and they are probably of the greatest importance in making abstract thought possible. They are also especially important because, in learning the system of symbols developed by his race, the individual can utilize, in ordering his current experience, not only his own experience but in some measure also the experience of his race.

6.11. But although communication (or at least communication by language proper, as distinguished from communication by gestures, facial expression, etc.) will as a rule be the result of conscious processes and 'give an account' of such processes, this means no more than that communication, being normally itself conscious action, is connected with (or can be influenced by) all other conscious processes. As a criterion of consciousness the possibility of 'giving an account' of conscious processes is therefore no more than a special instance of the second of the three criteria mentioned before, namely, of the fact that in conscious action we can 'take account' of all other processes which are also conscious.

6.12. The same applies to another supposed criterion of consciousness which is often mentioned but to which we have not yet referred, namely, to the fact that conscious experiences can be remembered and will be recognized as already experienced before when they occur again. 'Memory' or 'recognition' means here no more than the reappearance in consciousness, in combination with circumstances with which it has become associated, of what has been consciously experienced before. This is not a helpful criterion, if for no other reason so because it seems to be the case that we can sometimes in this manner 'remember' sense experiences of which we were not aware at the time when they first occurred. Moreover, memory in the general sense of learning clearly occurs also on pre-conscious levels.[3] With regard to conscious events the possibility of remembering or recognizing them thus means no more than that events which have occurred within the sphere of consciousness may do so again, but it tells us nothing about how conscious phenomena differ from nonconscious ones. All that it suggests is that in some sense all conscious phenomena belong to a common sphere, so that any conscious experience may appear in the company of any other.

6.13. The possibility of 'giving an account of' and of 'remembering' conscious events therefore merely leads us to that specially close connection between all events which are at the same time conscious, which before we have described by saying that in conscious processes a person will be able to 'take account' of other events which are conscious at the same time.

6.14. This close connection between *all* conscious events, often described as the 'unity of the consciousness', can be regarded as a distinguishing attribute of conscious events, since the same does not seem to apply to unconscious mental events. While such unconscious mental processes which occur at the same time *may* also affect each other, this is not necessarily always the case. Even when they take place at the same time, they may proceed largely independently of each other (possibly in different sub-centers) and without affecting each other's course. In other words, there is more than one 'unconscious-

---

[3] See above (5.10–5.12) and J. G. Miller, 1940.

ness' (or coherent system of unconscious mental events) while there exists (normally) in any individual only one consciousness.

6.15. Another familiar fact which is connected with this 'unity of the consciousness' may be mentioned here. This is the so-called 'narrowness of the consciousness', or the fact that, at any one time, only a limited range of experience can be fully conscious. Though the focus of consciousness may rapidly shift from one object to another, this often seems to mean that processes which have been fully conscious may temporarily recede into a semi-conscious or sub-conscious condition and persist there, ready to spring again into full consciousness at any moment.

3. The Common Space-Time Framework

6.16. The 'unity of consciousness' means, above all, that conscious events occupy a definite position in the same spatial and temporal order, that they are 'dated' and 'placed' in relation to other conscious events, and that all sensory and affective events which 'enter consciousness', together with the reproductions or images of such experiences, belong to the same order or universe. This means that within the range of conscious events the 'generality' (as distinguished from the 'specificity', see 5.34 and 5.49) of their classification or evaluation has reached the highest degree: they are discriminated not only with respect to particular responses but with respect to all responses guided by conscious processes. This comprehensiveness of the system of relationships which connect and order all conscious events with respect to each other is probably the most characteristic attribute of these events.

6.17. This highest degree of comprehensiveness of the order of the system of relations prevailing on the conscious level does not necessarily mean that all the stimuli recorded by impulses proceeding at a lower level must also be capable of obtaining a distinct position at that higher level (4.53), or even that the number of different impulses which may be connected at that highest level must necessarily be larger than that of those which can possess connections at some lower level. The comprehensiveness of which we speak is rather that of the top level of a hierarchic order at which all the elements belonging to that level are interconnected, while many elements belonging to lower levels may be connected with many other elements of the same level only *via* that higher level. It may be because all *classes* of impulses at this highest level form a common order, rather than because symbolic representations of all individual stimuli can reach this highest level, that it possesses this specially comprehensive character which distinguishes the system of relations on this level.

6.18. The existence of a common spatio-temporal framework, in which all the events which occur at that level are given a definite place, means that all reproductions or images of past or possible events will there be related to the experiences which are 'here' and 'now', and that this universal relatedness of all events to this common point of reference constitutes them into a continuum, the 'I'. The ever-presence of this common framework so long as consciousness is awake presupposes the continuous existence of certain representations of a most abstract kind: of a skeleton outline of the (spatial and temporal) surroundings within which we place the picture of the particular objects of which we are consciously aware or which we consciously imagine.

6.19. The continuous presence, while consciousness lasts, of these mental contents of a most abstract character, representing the spatial and temporal structure of the environment, is not always recognized. This is probably due to the pre-conception that concrete perceptions always precede the more abstract mental contents. There can be little doubt, however, that the distinct conscious picture of particular phenomena is always embedded in, or surrounded by, a semi-conscious and more shadowy outline of the rest of the surroundings, which is co-present with, although much less distinct and detailed than, the conscious picture itself.

6.20. Of this co-presence of sub-conscious representations of the environment with the conscious representations of those parts of which we are clearly aware we can easily convince ourselves, if we remember the common experience of suddenly feeling to 'have the ground withdrawn under our feet' if something pre-supposed by the conscious picture proves to be missing. If, e.g., after our conscious sensations were interpreted on the assumption that we were in an enclosed room, we discover that the walls behind us are missing, or when, walking on what seemed to be level ground, we suddenly come to a precipice, this alters our view even of those things of which we were fully aware before. In all such instances the sub-consciously pre-supposed background of our experience is discovered to be missing, and the firm 'placing' of the consciously experienced events in a sub-consciously pre-supposed framework is upset. The result is usually a characteristic feeling of dizziness and of disturbed orientation.

6.21. Conscious experience thus rests on a much more extensive basis of less fully conscious or sub-conscious images of the rest of the surroundings, which nevertheless (like the following of a sensory impulse which determines its quality) give to the conscious representations their place and value. Conscious experiences have in this respect justly been compared to mountain tops rising above the clouds which, while alone visible, yet pre-suppose an invisible sub-structure determining their position relative to each other.

4. Attention

6.22. Before we can attempt a more definite characterization of the peculiar attributes of conscious experience, it will be necessary to consider another phenomenon which is so closely related to consciousness that it must be regarded as little more than a specially high degree of awareness. This is 'attention'.[4] Our awareness of events to which we 'give our attention' certainly differs from that of other events of which we are merely co-conscious very much in the same manner in which the latter differ from conscious experiences.

6.23. The experiences to which our attention is directed are more fully discriminated and perceived in greater detail than others of which we are also aware. They stand out altogether more clearly than those which occupy merely the fringe of consciousness. We notice more in them and are more fully prepared to respond adequately to their occurrence.

6.24. At the same time, it is characteristic of attention that it has these effects only with regard to events which are in some sense expected or anticipated, and that, however attentive we may endeavour to be, an altogether unexpected event will take us as much by surprise and escape as much our detailed notice as if we had not been attentive at all. Attention is thus always directed,[5] or confined to a particular class of events for which we are on the look-out and which, in consequence, we perceive with greater distinctness when one of them occurs.

6.25. These characteristic attributes of attention fit readily into our account of the process of perception. Events or objects whose probable occurrence is suggested by the perceptions or images of which we are aware will form part of the following of these experiences. The corresponding physiological following will therefore be in a state of excitatory preparedness, and this will facilitate the evaluation of any of the corresponding stimuli should they actually occur. The excitation produced by any such stimulus will as a result penetrate further, the network of relations determining its position will be more extensively activated, and the sensory impulse will therefore be more completely discriminated.

6.26. The fact that the following of certain impulses or groups of impulses, or certain parts of this following, will be more completely activated because

---

[4] Cf., E. G. Boring, 1933, pp. 231–32: 'Consciousness is attentive, attention is selective; consciousness is selective. Attention and consciousness are almost synonymous, and selection is the fundamental principle of both.'

[5] Cf., W. Stern, 1938, p. 474. [William Stern (1871–1938) was a prominent German psychologist who made significant contributions to the psychology of personality and intelligence. He was a cofounder of the University of Hamburg where, with Heinz Werner (see 5.19, fn. 3), he directed the Psychological Institute. He also was a cofounder of the German Psychological Association (Deutsche Gesellschaft für Psychologie) and of the *Zeitschrift für angewandte Psychologie* (*Journal of Applied Psychology*). As a Jew he was dismissed in 1933 from his academic post and fled first to the Netherlands and then to the United States, where he taught at Duke University until his death in 1938. In 1909 he had been awarded (together with Sigmund Freud and Carl Gustav Jung) an honorary doctoral degree from Clark University, where Heinz Werner had found refuge after he left Germany in 1933.—Ed.]

the new impulses will be supported by an anticipatory stream of impulses tending in the same direction, will bring it about that these impulses will be evaluated more fully than others which may also be present; and the corresponding sensations will be lifted above others in intensity and distinctness.

6.27. This kind of anticipatory excitation of parts of the following of certain kinds of sensory impulses will mean that we shall not only be more ready to perceive the corresponding stimulus, but also that we shall perceive them from a certain angle or a certain 'point of view'; we shall discriminate them more fully with respect to certain types of responses towards which the whole organism is disposed at the moment. The conception of 'disposition' or 'set' which we have discussed before in connection with 'purposiveness' (4.60–4.63) is indeed the most general manifestation of the process of which attention is a special instance.[6]

6.28. It is worth noting in this connection that something similar to attention can be observed also on a semi-conscious or sub-conscious level. A person may be interested in finding some object or in noticing a particular event, and, although not thinking about it, will at once observe it when it presents itself to his senses, merely because his mind has been prepared for it. The same is probably true of certain suggestions in a hypnotic state which are carried out when the occasion arises. These states of preparedness for certain actions, like attention proper, or the set or disposition corresponding to a particular urge or drive, must probably be conceived as determined by a state of excitatory preparedness of the following of the classes of impulses corresponding to the objects to which they are directed.

5. The Functions of Consciousness

6.29. The phenomenon of attention is of special significance for the understanding of consciousness because in the case of attention as well as in that of consciousness, it is not merely the character of the particular stimulus, or the place of the impulse in the network of connections, which will determine whether it will or will not become conscious or receive our attention; but it will be the pre-existing excitatory state of the higher centers which will decide whether the evaluation of the new impulses will be of the kind characteristic of attention or consciousness. It will depend on the pre-disposition (or set) how fully the newly arriving impulses will be evaluated or whether they will be consciously perceived, and what the responses to them will be.

6.30. It is probable that the processes in the highest centers which become

[6] Cf., J. G. Miller, 1942, p. 159: 'Closely related to attention, perhaps its outward manifestation, is the phenomenon of set'.

conscious require the continuous support from nervous impulses originating at some source within the nervous system itself, such as the 'wakefulness center' for whose existence a considerable amount of physiological evidence has been found.[7] If this is so, it would seem probable also that it is these reinforcing impulses which, guided by the expectations evoked by pre-existing conditions, prepare the ground and decide on which of the new impulses the search-light beam of full consciousness and attention will be focused. The stream of impulses which is thus strengthened becomes capable of dominating the processes in the highest center, and of overruling and shutting out from full consciousness all the sensory signals which do not belong to the object on which attention is fixed, and which are not themselves strong enough (or perhaps not sufficiently in conflict with the underlying outline picture of the environment) to attract attention.

6.31. There would thus appear to exist within the central nervous system a highest and most comprehensive center at which at any one time only a limited group of coherent processes can be fully evaluated; where all these processes are related to the same spatial and temporal framework; where the 'abstract' or generic relations form a closely knit order in which individual objects are placed; and where, in addition, a close connection with the instruments of communication has not only contributed a further and very powerful means of classification, but has also made it possible for the individual to participate in a social or conventional representation of the world which he shares with his fellows.

6.32. Of these various characteristics of consciousness the pre-dominance of 'abstract' features requires further discussion. This will be combined in the next two sections with some further examination of the nature of abstract thought.

6. 'Concrete' and 'Abstract'

6.33. While the 'consciousness' of consciously experienced qualities implies their being closely related to each other, the relationships which determine these qualities are not in turn themselves conscious. These relationships determine how different conscious experiences will act upon or affect each other, but they are present in consciousness only in this 'implicit' manner and are not explicitly experienced.

6.34. Since the relations which determine the character of mental qualities are not themselves consciously experienced but show themselves solely in the different effects which the different experienced qualities produce, the

---

[7] Cf., C. T. Morgan, 1943, p. 283 et seq.

latter appear to us as the absolute and irreducible data of consciousness. This is often expressed by the statement that sensory experience gives us acquaintance with the 'concrete' phenomena while the higher mental processes derive 'abstractions' from those immediate data.

6.35. This distinction between the 'concrete' character of immediate experience and the 'abstract' character of 'concepts' is misleading in several respects. It is closely connected with the old belief that the sensory qualities constitute in some sense a reproduction of corresponding attributes of the objects of the external world, and with that mosaic theory of perception which conceives of all mental events as being built up from fixed sensory 'elements'.

6.36. If sensory perception must be regarded as an act of classification, what we perceive can never be unique properties of individual objects but always only properties which the objects have in common with other objects. Perception is thus always an interpretation, the placing of something into one or several classes of objects. An event of an entirely new kind which has never occurred before, and which sets up impulses which arrive in the brain for the first time, could not be perceived at all.[8]

6.37. All we can perceive of external events are therefore only such properties of these events as they possess as members of classes which have been formed by past 'linkages'. The qualities which we attribute to the experienced objects are strictly speaking not properties of that object at all, but a set of relations by which our nervous system classifies them[9] or, to put it differently, *all* we know about the world is of the nature of theories and all 'experience' can do is to change these theories.[10]

6.38. This means also that what we perceive of the external world are never either all the properties which particular objects can be said to possess objectively, nor even only some of the properties which these objects in fact do possess physically, but always only certain 'aspects', relations to other kinds of objects which we assign to all elements of the classes in which we place the perceived objects. This may often comprise relations which objectively do not at all belong to the particular object, but which we merely ascribe to it as the member of the class in which we place it as a result of some accidental collocation of circumstances in the past.

6.39. In any sense in which we can contrast our knowledge of the per-

---

[8] Cf., H. Henning, 1924, p. 304.

[9] Cf., E. G. Boring, 1933, p. 30: 'The thesis of this book is that nothing is "directly observed", that every fact is an implication.' It is curious that an author holding this view should still describe himself as a positivist.

[10] I owe this way of putting it to my friend K. R. Popper, who, however, may not entirely agree with this use I am making of his ideas. [On Popper's reaction to *The Sensory Order* see my comments in the editor's introduction, above pp. 52f.—Ed.]

ceived properties of an external object with its physical or objective properties, all sensory perception is therefore in a sense 'abstract'; it always selects certain features or aspects of a given situation. We shall presently see that the assumption that there exists a physical world different from the phenomenal world involves the assumption that the former possesses properties which we cannot directly perceive, and even some which we do not know. Even the so-called elementary sensory qualities are in this sense 'abstractions', since they are determined by bundles of relationships which we have learnt to attach to certain stimuli which in a physical sense may or may not possess identical properties.

6.40. We already have stressed repeatedly the fact that the immediate data of consciousness are not in fact built up in mosaic fashion from elementary sensations. We perceive directly such complexes as configurations (Gestalts), and there can be little doubt that we often consciously perceive only the Gestalt qualities without being aware of the 'elementary' sensations (such as colors) of which the former were once supposed to be built up.[11] It is at least probable that even on a pre-conscious level we can learn to respond similarly to certain 'abstract' features of an external situation irrespective of the different elements of which the Gestalt may be built up in the particular case.

6.41. The immediate data of consciousness will therefore be 'abstract' not only in the sense that they can never convey to us more than certain generic 'attributes' of the perceived objects, but also in the sense that they will always reflect only some of these generic properties which might be ascribed to the perceived object. If, with regard to current perceptions, we are usually little aware of their partial or incomplete character, this is probably due to the fact that while the experience is present we are in a position to supplement it by directing our attention to particular features.

6.42. This possibility of 'filling in' at first unperceived details by directing our attention to them probably constitutes also one of the main differences between current perceptions and memory images (though some people of the eidetic type appear to be able by recalling vivid images to discover details in them which they had not noticed at the time of the original experience). But the memory images need not always to be more 'abstract' than current perceptions. If frequently only certain abstract features of a perceived situation can be remembered, this is maybe a consequence of the fact that only those abstract features were perceived in the first instance.

6.43. While there thus exists little justification for any sharp distinction between the 'concrete' picture supplied by sense perception and the 'abstractions' which are derived from the former by the higher mental processes (or between the complete picture of a unique situation built up by the 'senses'

[11] J. von Kries, 1923, p. 99.

from fixed elements, and the abstract features which the 'intellect' singles out from the picture which is supposed to be given prior to any abstraction, cf. 5.19), there is a legitimate sense in which we can at any moment distinguish between the immediate data of consciousness and the further processes of rearrangement and reclassification to which they can be subjected on a conscious level.

7. Conceptual Thought

6.44. We have seen that the classification of the stimuli performed by our senses will be based on a system of acquired connections which reproduce, in a partial and imperfect manner, relations existing between the corresponding physical stimuli. The 'model' of the physical world which is thus formed will give only a very distorted reproduction of the relationships existing in that world (5.20–5.24); and the classification of these events by our senses will often prove to be false, that is, give rise to expectations which will not be borne out by events.

6.45. But, although the conscious mind can know of the external world only in terms of the classes which earlier experience has created, and although all its conscious experience must always refer to elements of such given classes rather than to individual objects, the experience of these data of consciousness will provide the foundation for a revision of the classification from which it starts. Further experience will show that parts of different situations which our senses represent as being alike will, according to the different accompanying circumstances, have to be treated as different. The mind will perform on the initial sensory experiences a process of reclassification, the objects of which are no longer the original stimuli but the elements of the classes formed by the preconscious sensory mechanism.

6.46. The experience that objects which individually appear as alike to our sense will not always behave in the same manner in relation to other classes of apparently similar objects, and that objects which to our senses appear to be different may in all other respects prove to behave in the same manner, will thus lead to the formation of new classes which will be determined by explicitly (consciously) known relations between their respective elements. These new classes formed by a rearrangement of the objects of the sensory world are what are usually described as abstract concepts.

6.47. The formation of abstract concepts thus constitutes a repetition on a higher level of the same kind of process of classification by which the differences between the sensory qualities are determined.[12] This continuous

---

[12] Cf., H. Margenau, 1950, pp. 54–56, and H. Werner, 1948, pp. 222, 224.

process of reclassification is forced on us because we find that the classification of objects and events which our senses effect is only a rough and imperfect approximation to a reproduction of the differences between the physical objects which would enable us correctly to predict their behavior[13]—an approximation determined by the accidents of evolution, the physiological capacities and the pragmatic needs of the individual and the species.

6.48. Perhaps we may go still further and regard conceptual thought and the processes of inference as a further repetition of the process of classification on a still higher level. It is probably no accident that the formation of classes and the relation between classes were first studied in the attempt to analyse the principles of conceptual reasoning. It should be clear now that the same kind of relationship which in logic has been developed as the theory of classes and relations is immediately applicable to that physiological process of multiple grouping or classification which we have been examining. And it should not be difficult to conceive of the conscious mental process which logic analyses as a repetition on a higher level of similar processes which, on a pre-conscious level, have produced the material on which the conscious processes operate.

6.49. We cannot attempt here further to distinguish the different levels on which this kind of process of constantly repeated classifications proceeds, and we must be content with the suggestion that all the 'higher' mental processes may be interpreted as being determined by the operation of the same general principle which we have employed to explain the formation of the system of basic sensory qualities. We have throughout to deal with an ever-repeated process of classification of the kind described earlier.

6.50. With this suggestion of the essential unity of the character of the physiological mechanism underlying all kinds of mental processes we have concluded the exposition of the theory which is the main object of this study. There remain yet, however, two complementary tasks to which the two concluding chapters will be devoted. We shall first consider what kind of empirical confirmation or refutation we may hope to find for our theory. The final chapter will examine certain philosophical consequences which would follow from this theory and which are closely connected with certain topics merely touched upon in this and the preceding chapters.

[13] Cf., F. A. Hayek, 1942, p. 271 *et seq.*

CHAPTER VII

CONFIRMATIONS AND VERIFICATIONS OF THE THEORY

1. Observed Facts for which the Theory Accounts

7.1. The value of a theory of the kind presented here may prove itself by accounting for known facts as consequences of other known phenomena, by enabling us to eliminate phantom problems, by showing that certain earlier theories are special cases of a more general principle, or, finally, by suggesting new questions which can be experimentally investigated. On all these scores our theory appears to have a certain amount of *prima facie* evidence in its favour.

7.2. The main aim of the theory presented is to show that the range of mental phenomena such as discrimination, equivalence of response to different stimuli, generalization, transfer, abstraction, and conceptual thought, may all be interpreted as different forms of the same process which we have called classification, and that such classifications can be effected by a network of connections transmitting nervous impulses. From the fact that this classification is determined by the position of the individual impulse or group of impulses in a complex structure of connections, extending through a hierarchy of levels, follow certain important conclusions concerning the effects which physiological or anatomical changes must be expected to have on mental functions. We shall confine ourselves here to point out a few of the more important consequences of our theory which are in accordance with observed fact.

7.3. Since the qualities of mental events produced by particular impulses or groups of impulses according to this view depend not on any property which these impulses possess by themselves, but on their position in the whole network of connections, it would follow that the different mental functions need not be localized in any particular part of the cortex.

7.4. While the possibility of a peripheral stimulus producing a sensory quality will in general[1] depend on the preservation of the central endings of the

---

[1] In view of what has been said before (4.37–4.42) about the role of the low-level responses it is, however, not entirely inconceivable that in the case of a local destruction of the cortical endings of particular sensory fibers, the proprioceptive fibers recording short-arc responses may come to deputize for them.

corresponding afferent fibers, there is no reason for expecting that beyond this the capacity of experiencing particular qualities will depend on particular parts of the cortex. We should rather expect to find, as in fact we do find, that a destruction of a limited part of the cortex will lead to some weakening of most or all mental functions, rather than to the extinction of some particular capacities.[2]

7.5. Similar considerations would lead us also to expect that particular mental functions will not depend entirely on the existence of particular nervous connections but will be capable of being produced by alternative channels. If the complete classification which determines the peculiar mental quality of an impulse depends on a multiplicity of connections extending throughout the greater part of the cortex, this does not mean that for any particular effect any one of these connections will be indispensable. Partial classifications based on certain bundles of connections may often alternatively be capable of bringing about a discrimination sufficient to maintain the particular effect.

7.6. This may mean either that certain mental processes which are normally based on impulses proceeding in certain fibers may, after these fibers have been destroyed, be relearned by the use of some other fibers, or that certain associations may be effectively brought about through several alternative bundles of connections, so that, if any one of these paths is severed, the remaining ones will still be able to bring about the result. Such effects have been observed and described under the names of 'vicarious functioning' and 'equipotentiality'.[3]

7.7. Our account of the translation of the neural impulse into a mental event as a process of classification leads us to expect that we will find that this process not only takes perceptible time but also that it can be observed in different successive stages in which the classification or evaluation is developed to different degrees. This expectation is amply borne out by observation. From the unconscious responses to stimuli and the still unconscious 'subception'[4] through the 'pre-sensation'[5] and the various degrees of clarity of the sensation,[6] perception and 'apperception',[7] to judgements and concept forma-

[2] See K. S. Lashley, 1929, and already J. von Kries, 1898.
[3] K. S. Lashley, 1929.
[4] R. A. McCleary and R. S. Lazarus, 1949, p. 178. ["Subception" or, alternatively, "subliminal perception" describes the fact that a stimulus may be too weak for a person to consciously perceive it and nevertheless be influenced by it. A prominent example is subliminal advertising, yet research on this phenomenon produced controversial results.—Ed.]
[5] F. R. Bichowsky, 1925, p. 589; R. B. Cattell, 1930. [On the concept of "pre-sensation," see above, 5.7, fn. 2.—Ed.]
[6] H. Henning, 1922, p. 71.
[7] ["Apperception" is the mental process by which new experience is, consciously or unconsciously, integrated into an already existing mental framework.—Ed.]

tion, there exists clearly a chain of events in which the full evaluation of any mental quality gradually unfolds itself.

7.8. From the account we have given of the determination of sensory qualities it would further follow that the quality of any sense experience attached to certain impulses or group of impulses will not always be the same but will be different in different circumstances. The same individual stimulus, affecting the same receptor organs, must thus be expected to produce different sensory qualities according as different other stimuli operate at the same time.

7.9. As we have already seen (4.45–4.47), this expectation is fully borne out by experimental work. Many stimuli are perceived 'correctly' only if received under normal conditions, but lead to different sensations if the setting is not normal.[8]

2. Older Theories Comprised as Special Cases

7.10. There is no need here to mention again the various instances where our approach eliminates what now appear to be false questions. We can at once turn to the several instances where our theory embraces as special cases theories which in the past have been advanced in order to explain particular phenomena. Some of these instances have been noticed earlier and now need be mentioned only briefly.

7.11. The first instance of this kind which has been discussed earlier (3.40–3.45) is Berkeley's theory of spatial vision and the more general theories of space perception which have developed from it. The account of the determination of the spatial order of perception by the co-ordination between the various sense modalities and the kinesthetic sensations is of course merely one particular instance of the theory of the determination of sensory qualities developed here.

7.12. Another similar instance of an anticipation in a particular field which we have already mentioned is the James-Lange theory of emotions. As has been shown before (4.70–4.72), this theory, carefully restated, might be regarded as a special case of our theory.

7.13. In the case at least of von Helmholtz the emphasis on the effect of experience in determining sensory qualities goes far beyond ascribing to experience the creation of their spatial order, and it probably is due mainly to his influence that it is today widely recognized that 'the manner in which we see things of the external world is sometimes affected by experience to an overwhelming extent', and that 'it is often difficult to decide which of our visual experiences are determined immediately by sensation and which, on the con-

---

[8] See on this now the German works by W. Metzger, 1941, and V. von Weizsäcker, 1947.

trary, are determined by experience and practice'.[9] His conception of the 'unconscious inference'[10] by which stimuli which do not lead to conscious experience are yet utilized in the perception of a complex position comes very close to the theory developed here. Yet von Helmholtz, like all later writers following on these lines, instead of drawing the conclusion that the factors to which he attributed 'overwhelming importance' in determining the sensory qualities might be the sole factors which determine them, in fact insisted that nothing could be recognized as sensation which is demonstrably due to experience[11]— thus giving, in fact, support to the conception of a pure core of sensation.

7.14. The same applies to the group of theories which have furthest developed this line of thought, the *Reproduktionspsychologie* of B. Erdmann, R. Dodge, H. Henning and F. Schumann, which, with its stress on the 'residua' which determine sensory qualities, came very close to the position taken here, yet never ceased to distinguish between a 'stimulus component' and a 'residual component', the former of which still corresponds to the 'pure core' of sensation.[12]

7.15. The relation which exists between our theory and the views of the Gestalt school is of a somewhat different character and has already been discussed (3.70–3.79). As was then pointed out, the present approach may be regarded as an attempt to raise, with regard to all kinds of sensory experiences, the question which the Gestalt school raised in connection with the perception of configurations. And it seems to us, that in some respects at least, our theory may be regarded as a consistent development of the approach of the Gestalt school.[13]

---

[9] I cannot now trace the source of this quotation, but similar statements can be found in many passages of Helmholtz, e.g., 1925, III, p. 12. [The statement Hayek may have had in mind appears on p. 10 of Helmholtz 1925, III (electronic edition 2001, University of Pennsylvania, http://psych.upenn.edu/backuslab/Helmholtz): "Consequently, it may be rather hard to say how much of our apperceptions (*Anschauungen*) as derived by the sense of sight is due directly to sensation, and how much of them, on the other hand, is due to experience and training."—Ed.] W. Wundt's theory of 'assimilation', which ought also to be mentioned in this connection, is essentially a development of these ideas.

[10] H. von Helmholtz, 1925, III, p. 4, where '*unbewusster Schluss*' is, however, inadequately translated as 'unconscious conclusions'. The correct translation 'unconscious inference' is suggested by E. G. Boring.

[11] H. von Helmholtz, 1925, III, p. 13.

[12] B. Erdmann, 1886, 1907, and especially 1920, pp. 7, 16, 18, 63–64, 74–75, and 127; R. Dodge, 1931, p. 126; H. Henning, 1917, p. 198; 1924, pp. 303–04; F. Schumann, 1909, II, p. 19; 1922, pp. 207, 216. It may be worth mentioning that the fullest exposition of this view, Erdmann's *Reproduktionspsychologie*, appeared in the same year, 1920, when the first draft of the present theory was completed. [Benno Erdmann (1851–1921) was a German philosopher and psychologist. He had studied with H. von Helmholtz and was a known Kant specialist and editor of Kant's works. *Grundzüge der Reproduktionspsychologie* is a summary of his psychology of perception and cognition. See also above, 5.61, fn. 10.—Ed.]

[13] This applies particularly to the formulation of the basic problems by K. Koffka, 1935.

7.16. Another instance of a connection between our theory and a familiar older view has not yet been explicitly mentioned: the obvious relations that exist between it and the basic ideas of the old association psychology. Our view agrees, of course, with associationism in the endeavour to trace all mental processes to connections established by experience between certain elements. It differs from it by regarding the elements between which such connections are established as not themselves mental in character but as material events which only through those connections are arranged in a new order in which they obtain the specific significance characteristic of mental events (5.52).

7.17. This is a step which James Mill[14] very nearly made when he briefly suggested that similarity ('resemblance') might be dispensed with as a 'principle of association' and be reduced to a 'particular case' of the 'law of frequency' of co-occurrence.[15] This promising beginning was, however, cut short by the somewhat uncomprehending comment added to this passage by his son, who described the brief hint as 'perhaps the least successful attempt at simplification and generalization of the laws of mental phenomena to be found in the work.'[16] The only further development of this idea is to be found in the writings of the last of the old association psychologists, G. H. Lewes, which never seem to have received the attention which they deserve.[17]

7.18. Finally, we may perhaps once more mention that within the framework of this theory the conception of events which are mental but not conscious receives, for the first time so far as we are aware, a clear meaning. In consequence it provides a systematic place for whatever of the various theories of the unconscious will prove permanent additions to knowledge.

3. New Experiments Suggested

7.19. The theory developed here is not the kind which one could hope to confirm or refute by a single crucial experiment. Its value ought to show itself rather in suggesting new directions in which experimental work should pro-

---

[14] [James Mill (1773–1836) developed, in his two-volume work *Analysis of the Phenomena of the Human Mind* (1829), an associationist epistemology which postulates that ideas derive their order from the order of sensations and that the strength of their association is a function of "vividness" and "frequency." Complex ideas are assumed to be formed in the same manner as compounds of simple ideas.—Ed.]

[15] J. Mill, 1829 (1869), vol. I, p. 111.

[16] [John Stuart Mill (1806–73) reprinted his father's *Analysis of the Phenomena of the Human Mind* in 1869 with extensive comments. Hayek quotes here from footnote 35, on p. 111, the first sentence of which reads: "The reason assigned by the author for considering association by resemblance as a case of association by contiguity is perhaps the least successful attempt at a generalization and simplification of the laws of mental phenomena to be found in the work."—Ed.]

[17] G. H. Lewes, 1879.

duce interesting results. The main thesis for which one may hope to find experimental confirmation is that the sensory qualities can be changed by the acquisition of new connections between sensory impulses. If this central contention is correct it should in principle be possible both, to attach conscious sensory qualities to sensory impulses which before carried no conscious values, and to create discriminations between such impulses which before caused undistinguishable sensations. It should even be possible to create altogether new sensory qualities which have never been experienced before.

7.20. There exists a great deal of evidence that the capacities for sensory discrimination can be greatly developed by practice. The greatly heightened capacities for tactual, auditory and olfactory discrimination often acquired by the blind,[18] the development of taste, smell, vision and touch by the professional tasters and samplers of wine,[19] spirits, tobacco, chocolate, perfumes, wool,[20] cheese,[21] and the like, the development of the sense of smell by some doctors and chemists,[22] of the auditory sense of musicians,[23] and of the color sense of artists and dyers[24] are familiar, although quite inadequately studied, examples.

7.21. In more recent times, largely under the influence of the Gestalt school, the effect of experience and practice on what has come to be known as 'perceptual organization' has received a good deal of attention. It appears to have been established beyond doubt that the perception of the various configurations and complexes can be profoundly altered by experience.[25] But although this fact is closely connected with our problem, and (if the belief, held both by the Gestalt school and ourselves, is correct, that there is no real difference between sensation and perception) goes far to make the variability of even the most elementary sensory qualities probable, it does not directly confirm that the latter is the case.

7.22. Most of this discussion of sensory organization—not excluding much of the work of the Gestalt school, in spite of its fight against the 'constancy assumption'—however, still suffers from an underlying belief that this problem is one of how given sensations become 'organized', as if there could be unorganized sensory data, something like W. James's 'blooming buzzing con-

[18] In addition to such older studies as the classic investigation of J. N. Czermak, 1855, and the more recent works of T. J. Williams, 1922, and M. von Senden, 1932, see the recent summary by E. von Skramlik, 1937, p. 173, which seems to show that the pre-dominant evidence is against the contrary results obtained by some investigators.

[19] H. Henning, 1924, p. 55.

[20] H. Binns, 1926.

[21] G. W. S. Blair and F. M. V. Coppen, 1939.

[22] R. W. Moncrieff, 1944 (1946), pp. 9, 76.

[23] F. L. Dimmick, 1946, p. 19.

[24] E. G. Boring, 1942, pp. 339–40.

[25] K. W. Braly, 1933; R. W. Leeper, 1935; K. Duncker, 1939.

fusion'[26] in the mind of the newly born, and that it is these initial fixed sense data which perception organizes in a pattern.[27] These remnants of the old 'mosaic theory' which still pervade the discussion cannot be finally eliminated until it is realized that sensory organization and the determination of the individual qualities are one and the same problem.

7.23. Connected with the studies of the effect of experience on sensory organization are the known facts about the manner in which congenitally blind who by an operation have become able to see (and animals reared in darkness),[28] learn to perceive visual objects. The ample material collected on this problem by Senden[29] shows clearly that at least the ordering of the individual sensations has to be gradually learnt, but also that apparently such persons are able from the first moment to distinguish colors. But as it appears that no completely blind person has ever gained vision in this manner[30] and that all those operated persons whose vision had been obstructed by cataract were, before the operation, able to distinguish shades of light and probably also colors, this information is of little direct use for our purpose.

7.24. Perhaps the most significant experimental findings in this field are the extensive investigations of Stratton, Ewert and, more recently, Erismann on the effect of the prolonged wearing of various kinds of spectacles which either invert or distort vision,[31] and the corresponding experiments by P. T. Young with the 'pseudo-phone', an apparatus which effects an acoustical transposi-

---

[26] [James's reference to a baby's impression of the world "as one great blooming, buzzing confusion" appears on p. 462 of *The Principles of Psychology* (1890). In his article "The Primacy of the Abstract," Hayek comments on this notion: "James speaks of the 'blooming, buzzing confusion' of the baby's sensory experience of his environment. This presumably means that the baby can fully perceive such particulars as colored spots, particular sounds, etc., but that for him these particulars are unordered. I am inclined to believe that, in the case of the baby as well in that of higher animals, almost the exact opposite is true, namely that they experience a structured world in which the particulars are very indistinct" (F. A. Hayek, *The Market and Other Orders*, ed. Bruce Caldwell, vol. 15 (2014) of *The Collected Works of F. A. Hayek*, 322).—Ed.]

[27] As R. S. Woodworth rightly points out with regard to form perception (1938, p. 624), 'the empiricist theory aims to get along with a minimum number of concepts: it uses only the concept of a pure mosaic of elementary sensation and the concept of associations established by experience. To the associations are assigned the functions (*a*) of combining the elements into forms and (*b*) of giving objective meaning to these forms.'

[28] A. H. Riesen, 1947.

[29] M. von Senden, 1932.

[30] J. B. Miner, 1905, p. 103.

[31] G. M. Stratton, 1897 [George Malcolm Stratton (1865–1957) was an American experimental psychologist who had studied from 1894–96, and received his doctorate, at W. Wundt's Institute for Experimental Psychology in Leipzig, Germany.—Ed.]; P. H. Ewert, 1930, and 1936; T. Erismann, 1948. [Theodor Erismann (1883–1961) was a Swiss psychologist and philosopher who, from 1926 until his retirement in 1956, taught at the University of Innsbruck, where he conducted vision experiments with Ivo Kohler. See above, introduction, fn. 12.—Ed.]

tion of sound between the two ears.[32] All these experiments show that the significance or position of different stimuli of one modality relative to stimuli of another modality can be altered if they are regularly made to occur in a new combination.

7.25. The older treatises on psychology contain a good deal of discussion on the effect of practice on sensory discrimination. William James, e.g., in a section headed 'the improvement of discrimination by practice' even explicitly mentions as the first cause 'which we can see at work whenever experience improves discrimination' the fact that 'the terms whose difference comes to be felt contract disparate associates and these help to draw them apart'.[33]

7.26. Little systematic work, however, has been done on this problem and even the meaning of the concept of practice as applied to sensory discrimination, and of the conception of new or improved discriminations, has been left somewhat obscure. Indeed the older psychologists, who paid at least some attention to the effect of practice in this connection, were inclined to regard it mainly as a nuisance, an effect which had to be eliminated before serious experimental work could start, rather than as a phenomenon which deserved investigation for its own sake.

7.27. The earliest and for a long time the only systematic experiments in these fields were those performed nearly a hundred years ago by A. W. Volkmann[34] on the effect of practice on the threshold for discrimination between two neighbouring points on the skin. Later experiments[35] have amply confirmed his findings that not only these thresholds could be decreased by short practice by as much as from 50 mm. to 0.5 mm., but also that practice with such tactual stimuli on a part of the skin on one side of the body would similarly decrease the threshold for discrimination between symmetrically corresponding points on the other side of the body.

7.28. Almost the only systematic work done in this field in more recent times are a number of somewhat inconclusive studies on the effect of practice

---

[32] P. T. Young, 1928. [Paul Thomas Young (1892–1978) was an American psychologist who had received his doctorate under E. B. Titchener. In 1926, he spent a sabbatical year in Berlin with Köhler, Wertheimer, and Lewin.—Ed.]

[33] W. James, 1890, I, pp. 508, 510. For other similar earlier references *see* O. Külpe, 1895, pp. 42, 302, 340; L. J. Martin and G. E. Müller, 1899, pp. 128ff.; E. B. Titchener, 1905, I, ii, p. 57; E. L. Thorndike, 1913, p. 152; F. Krüger, 1915, pp. 95–96 [Felix Krüger (1874–1948) was a German psychologist and philosopher who in 1917 became director of the Leipzig Institute for Experimental Psychology, founded by Wilhelm Wundt (see above, preface, fn. 8).—Ed.]; J. von Kries, 1923, p. 144. The explicit and categorical denial of any improvement of the capacity of sensing, or sensory acuity, by H. L. Kingsley, 1946, p. 265, is rather exceptional and apparently based on as little precise information as the prevalent contrary view.

[34] A. W. Volkmann, 1858.

[35] See V. Henri, 1898, and the summary of the work of F. B. Dressler, G. A. Tawney, and L. Solomons in C. L. Friedline, 1918.

on pitch discrimination in hearing, conducted by various students interested mainly in musical education.[36] These studies are not very helpful for our purpose because they addressed themselves in the main to the question whether practice would improve discrimination, rather than to the problem of the conditions under which it would do so. The one significant point which emerges is that it seems to be generally true that no mere repetition but only knowledge of results of the attempts to discriminate will lead to an improvement of discrimination.

7.29. This unsatisfactory state of knowledge of the whole subject is probably in a great measure due to the uncertain meaning of the concept of practice when applied to these problems. Although this meaning is usually taken (and sometimes explicitly said[37]) to be obvious, it is by no means clear that the sense of improving an existing capacity by repeated exercise, which is probably roughly what is meant by the effect of practice in other fields, fits the case of sensory discrimination.

7.30. There is little difficulty about understanding why the repetition of any particular series of movements should enable us to perform them afterwards more quickly, surely, smoothly, or otherwise more efficiently. But there seems to be no similar obvious reason why any number of attempts to distinguish between two stimuli which we have not been able to distinguish before should teach us to do so. The whole approach to the problem seems still to be determined by the rather meaningless conception that these different sensations are always 'there' in some concealed sense, and that the problem is merely to learn to notice these 'unnoticed' sensations which are assumed to be necessarily and invariably coupled with the sensory impulse.

7.31. With regard to any kind of movements, practice clearly means some effect of memory and, as we have seen (5.10–5.12), it is difficult to see what other meaning 'memory' can have but the retention of connections or relations. But while this conception applies directly to the acquisition of new series of movements which can become coupled with each other, and makes it easy to see why, e.g., such a series of movements which at first could be performed only by conscious effort, comes later to be performed automatically, at least the traditional view of the character of sensations does not fit into this pattern.

7.32. To acquire the capacity for new sensory discrimination is not merely to learn to do better what we have done before; it means doing something altogether new. It means not merely to discriminate better or more efficiently between two stimuli or groups of stimuli: it means discriminating between

---

[36] H. T. Moore, 1914; J. F. Humes, 1930; A. A. Capurso, 1934; E. Connette, 1941; C. H. Wedell, 1934; R. F. Wyatt, 1945; B. L. Riker, 1946.

[37] E.g., B. J. Underwood, 1949, p. 118.

stimuli which before were not discriminated at all. If qualities are, as we have maintained, subjective, then, if new discriminations appear for the first time, this means the appearance of a new quality. There is no sense in saying that, if a chemist learns to distinguish between two smells which nobody has ever distinguished before, he has learnt to distinguish between given qualities: these qualities just did not exist before he learnt to distinguish between them.

7.33. Of course, such a 'new' quality can never be unlike any quality ever experienced before: to be recognizable as a distinct quality it must, in certain ways, be related to already familiar qualities, be in various respects similar to, or different from them. It will be a quality only by occupying a certain position in the order of all qualities, an order which can only be gradually extended and more finely sub-divided. But although thus most 'new' qualities will constitute merely a new step in a pre-existing gradation or scale, and share their various attributes with different other qualities, they will nevertheless be new qualities which did not exist before.

7.34. The prevalent uncritical attitude towards the whole problem probably has been much assisted by the fact that the very term 'discrimination' suggests something like a 'recognition' of objective differences between the stimuli (2.32) and belongs thus to an earlier stage of theoretical development.[38] To this idea probably is also due the still widely held view that what is affected by practice is merely the 'interpretation' of a 'given' sensory quality or datum. The whole problem is still largely approached as if the differences between sensory qualities could be accounted for by a different physiological sensitivity of the sense organs—a physiological 'capacity' which needs merely to be 'developed' and which at the same time sets a 'physiological limit' to the extent to which discrimination can be improved. These concepts of the 'capacity' and the 'physiological limit' are as obscure and need as much clearing up as the concept of practice itself.

7.35. Discrimination in the relevant sense (better described as classification) involves not only the learning to respond differently to different physical stimuli, but also the learning to respond similarly to stimuli which physically may be different or similar, and to respond differently to the same stimulus in different contexts. In order that a problem of discrimination should arise, it is necessary, of course, that the different stimuli should cause impulses in different sensory fibers (or, though this does not seem to be the case, different kinds of impulses in the same fiber). But this condition would appear to be the only 'physiological limit': different impulses which affect the same receptor

---

[38] It is interesting to note that E. G. Boring, who at one stage had defined consciousness as discrimination (1933, p. 187), later came to the conclusion that it is 'probably best to abandon the word *discrimination*, which implies a freely acting, conscious observer, and to limit ourselves to the descriptive terms of successive differentiation and relations between them' (1937, p. 451).

organs in the same manner must under the same conditions produce undistinguishable effects.

7.36. Unless we assume the theory of the specific energy of the nerves to be true in its illegitimate interpretation (1.33), there is indeed no reason why it should not be possible to learn to attach different qualities to impulses caused by stimuli which are physically identical, and proceeding in fibers which belong to the same sense modality. Cases are, of course, known where identical physical stimuli, acting on receptors belonging to different modalities ('paradoxical cold', vibration and sound, and the different sensory qualities produced by the same physical stimulus acting on the mucous membranes of the eye and the mouth—1.40) produce different sensations, but the same should in principle also be possible where otherwise identical receptors at different points of the body are involved.

7.37. From the whole approach followed in the present inquiry it would follow that learning to distinguish between different individual stimuli can only mean that we come to attach to these stimuli different effects irrespective of the manner in which these stimuli differ objectively. Learning to discriminate does not necessarily produce a better reproduction of the physical order of the stimuli; it merely means the creation of a new distinction in the phenomenal order which, if it were the result of a non-recurring, accidental or artificial combination of stimuli during a particular period, might indeed prove later not a help but an obstacle to orientation and appropriate behavior.

7.38. The only sense in which the improvement of sense discrimination by practice can be said to be a 'development' of pre-existing capacities is that, in order that such discrimination at the higher levels should become possible, the occurrence of distinct processes at some lower level (at least the receptor level) must be pre-supposed. That is, the organism must initially respond in some way differently to the different stimuli (even if it only be that impulses are set up in the first instance in different fibers), if it is to be possible that these stimuli should acquire different significance for the higher nervous centers. It is at least likely that in most instances different responses to the impulses in the different fibers will already have taken place on a reflex or spinal level before the higher centers learn to discriminate between those impulses, since the development of distinct receptors for different physical stimuli probably goes hand in hand with the development of different responses to those stimuli.

7.39. There appear to exist three principal ways in which the attaching of new connections to sensory impulses which arrive at the higher centers might lead to the appearance of new sensory qualities: 1. impulses which before did not produce a distinct sensation might come to do so; 2. different impulses produced by different physical stimuli which formerly produced the same sensory quality might be made to be perceived as different sensory qualities; and 3. impulses produced by the action of physically identical stimuli on similar receptor organs at different points of the body might also acquire different sensory qualities.

7.40. The task of experimentation in all these instances would be to ascertain whether we could either become aware of particular sensory impulses of which we were before not conscious, or whether sensory impulses could be given distinct qualitative significance different from that of other such impulses from which they were formerly indistinguishable; this might be done by attaching to them a distinct set of connections which are different from those attached to other such impulses which before were perceived as identical.

7.41. It would seem that in any such experiments we must be able to rely on verbal reports of the subject and that therefore animal experiments cannot be used for our purpose. It would be necessary to ascertain before experiments start that the subject is either unaware of the stimulus, or unaware of any qualitative difference between the effects of different stimuli. And although we can teach animals to discriminate between stimuli with respect to certain responses, it would be impossible to decide whether an animal has merely learnt to attach a new response to distinct sensations which it perceived before, or whether it has acquired a new capacity for discrimination. Considering the difficulty of merely ascertaining, e.g., whether particular animals possess our color vision or not,[39] it would seem that animal experiments must be ruled out in this connection.

7.42. With human subjects the chances of successful experiments on these lines probably differ greatly between the different sense modalities. With a sense as highly developed and as fully used in humans as sight, practice in most instances probably has been carried to a point where a definite order has been so deeply engrained that it would at least take very long to obtain any results. It should be noted, however, that as von Kries has pointed out,[40] in another sense this most highly developed of human sensory capacities is the most imperfect of the senses: the correspondence between physical differences between the stimuli and the differences between the sensory qualities is probably less close here than it is with other senses. Every color can be produced by a great variety of mixtures of wave lengths in addition to (in most instances) a monochromatic (homogeneous) light. We do not know whether this equivalence of various combinations of stimuli is determined by a peripheral (i.e. receptor) or by a central mechanism. If the latter were the case, it should not be impossible to learn to see as different colors different mixtures of light waves which initially appear to be indistinguishable.

7.43. Better chances of experimental results exist probably in the less practised sense modalities, particularly those, such as the human sense of smell,

[39] G. L. Walls, 1942, p. 472.
[40] J. von Kries, 1923, p. 80.

of which in an earlier state of development man made greater use than he does in civilized life, and where the physiological capacity of distinguishing between different stimuli is probably much greater than that which we use. It has been pointed out by a competent observer that in this field 'the influence of practice is so enormous, particularly in the beginning, that some people require on the second day of experimentation only small fractions of the threshold values necessary on the first day; and that they then easily solve qualitative analyses which on the previous day seemed impossible to them'.[41]

7.44. As against this advantage of the relative unpractised state of olfaction in civilized men, and the consequent high degree of educability of this sense, stands our ignorance of the nature of the proximal stimuli[42] and of the differential sensitivity of the receptor organs for these stimuli. We shall nevertheless outline the kind of experiments which might be attempted with respect to this sense as the one which seems on the whole to be the most promising one for our purposes.

7.45. The task of the experiment would be to attempt to attach to originally undiscriminated stimuli as many distinct connections with other sensory stimuli and emotional states as possible. That such intersensory associations can be created has, of course, been demonstrated by the recent work on sensory conditioning.[43] The problem is whether by attaching such distinct associations to initially indistinguishable stimuli new discriminations can be created.

7.46. Experiments had probably best start with stimuli which highly practised persons are known to distinguish, but which to an unpractised person are undistinguishable. The points to be ascertained would be not only whether by repeated exposure to the stimuli people can be taught to discriminate between them, but whether this process is considerably speeded up if the different stimuli are made to act under completely different accompanying circumstances. This implies of course the necessity of parallel control experiments in which the conditions under which the two stimuli act are the same.

7.47. For such experiments it would be desirable to alter the whole surroundings and the state of the organism in which the different stimuli were made to act: one of two stimuli might, e.g., be made to act regularly at a particular time of the day (say on awakening in the morning) so that it always coincided with the same phase of the rhythm of the body, in a state of restedness, warmth and inactivity, immediately preceding food and in combinations with a constant combination of colors, tones, etc.; while the other stimulus should as regularly be made to act in circumstances which were in all respects different from those just described: say in the late afternoon, out of doors, in

---

[41] H. Henning, 1927, p. 745.
[42] See, however, the reports on recent work by L. H. Beck and W. R. Miles, 1947.
[43] W. J. Brogden, 1939, 1942, 1947, 1950.

a state of considerable activity and exhilaration, nervous excitement, cold and hunger and in combination with an altogether different set of visual and auditory perceptions.

7.48. In using sensory associations to assist the discrimination between stimuli, care would have to be taken not to run counter to well-established synesthetic relations between the qualities of the different senses. The existence of such synesthetic relations between two scales or dimensions of different modalities might, however, well be used to transfer to the other the finer distinctions which the scale of the one modality possesses. Our inadequate knowledge of the character of the stimuli at present probably makes it impossible to use the technique of differential thresholds with regard to olfaction. But as between colors and tones, for instance, persons who have the capacity of color hearing might well be tested on whether, by deliberately making connections even closer, the greater capacity of discrimination which they possess in one sense can be transferred to the other.

7.49. It is evident that such a technique for the education of the senses might prove to be of considerable practical importance and should thus be studied even apart from its theoretical significance. It is, of course, more than likely that in such attempts it will be found that the crude approach suggested here is inadequate and that, before much can be accomplished in this direction, much more knowledge about the nature of the sensory order, that is about the interrelations between the dimensions of the various sense modalities, will have to be acquired.

7.50. In addition to such attempts to teach new discriminations between stimuli which were already consciously perceived but not distinguished, the possibility should not be overlooked of attaching conscious values to impulses which did not possess them before. In this connection perhaps stimuli acting inside the body might offer the most interesting field, and the new techniques of deep heating would seem to open possibilities which ought to be explored. Also the possibility of extending the range of the more familiar senses in this manner should not be disregarded. Although the upper and lower limits of the visible spectrum and the range of audible sounds may well be true physiological limits determined by the nature of the receptor organs, they may in part be centrally determined, and in this case be alterable by training. The considerable inter-individual differences between these limits rather suggest that this may be so, and even such reports as that a blind person has acquired the capacity of smelling colors[44] should not be dismissed as altogether impossible.

7.51. It is not at all improbable that man possesses a considerable number of 'reflex senses', as the action of the semi-circular canals in controlling bal-

---

[44] T. J. Williams, 1922, p. 1333. This deserves examination, especially in view of the recent conclusions of Beck and Miles concerning the radiation character of olfactory stimulation.

ance has been aptly described,[45] a sensitivity of the body for certain specific stimuli to which a specific response is effected at lower levels, but which have not occurred with sufficient regularity in the company of particular other stimuli to give them a distinct conscious quality. In all such instances it might be possible to raise these impulses to a conscious level by deliberately attaching to them that characteristic following which they did not have occasion to acquire in natural surroundings.

4. Possibilities of Experimental Refutation

7.52. It will assist further to define the content of our main thesis if we state briefly the main alternative theories whose confirmation would at the same time disprove the theory here developed.

7.53. Disregarding all those theories which, like parallelism, assume the existence of some mind-substance and which are unverifiable almost by definition, the first of the alternative theories which might be mentioned is that of a cell-memory or of the 'storage' of impressions in the individual cell, such as underlies R. Semon's conception of the 'engram'.[46] This conception implies, of course, the assumption that whatever it is that is thus stored possesses by itself the different attributes by which different sensory qualities are distinguished. Although it is difficult to see how this assumption could ever be experimentally verified, its confirmation would, of course, refute our theory and in fact eliminate the problem which the latter is intended to solve.

7.54. A more direct refutation of our theory would be obtained by the discovery of such difference in the physical properties transmitted by the different nerve fibers that these could be said to correspond to the differences in the sensory qualities produced by those impulses—that is, if the theory of the specific energy of nerves, in what we have called its illegitimate interpretation (1.33), should prove to be correct. It was by suggesting the search for such physiological differences between the individual impulses that the theoretical views widely held in the past have posed a problem to physiological research to which, if our view is correct, no answer can be found.

7.55. A special modern form of that theory is the resonance theory developed (for efferent nervous impulses) by P. A. Weiss[47] which suggests that it is not the fact of a transmission of impulses through special pathways but rather the character of the impulses in some fibers which determines that similar impulses are being set up in other distant fibers. This view, if proved correct

[45] E. Cyon, quoted by E. G. Boring, 1942, p. 544.
[46] R. Semon, 1904, 1909.
[47] P. A. Weiss, 1941.

for afferent impulses, would also disprove most of the present theory. The same would be true if the views of some modern Gestaltists were confirmed, who seem to suggest that it is not the topological position of the group of impulses in the whole structure of connections but the spatial configuration[48] of these impulses, irrespective of the particular fibers in which they occur, which counts.

7.56. Finally we might mention as a conceivable alternative theory, although it seems doubtful whether it has ever been carried to its ultimate consequences, the view that sensory discrimination is determined entirely by peripheral motor events. Although we do certainly not wish to minimize the importance of motor responses at all the various levels of the hierarchy of the central nervous system, it is difficult to see how they should ever make those central 'symbolic' or classificatory processes unnecessary with whose functions we were mainly concerned.

[48] W. Köhler and R. Held, 1949.

CHAPTER VIII

PHILOSOPHICAL CONSEQUENCES

1. Pre-Sensory Experience and Pure Empiricism

8.1. If the account of the determination of mental qualities which we have given is correct, it would mean that the apparatus by means of which we learn about the external world is itself the product of a kind of experience (5.1–5.16). It is shaped by the conditions prevailing in the environment in which we live and it represents a kind of generic reproduction of the relations between the elements of this environment which we have experienced in the past; and we interpret any new event in the environment in the light of that experience. If this conclusion is true, it raises necessarily certain important philosophical questions on which in this last chapter we shall attempt some tentative observations.

8.2. These consequences arise mainly from the role which we have assigned to the action of the pre-sensory experience or 'linkages' in determining the sensory qualities. Especially the elimination of the hypothetical 'pure' or 'primary' core of sensations, supposed not to be due to earlier experience, but either to involve some direct communication of properties of the external objects, or to constitute irreducible mental atoms or elements, disposes of various philosophical puzzles which arise from the lack of meaning of those hypotheses.

8.3. According to the traditional view, experience begins with the reception of sensory data possessing constant qualities which either reflect corresponding attributes belonging to the perceived external objects, or are uniquely correlated with such attributes of the elements of the physical world. These sensory data are supposed to form the raw material which the mind accumulates and learns to arrange in various manners. The theory developed here challenges the basic distinction implied in that conception: the distinction between sensory perception of given qualities and the operations which the intellect is supposed to perform on these data in order to arrive at an understanding of the given phenomenal world (5.19, 6.44).

8.4. According to our theory, the characteristic attributes of the sensory qualities, or the classes into which different events are placed in the process of perception, are not attributes which are possessed by these events and which are in some manner 'communicated' to the mind; they are regarded as consisting entirely in the 'differentiating' responses of the organism by which the qualitative classification or order of these events is created; and it is contended that this classification is based on the connections created in the nervous system by past linkages. Every sensation, even the 'purest', must therefore be regarded as an interpretation of an event in the light of the past experience of the individual or the species.

8.5. The process of experience thus does not begin with sensations or perceptions, but necessarily precedes them: it operates on physiological events and arranges them into a structure or order which becomes the basis of their 'mental' significance; and the distinction between the sensory qualities, in terms of which alone the conscious mind can learn about anything in the external world, is the result of such pre-sensory experience. We may express this also by stating that experience is not a function of mind or consciousness, but that mind and consciousness are rather products of experience (2.50).

8.6. Every sensory experience of an event in the external world is therefore likely to possess 'attributes' (or to be in a manner distinguished from other sensory events) to which no similar attributes of the external events correspond. These 'attributes' are the significance which the organism has learnt to assign to a class of events on the basis of the past associations of events of this class with certain other classes of events. It is only in so far as the nervous system has learnt thus to treat a particular stimulus as a member of a certain class of events, determined by the connections which all the corresponding impulses possess with the same impulses representing other classes of events, that an event can be perceived at all, i.e., that it can obtain a distinct position in the system of sensory qualities.

8.7. If the distinctions between the different sensory qualities of which our conscious experience appears to be built up are thus themselves determined by pre-sensory experiences (linkages), the whole problem of the relation between experience and knowledge assumes a new complexion. So far as experience in the narrow sense, i.e., conscious sensory experience, is meant, it is then clearly not true that all that we know is due to such experience. Experience of this kind would rather become possible only after experience in the wider sense of linkages has created the order of sensory qualities—the order which determines the qualities of the constituents of conscious experience.

8.8. Sense experience therefore pre-supposes the existence of a sort of accumulated 'knowledge' of an acquired order of the sensory impulses based on their past co-occurrence; and this knowledge, although based on (pre-sensory) experience, can never be contradicted by sense experiences and will determine the forms of such experiences which are possible.

8.9. John Locke's famous fundamental maxim of empiricism that *nihil est in intellectu quod non antea fuerit in sensu* is therefore not correct if meant to refer to conscious sense experience. And it does not justify the conclusion that all we know (*quod est in intellectu*) must be subject to confirmation or contradiction by sense experience. From our explanation of the formation of the order of sensory qualities itself it would follow that there will exist certain general principles to which all sensory experiences must conform (such as that two distinct colors cannot be in the same place)—relations between the parts of such experiences which must always be true.

8.10. A certain part at least of what we know at any moment about the external world is therefore not learnt by sensory experience, but is rather implicit in the means through which we can obtain such experience; it is determined by the order of the apparatus of classification which has been built up by pre-sensory linkages. What we experience consciously as qualitative attributes of the external events is determined by relations of which we are not consciously aware but which are implicit in these qualitative distinctions, in the sense that they affect all that we do in response to these experiences.

8.11. All that we can perceive is thus determined by the order of sensory qualities which provides the 'categories' in terms of which sense experience can alone take place. Conscious experience, in particular, always refers to events defined in terms of relations to other events which do not occur in that particular experience.[1]

8.12. We thus possess 'knowledge' about the phenomenal world which, because it is in this manner implicit in all sensory experience, must be true of all that we can experience through our senses. This does not mean, however, that this knowledge must also be true of the physical world, that is, of the order of the stimuli which cause our sensations. While the conditions which make sense perception possible—the apparatus of classification which treats them as similar or different—must affect all sense perception, it does not for this reason also govern the order of the events in the physical world.

8.13. It requires a deliberate effort to divest oneself of the habitual assumption that all we have learned from experience must be true of the external (physical) world.[2] But since all we can ever learn from experience are generalizations about certain kinds of events, and since no number of particular instances can ever prove such a generalization, knowledge based entirely on experience may yet be entirely false. If the significance which a certain group of stimuli has acquired for us is based entirely on the fact that in the past

[1] K. Lorenz, 1942, p. 352.
[2] H. von Helmholtz, 1925, III, p. 14: 'Here we still have to explain how experience counteracts experience, and how illusion can be produced by factors derived from experience, when it might seem *as if experience could not teach anything except what was true*. In this matter we must remember, as was intimated above, that the sensations are interpreted just as they arise when they are stimulated in the normal way, and when the organ of sense is used normally.' (Italics ours.)

they have regularly occurred in combination with certain other stimuli, this may or may not be an adequate basis for a classification which will enable us to make true predictions. We have earlier (5.20–5.24) given a number of reasons why we must expect that the classifications of events in the external world which our senses perform will not strictly correspond to a classification of these events based solely on the similarity or the differences of their behavior towards each other.

8.14. While there can thus be nothing in our mind which is not the result of past linkages (even though, perhaps, acquired not by the individual but by the species), the experience that the classification based on the past linkages does not always work, i.e., does not always lead to valid predictions, forces us to revise that classification (6.45–6.48). In the course of this process of reclassification we not only establish new relations between the data given within a fixed framework of reference, i.e., between the elements of given classes: but since the framework consists of the relations determining the classes, we are led to adjust that framework itself.

8.15. The reclassification, or breaking up of the classes formed by the implicit relations which manifest themselves in our discrimination of sensory qualities, and the replacement of these classes by new classes defined by explicit relations, will occur whenever the expectations resulting from the existing classification are disappointed, or when beliefs so far held are disproved by new experiences. The immediate effects of such conflicting experiences will be to introduce inconsistent elements into the model of the external world; and such inconsistencies can be eliminated only if what formerly were treated as elements of the same class are now treated as elements of different classes (5.72).

8.16. The reclassification which is thus performed by the mind is a process similar to that through which we pass in learning to read aloud a language which is not spelled phonetically. We learn to give identical symbols different values according as they appear in combination with different other symbols, and to recognize different groups of symbols as being equivalent without even noticing the individual symbols.

8.17. While the process of reclassification involves a change of the frame of reference, or of what is *a priori* true of all statements which can be made about the objects defined with respect to that frame of reference, it alters merely the particular presuppositions of all statements, but does not change the fact that such suppositions must be implied in all statements that can be made. In fact, far from being diminished, the *a priori* element will tend to increase as in the course of this process the various objects are increasingly defined by explicit relations existing between them.

8.18. The new experiences which are the occasion of, and which enter into, the new classifications or definitions of objects, are necessarily pre-supposed by anything which we can learn about these objects and cannot be contradicted by anything which we can say about the objects thus defined. There is, therefore, on every level, or in every universe of discourse, a part of our knowledge which, although it is the result of experience, cannot be controlled by experience, because it constitutes the ordering principle of that universe by which we distinguish the different kinds of objects of which it consists and to which our statements refer.

8.19. The more this process leads us away from the immediately given sensory qualities, and the more the elements described in terms of these qualities are replaced by new elements defined in terms of consciously experienced relations, the greater becomes the part of our knowledge which is embodied in the definitions of the elements, and which therefore is necessarily true. At the same time the part of our knowledge which is subject to control by experiences becomes correspondingly smaller.

8.20. This progressive growth of the tautological character of our knowledge is a necessary consequence of our endeavour so to readjust our classification of the elements as to make statements about them true. We have no choice but either to accept the classification effected by our senses, and in consequence to be unable correctly to predict the behavior of the objects thus defined; or to redefine the objects on the basis of the observed differences in their behavior with respect to each other, with the result that not only the differences which are the basis of our classification become necessarily true of the objects thus classified, but also that it becomes less and less possible to say of any particular sensory object with any degree of certainty to which of our theoretical classes it belongs.

8.21. This difficulty does not become too serious so long as we merely redefine a particular object in relational terms. But as we continue this process of reclassification, those other objects must in turn also be redefined in a similar manner. In the course of this process we are soon forced to take into account not only relations existing between a given object and other objects which are actually observed in conjunction with the former, but also relations which have existed in the past between that and other objects, and even relations which can be described only in hypothetical terms: relations which might have been observed between this and other objects in circumstances which did not in fact exist and which, if they had existed, would not have left the identity of the object unchanged.

8.22. Several chemical substances may, e.g., be completely indistinguishable to the senses so long as they remain in their given state. The reason why chemistry classifies them as different substances is that in certain circumstances and in combination with certain other substances they will 'react' differently. But most of these chemical reactions involve a change in the character of the substance, so that the identical quantity of a given substance, which has been tested for the reaction which is the basis of its classification, cannot be available after it has been established to which class it belongs. Only by such unverifiable assumptions as that the quantity of the substance from which we have drawn the sample is completely homogeneous, so that what we have found out about various samples applies also to the rest, can we arrive at the conclusion that the particular sensory object belongs to a definite theoretical class.

8.23. The sense data, or the sensory qualities of the objects about which we make statements, thus are pushed steadily further back; and when we complete the process of defining all objects by explicit relations instead of by the implicit relations inherent in our sensory distinctions, those sense data disappear completely from the system. In the end the system of explicit definitions becomes both all-comprehensive and self-contained or circular; all the elements in the universe are defined by their relations to each other, and all we know about that universe becomes contained in those definitions. We should obtain a self-contained model capable of reproducing all the combinations of events which we can observe in the external world, but should have no way of ascertaining whether any particular event in the external world corresponded to a particular part of our model.

8.24. Science thus tends necessarily towards an ultimate state in which all knowledge is embodied in the definitions of the objects with which it is concerned; and in which all true statements about these objects therefore are analytical or tautological and could not be disproved by any experience. The observation that any object did not behave as it should, could then only mean that it was not an object of the kind it was thought to be. With the disappearance of all sensory data from the system, laws (or theories) would no longer exist in it apart from the definitions of the objects to which they applied, and for that reason could never be disproved.

8.25. Such a completely tautological or self-contained system of knowledge about the world would not be useless. It would constitute a model of the world from which we could read off what kind of events are possible in that world and what kind are not. It would often allow us, on the basis of a fairly complete history of a particular sensory object, to state with a high degree of probability that it fits into one and only one possible place in our model, and that in consequence it is likely to behave in a certain manner in circumstances which would have to be similarly described. But it would never enable us to identify with certainty a particular sensory object with a particular part of our model, or with certainty to predict how the former will behave in given circumstances.

8.26. A strict identification of any point of our theoretical model of the world with a particular occurrence in the sensory world would be possible only if we were in a position to complete our model of the physical world by including in it a complete model of the working of our brain (cf. 5.77–5.91)—that is, if we were able to explain in detail the manner in which our senses classify the stimuli. This, however, as will be shown in section 6 of this chapter, is a task which that same brain can never accomplish.

8.27. In conclusion of this section it should, perhaps, be emphasized that, in so far as we have been led into opposition to some of the theses traditionally associated with empiricism, we have been led to their rejection not from an opposite point of view, but on the contrary, by a more consistent and radical application of its basic idea. Precisely because all our knowledge, including the initial order of our different sensory experiences of the world, is due to experience, it must contain elements which cannot be contradicted by experience. It must always refer to classes of elements which are defined by certain relations to other elements, and it is valid only on the assumption that these relations actually exist. Generalization based on experience must refer to classes of objects or events and can have relevance to the world only in so far as these classes are regarded as given irrespective of the statement itself. Sensory experience pre-supposes, therefore, an order of experienced objects which precedes that experience and which cannot be contradicted by it, though it is itself due to other, earlier experience.

2. Phenomenalism and the Inconstancy of Sensory Qualities

8.28. If the classification of events in the external world effected by our senses proves not to be a 'true' classification, i.e., not one which enables us adequately to describe the regularities in this world, and if the properties which our senses attribute to these events are not objective properties of these individual events, but merely attributes defining the classes to which our senses assign them, this means that we cannot regard the phenomenal world in any sense as more 'real' than the constructions of science: we must assume the existence of an objective world (or better, of an objective order of the events which we experience in their phenomenal order) towards the recognition of which the phenomenal order is merely a first approximation. The task of science is thus to try and approach ever more closely towards a reproduction of this objective order—a task which it can perform only by replacing the sensory order of events by a new and different classification.[3]

8.29. By saying that there 'exists' an 'objective' world different from the

---

[3] Cf., M. Planck, 1949, p. 108.

phenomenal world we are merely stating that it is possible to construct an order or classification of events which is different from that which our senses show us and which enables us to give a more consistent account of the behavior of the different events in that world. Or, in other words, it means that our knowledge of the phenomenal world raises problems which can be answered only by altering the picture which our senses give us of that world, i.e., by altering our classification of the elements of which it consists. That this is possible and necessary is, in fact, a postulate which underlies all our efforts to arrive at a scientific explanation of the world.

8.30. Any purely phenomenalistic interpretation of the task of science, or any attempt to reduce this task to merely a complete description of the phenomenal world, thus must break down because our senses do not effect such a classification of the different events that what appears to us as alike will also always behave in the same manner. The basic thesis of phenomenalism (and positivism) that 'all *phenomena* are subject to invariable laws' is simply not true if the term phenomenon is taken in its strict meaning of things as they appear to us.

8.31. The ideal of science as merely a complete description of phenomena, which is the positivist conclusion derived from the phenomenalistic approach, therefore proves to be impossible. Science consists rather in a constant search for new classes, for 'constructs' which are so defined that general propositions about the behavior of their elements are universally and necessarily true. For this purpose these classes cannot be defined in terms of sensory properties of the particular individual events perceived by the individual person; they must be defined in terms of their relations to other individual events.

8.32. Such a definition of any class of events, in terms of their relations to other classes of events instead of in terms of any sensory properties which they individually possess, cannot be confined to the former, or even to all the events which together constitute the complete situation existing at a particular moment. The events referred to in the definition of those with which we have actually to deal have to be defined in a similar purely 'relational' manner. The ultimate aim of this procedure must be to define all classes of events exclusively in terms of their relations to each other and without any reference to their sensory properties. It has been well said that 'for science an object expresses itself in the totality of relations possible between it and other objects.'[4] We have already seen (8.24–8.25) that such a complete system of explanation would necessarily be tautological, because all that could be predicted by it would necessarily follow from the definitions of the objects to which it referred.

[4] *Fundamental Mathematics*, 1948, I, p. 92.

8.33. If the theory outlined here is correct, there exists an even more fundamental objection to any consistently phenomenalist interpretation of science.
It would appear that not only are the events of the world, if defined in terms
of their sensory attributes, not subject to invariable laws, so that situations presenting the same appearance to our senses may produce different results; but
also that the phenomenal world (or the order of the sensory qualities from
which it is built up) is itself not constant but variable, and that it will in some
measure change its appearance as a result of that very process of reclassification which we must perform in order to explain it.

8.34. If it is true, as we have argued, that the 'higher' mental activities are
merely a repetition at successive levels of processes of classification of essentially the same character as those by which the different sensory qualities have
come to be distinguished in the first instance, it would seem almost inevitable
that this process of reclassification will in some measure also affect the distinctions between the different sensory qualities from which it starts. The nature
of the process by which the differences between sensory qualities are determined makes it probable that they will remain variable and that the distinctions between them will be modified by new experiences. This would mean
that the phenomenal world itself would not be constant but would be inces-
santly changing in a direction to a closer reproduction of the relations existing
in the physical world. If in the course of this process the sensory data themselves alter their character, the ideal of a purely descriptive science becomes
altogether impossible.

8.35. That the sensory qualities which attach to particular physical events
are thus in principle themselves variable[5] is no less important even though we
must probably regard them as *relatively* stable compared with the continuous
changes of the scheme of classification in terms of which abstract thought
proceeds, almost certainly in so far as the course of the life of the individual is concerned. But we should still have to consider more seriously than we
are wont to do, what is amply confirmed by ordinary experience, namely that
as a result of the advance of our explanation of the world we also come to
'see' this world differently, i.e., that we not merely recognize new laws which
connect the given phenomena, but that these events are themselves likely to
change their appearance to us.

8.36. Such variations of the sensory qualities attributed to given events
could, of course, never be ascertained by direct comparisons of past and pres-

[5] This changeability of the sensory qualities apparently was already recognized by Protago-
ras, who according to Sextus Empiricus taught that the sensations 'are transformed and altered
according to the times of life and to all the other conditions of the body.' *Outlines of Pyrrhonianism*,
translation R. G. Bury, *Loeb Classical Library*, I, Book I, p. 218.

ent sensations, since the memory images of past sensations would be subject to the same changes as the current sensations. The only possibility of testing this conclusion would be provided by experiments with discrimination such as have been suggested in the preceding chapter (7.38–7.51).

8.37. It deserves, perhaps, to be mentioned that, although the theory developed here was suggested in the first instance by the psychological views which Ernst Mach has outlined in his *Analysis of Sensations* and elsewhere, its systematic development leads to a refutation of his and similar phenomenalist philosophies: by destroying the conception of elementary and constant sensations as ultimate constituents of the world, it restores the necessity of a belief in an objective physical world which is different from that presented to us by our senses.[6]

8.38. Similar considerations apply to the views expounded on these matters by William James, John Dewey[7] and the American realists and developed by Bertrand Russell. The latter's view according to which 'the stuff of the world' consists of 'innumerable transient particulars' such as a patch of color which is 'both physical and psychical' in fact is explicitly based on the assumption that 'sensations are what is common to the mental and the physical world', and that their essence is 'their independence from past experience'. The whole of this 'neutral monism' seems to be based on entirely untenable psychological conceptions.[8]

8.39. Another interesting consequence following from our theory is that a stimulus whose occurrence in conjunction with other stimuli showed no regularities whatever could never be perceived by our senses (6.36). This would seem to mean that we can know only such kinds of events as show a certain degree of regularity in their occurrence in relations with others, and that we could not know anything about events which occurred in a completely irregular manner. The fact that the world which we know seems wholly an orderly world may thus be merely a result of the method by which we perceive it. Everything which we can perceive we perceive necessarily as an element of a class of events which obey certain regularities. There could be in this sense no

---

[6] Cf., K. Koffka, 1935, p. 63: 'Mach was an excellent psychologist, who saw many of the most fundamental problems of psychology which, a whole generation later, many psychologists failed even to understand; at the same time he had a philosophy which made it impossible to give fruitful solutions to these problems.'

[7] [John Dewey (1859–1952), strongly influenced by William James's (see above, preface, fn. 9) pragmatism and inspired by Charles Darwin's theory of natural selection, advocated a naturalistic approach to the theory of knowledge, viewing knowledge as a product of the organism's adaptation to the contingencies of its environment. The test of the validity or "truth" of knowledge, from everyday knowledge to scientific theories, is seen in the instrumental guidance it provides for problem-solving action.—Ed.]

[8] B. Russell, 1921, p. 144.

class of events showing no regularities, because there would be nothing which could constitute them for us into a distinct class.

3. Dualism and Materialism

8.40. Because the account of the determination of mental qualities which has been given here explains them by the operation of processes of the same kind as those which we observe in the material world, it is likely to be described as a 'materialistic' theory. Such a description in itself would matter very little if it were not for certain erroneous ideas associated with the term materialism which not only would prejudice some people against a theory thus described but, what is more important, would also suggest that it implies certain conclusions which are almost the opposite of those which in fact follow from it. In the true sense of the word 'materialistic' it might even be argued that our theory is less materialistic than the dualistic theories which postulate a distinct mind 'substance'.

8.41. The dualistic theories are a product of the habit, which man has acquired in his early study of nature, of assuming that in every instance where he observed a peculiar and distinct process it must be due to the presence of a corresponding peculiar and distinct substance. The recognition of such a peculiar material substance came to be regarded as an adequate explanation of the process produced.

8.42. It is a curious fact that, although in the realm of nature in general we no longer accept as an adequate explanation the postulate of a peculiar substance possessing the capacity of producing the phenomena we wish to explain, we still resort to this old habit where mental events are concerned. The mind 'stuff' or 'substance' is a conception formed in analogy to the different kinds of matter supposedly responsible for the different kinds of material phenomena. It is, to use an old term in its literal sense, the result of a 'hylomorphic' manner of thinking. Yet, in whatever manner we define substance, to think of mind as a substance is to ascribe to mental events some attributes for whose existence we have no evidence and which we postulate solely on the analogy of what we know of material phenomena.[9]

8.43. In the strict sense of the terms employed an account of mental phenomena which avoids the conception of a distinct mental substance is therefore the opposite of materialistic, because it does not attribute to mind any property which we derive from our acquaintance with matter. In being con-

---

[9] This seems to me to be true in spite of the efforts of C. D. Broad, 1925, to give 'substance' a meaning independent of its material connotations. On the mind-substance theory see now G. Ryle, 1949.

tent to regard mind as a peculiar order of events, different from the order of events which we encounter in the physical world, but determined by the same kind of forces as those that rule in that world, it is indeed the only theory which is not materialistic.[10]

8.44. Superficially there may seem to exist a closer connection between the theory presented here and the so-called 'double-aspect theories' of the relations between mind and body. To scribe our theory as such, however, would be misleading. What could be regarded as the 'physical aspect' of this double-faced entity would not be the individual neural processes but only the complete order of all these processes; but this order, if we knew it in full, would then not be another aspect of what we know as mind but would be mind itself. We cannot directly observe how this order is formed by its physical elements, but can only infer it. But if we could complete the theoretical reconstruction of this order from its elements and then disregard all the properties of the elements which are not relevant to the existence of this order as a whole, we should have a complete description of the order we call mind, just as in describing a machine we can disregard many properties of its parts, such as their color, and consider only those which are essential to the functioning of the machine as a whole (cf. 2.28–2.30).

8.45. This order which we call mind is thus the order prevailing in a particular part of the physical universe—that part of it which is ourselves. It is an order which we 'know' in a way which is different from the manner in which we know the order of the physical universe around us. What we have tried to do here is to show that the same kind of regularities, which we have learnt to discover in the world around us, are in principle also capable of building up an order like that constituting our mind. That such a kind of sub-order can be formed within that order which we have discovered in the external universe does not yet mean, however, that we must be able to explain how the particular order which constitutes our mind is placed in that more comprehensive order. In order to achieve this it would be necessary to construct, with special reference to the human mind, a detailed reproduction of the model-object relation which it involves such as we have sketched schematically before in order to illustrate the general principle (5.77–5.91).

8.46. While our theory leads us to deny any ultimate dualism of the forces governing the realms of mind and that of the physical world respectively, it forces us at the same time to recognize that for practical purposes we shall always have to adopt a dualistic view. It does this by showing that any expla-

---

[10] Cf., W. Metzger, 1941, p. 23: 'Diese, im eigentlich Sinn "materialistische" Auffassung . . . lebt in der Psychologie bis an die Schwelle unserer Zeit fort: in der Alltagspsychologie in der kaum ausrottbaren Ansicht von der Seele als zweitem, stofflichen Etwas, das mit dem Körper während des Lebens "verbunden sei", in ihm wohne . . .'

nation of mental phenomena which we can hope ever to attain cannot be sufficient to 'unify' all our knowledge, in the sense that we should become able to substitute statements about particular physical events (or classes of physical events) for statements about mental events without thereby changing the meaning of the statement.

8.47. In this specific sense we shall never be able to bridge the gap between physical and mental phenomena; and for practical purposes, including in this the procedure appropriate to the different sciences, we shall permanently have to be content with a dualistic view of the world. This, however, raises a further problem which must be more systematically considered in the remaining sections of this chapter.

4. The Nature of Explanation

8.48. What remains now is to restate briefly what the theory outlined in the preceding pages is meant to explain, and how far it can be expected to account for particular mental processes. This makes it necessary to make more precise than we have yet done what we mean by 'explanation'. This is a peculiarly relevant question since 'explanation' is itself one of the mental processes which the theory intends to explain.

8.49. It has been suggested before (5.44–5.48) that explanation consists in the formation in the brain of a 'model' of the complex of events to be explained, a model the parts of which are defined by their position in a more comprehensive structure of relationships which constitutes the semi-permanent framework from which the representations of individual events receive their meaning.

8.50. This notion of the 'model', which the brain is assumed to be capable of building, has, of course, been often used in this connection,[11] and by itself it does not get us very far. Indeed, if it is conceived, as is usually the case, as a separate model of the particular phenomenon to be explained, it is not at all clear what is meant by it. The analogy with a mechanical model is not directly applicable. A mechanical model derives its significance from the fact that the properties of its individual parts are assumed to be known and in some respects to correspond to the properties of the parts of the phenomenon which it reproduces. It is from this knowledge of the different properties of the parts that we derive our knowledge of how the particular combination of these parts will function.

8.51. In general, the possibility of forming a model which explains anything pre-supposes that we have at our disposal distinct elements whose action

---

[11] See particularly K. J. W. Craik, 1943; and K. Lorenz, 1942, pp. 343 and 351.

in different circumstances is known irrespective of the particular model in which we use them. In the case of a mechanical model it is the physical properties of the individual parts which are supposed to be known. In a mathematical 'model' the 'properties' of the parts are defined by functions which show the values they will assume in different circumstances, and which are capable of being combined into various systems of equations which constitute the models.

8.52. The weakness of the ordinary use of the concept of the model as an account of the process of explanation consists in the fact that this conception pre-supposes, but does not explain, the existence of the different mental entities from which such a model could be built. It does not explain in what sense or in which manner the parts of the model correspond to the parts of the original, or what are the properties of the elements from which the model is built.

8.53. The concept of a model that is being formed in the brain is helpful only after we have succeeded in accounting for the different properties of the parts from which it is built. Such an account is provided by the explanation of the determination of sensory (and other mental) qualities by their position in the more comprehensive semi-permanent structure of relationships, the 'map' of the world which past experience has created in the brain, which has been described in the preceding pages. It is the position of the impulse in the connected network of fibers which brings it about that its occurrence together with other impulses will produce certain further impulses. The formation of the model appears thus merely a particular case of that process of joint or simultaneous classification of a group of impulses of which each has its determined significance apart from the particular combination or model in which it now occurs.

8.54. We can schematically represent this process of joint classification which produces a model in the following manner: the different elements, the mental qualities from which the model is built, are classes of impulses which we may call A, B, C, etc., and which are defined as an a (member of A) producing x (and perhaps some other impulses) when it occurs in company with $o, p, \ldots$, but producing $v, z, \ldots$ when it occurs in company with $r, s, \ldots$ etc., etc., and similarly for all members of the classes B, C, etc. In this definition any given class of impulses may, of course, occur both in a 'primary' character, that is as an element of a class to be defined by the impulses which any element of this class will evoke, and in a 'secondary' character as an evoked impulse which determines the class to which some other impulses belong (3.38, 3.55ff.). Impulses of the class A will appear not only in statements like 'if (a, o, p), then x', and 'if (a, r, s), then$(y, z \ldots)$', but also in statements like 'if (b, c, q), then (a, t)', etc.

8.55. Given such a determination of the different significance of impulses of the different classes, it follows that any given combination of such impulses will produce impulses standing for other classes; and these in turn others, and so on, somewhat as in the following schematic representation:

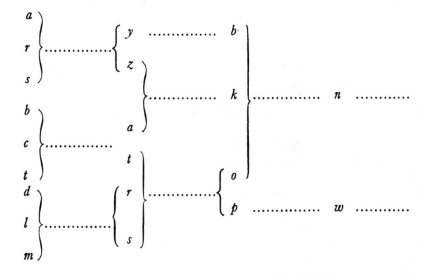

8.56. The particular result produced is thus recognized to be the effect of the simultaneous occurrence of certain elements in a particular constellation which, if we had known of their presence, would have enabled us to predict the result. Once we have formed such a model we are in a position to say on which of the various elements in the actual situation the observed result depends, and how it would be modified if any of these elements were changed; this is what an explanation enables us to do.

5. Explanation of the Principle

8.57. It follows from what has been said so far about explanation that it will always refer to classes of events, and that it will account only for those properties which are common to the elements of the class. Explanation is always generic in the sense that it always refers to features which are common to all phenomena of a certain kind, and it can never explain everything to be observed on a particular set of events.

8.58. But although all explanation must refer to the common features of a class of phenomena, there are evidently different degrees to which an explanation can be general, or to which it may approach to a full explanation of a particular set of events. The model may reproduce only the few common features of a great variety of phenomena, or it may reproduce a much larger number of features common to a smaller number of instances. In general, it will be true that the simpler the model, the wider will be the range of particular phenomena of which it reproduces one aspect, and the more complex the model, the more will its range of application be restricted.[12] In this respect the relation of the model to the object is similar to that between the connotation and the denotation (or the 'intension' and the 'extension') of a concept.

8.59. Most explanations (or theories) with which we are familiar are intended to show a common principle which operates in a large number of particular instances which in other respects may differ widely from each other. We have referred already earlier (2.18–2.19) to such explanations as 'explanations of the principle'.[13] The difference between such 'explanations of the principle' and more detailed explanations is, of course, merely one of the degree of their generality, and strictly speaking no explanation can be more than an explanation of the principle. It will be convenient, however, to reserve the name 'explanation of the principle' for explanations of a high degree of generality, and to contrast them with explanations of the detail.

8.60. The usual kind of explanation which we give, e.g., of the functioning of a clockwork, will in our sense be merely an explanation of the principle. It will merely show how the kind of phenomena which we call clockworks are produced: the manner in which a pair of hands can be made to revolve at constant speeds, etc. In the same 'general' way most of us are familiar with the principles on which a steam engine, an atomic bomb, or certain kinds of simple organisms function, without therefore necessarily being able to give a sufficiently detailed explanation of any one of these objects so that we should be able to construct it or precisely to predict its behavior. Even where we are able to construct one of these objects, say a clockwork, the knowledge of the principle involved will not be sufficient to predict more than certain general aspects of its operation. We should never be able, for instance, before we have built it, to predict precisely how fast it will move or precisely where its hands will be at a particular moment of time.

8.61. If in general we are not more aware of this distinction between explanations merely of the principle and more detailed explanations, this is because usually there will be no great difficulty about elaborating any explanation of the principle so as to make it approximate to almost any desired degree to the circumstances of a particular situation. By increasing the complexity of the model we can usually obtain a close reproduction of any particular feature in which we are interested.

8.62. The distinction between the explanation of the principle on which a

---

[12] Cf., M. Petrovitch, 1921, *passim.*

[13] See also F. A. Hayek, 1942, p. 290. [See now F. A. Hayek, *Studies on the Abuse and Decline of Reason*, ed. Bruce Caldwell, vol. 13 (2010) of *The Collected Works of F. A. Hayek*, 106f., 112f.—Ed.]

wide class of phenomena operate and the more detailed explanation of particular phenomena is reflected in the familiar distinction between the 'theoretical' and the more 'applied' parts of the different sciences. 'Theoretical physics', 'theoretical chemistry', or 'theoretical biology' are concerned with the explanation of the principles common to all phenomena which we call physical, chemical or biological.

8.63. Strictly speaking we should, of course, not be entitled to speak at all of phenomena of a certain kind unless we know some common principles which apply to the explanation of the phenomena of that kind. The various ways in which atoms are combined into molecules, e.g., constitute the common principles of all the phenomena which we call chemical. It is quite possible that an observed phenomenon, supposed to be, say, chemical, such as a change in the color of a certain substance, may on investigation prove to be an event of a different kind, e.g., an optical event, such as a change in the light falling on the substance.

8.64. While it is true that a theoretical class of phenomena can be definitely established only after we have found a common principle of explanation applying to all its members, that is, a model of high degree of generality reproducing the features they all have in common, we will yet often know of a range of phenomena which seem to be similar in some respect and where we therefore expect to find a common principle of explanation without, however, as yet knowing such a principle. The difference between such *prima facie* or 'empirical' classes of phenomena and the theoretical classes derived from a common principle of explanation is that the empirical class is limited to phenomena actually observed, while the theoretical class enables us to define the range over which phenomena of the kind in question may vary.

8.65. The class of events which we call 'mental' has so far on the whole been an empirical class in this sense. What has been attempted here might be described as a sketch of a 'theoretical psychology' in the same sense in which we speak of theoretical physics or theoretical biology. We have attempted an explanation of the principle by which we may account for the peculiarities which are common to all processes which are commonly called mental. The question which arises now is how far in the sphere of mental processes we can hope to develop the explanation of the principle into more detailed explanations, especially into explanations that would enable us to predict the course of particular mental events.

6. The Limits of Explanation

8.66. It is by no means always and necessarily true that the achievement of an explanation of the principle on which the phenomena of a certain class operate enables us to proceed to explanations of the more concrete detail. There are several fields in which practical difficulties prevent us from thus elaborating known explanations of the principle to the point where they would enable us to predict particular events. This is often the case when the phenomena are very complex, as in meteorology or biology; in these instances, the number of variables which would have to be taken into account is greater than that which can be ascertained or effectively manipulated by the human mind. While we may, e.g., possess full theoretical knowledge of the mechanism by which waves are formed and propagated on the surface of water, we shall probably never be able to predict the shape and movements of the wave that will form on the ocean at a particular place and moment of time.

8.67. Apart from these practical limits to explanation, which we may hope continuously to push further back, there also exists, however, an absolute limit to what the human brain can ever accomplish by way of explanation—a limit which is determined by the nature of the instrument of explanation itself, and which is particularly relevant to any attempt to explain particular mental processes.

8.68. If our account of the process of explanation is correct, it would appear that any apparatus or organism which is to perform such operations must possess certain properties determined by the properties of the events which it is to explain. If explanation involves that kind of joint classification of many elements which we have described as 'model-building', the relation between the explaining agent and the explained object must satisfy such formal relations as must exist between any apparatus of classification and the individual objects which it classifies (cf. 5.77–5.91).

8.69. The proposition which we shall attempt to establish is that any apparatus of classification must possess a structure of a higher degree of complexity than is possessed by the objects which it classifies; and that, therefore, the capacity of any explaining agent must be limited to objects with a structure possessing a degree of complexity lower than its own. If this is correct, it means that no explaining agent can ever explain objects of its own kind, or of its own degree of complexity, and, therefore, that the human brain can never fully explain its own operations. This statement possesses, probably, a high degree of *prima facie* plausibility. It is, however, of such importance and far-reaching consequences, that we must attempt a stricter proof.

8.70. We shall attempt such a demonstration at first for the simple processes of classification of individual elements, and later apply the same reasoning to those processes of joint classification which we have called model-building. Our first task must be to make clear what we mean when we speak of the 'degree of complexity' of the objects of classification and of the classifying apparatus. What we require is a measure of this degree of complexity which can be expressed in numerical terms.

8.71. So far as the objects of classification are concerned, it is necessary in the first instance to remember that for our purposes we are not interested in all the properties which a physical object may possess in an objective sense, but only in those 'properties' according to which these objects are to be classified. For our purposes the complete classification of the object is its complete definition, containing all that with which we are concerned in respect to it.

8.72. The degree of complexity of the objects of classification may then be measured by the number of different classes under which it is subsumed, or the number of different 'heads' under which it is classified. This number expresses the maximum number of points with regard to which the response of the classifying apparatus to this object may differ from its responses to any one other object which it is also capable of classifying. If the object in question is classified under n heads, it can evidently differ from any one other object that is classified by the same apparatus in n different ways.

8.73. In order that the classifying apparatus should be able to respond differently to any two objects which are classified differently under any one of these n heads, this apparatus will clearly have to be capable of distinguishing between a number of classes much larger than n. If any individual object may or may not belong to any one of the n classes $A, B, C, \ldots N$, and if all individual objects differing from each other in their membership of any one of these classes are to be treated as members of separate classes, then the number of different classes of objects to which the classifying apparatus will have to be able to respond differently will, according to a simple theorem of combinatorial analysis, have to be 2^{n+1}.

8.74. The number of different responses (or groups of responses) of which the classifying apparatus is capable, or the number of different classes it is able to form, will thus have to be of a definitely higher order of magnitude than the number of classes to which any individual object of classification can belong. This remains true when many of the individual classes to which a particular object belongs are mutually exclusive or disjunct, so that it can belong only to either A_1 or A_2 or $A_3 \ldots$, and to either B_1 or B_2 or $B_3 \ldots$, etc. If in such a case the number of variable 'attributes' which distinguish elements of A_1 from elements of A_2 and of A_3, and elements of B_1 from those of B_2 and B_3, etc., is m, and each of these m different variable attributes may assume n different 'values', although any one element will belong to at most m different classes, the number of distinct combinations of attributes to which the classifying apparatus will have to respond will still be equal to n^m.

8.75. In the same way in which we have used the number of different classes to which any one element can be assigned as the measure of the degree of its complexity, we can use the number of different classes to which the classifying apparatus will have to respond differently as the measure of complexity of that apparatus. It is evidently this number which indicates the variety of ways in which any one scheme of classification for a given set of elements may differ from any other scheme of classification for the different schemes of classification which can be applied to the given set of elements. Such a scheme for classifying the different possible schemes of classification would in turn have to possess a degree of complexity as much greater than that of any of the latter as their degree of complexity exceeds the complexity of any one of the elements.

8.76. What is true of the relationship between the degree of complexity of the different elements to be classified and that of the apparatus which can perform such classification, is, of course, equally true of that kind of joint or simultaneous classification which we have called 'model-building'. It differs from the classification of individual elements merely by the fact that the range of possible differences between different constellations of such elements is already of a higher order of magnitude than the range of possible differences between the individual elements, and that in consequence any apparatus capable of building models of all the different possible constellations of such elements must be of an even higher order of complexity.

8.77. An apparatus capable of building within itself models of different constellations of elements must be more complex, in our sense, than any particular constellation of such elements of which it can form a model, because, in addition to showing how any one of these elements will behave in a particular situation, it must be capable also of representing how any one of these elements would behave in any one of a large number of other situations. The 'new' result of the particular combination of elements which it is capable of predicting is derived from its capacity of predicting the behavior of each element under varying conditions.

8.78. The significance of these abstract considerations will become clearer if we consider as illustrations some instances in which this or a similar principle applies. The simplest illustration of the kind is probably provided by a machine designed to sort out certain objects according to some variable property. Such a machine will clearly have to be capable of indicating (or of differentially responding to) a greater number of different properties than any one of the objects to be sorted will possess. If, e.g., it is designed to sort out objects according to their length, any one object can possess only one length, while the machine must be capable of a different response to many different lengths.

8.79. An analogous relationship, which makes it impossible to work out on any calculating machine the (finite) number of distinct operations which can be performed with it, exists between that number and the highest result which the machine can show. If that limit were, e.g., 999,999,999, there will already be 500,000,000 additions of two different figures giving 999,999,999 as a result, 499,999,999 pairs of different figures the addition of which gives 999,999,998 as a result, etc., etc., and therefore a very much larger number of different additions of pairs of figures only than the machine can show. To this would have to be added all additions of more than two figures and all the different instances of the other operations which the machine can perform. The number of distinct calculations it can perform therefore will be clearly of a higher order of magnitude than the highest figure it can enumerate.

8.80. Applying the same general principle to the human brain as an apparatus of classification it would appear to mean that, even though we may understand its *modus operandi* in general terms, or, in other words, possess an explanation of the principle on which it operates, we shall never, by means of the same brain, be able to arrive at a detailed explanation of its working in particular circumstances, or be able to predict what the results of its operations will be. To achieve this would require a brain of a higher order of complexity, though it might be built on the same general principles. Such a brain might be able to explain what happens in our brain, but it would in turn still be unable fully to explain its own operations, and so on.

8.81. The impossibility of explaining the functioning of the human brain in sufficient detail to enable us to substitute a description in physical terms for a description in terms of mental qualities applies thus only in so far as the human brain is itself to be used as the instrument of classification. It would not only not apply to a brain built on the same principle but possessing a higher order of complexity, but, paradoxical as this may sound, it also does not exclude the logical possibility that the knowledge of the principle on which the brain operates might enable us to build a machine fully reproducing the action of the brain and capable of predicting how the brain will act in different circumstances.

8.82. Such a machine, designed by the human mind, yet capable of 'explaining' what the mind is incapable of explaining without its help, is not a self-contradictory conception in the sense in which the idea of the mind directly explaining its own operations involves a contradiction. The achievement of constructing such a machine would not differ in principle from that of constructing a calculating machine which enables us to solve problems which have not been solved before, and the results of whose operations we cannot, strictly speaking, predict beyond saying that they will be in accord with the principles built into the machine. In both instances our knowledge merely of the principle on which the machine operates will enable us to bring about results of which, before the machine produces them, we know only that they will satisfy certain conditions.

8.83. It might appear at first as if this impossibility of a full explanation of mental processes would apply only to the mind as a whole, and not to particular mental processes, a full explanation of which might still enable us to substitute for the description of a particular mental process a fully equivalent statement about a set of physical events. Such a complete explanation of any particular mental process would, if it were possible, of course be something different from, and something more far-reaching than, the kind of partial explanation which we have called 'explanation of the principle'.

8.84. In order to provide a full explanation of even one particular mental process, such an explanation would have to run entirely in physical terms, and would have to contain no references to any other mental events which were not also at the same time explained in physical terms. Such a possibility is ruled out, however, by the fact, that the mind as an order is a 'whole' in the strict sense of the term: the distinct character of mental entities and of their mode of operation is determined by their relations to (or their position in the system of) all other mental entities. No one of them can, therefore, be explained without at the same time explaining all the others, or the whole structure of relationships determining their character.

8.85. So long as we cannot explain the mind as a whole, any attempt to explain particular mental processes must therefore contain references to other mental processes and will thus not achieve a full reduction to a description in physical terms. A full translation of the description of any set of events from the mental to the physical language would thus presuppose knowledge of the complete set of 'rules of correspondence'[14] by which the two languages are related, or a complete account of the orders prevailing in the two worlds.

8.86. This conclusion may be expressed differently by saying that a mental process could be identified with (or 'reduced to') a particular physical process only if we were able to show that it occupies in the whole order of mental events a position which is identical with the position which the physical events occupy in the physical order of the organism. The former is a mental process because it occupies a certain position in the whole order of mental processes (i.e., because of the manner in which it can affect, and be affected by, other mental processes), and this position in an order can be explained in physical terms only by showing how an equivalent order can be built up from physical elements. Only if we could achieve this could we substitute for our knowledge of mental events a statement of the order existing in a particular part of the physical world.

7. The Division of the Sciences and the 'Freedom of the Will'

8.87. The conclusion to which our theory leads is thus that to us not only mind as a whole but also all individual mental processes must forever remain phenomena of a special kind which, although produced by the same prin-

[14] H. Margenau, 1950, pp. 60, 69, 450.

ciples which we know to operate in the physical world, we shall never be able fully to explain in terms of physical laws. Those whom it pleases may express this by saying that in some ultimate sense mental phenomena are 'nothing but' physical processes; this, however, does not alter the fact that in discussing mental processes we will never be able to dispense with the use of mental terms, and that we shall have permanently to be content with a practical dualism, a dualism based not on any assertion of an objective difference between the two classes of events, but on the demonstrable limitations of the powers of our own mind fully to comprehend the unitary order to which they belong.

8.88. From the fact that we shall never be able to achieve more than an 'explanation of the principle' by which the order of mental events is determined, it also follows that we shall never achieve a complete 'unification' of all sciences in the sense that all phenomena of which it treats can be described in physical terms.[15] In the study of human action, in particular, our starting point will always have to be our direct knowledge of the different kinds of mental events, which to us must remain irreducible entities.

8.89. The permanent cleavage between our knowledge of the physical world and our knowledge of mental events goes right through what is commonly regarded as the one subject of psychology. Since the theoretical psychology which has been sketched here can never be developed to the point at which it would enable us to substitute for the description of particular mental events descriptions in terms of particular physical events, and since it has therefore nothing to say about particular kinds of mental events, but is confined to describing the *kind* of physical processes by which the various types of mental processes can be produced, any discussion of mental events which is to

---

[15] The term 'physical' must here be understood in the strict sense in which it has been defined in the first chapter and not be confused with the sense in which it is used, e.g., by O. Neurath [Otto Neurath (1882–1945) had been—along with Joseph Schumpeter and Ludwig von Mises—a participant in the famous Böhm-Bawerk seminar. He played a leading role in the Vienna Circle, emphasizing the intrinsic connection between positivism and socialism (see B. Caldwell, introduction to F. A. Hayek, *Studies on the Abuse and Decline of Reason*, ed. Bruce Caldwell, vol. 13 (2010) of *The Collected Works of F. A. Hayek*, 17f.). As Hayek (*Hayek on Hayek* [London: Routledge, 1994], 50) recollects, it was Neurath's extreme "physicalism" and "naïve economics" that kept him from joining the Vienna Circle, despite his close contacts to several of its members.—Ed.] or R. Carnap when they speak of the 'physical language'. In our sense their 'physical language', since it refers to the phenomenal or sensory qualities of the objects, is not 'physical' at all. Their use of this term rather implies a metaphysical belief in the ultimate 'reality' and constancy of the phenomenal world for which there is little justification. Cf., O. Neurath, 1933, and R. Carnap, 1938. [Jointly with Hans Hahn and Rudolf Carnap, Neurath had published in 1929 the so-called "manifesto of the Vienna Circle": *Wissenschaftliche Weltauffassung. Der Wiener Kreis* (*The Scientific Conception of the World: The Vienna Circle*).—Ed.]

get beyond such a mere 'explanation of the principle' will have to start from the mental entities which we know from direct experience.

8.90. This does not mean that we may not be able in a different sense to 'explain' particular mental events: it merely means that the type of explanation at which we aim in the physical sciences is not applicable to mental events. We can still use our direct ('introspective') knowledge of mental events in order to 'understand', and in some measure even to predict, the results to which mental processes will lead in certain conditions. But this introspective psychology, the part of psychology which lies on the other side of the great cleavage which divides it from the physical sciences, will always have to take our direct knowledge of the human mind for its starting point. It will derive its statements about some mental processes from its knowledge about other mental processes, but it will never be able to bridge the gap between the realm of the mental and the realm of the physical.

8.91. Such a *verstehende* psychology, which starts from our given knowledge of mental processes, will, however, never be able to explain why we must think thus and not otherwise, why we arrive at particular conclusions. Such an explanation would pre-suppose a knowledge of the physical conditions under which we would arrive at different conclusions. The assertion that we can explain our own knowledge involves also the belief that we can at any one moment of time both act on some knowledge and possess some additional knowledge about how the former is conditioned and determined. The whole idea of the mind explaining itself is a logical contradiction—nonsense in the literal meaning of the word—and a result of the prejudice that we must be able to deal with mental events in the same manner as we deal with physical events.[16]

8.92. In particular, it would appear that the whole aim of the discipline known under the name of 'sociology of knowledge' which aims at explaining why people as a result of particular material circumstances hold particular views at particular moments, is fundamentally misconceived. It aims at precisely that kind of specific explanation of mental phenomena from physical facts which we have tried to show to be impossible. All we can hope to do in this field is to aim at an explanation of the principle such as is attempted by the general theory of knowledge or epistemology.

8.93. It may be noted in passing that these considerations also have some bearing on the age-old controversy about the 'freedom of the will'. Even though we may know the general principle by which all human action is causally determined by physical processes, this would not mean that to us a par-

---

[16] On this and the subject of the next paragraph: Cf., F. A. Hayek, 1944, pp. 31 *et seq.* [See now F. A. Hayek, *Studies on the Abuse and Decline of Reason*, ed. Bruce Caldwell, vol. 13 (2010) of *The Collected Works of F. A. Hayek*, 150ff.—Ed.]

ticular human action can ever be recognizable as the necessary result of a particular set of physical circumstances. To us human decisions must always appear as the result of the whole of a human personality—that means the whole of a person's mind—which, as we have seen, we cannot reduce to something else.[17]

8.94. The recognition of the fact that for our understanding of human action familiar mental entities must always remain the last determinants to which we can penetrate, and that we cannot hope to replace them by physical facts, is, of course, of the greatest importance for all the disciplines which aim at an understanding and interpretation of human action. It means, in particular, that the devices developed by the natural sciences for the special purpose of replacing a description of the world in sensory or phenomenal terms by one in physical terms lose their raison d'être in the study of intelligible human action. This applies particularly to the endeavour to replace all qualitative statements by quantitative expressions or by descriptions which run exclusively in terms of explicit relations.[18]

8.95. The impossibility of any complete 'unification' of all our scientific knowledge into an all-comprehensive physical science has hardly less significance, however, for our understanding of the physical world than it has for our study of the consequences of human action. We have seen how in the physical sciences the aim is to build models of the connections of the events in the external world by breaking up the classes known to us as sensory qualities and by replacing them by classes explicitly defined by the relations of the events to each other; also how, as this model of the physical world becomes more and more perfect, its application to any particular phenomenon in the sensory world becomes more and more uncertain (8.17–8.26).

8.96. A definite co-ordination of the model of the physical world thus constructed with the picture of the phenomenal world which our senses give us would require that we should be able to complete the task of the physical sciences by an operation which is the converse of their characteristic procedure (1.21): we should have to be able to show in what manner the different parts of our model of the physical world will be classified by our mind. In other words, a complete explanation of even the external world as we know it would pre-suppose a complete explanation of the working of our senses and our

---

[17] It may also be mentioned, although this has little immediate connection with our main subject, that since the word 'free' has been formed to describe a certain subjective experience and can scarcely be defined except by reference to that experience, it could at most be asserted that the term is meaningless. But this would make any denial of the existence of free will as meaningless as its assertion.

[18] For a fuller discussion of this point see F. A. Hayek, 1942, pp. 290ff. [See now F. A. Hayek, *Studies on the Abuse and Decline of Reason*, ed. Bruce Caldwell, vol. 13 (2010) of *The Collected Works of F. A. Hayek*, 113ff.—Ed.]

mind. If the latter is impossible, we shall also be unable to provide a full explanation of the phenomenal world.

8.97. Such a completion of the task of science, which would place us in a position to explain in detail the manner in which our sensory picture of the external world represents relations existing between the parts of this world, would mean that this reproduction of the world would have to include a reproduction of that reproduction (or a model of the model-object relation) which would have to include a reproduction of that reproduction of that reproduction, and so on, *ad infinitum*. The impossibility of fully explaining any picture which our mind forms of the external world therefore also means that it is impossible ever fully to explain the 'phenomenal' external world. The very conception of such a completion of the task of science is a contradiction in terms. The quest of science is, therefore, by its nature a never-ending task in which every step ahead with necessity creates new problems.

8.98. Our conclusion, therefore, must be that *to us* mind must remain forever a realm of its own which we can know only through directly experiencing it, but which we shall never be able fully to explain or to 'reduce' to something else. Even though we may know that mental events of the kind which we experience can be produced by the same forces which operate in the rest of nature, we shall never be able to say which are the particular physical events which 'correspond' to a particular mental event.

BIBLIOGRAPHY

In addition to the works quoted in the text this bibliography contains the titles of the works of which I can now remember that they influenced me in the original formulation of the theory here developed (marked with an asterisk), and a few additional works on sensory learning not explicitly referred to in the text. Where the reference is to a translation or edition of a date different from the original, the date of the latter is given first and the former added in brackets.

Adrian, Edgar Douglas, 1947, *The Physical Background of Perception*, Oxford: Oxford University Press.

Argelander, Annelies, 1927, *Das Farbenhören und der synaesthetische Faktor in der Wahrnehmung*, Jena: Gustav Fischer.

*Ashby, W. Ross, 1945, 'The physical origin of adaptation by trial and error', *The Journal of General Psychology*, 32, pp. 13–25.

*————, 1946, 'Dynamics of the cerebral cortex: The behavioral properties of systems in equilibrium', *American Journal of Psychology*, 59, pp. 682–89.

————, 1947a, 'Principles of self-organizing dynamic systems', *Journal of General Psychology*, 37(2), pp. 125–28.

————, 1947b, 'Dynamics of the cerebral cortex: Automatic development of equilibrium in self-organizing systems', *Psychometrika*, 12, pp. 135–40.

————, 1948, 'Design for a brain', *Electronic Engineering*, 20, pp. 379–83.

————, 1949, 'Critical Review, The facts and methods of cybernetics', (Review of N. Wiener, *Cybernetics*) *Journal of Mental Science*, 95, pp. 716–24.

Bargmann, Wolfgang, 1947, 'Das Substrat des nervösen Geschehens', *Universitas*, 2, pp. 57–65.

*Becher, Erich, 1911, *Gehirn und Seele*, Heidelberg: Winter.

*Bechterew, Wladimir Michailovic, 1913, *Objektive Psychologie*, Leipzig: Teubner.

Beck, Lloyd H., and Miles, Walter R., 1947, 'Some theoretical and experimental relationships between infrared absorption and olfaction', *Science*, 106, p. 511.

Bertalanffy, Ludwig von, 1942, *Theoretische Biologie*, 2, Berlin: Julius Springer.

————, 1949, *Das biologische Weltbild*, 1, Bern: A. Francke A.G.

*————, 1950a, 'The theory of open systems in physics and biology', *Science, New Series* 111(2872), pp. 23–29.

*————, 1950b, 'An outline of general system theory', *British Journal for the Philosophy of Science*, 1(12), pp. 134–65.

Bichowsky, F. Russell, 1925, 'The mechanism of consciousness: Pre-sensation', *American Journal of Psychology*, 36, pp. 588–96.

Binns, Henry, 1926, 'A comparison between the judgments of individuals skilled in the textile trade and the natural judgments of untrained adults and children', *Journal of the Textile Institute*, 16, pp. 615–41.

*————, 1937, 'Visual and tactual "judgment" as illustrated in a practical experiment', *British Journal of Psychology*, 27, pp. 404–10.

Blair, George William S., and Coppen, Flora Margaret V., 1939, 'The subjective judgment of the elastic and plastic properties of soft bodies; the "differential thresholds" for viscosities and compression moduli', *Proceedings of The Royal Society of London*, 128, pp. 109–25.

*————, 1940, 'The subjective judgment of the elastic and plastic properties of soft bodies—reproducibility in complex systems', *British Journal of Psychology*, 31(1), pp. 61–79.

Boring, Edwin G., 1930, 'Psychology for Eclectics', in Carl Murchison (ed.), *Psychologies of 1930*, Worcester, MA: Clark University Press, pp. 115–27.

————, 1933, *The Physical Dimensions of Consciousness*, New York: The Century Co.

————, 1935, 'The relation of the attributes of sensation to the dimensions of the stimulus', *Philosophy of Science*, 2, pp. 236–45.

————, 1936, 'Psychological systems and isomorphic relations', *Psychological Review*, 43, pp. 565–87.

————, 1937, 'A psychological function is a relation of successive differentiations of events in the organism', *Psychological Review*, 44, pp. 445–61.

————, 1942, *Sensation and Perception in the History of Experimental Psychology*, New York: Appleton-Century-Crofts.

————, 1946, 'Mind and Mechanism', *American Journal of Psychology*, 59(2), pp. 173–92.

Boring, Edwin G., Langfeld, H. S., and Weld, H. P. (eds.), 1948, *Foundations of Psychology*, Hoboken, NJ: Wiley.

Braly, Kenneth Walter, 1933, 'The influence of past experience in visual perception', *Journal of Experimental Psychology*, 16(5), pp. 613–43.

Broad, Charlie D., 1925, *The Mind and Its Place in Nature*, London: Kegan Paul.

Brogden, Wilfred J., 1939, 'Sensory pre-conditioning', *Journal of Experimental Psychology*, 25(4), pp. 323–32.

————, 1942, 'Test of sensory pre-conditioning with human subjects', *Journal of Experimental Psychology*, 31, pp. 505–17.

————, 1947, 'Sensory pre-conditioning of human subjects', *Journal of Experimental Psychology*, 37, pp. 527–39.

————, 1950, 'Sensory pre-conditioning measured by the facilitation of auditory acuity', *Journal of Experimental Psychology*, 40, pp. 512–19.

Cannon, Walter B., 1932, *The Wisdom of the Body*, New York: Norton.

Capurso, Alexander A., 1934, 'The effect of an associative technique in teaching pitch and interval discrimination', *Journal of Applied Psychology*, 18, pp. 811–18.

Carnap, Rudolf, 1928, *Der logische Aufbau der Welt*, Berlin: Weltkreis Verlag.

————, 1938, 'Logical Foundations of the Unity of Science', *International Encyclopaedia of Unified Science*, Chicago: University of Chicago Press, 1(1), pp. 42–62.

*Carneri, Bartholomäus von, 1893, *Empfindung und Bewußtsein. Monistische Bedenken*, Bonn: E. Strauss.

Cattell, Raymond B., 1930, 'The subjective character of cognition and the presensational development of perception', *British Journal of Psychology, Monograph Supplements*, 14.

Connette, Earle, 1941, 'The effect of practice with knowledge of results upon pitch discrimination', *Journal of Educational Psychology*, 32, pp. 523–32.

Craik, Kenneth John William, 1943, *The Nature of Explanation*, Cambridge: Cambridge University Press.

Czermák, Johan N., 1855, 'Weitere Beiträge zur Physiologie des Tastsinnes', *Sitzungsberichte der Kaiserlichen Akademie der Wissenschaften*, Vienna, XVIII.

Dimmick, Forrest L., 1946, 'A color aptitude test, 1940 experimental edition', *Journal of Applied Psychology*, 30, pp. 10–22.

————, 1948, 'Visual Space Perception', in Boring, E. G., Langfeld, H. S., and Weld, H. P. (eds.), *Foundations of Psychology*, pp. 297–312.

Dodge, Raymond, 1931, *Conditions and Consequences of Human Variability*, New Haven, CT: Yale University Press.

Duncker, Karl, 1939, 'The influence of past experience on perceptual properties', *American Journal of Psychology*, 52, pp. 255–65.

*Edinger, Ludwig, 1909, 'Die Beziehungen der vergleichenden Anatomie zur vergleichenden Psychologie', *Bericht des 3. Kongresses für experimentelle Psychologie, 1908*, Leipzig.

Edmonds, E. M., and Smith, M. E., 1923, 'The phenomenological description of musical intervals', *American Journal of Psychology*, 34(2), pp. 287–91.

Erdmann, Benno, 1886, *Die psychologischen Grundlagen der Beziehungen zwischen Sprechen und Denken*, Leipzig: Reisland.

————, 1907, *Wissenschaftliche Hypothesen über Leib und Seele*, Vorträge, gehalten an der Handelshochschule zu Köln, Köln: M. Dumont-Schauberg'sche Buchhandlung. [Hayek refers to Erdmann 1886 and Erdmann 1907 in § 7.14, footnote 12, without listing corresponding titles in the bibliography. In 1907 several works by Erdmann were published, of which the one referenced here seems most likely what Hayek meant.—Ed.]

————, 1920, *Grundzüge der Reproduktionspsychologie*, Berlin: de Gruyter.

Erismann, Theodor, 1948, 'Das Werden der Wahrnehmung', *Kongress der deutschen prak-tischen Psychologen*, I., pp. 61–86.

Ewert, P. Harry, 1930, 'A study of the effect of inverted retinal stimulation upon spa-tially coordinated behavior', *Genetic Psychology Monographs: Child Behavior, Animal Behavior, and Comparative Psychology*, Worcester, MA: Clark University Press, 7(3/4), pp. 177–363.

———, 1936, 'Factors in space localization during inverted vision: I. Interference', *Psychological Review*, 43(6), pp. 522–46.

*Exner, Sigmund, 1894, *Entwurf zu einer physiologischen Erklärung der psychischen Erscheinun-gen*, Leipzig and Vienna: Deuticke.

Friedline, Cora L., 1918, 'The discrimination of cutaneous patterns below the two-point limen', *American Journal of Psychology*, 29, pp. 400–419.

Fundamental Mathematics, 1948, Prepared for the general course Mathematics I in the College by the College Mathematics Staff: E. P. Northrop, Chairman and others, 3rd ed., Chicago: University of Chicago Press.

Gibson, James J., 1941, 'A critical review of the concept of set in contemporary exper-imental psychology', *Psychological Bulletin*, 38, pp. 781–817.

*Gilbert, G. M., 1941, 'Inter-sensory facilitation and inhibition', *Journal of General Psy-chology*, 24, pp. 381–407.

Goldstein, Kurt, 1939, *The Organism. A Holistic Approach to Biology Derived from Biological Data in Man*, New York: American Book Company.

Green, Thomas Hill, 1883 (1884), *Prolegomena to Ethics*, Oxford: Clarendon Press.

Hartmann, George Wilfried, 1935, *Gestalt Psychology, A Survey of Facts and Principles*, New York: Ronald Press.

Hayek, Friedrich A. von, 1942–1944, 'Scientism and the Study of Society', *Econom-ica*, N.S., 9 (Aug. 1942), pp. 267–91; *Economica*, N.S., 10 (Feb. 1943), pp. 34–63; *Economica*, N.S., 11 (Feb. 1944), pp. 27–39; reprinted in F. A. Hayek, 1952, *The Counter-Revolution of Science. Studies in the Abuse of Reason*, Glencoe, IL: Free Press, pp. 17–182. [Now reprinted in F. A. Hayek, *Studies in the Abuse and Decline of Rea-son, Text and Documents*, ed. Bruce Caldwell, vol. 13 (2010) of *The Collected Works of F. A. Hayek*, Chicago: University of Chicago Press; London: Routledge, Part I, pp. 75–166.—Ed.]

Hazzard, Florence W., 1930, 'A descriptive account of odors', *Journal of Experimental Psychology*, 13(4), pp. 297–331.

Head, Henry, in conjunction with W. H. R. Rivers et al., 1920, *Studies in Neurology*, London: H. Frowde, Hodder & Stoughton.

Hebb, Donald O., 1949, *The Organization of Behavior: A Neuropsychological Theory*, New York: Wiley.

*Helmholtz, Hermann von, 1879, *Die Thatsachen in der Wahrnehmung*, Berlin: Hirschwald.

———, 1925, *Helmholtz's Treatise on Physiological Optics*, 3 vols., transl. by James P. C. Southall from the third German edition, 1909. Vol. III: *The Perception of Vision*,

Rochester, NY: The Optical Society of America. (German original: *Handbuch der physiologischen Optik*, 1867, Leipzig: Voss.)

Henning, Hans, 1917, 'Versuche über die Residuen', *Zeitschrift für Psychologie*, 78, pp. 198–269.

*———, 1919, 'Experimentelle Untersuchung zur Denkpsychologie. I. Die assoziative Mitwirkung, das Vorstellen von noch nie Wahrgenommenem und deren Grenzen', *Zeitschrift für Psychologie*, 81, pp. 1–96.

———, 1922, 'Assoziationsgesetz und Geruchsgedächtnis', *Zeitschrift für Psychologie*, 89, pp. 38–80.

———, 1924, *Der Geruch. Ein Handbuch für die Gebiete der Psychologie, Physiologie, Zoologie, Botanik, Chemie, Physik, Neurologie, Ethnologie, Sprachwissenschaft, Literatur, Ästhetik und Kulturgeschichte*, Leipzig: J. A. Barth.

———, 1927, 'Psychologische Studien am Geschmacksinn' and 'Psychologische Studien am Geruchsinn', in Abderhalden, E. (ed.), *Handbuch der biologischen Arbeitsmethoden*, vol. VI, Part A, pp. 627–740, and pp. 742–836.

Henri, Victor, 1898, *Die Raumwahrnehmungen des Tastsinnes*, Berlin: Reuther and Reichard.

*Hering, Ewald, 1870, *Über das Gedächtnis als eine allgemeine Funktion der organisierten Materie*, Vortrag gehalten in der feierlichen Sitzung der Kaiserlichen Akademie der Wissenschaften in Wien, 30.5.1870, Leipzig: Akademische Verlagsgesellschaft.

———, 1884, *Über die spezifischen Energien des Nervensystems*, Lotos, NF, vol. 5, Prag; English transl. 1913 in *Memory: Lectures on the specific energies of the nervous system*, 4th ed., Chicago: Open Court Publishing Co.

Herrick, C. Judson, 1926, *Brains of Rats and Men*, New York: Hafner.

*Hilgard, Ernest R., Campbell, Albert A., and Sears, W. Norman, 1937, 'Conditioned discrimination: The development of discrimination with and without verbal report', *American Journal of Psychology*, 49(4), pp. 564–80.

Hilgard, Ernest R., and Marquis, Donald G., 1940, *Conditioning and Learning*, New York: Appleton-Century.

Hillarp, Nils-Ake, 1946, 'Structure of the synapse and the peripheral innervation apparatus of the autonomic nervous system', *Acta Anatomica*, 2, Supplement 4.

Holt, Edwin B., 1937, 'Materialism and the criterion of the psychic', *Psychological Review*, 44(1), pp. 33–53.

Hornbostel, Erich M. von, 1925, 'Die Einheit der Sinne', *Melos, Zeitschrift für Musik*, 4, pp. 290–97. Engl. transl. 1926, 'Unity of the Senses', *Psyche*, 7, pp. 83–89.

*———, 1931, 'Über Geruchshelligkeit', *Pflüger's Archiv für die gesamte Physiologie des Menschen und der Tiere*, 227, pp. 517–38.

*Hull, Clark Leonard, 1943, *Principles of Behavior*, New York: Appleton-Century-Crofts.

Humes, John F., 1930, 'The effect of practice upon the upper limen of tonal discrimination', *American Journal of Psychology*, 42, pp. 1–16.

*Humphrey, George, 1923 (1932), *The Story of Man's Mind*, rev. and enl. ed., New York: Dodd, Mead and Co.

James, William, 1890, *Principles of Psychology*, London: Macmillan.

Jennings, Herbert Spencer, 1906, *The Behavior of the Lower Organisms*, New York: Columbia University Press.

*Jodl, Friedrich, 1916, *Lehrbuch der Psychologie*, 4th ed., Stuttgart and Berlin: Cotta.

Katz, David, 1944, *Gestaltpsychologie*, Basel: Schwabe.

*Kenneth, John H., 1927, 'An experimental study of affects and associations due to certain odors', *Psychological Monographs*, 37(2), pp. 1–64.

Kingsley, Howard L., 1946, *The Nature and Conditions of Learning*, New York: Prentice Hall.

Kleint, Herbert, 1937–1940, 'Versuche über Wahrnehmung', *Zeitschrift für Psychologie*, 140, pp. 109–38; 142, pp. 259–90; 143, pp. 299–316; 148, pp. 145–204; 149, pp. 31–82.

*Klüver, Heinrich, 1931, 'The equivalence of stimuli in the behavior of monkeys', *Journal of Genetic Psychology*, 39, pp. 3–27.

———, 1933, *Behavior Mechanisms in Monkeys*, Oxford: University of Chicago Press.

———, 1936, 'The study of personality and the method of equivalent and non-equivalent stimuli', *Journal of Personality*, 5(2), pp. 91–112.

———, 1949, 'Psychology at the beginning of World War II: Meditations on the impending dismemberment of Psychology written in 1942', *Journal of Psychology*, 28, pp. 383–410.

Köhler, Wolfgang, 1913, 'Über unbemerkte Empfindungen und Urteilstäuschungen', *Zeitschrift für Psychologie*, 66, pp. 51–80.

*———, 1920, *Die physischen Gestalten in Ruhe und im stationären Zustand*, Braunschweig: Vieweg.

———, 1929, *Gestalt Psychology*, New York: Liveright.

Köhler, Wolfgang, and Held, Richard, 1949, 'The cortical correlate of pattern vision', *Science*, 110, pp. 414–19.

*Koffka, Kurt, 1928, 'On the structure of the unconscious', in: *The Unconscious: A Symposium*, New York: Knopf, pp. 43–68.

———, 1935, *Principles of Gestalt Psychology*, New York: Harcourt Brace and Routledge Kegan Paul.

Kries, Johannes von, 1898, *Über die materiellen Grundlagen der Bewußtseinserscheinungen*, Freiburg i. Br.: Lehmann.

———, 1923, *Allgemeine Sinnesphysiologie*, Leipzig: F. C. W. Vogel.

Krüger, Felix, 1915, *Über Entwicklungspsychologie, ihre sachliche und geschichtliche Notwendigkeit*, vol.1(1) of the series *Arbeiten zur Entwicklungspsychologie*, ed. by F. Krüger, Leipzig: W. Engelmann.

Külpe, Oswald, 1895, *Outlines of Psychology*, London: Swan Sonnenschein and Co. Ltd. Translation by E. B. Titchener of the German original *Grundriss der Psychologie*, Leipzig, 1893.

Lashley, Karl Spencer, 1923, 'The behavioristic interpretation of consciousness', *Psychological Review*, 30(4), Part I, pp. 237–72; Part II, pp. 329–53.

———, 1929, *Brain Mechanisms and Intelligence*, Chicago: University of Chicago Press.

*——, 1934, 'Learning: III. Nervous mechanisms in learning', in: Murchison, C. (ed.), *A Handbook of General Experimental Psychology*, pp. 456–96.

——, 1942, 'The problem of cerebral organization in vision', in: Klüver, Heinrich (ed.), *Visual Mechanisms, Biological Symposia*, 7, pp. 301–22.

Leeper, Robert W., 1935, 'A study of a neglected portion of the field of learning—the development of sensory organization', *Journal of Genetic Psychology*, 46, pp. 41–75.

Lewes, George Henry, 1874–1879, *Problems of Life and Mind*, London: Truebner.

Locke, John, 1690, *An Essay Concerning Human Understanding*, London: Scolar Press.

Lorenz, Konrad, 1942, 'Die angeborenen Formen möglicher Erfahrung', *Zeitschrift für Tierpsychologie*, 5(2), pp. 235–409.

Mach, Ernst, 1886, *Beiträge zur Analyse der Empfindungen*, Jena: G. Fischer. Engl. Transl. 1897, *Contributions to the analysis of the sensations*, La Salle, IL: Open Court Publishing.

*——, 1905, *Erkenntnis und Irrtum*, Leipzig: I. A. Barth.

Mahling, Friedrich, 1926, 'Das Problem der "Audition colorée"', *Archiv für die gesamte Psychologie*, 57, pp. 165–301.

Margenau, Henry, 1950, *The Nature of Physical Reality*, New York: McGraw-Hill.

Martin, Lillien Jane, and Müller, Georg Elias, 1899, *Zur Analyse der Unterschiedsempfindlichkeit: Experimentelle Beiträge*, Leipzig: I. A. Barth.

McCleary, Robert A., and Lazarus, Richard S., 1949, 'Autonomic discrimination without awareness: An interim report', *Journal of Personality*, 18(2), pp. 171–79.

McCulloch, Warren S., 1948, 'A recapitulation of the theory, with a forecast of several extensions', *Annals of the New York Academy of Science*, 50, pp. 259–77.

McDougall, William, 1923, *An Outline of Psychology*, London: Methuen.

*McGeoch, John Alexander, 1936, 'The vertical dimensions of mind', *Psychological Review*, 43, pp. 107–29.

Mees, C. E. Kenneth, 1946, *The Path of Science*, New York: Wiley.

Metzger, Wolfgang, 1941, *Psychologie: Die Entwicklung ihrer Grundannahmen seit der Einführung des Experiments*, Wissenschaftliche Forschungsberichte: Naturwissenschaftliche Reihe, 52, Dresden: Theodor Steinkopff.

Mill, James, 1829 (1869), *Analysis of the Phenomena of the Human Mind*, a new edition by J. S. Mill, London: Longmans Green Reader and Dyer.

*Miller, James Grier, 1939, 'Discrimination without awareness', *American Journal of Psychology*, 52, pp. 562–78.

——, 1940, 'The role of motivation in learning without awareness', *American Journal of Psychology*, 53, pp. 229–39.

——, 1942, *Unconsciousness*, New York: Wiley.

Miner, James Burt, 1905, 'A case of vision acquired in adult life', *Psychological Review Monograph*, 6(5), pp. 103–18.

Moncrieff, Robert Wighton, 1946, *The Chemical Senses*, New York: Wiley. (First published 1944, London: Hill.)

Moore, Henry Thomas, 1914, 'The genetic aspects of consonance and dissonance', *Psychological Monographs*, 17(73), pp. 1–68.

Morgan, Clifford Thomas, 1943, *Physiological Psychology*, New York: McGraw Hill.

Müller, Georg Elias, 1896, 'Zur Psychophysik der Gesichtsempfindungen', *Zeitschrift für Psychologie und Physiologie der Sinnesorgane*, 10, pp. 1–82.

Müller, Johannes Peter, 1833–1840, *Handbuch der Physiologie des Menschen für Vorlesungen*, 2 vols., Koblenz: Hölschen.

Neurath, Otto von, 1933, *Einheitswissenschaft und Psychologie*, Vienna: Gerold.

*Northway, Mary L., 1940, 'The concept of the "schema"', *British Journal of Psychology*, 31, pp. 22–36.

*Noyes, Charles R., 1950, 'What kind of psychology does economics need?', *Canadian Journal of Economics and Political Science*, 16(2), pp. 210–15.

*Ogden, Robert Morris, 1926, *Psychology and Education*, New York: Harcourt, Brace and Co.

*Peak, Helen, 1933, 'An evaluation of the concepts of reflex and voluntary action', *Psychological Review*, 40, pp. 71–89.

*Peterson, Joseph, 1933, 'Aspects of learning', *Psychological Review*, 42, pp. 1–27.

Petrovitch, M. Michel, 1921, *Mécanismes communs aux phénomènes disparates*, Paris: Félix Alcan.

*Piaget, Jean, 1942, *Classes, Relations et Nombres: Essai sur les Groupements de la logistique et sur la réversibilité de la pensée*, Paris: Vrin.

———, 1947, *La psychologie de l'intelligence*, Paris: Armand Colin. Engl. transl., 1950, *The Psychology of Intelligence*, London: Routledge & Kegan Paul.

*———, 1949, *Traité de Logique: Essai de logistique opératoire*, Paris: Armand Colin.

*Pitts, Walter, and McCulloch, Warren S., 1947, 'How we know universals. The perception of auditory and visual forms', *Bulletin of Mathematical Biophysics*, 9(3), pp. 127–47.

Planck, Max, 1925, *A Survey of Physics*, transl. by R. Jones and D. H. Williams, London: Methuen.

———, 1949, 'The Meaning and Limits of Exact Science', in: *Scientific Autobiography and Other Papers*, New York: Philosophical Library, pp. 80–120. (A lecture delivered by Max Planck in November 1941; translated from German by Frank Gaynor.)

Pratt, Carrol C., 1939, *The Logic of Modern Psychology*, New York: Macmillan.

*Renshaw, Samuel, 1930, 'The errors of cutaneous localization and the effect of practice on the localizing movement in children and adults', *Journal of Genetic Psychology*, 38, pp. 223–38.

*Renshaw, Samuel, Wheery, R. J., and Newlin, J. C., 1930, 'Cutaneous localization in congenitally blind versus seeing children and adults', *Journal of Genetic Psychology*, 38, pp. 239–48.

Révész, Géza, 1924, 'Experiments on animal space perception', *British Journal of Psychology*, 14, pp. 388–414.

*Ries, G., 1922, 'Untersuchungen über die Sicherheit der Aussage', *Zeitschrift für Psychologie*, 88, pp. 145–204.

Riesen, Austin H., 1947, 'The development of visual perception in man and chimpanzee', *Science*, 106, pp.107–8.

*———, 1950, 'Arrested vision', *Scientific American*, 183(1), pp. 16–19.

Riker, B. L., 1946, 'The ability to judge pitch', *Journal of Experimental Psychology*, 36(4), pp. 331–46.

*Robinson, Edward Stevens, 1932, *Association Theory Today: An Essay in Systematic Psychology*, London: Century/Random House.

Rosenblüth, Arturo, Wiener, Norbert, and Bigelow, Julian, 1943, 'Behavior, purpose, and teleology', *Philosophy of Science*, 10(1), pp. 18–24.

Russell, Bertrand, 1921, *The Analysis of Mind*, London: Allen & Unwin.

*———, 1927, *The Analysis of Matter*, London: Kegan Paul.

*Ryan, T. A., 1940, 'Interrelations of sensory systems in perception', *Psychological Bulletin*, 37(9), pp. 659–98.

Ryle, Gilbert, 1945–46, '"Knowing How" and "Knowing That": The Presidential Address', *Proceedings of the Aristotelian Society, New Series*, 46, pp. 1–16.

———, 1949, *The Concept of Mind*, London: Hutchinson's University Library.

Schiller, Paul von, 1932, 'Die Rauhigkeit als intermodale Erscheinung', *Zeitschrift für Psychologie*, 127, pp. 265–89.

*Schlick, Moritz, 1918, *Allgemeine Erkenntnislehre*, Berlin: J. Springer.

*Schnabel, R., 1881, 'Beiträge zu der Lehre von der Schlechtsichtigkeit durch Nichtgebrauch der Augen', *Berichte des naturwissenschaftlich-medizinischen Vereins in Innsbruck*, 11, pp. 32–59.

Schumann, Friedrich, 1909, *Beiträge zur Analyse der Gesichtswahrnehmungen*, vol. 3(1) of *Psychologische Studien*, 1904–23, ed. by F. Schumann, Leipzig: Barth.

———, 1922, 'Das Erkennungsurteil', *Zeitschrift für Psychologie*, 88, pp. 205–24.

Semon, Richard Wolfgang, 1904, *Die Mneme als erhaltendes Prinzip im Wechsel des organischen Geschehens*, Leipzig: Engelmann.

———, 1909, *Die Mnemischen Empfindungen in ihren Beziehungen zu den Originalempfindungen*, Leipzig: Engelmann.

Senden, Marius von, 1932, *Raum- und Gestaltauffassung bei operierten Blindgeborenen vor und nach der Operation*, Leipzig: J. A. Barth.

*Sherrington, Sir Charles, 1933, *The Brain and Its Mechanism*, Cambridge: Cambridge University Press.

*———, 1940, *Man: On His Nature*, Cambridge: Cambridge University Press.

———, 1949, 'Mystery of mysteries: The human brain', *New York Times Magazine*, December 4.

Skramlik, Emil von, 1937, 'Psychophysiologie der Tastsinne', Supplement 4, *Archiv für die gesamte Psychologie*.

*Spence, Kenneth W., 1944, 'The nature of theory construction in contemporary psychology', *Psychological Review*, 51(1), pp. 47–68.

———, 1948, 'The postulates and methods of "behaviorism"', *Psychological Review*, 55(2), pp. 67–78.

Sperry, Robert Wolcott, 1945a, 'The problem of central nervous reorganization after nerve regeneration and muscle transposition', *Quarterly Review of Biology*, 20(4), pp. 311–69.

———, 1945b, 'Restoration of vision after crossing of optic nerves and after contralateral transplantation of eye', *Journal of Neurophysiology*, 8, pp.15–28.

Stern, William, 1938, *General Psychology from the Personalistic Standpoint*, New York: Macmillan.

Stevens, Stanley Smith, 1934, 'The attributes of tones', *Proceedings of the National Academy of Sciences*, 20, pp. 457–59.

*———, 1935a, 'The operational definition of psychological concepts', *Psychological Review*, 42, pp. 517–27.

*———, 1935b, 'The operational basis of psychology', *American Journal of Psychology*, 47, pp. 323–30.

*———, 1936, 'Psychology: The propaedeutic science', *Philosophy of Science*, 3, pp. 90–103.

*———, 1939a, 'Psychology and the science of science', *Psychological Bulletin*, 36, pp. 221–63.

*———, 1939b, 'On the problem of scales for the measurement of psychological magnitudes', *Journal of Unified Science*, 9, pp. 94–99.

*———, 1946a, 'On the theory of scales of measurement', *Science*, 103, pp. 677–80.

*———, 1946b, 'The two basic mechanisms of sensory discrimination', *Federation of the American Society of Experimental Biology, Proceedings*, 5(1), Part 2, p. 101.

*———, 1948, 'Sensation and psychological measurement', in: E. G. Boring, H. S. Langfeld, and H. P. Weld (eds.), *Foundations of Psychology*, New York: Wiley, pp. 250–68.

Stevens, Stanley Smith, and Davis, Hallowell, 1938, *Hearing: Its Psychology and Physiology*, New York: Wiley.

Stevens, Stanley Smith, Morgan, C. T., and Volkman, J., 1941, 'Theory of the neural quantum in the discrimination of loudness and pitch', *American Journal of Psychology*, 54, pp. 315–35.

Stevens, Stanley Smith, and Volkmann, J., 1940a, 'The quantum theory of sensory discrimination', *Science*, 92, pp. 583–85.

———, 1940b, 'The relation of pitch to frequency: A revised scale', *American Journal of Psychology*, 53, pp. 329–53.

*Stöhr, Adolf, 1917, *Psychologie*, Vienna: Braumüller.

Stout, George Frederick, 1915, *Manual of Psychology*, 3rd rev. and enl. ed., London: Clive.

Stratton, George M., 1897, 'Vision without inversion of the retinal image', *Psychological Review*, 4(4), pp. 341–60; 4(5), pp. 463–81.

Thompson, D'Arcy Wentworth, 1942, *On Growth and Form*, a new ed., Cambridge: Cambridge University Press.

Thorndike, Edward L., 1913, *The Psychology of Learning, Educational Psychology*, vol. 2, New York: Teachers College, Columbia University Press.

Titchener, Edward B., 1905, *Experimental Psychology: A Manual of Laboratory Practice*, New York: Macmillan.

*Tolman, Edward Chace, 1932, *Purposive Behavior in Animals and Men*, New York: Century.

———, 1948, 'Cognitive maps in rats and men', *Psychological Review*, 55, pp. 189–208.

*———, 1949, 'There is more than one kind of learning', *Psychological Review*, 56, pp. 144–55.

*Troland, Leonard T., 1928, *The Fundamentals of Human Motivation*, New York: D. Van Nostrand &Co.

*———, 1929, *The Principles of Psychophysiology: A Survey of Modern Scientific Psychology*, New York: D. Van Nostrand & Co.

Underwood, Benton J., 1949, *Experimental Psychology: An Introduction*, New York: Appleton-Century-Crofts.

*Urbantschitsch, Viktor, 1888, 'Über den Einfluss einer Sinneserregung auf die übrigen Sinnesempfindungen', *Plügers Archiv für die gesamte Physiologie der Menschen und der Tiere*, 42.

*Verworn, Max, 1907, *Die Mechanik des Geisteslebens*, Leipzig: Teubner.

*———, 1920, *Die Entwicklung des menschlichen Geistes, ein Vortrag*, 4th ed., Jena: G. Fischer.

Volkmann, Alfred Wilhelm, 1858, 'Über den Einfluss der Übung auf das Erkennen räumlicher Distanzen', *Berichte über die Verhandlungen der Königlich Sächsischen Gesellschaft der Wissenschaften zu Leipzig*, 10, pp. 38–69.

Walls, Gordon L., 1942, *The Vertebrate Eye and Its Adaptive Radiation*, Bloomfield Hill, MI: The Cranbrook Institute of Science.

Walter, William Grey, 1950, 'An imitation of life', *Scientific American*, 182(5), pp. 42–45.

Wedell, Carl Havelock, 1934 'The nature of the absolute judgment of pitch', *Journal of Experimental Psychology*, 17(4), pp. 485–503.

Weiss, Albert Paul, 1925, *A Theoretical Basis of Human Behavior*, Columbus, OH: R. G. Adams & Co.

Weiss, Paul Alfred, 1941, *Self-differentiation of the Basic Patterns of Coordination*, vol. 17(4), (88) of *Comparative Psychology Monographs*, Baltimore, MD: Williams and Wilkins.

Weizsäcker, Viktor von, 1940 (1947), *Der Gestaltkreis. Theorie der Einheit von Wahrnehmen und Bewegen*, 3rd ed., Stuttgart: Georg Thieme.

Wellek, Albert, 1931, 'Zur Geschichte und Kritik der Synästhesie-Forschung', *Archiv für die gesamte Psychologie*, 79, pp. 325–84.

*Werner, Heinz, 1926a, 'Mikromelodik und Mikroharmonik', *Zeitschrift für Psychologie*, 98, pp. 74–89.

*———, 1926b, 'Untersuchungen über Empfindung und Empfinden: Die Ausprägung von Tongestalten', *Zeitschrift für Psychologie*, 101, pp. 159–81.

*———, 1930, 'Untersuchungen über Empfindung und Empfinden: Das Problem des Empfindens und die Methoden seiner experimentellen Prüfung', *Zeitschrift für Psychologie*, 114, pp. 152–66.

———, 1948, *Comparative Psychology of Mental Development*, rev. ed., Chicago: Follet Publications Co.

Wiener, Norbert, 1948a, *Cybernetics: Or Control and Communication in the Animal and the Machine*, New York: Wiley.

———, 1948b, 'Time, communications, and the nervous system', in: L. K. Frank (ed.), *Teleological Mechanisms, Annals of the New York Academy of Sciences*, 50, pp. 197–278. (See also Rosenblüth, Wiener and Bigelow, 1943.)

Williams, Thomas J., 1922, 'Extraordinary development of the tactile and olfactory senses compensatory for loss of sight and hearing', *Journal of the American Medical Association*, 79(16), pp. 1331–34.

Winslow, Charles Nelson, 1933, 'Visual illusions in the chick', *Archives of Psychology*, 153, pp. 5–83.

Woodger, Joseph Henry, 1929, *Biological Principles*, London: Kegan Paul.

Woodworth, Robert S., 1938, *Experimental Psychology*, New York: Henry Holt.

*Wundt, Wilhelm, 1902–3, *Grundzüge der physiologischen Psychologie*, 3 vols., 5th ed., Leipzig: Engelmann.

Wyatt, Ruth F., 1945, 'Improvability of pitch discrimination', *Psychological Monographs*, 58(2), (No. 267). Evanston, IL: American Psychological Association.

Young, Paul T., 1928, 'Auditory localization with acoustical transposition of the ears', *Journal of Experimental Psychology*, 11, pp. 399–429.

Note

While there would be little point in adding to this bibliography the titles of the various relevant American and English works which have appeared since the middle of 1950, when the final text of the present book was completed, I should like to draw special attention to the full account of some interesting experiments on sensory learning (of which I then knew only through the preliminary accounts in T. Erismann, 1948), given in:

Kohler, Ivo, 1951, 'Über Aufbau und Wandlungen der Wahrnehmungswelt. Insbesondere über bedingte Empfindungen', *Österreichische Akademie der Wissenschaften, Philosophisch-Historische Klasse, Sitzungsberichte*, 227(1), pp. 1–118.

OTHER WRITINGS ON THE
FOUNDATIONS OF THEORETICAL
PSYCHOLOGY

CONTRIBUTIONS TO A THEORY OF HOW CONSCIOUSNESS DEVELOPS

This study is an attempt to create a basis for a general physiological explanation of consciousness phenomena by investigating the simplest conscious experiences, particularly those of a sensory nature, and explaining them in terms of the operation of established physiological laws. What we mean here by explanation is advancing a theory capable of reconstructing the functions encompassed by the concept of "consciousness" with the help of recognized regularities. Until now, psychology has endeavored to base this explanation on "elementary psychic processes," whereas the study presented here seeks to show how the simple physiological processes at the root of these elementary processes are converted into characteristic markers indicative of certain external stimuli. The author's views on this matter are in the sharpest opposition to the prevalent "dogmatic-atomistic concept of sensations" and to any concept relying on a primal, clear-cut association of consciousness event and brain process. Instead, this study focuses on the context within which effects on the organism take place, making experience the source of different sensory qualities. Here the author seeks to base his explanation exclusively on the physiological processes that underlie association processes, without reliance on any special psychic capacity for comprehension or any special physiological hypothesis (such as cell memory!). He hopes thereby to limit the explanation to a single recognized physiological law compatible with the perspective of the natural sciences. The second part of the study attempts to apply this explanation to other elementary consciousness phenomena (emotions) as well, and to draw appropriate conclusions for more complicated consciousness processes (association processes, recognition, conceptualization, abstraction). The author has no intention to deal with philosophical questions head-on. Yet the

[The original German typescript, entitled "Beiträge zur Theorie der Entwicklung des Bewußtseins," dated September 1920, is kept in the Hoover Institution Archives, Friedrich A. von Hayek Papers, box 93, folder 1. The paper remained unpublished until 2006, when it was included in the German edition of *The Sensory Order*. See Friedrich A. von Hayek, *Die sensorische Ordnung—Eine Untersuchung der Grundlagen der theoretischen Psychologie*, Übersetzt und mit ergänzenden Beiträgen herausgegeben von Manfred E. Streit (Tübingen: Mohr Siebeck, 2006), 199–226. The English translation has been prepared by Dr. Grete Heinz.—Ed.]

findings of this study could have far-reaching implications for epistemology, should its hypotheses—that subjective sensory qualities emanate from the objective constellation of triggering external events and that no fundamental opposition exists between sensory perception and conceptualization and thought—be confirmed.

1. Critical Comments on the Concept of Sensations

By positing a parallelism between psychic and physiological phenomena, conventional psychology circumvents the very problem that is common to the totality of psychic phenomena, to wit, the manner in which a physiological stimulus is converted to a consciousness entity.—The physiological excitation of the brain's target ganglion cells is the last observable aspect in the process whereby a stimulus is finally converted into an evoked sensation (and we will limit ourselves to sensations in the first part of this study). Beyond that point there is a gaping hole until the external stimulus reemerges in our consciousness as a sensation. The doctrine of psycho-physiological parallelism typically interprets this conversion of the stimuli reaching the brain as the unfathomable elementary process underlying all consciousness phenomena, and it is therefore dispensed from further investigation. A parallelism is established between the induced change of consciousness, which is usually designated as a special "psychic element," and the excitatory physiological process, or the physiological element. The content of the former cannot be separated from the occurrence of the physiological element and is primarily associated with it, a view that has some grave consequences.[1] The psychic elements in question were seen as unchangeable qualitative entities that would serve as the building blocks for all consciousness phenomena. Other psychologists viewed psychological and physiological processes as interdependent or regarded the former as products of the latter and made special efforts to attribute the specific impacts on consciousness by the individual elements to dif-

---

[1] Typical of this interpretation, though its author is not a parallelist in the strict sense of the word, are the following sentences cited from Wilhelm Jerusalem's popular *Lehrbuch der Psychologie*, 4th ed. (Vienna and Leipzig: Braumüller, 1907), p.18: "When the excitation penetrates as far as the cerebrum, it is converted there, inexplicably, into a psychic state, or, in the case of a simple stimulus, into a sensation." And: "Simple or pure sensations are an elementary psychic process, which we elucidate by analysis" (ibid., p. 34). [Here and in the remainder of this essay, German citations are reproduced in English translation.—Ed.] [Wilhelm Jerusalem (1854–1923) was an Austrian philosopher and psychologist who had studied at Wilhelm Wundt's (see above, *TSO*, preface, fn. 8) psychological institute in Leipzig. He was influenced by William James (see above, *TSO*, preface, fn. 9), whose *Pragmatism* Jerusalem translated into German. Jerusalem became particularly known for his research on the education of the deaf-blind. He corresponded with Helen Keller (see above, *TSO*, 1.96, fn. 58).—Ed.]

ferences in their metabolic processes (notably Max Verworn[2]). This approach failed to clarify the processes in question and did not emancipate itself from the doctrine implicit in parallelism, namely the existence of a primal association between the stimulation of individual physiological elements and consciousness entities.

Before examining more closely the process—to be designated as uptake [*Auffassung*][3] for short—whereby something is incorporated into consciousness, we must try to understand what the term "consciousness" really means. It means, above all, that we know about something, that is, that we are capable of remembering it in the future. Since the act of remembering is itself merely an uptake into consciousness of sorts, that is, a re-uptake, the capacity to remember an impression may thus be an indication that it is present in consciousness. But the distinctive feature that the first uptake into consciousness shares with its being taken up again later is not captured by simply pointing to the possibility of its re-uptake. Nor can the control of our behavior that we exert when an impression becomes conscious tell us more, since "controlling" something is just synonymous with "being conscious" of something. We come closer to an explanation when we say that it is the specific sort of influence an impression exerts on an action—its "meaning" for the execution of an action—that constitutes the distinctive feature of a consciousness entity. Yet the act of becoming conscious includes more, namely a connection with the apprehending subject's entire being,[4] particularly a specific relationship

[2] Max Verworn, *Die Entwicklung des menschlichen Geistes*, Lecture, 4th ed. (Jena: Fischer, 1920), p. 21: "There is one thing that has remained wholly impenetrable for us so far: the mystery of what each individual type of nerve specifically contributes. All we can do here is to state that fact and accept the meager truth that a specific metabolic process occurs in each type of cell. But the specific differences in the metabolism of individual neurons continue to remain a mystery, if for no other reason than that so far we have been unable to acquire even a sketchy notion of how the whole metabolic process functions for a single cell type." See also his *Die Mechanik des Geisteslebens*, 3rd ed. (Berlin and Leipzig: Teubner, [1907] 1914a), p. 41. [Max Verworn (1863–1921) was a German physiologist and founder of the *Zeitschrift für Allgemeine Physiologie* (*Journal of General Physiology*). He was known for his research on elementary physiological processes and the function of nerve cells.—Ed.]

[3] [Where English equivalents are not readily available the original term is added in brackets.—Ed.]

[4] Cf., Bartholomäus von Carneri, *Empfindung und Bewusstsein. Monistische Bedenken* (Bonn: E. Strauss, 1893), p. 17: "Should we now ask by what means sensation becomes conscious, we would recognize that this presupposes the existence of an individual relating the sensation to himself. This requires an individual with a nervous system such as the one to which we referred above, and in whose gray brain matter all activity of the senses is uniformly assembled with the help of a complete set of connections. This centralization represents the whole individual, to whom any sensation that is conducted there represents itself—becomes a representation—in that the sensation experienced by a part becomes a sensation of the whole." See also the quotations from Riehl (fn. 42) and Jodl (fn. 9 and 15) below. [Bartholomäus von Carneri (1821–1909) was an Austrian philosopher and politician who advocated an evolutionary ethics, arguing that

between the most recently acquired and all previous impressions, whereby the recently acquired impression is subsumed in a system of qualities defined by their interrelations. The interrelations among all these impressions and with the actions are what constitute their significance for the subject. From their multiplicity results the unique and unpredictable response they elicit in each human being. We are therefore justified in saying that becoming conscious means integrating an impression into a preexisting nexus of meanings, a system of qualities, and it is this process that we shall designate as uptake into consciousness [*Wertung* or *Auffassung*].

Proceeding from our starting point, the physiological element, we only need to model the final stages of a familiar physiological process to obtain a similar picture: the phenomenon that the simultaneous excitation of two ganglion cells in the brain forges a permanent connection between the two cells, so that future excitation of one cell also stimulates the other cell. How this phenomenon, which has been called facilitation or smoothing, can be explained need not concern us here, since its existence appears to be beyond doubt. Keeping in mind that organisms are never bombarded by just a single stimulus but always by a large number of stimuli, and that on these occasions linkages are always created between the ganglion cells, we realize that during an individual's entire life span each of these cells nearly continuously acquires new linkages, that old linkages are reinforced as well, and that, according to the origin of the causing stimulus, this is particularly true for such other elements whose stimulus source is likely to occur simultaneously. Each ganglion cell thus has a large number of unique linkages, so that a whole network of linkages will spread between the cells, whose ordering will reflect the relative strength or weakness of the linkages.

Whenever a cell is stimulated, it will at once communicate this stimulus to the other cells with which it is directly linked, according to the strength of the linkage. From these cells the stimulus will be communicated to other cells. Because of its position within a certain retinue of connected cells and, indirectly, within an order of sensory events, and analogously (directly and indirectly) because of its relation to the elements of the emotional and motor processes, each cell or group of cells acquires a particular and usually unique character that distinguishes it from all other cells. At the same time it acquires a position in the general nexus of effects and consciousness. I would say that this sums up all the indispensable features of consciousness. To clarify these

---

man's consciousness is a function of the "centralized organism." Alois Riehl (1844–1924) was an Austrian philosopher and neo-Kantian who in 1905, after teaching at several other universities, succeeded Wilhelm Dilthey as professor of philosophy at the University of Berlin. Friedrich Jodl (1849–1914) was a German philosopher and psychologist who advocated a positivist psychology and a naturalistic ethics.—Ed.]

concepts, we could visualize a similar process taking place at a central telephone switchboard, where previous connections would have had such a strong impact on the different lines in question that a call from one of these lines would automatically reestablish prior connections with the other lines. For each line, we would obtain a particular, characteristic constellation when a call was made, which would not only characterize this line in a very specific way but would also show those of its characteristics that are essential for the activation of the mechanism—its relations to the other lines. Even if such spatial analogies are not applicable, this illustration should help to clarify the process whereby the physiological elements in the brain are converted to attributes of consciousness. In both cases, the special character and the significance of a given element for the functioning of the entire system are determined by many other elements, which are activated by this element and represent its functioning within the totality. Here too we have a comparable insertion into a system of entities like the one we encountered in defining the concept of consciousness. We can therefore think of the two processes as being identical and merely viewed from two different angles. We can thus apply the concept of uptake [*Wertung*] to the above-mentioned process and designate those other elements, through whose activation the element that is taken up is integrated in the qualitative order and hence converted to consciousness, as its retinue or its field of uptake [*Wertungsfeld*].[5]

If, however, we deny the attribute of consciousness to isolated physiological processes, as we have done here, and if we consider their conversion to consciousness as an effect of the field of uptake that they have acquired, we must once and for all give up the basic dogma of the parallelism, the primal one-to-one linkage between physiological events and consciousness attributes. As Langley,[6] Donders,[7] and Du Bois-Reymond[8] have demonstrated, there exists

[5] Cf. on this point particularly the assimilation theory of Wilhelm Wundt, who notes in his *Grundriss der Psychologie*, 3rd ed. (Leipzig: Körner, [1896] 1918), p. 284: "In ordinary sensations direct factors (of assimilation) are predominant, to the point where reproductive ones are generally overlooked, although they actually are always present and are often even of great importance for grasping the objects."

[6] [John Newport Langley (1852–1925) was a British physiologist who taught at Cambridge University. He laid the foundations for the "chemical receptor theory," which postulates that specific receptors mediate between chemicals and their effects on nerve cells.—Ed.]

[7] [Franciscus Cornelius Donders (1818–89) was a Dutch biologist, physiologist, and ophthalmologist. Along with Hermann von Helmholtz (see above, *TSO*, preface, fn. 7), he was one of the founders of scientific ophthalmology. His research included the study of the differences in physiological reaction time and cognitive processing.—Ed.]

[8] [Emil Du Bois-Reymond (1818–96), older brother of the mathematician Paul Du Bois-Reymond (see above, *TSO*, introduction, fn. 8), was a German physician and physiologist who, like von Helmholtz, had studied with Johannes Peter Müller (see above, *TSO*, 1.32, fn. 17). He pioneered the field of experimental electrophysiology.—Ed.]

no original quality shared by physiological stimuli that are identical to each other. Accordingly, a completely isolated element as the artificially constructed basis for any development of consciousness (in reality such a process could not happen, inasmuch as linkages of elements are probably partially inherited) cannot be reflected in a consciousness uptake. Such uptake requires its being linked with a series of other elements.[9] Just as an element acquires the first uptaking linkages at the very beginning of the development, it is continuously affected by the addition of new linkages, so that the attributes of consciousness keep changing even in a developed consciousness. This perpetual changeability demonstrated even by relatively very simple attributes of consciousness is another fact very much in conflict with the doctrine of parallelism.

From the standpoint of consciousness, the creation of linkages, which are at the root of all this, is nothing other than the acquisition of experience. And, in view of the constant, simultaneous intrusion of multitudinous stimuli on the nervous system, such acquisition of experience is associated with every uptake into consciousness. We can thus differentiate two facets in each instance: (1) uptake of the impression by means of the activation of the field of uptake, uptake in its narrower sense; and (2) creation of new linkages or reinforcement of old linkages between psychological entities, that is, experience, which forms the foundation for subsequent uptakes. The latter process is in keeping with a feature mentioned in our definition of the insertion of an impression into consciousness: the possibility of remembering it. Modern psychology is nearly unanimous in ascribing this—and memory in general—to association, that is, from the standpoint of consciousness, the reciprocal activation of impulses in ganglion cells that are interconnected. The following, it is believed, occurs when a sensory experience is re-evoked: the basic stimulus related to it is first activated by other stimuli, that is, by physiological means, and, when this basic stimulus is strong enough, it will pass on the stimulus to its field of uptake and insert itself into the nexus of consciousness. The concept of association, which was coined to describe the linking of consciousness attributes, should not target the evocation of the elements of the field of uptake, which remain unconscious; rather, it should confine itself to those activating mechanisms (caused by a merger of elements) strong enough to re-endow the evoked element with the attribute of consciousness.

---

[9] Cf. Friedrich Jodl, *Lehrbuch der Psychologie*, 3rd ed. (Stuttgart and Berlin: Cotta, [1896] 1908), vol. 1, p. 228: "The process whereby an individual mirrors events in the outside world in his consciousness is an extremely complex one. This is incontrovertibly proved (at least as far as man's psychic life is concerned) by the fact that the transformation of external stimuli into an orderly sensory world, which is so natural and seemingly effortless for the developed consciousness, must first be learned by human beings. As experience with children and persons with inborn sensory defects that were later cured indicates, it is not sufficient to have normal sensory organs. It takes the accumulation and fusing of impressions, their sorting and comparison, to transform what was initially chaos into a cosmos."

Physiological memory, which is based on sensory experiences, is in any case a precursor of this sensation. We have seen how sensation was created by memory. Memory in its physiological sense can occur when a connection is established between two isolated nerve cells, but a sensation or any other attribute of consciousness is possible only in the fully developed cerebrum.[10] *We do not first have sensations that are then preserved by memory, but it is as a result of physiological memory that the physiological impulses are converted into sensations.* The connections between the physiological elements are thus the primary phenomenon that creates the mental phenomena. In the dualist-parallelist doctrine, according to which there exists no perfect correspondence but only an unclarified parallelism between psychic association and physiological activation, sensation as such is the accepted point of departure. This doctrine implied that sensations as such are stored in the brain and reproduced by association. Both memory and association therefore had to be considered psychic forces influencing the attributes of consciousness. But once we abandon the dogmatic assumption of sensations as a preestablished given, memory can easily be ascribed to physiological linkages.

The idea of an absolute sensation, for its part, which is a component not only of the parallelist doctrine but of most other psychological doctrines as well, rests mainly on a biological concept that is a "remnant of the old notion that each representation has its own particular cell, a private little chamber of sorts."[11] Semon[12] sums this up characteristically by the concept of an "engram," according to which the preservation, or the "recording," of an impression takes place in the corresponding individual cell. As to the generally recognized concept of association (linkage, facilitation), which even here cannot be overlooked, Semon's hypothesis leaves it only a modest scope as a "reproductive pattern." Psychology, on the other hand, unanimously proclaims that "we are justified under all circumstances to consider association as the general and exclusive cause of memory processes."[13] Furthermore, several respected researchers[14] assert, on the strength of numerous earlier principles,

[10] [The cerebrum—Latin for "brain"—comprises the largest part of the human brain, surrounding the older parts of the brain. It is evolutionarily the newest part of the brain and controls complex behaviors such as thought, learning, judgment, imagination, memory, and speech.—Ed.]

[11] Erich Becher, *Gehirn und Seele*, Psychologie in Einzeldarstellungen, no. 5 (Heidelberg: Winter, 1911), p. 91. [Erich Becher (1882–1929) was a German philosopher and psychologist. He was a student of Benno Erdmann (see *TSO*, 7.14, fn. 12).—Ed.]

[12] Richard Semon, *Die Mneme als erhaltendes Prinzip im Wechsel des organischen Geschehens*, 2nd ed. (Leipzig: Engelmann, [1904] 1918a); Richard Semon, *Die mnemischen Empfindungen in ihren Beziehungen zu den Originalempfindungen* (Leipzig: Engelmann, [1909] 1918b). [On Semon see above, *TSO*, introduction, fn. 13.—Ed.]

[13] W. Wundt, 1918, p. 290.

[14] Ernst Mach, *Analyse der Empfindungen und das Verhältnis des Physischen zum Psychischen*, 7th ed. (Jena: Fischer, 1918) p. 195 [The original edition was published in 1886 under the title *Beiträge*

that association can be reduced to a single cause, the simultaneous appearance of associated consciousness contents. This implies that there is a perfect concordance between physiological and psychological processes. Thus, the hypothesis that, concurrent with the establishment of new linkages between the physiological elements, there exists a separate memory cell for each impression is, to say the least, superfluous. Because, moreover, this hypothesis provokes additional difficulties, to be discussed below, there is no reason to invoke it in explaining consciousness phenomena. Since it never happens that an organism is affected by a single stimulus limited to a single element of the nervous system, it is not possible to verify experimentally whether an impression is retained only when at least two cells are simultaneously stimulated and a connection is thus established (or reinforced) between them. In any case, if one insists on a hypothesis for explaining the physiological aspect of memory, which has so far remained unclarified, Heinrich E. Ziegler's[15] hypothesis is more plausible than Semon's engram theory. There are more physiological and psychological considerations that support Ziegler's theory about the connection between the way experience is processed and the multiplication of dendrites (ganglion cell extensions), than for the engram theory, which attempts to derive two quite different phenomena—the way individuals retain impressions and how morphological structure is transmitted by the germ cell from generation to generation—from a single common cause. Even to the extent that acquired experiences can at all be considered heritable, there is nothing that speaks in favor of a common cause for the two phenomena, since the complete reproduction of the structure of our forbears' nervous system would imply that the associations acquired by them would have to be reproduced as well.

The creation of connections, or experience, arranges originally meaningless physiological processes, whereby stimuli are recorded in the brain, by way of connections of different strengths into a structural network within which they occupy a *specific position contingent on the conditions of their occurrence*. From a psychological point of view, it is this system of relationships that constitutes consciousness. Each insertion into the system results in an "uptake" (*Wertung*), and

---

zu einer Analyse der Empfindungen.—Ed.]; R. Semon himself in 1918a, p. 132; and in R. Semon, 1918b, pp. 98–203.

[15] Heinrich Ernst Ziegler, "Theoretisches zur Tierpsychologie und vergleichenden Nervenpsychologie," *Biologisches Zentralblatt*, vol. 20, 1900, no.1. [Heinrich Ernst Ziegler (1858–1925) was a German zoologist.—Ed.] Cf. also F. Jodl, 1908, p. 55: "And as far as what we call mental development, mental growth, is concerned, during the years in which brain volume no longer increases (and this increase in volume itself is probably not tantamount to an increase in the number of neurons), what takes place is a more abundant ramification of the fibers extending from the cells, especially in the cerebrum, by means of which nerve elements that were previously unconnected with each other become interconnected."

the impression acquires a quality. It is experience that creates and enlarges this system. The processes taking place within it refer back to prior relationships between experiences. One might justly say that each human being thinks with his past.

Insertion into the system or uptake may involve a greater or lesser degree of differentiation. The degree of differentiation attained by specific impulses representing an external stimulus in the brain of a fully mature and verbally competent individual can be designated as sensation. The fact that sensory experiences always have a specific quality as their "content" as well as a specific localization (the "Lokalzeichen")[16] has led to the assumption that they had an intrinsic connection with the physiological process. It would be more correct to say that both these uptakes [*Wertungen*] pre-date language, which found them fully developed, and subsumed them under the concept of sensation.

In view of the ancientness of the two uptakes [*Wertungen*], it is reasonable to assume that they were created by linkages of impressions that most frequently occur simultaneously. Hence, they must be either stimuli of the same sort or stimuli that affect nerves whose receptors are immediately adjacent. Inasmuch as each stimulus normally affects more than one element of the nervous system and stimuli with the same origin usually affect various elements of the nervous system simultaneously, it is natural that those ganglion cells whose sensory organs are adjacent—and again, among these, the ones that respond to stimuli of the same origin (light, heat, pressure)—will be most closely associated. However, since stimuli of the same kind (i.e., physically similar stimuli) tend to affect all the responsive nerves in an organism while all neighboring receptors may simultaneously receive stimuli of a different kind, particularly close linkages will be formed between all impulses of the same kind and between neighboring impulses. Two networks of close linkages will therefore be established early in life and will be reinforced by every experience. One network relates each recurring impression to impressions of the same and, in the second instance, of a similar sort, and thereby assures its place in the system of qualities. The other network gives each impression its quality by its greater or lesser proximity and stronger or weaker linkages with impressions received elsewhere in the organism. This is what we usually characterize as a "localization clue" [*Lokalzeichen*].

The first ordering of impressions is reinforced by experiences that accompany each motion. This happens through the interconnection among impulses that follow each other in the wake of a motion and with the sensation of

[16] [The concept "*Lokalzeichen*" (localization clue) was used by the German philosopher Rudolf Hermann Lotze (1817–81), by Hermann von Helmholtz, and by Wilhelm Wundt as a label for the idea that sensations, in addition to their specific content, are also characterized by the location where the stimulus impinges on the organism. Such localization of sensations is crucial for the organism's ability to form a notion of space.—Ed.]

motion, a relationship of proximity. The experience that, for motions resulting from the same intervention, the stimulus remains unchanged establishes
a relationship of sameness. These two uptakes [*Wertungen*] contained in each
sensation are thus acquired, like all others, as a result of experience. To speak
of an original content of sensations is therefore legitimate only to the extent
that the concept of sensation already presupposes the relationship of sameness and differences and of proximity and remoteness. At a stage in the development of consciousness when these uptakes have not yet been acquired,
one cannot speak of sensations. Yet the same physiological process, which
would later produce this uptake and would therefore be envisaged as a sensory experience, may well manifest itself without sensory counterpart, without
"content," just as it may, even later, remain unconscious and without sensory
counterpart when the requisite resonance for its uptake is lacking because the
whole nervous system is already overstimulated or overstressed.

Sensations are not limited to these two basic contents, though, since their
quality is not exclusively contingent on their being identical with or different
from other impressions. It extends to their having a relative distinctness
beyond the relation of sameness or difference. All we have done so far is to
group together all similar impressions and all those sharing a same localization. Now that we are confronting the task of establishing their differentiation, many people will wonder, in the face of the fantastic multiplicity of sensations and emotions, where psychology will find all these qualities. We need
not hesitate to apply to the totality of consciousness phenomena the answer
Ernst Mach gave when faced with the same question about cognitive phenomena: "No need to worry! They will all turn up, just as did muscular sensations in spatial theory. The organism can supply enough of them to fill up
the show-windows of psychology in this respect. It is high time to give serious
thought to 'bodily resonance,' about which psychology is always talking."[17]
It must be remembered that for the uptakes [*Wertungen*] to which we have
referred so far, we limited ourselves entirely to the relations between sensations of a single sensory organ. That means that in explaining additional differentiations between impressions, we can still rely on the far more numerous relationships between stimuli that regularly affect several sensory organs
simultaneously. A case in point are the relationships by means of which light
(color) and temperature sensations, olfactory and taste sensations, as well as
these pairs and tactile sensations, can influence each other's uptake [*Wertung*].
The phenomenon of color-hearing demonstrates that even colors can contribute to the uptake of auditory sensations. E. Mach in particular demon-

---

[17] Ernst Mach, *Populärwissenschaftliche Vorlesungen*, 3rd enlarged and revised ed. (Leipzig: Johann
Ambrosius Barth, [1896] 1903), pp. 122f. The beginning of this passage is quoted on p. 342f.
below. [On Mach see above, *TSO*, preface, fn. 11.—Ed.]

strated the important role that nerve stimulations arising from movements play in the uptake of the most varied consciousness phenomena. And here we are not limited to linkages between stimuli that by necessity occur simultaneously. In many cases we are dealing with a regular coincidence produced by the individual's regimen, which often results in the concurrence of periodically intervening stimuli with periods in the organism's life processes. Generally speaking, the relation between external stimuli and the organism's normal life processes is of the greatest significance in this connection. Pavlov's[18] experiments on the salivation reflex in dogs have demonstrated to how large an extent the linkage with internal reactions can influence sensory experiences. The internal reaction to external impressions that are important in this respect are by no means limited to glandular processes, but also encompass activities of the heart, respiratory organs, stomach, colon, and bladder, as well as the muscles' expanding and constricting of the blood vessels (vasomotor, trophic, and caloric reactions, according to Bechterew[19]). The alterations in the general state of arousal that are produced by these reactions, in what is generally called frame of mind, influence the uptake of the triggering impression. And since there are always combinations of the most varied influences related to uptake at work, there is no question that the uptake can occur in at least as many ways as the number of sensory qualities. It should be one of the most urgent tasks of psychology to investigate which relationships characteristically contribute to the uptake of typical sensory qualities.

When dealing with the quality of consciousness entities determined by prior linkages, one cannot, of course, preclude that two distinctive physiological stimuli manifesting themselves simultaneously will result in the same uptake, that is, will not be differentiated by consciousness, since they possess identical linkages. This is something that we can actually observe when we experience pressure on our teeth. This pressure generally acts simultaneously on the upper and lower teeth facing each other and arouses a single sensation. Whenever pain is caused by clenching one's teeth, one must first touch each tooth separately to ascertain which one is the source of pain.

The objection has been raised that the initial nerve impulse could never induce any consciousness entity if we assume prior linkages to be indispensable for uptake into consciousness, since no such impulse had ever been previously encountered. This objection is not valid because there normally exists no nerve that receives absolutely no stimulation. Even a weak impulse would suffice as a basis for identifying this kind of impulse and would later allow the acquisition of uptakes [*Wertungen*] under the impetus of unusually powerful impulses. A nerve of this sort will, in any case, already be inserted into a sig-

---

[18] [On I. P. Pavlov see above, *TSO*, preface, fn. 2.—Ed.]
[19] [On Bechterew see above, *TSO*, preface, fn. 3.—Ed.]

nificant nexus by linkages of its weak impulses, and this nexus will provide it with a psychic value whenever it can excite its field of uptake with suffi-cient vigor.

Let me summarize the essential features involved in the creation of the rela-tively simplest consciousness entities, individual sensations, before turning to composite consciousness phenomena. The excitation of a ganglion cell in the cerebrum as such does not necessarily entail a consciousness entity. This ele-ment of the total physiological process produces a consciousness entity only by its insertion into the whole nexus by the linkages it acquires and that allow its uptake. These are linkages with all those elements with which the element in question was ever linked by an impression, and all impressions in which that element was ever contained therefore contribute to its uptake.

The psychic content of an impulse depends not on the impulse as such but how it resonates with other impulses, that is, on whatever field of uptake it has acquired. For this reason this content is not fully predetermined and unchang-ing. On the contrary, it is perpetually in flux and is dependent on the individ-ual's entire past. This relative theory of sensations, in which the consciousness quality associated with an impulse is not intrinsic to the impulse, challenges the currently prevailing absolute theory of sensations. This relative theory of sensations stipulates instead that the quality of consciousness arises from the relations of the stimulus to other stimuli. As a result of the uptake principle, all psychic phenomena involve a multiplicity of variable physiological processes, each of which contributes to the formation of a series of other psychic entities. In view of this fact, we can never speak of a psychic atom or element: each consciousness content is relative and changeable. The "dogmatic-atomistic concept of sensation"[20] that has held sway until now must be discarded, and with it the assumption that there exists a sensation pure and simple that repre-sents a basic psychic process. This assumption rests on the unwarranted iden-tification of a given sensation with the specific impulse that is supposed to acti-vate it, the physiological element, which is the only component that can be simple or pure.[21] All that we have just explained speaks against this concep-tion of sensations as constant elements of consciousness processes. This very

---

[20] Felix Krüger, *Über Entwicklungspsychologie, ihre sachliche und geschichtliche Notwendigkeit*, vol.1 of *Arbeiten zur Entwicklungspsychologie*, ed. F. Krüger (Leipzig: W. Engelmann, 1915). [On Krüger see above, *TSO*, 7.25, fn. 33.—Ed.]

[21] Cf. F. Jodl, 1908, pp. 225ff.: "Simple or pure sensations are an abstraction. It is a most inex-cusable error from the point of view of psychology to believe that the development of our con-sciousness results from what analysis refers to as simple elements. What we receive is always a configuration, and what happens in reality is not that this configuration is assembled from its ele-ments, but that it is decomposed into its parts. In life, the whole precedes the parts; the converse happens only in science."

conception of individual segments of consciousness existing unchanged and in isolation has so far been responsible for blocking a satisfactory theory of all psychic processes. It is noteworthy that Henri Bergson[22] reached very similar conclusions, though by entirely different paths, and that he too is a firm opponent of this atomistic conception.

Medical research as well has brought to light many findings that speak in favor of the view presented here. And it lends more support to my hypothesis than to his own when Kries notes that "pathologists in particular will not hesitate to confirm the resulting conclusion, to the effect that the memory of specific objects can in no way be interpreted anatomically as something unified or circumscribed" and, further, that "partial destructions of a field never wipe out the remembered image of a table, lion, or oak tree, while that of a chair, dog, and birch tree remains intact; in reality what takes place is a relative attenuation that evenly applies to everything, a loss of sharpness and definition."[23]

2. Implications

The preceding section has clarified the fact that it is improper to use individual physiological processes to explain consciousness phenomena. Consciousness phenomena must, on the contrary, be tied to a multiplicity of such processes, whose position in our experiential system and our total activity constitutes its input into our consciousness. In presenting these processes, science has gone too far in simplifying and isolating phenomena, in the belief that it could safely disregard the multiplicity of ongoing processes and deduce consciousness processes from simple chains of physiological processes. What it has failed to notice is that it has thereby omitted an essential feature of what it is seeking to explain. This simplification was not a response to the facts, but rather the result of unjustified reductionism, as demonstrated by the observation that "there is a disproportion between the richness of forms in the central nervous system as determined by anatomy and what I would call the sparse

[22] [Henri-Louis Bergson (1859–1941) was one of the most influential French philosophers of his time and the recipient of the 1927 Nobel Prize in Literature. He corresponded with and was a friend of William James, who introduced Bergson's work to the Anglo-American public. Hayek does not provide a specific reference here, but a likely source he may have had in mind is Bergson's *Matter and Memory* (New York: Macmillan Company, 1911), translated by N. M. Paul and W. S. Palmer from the French original *Matière et mémoire* (1896).—Ed.]

[23] Johannes von Kries, *Über die materiellen Grundlagen der Bewusstseinserscheinungen* (Festschrift der Universität Freiburg i.Br.: Lehmann, 1898), p. 15. [On J. von Kries see above, *TSO*, introduction, fn. 4.—Ed.]

simplicity of physiological concepts according to which we are accustomed to interpret and evaluate these processes and functions."[24]

Let us now attempt to reconstruct the unfolding of a consciousness process. A typical case would be the sequence of phenomena occurring between a sensation and an ensuing action. We must not lose sight of the fact that this is by no means a self-contained process: on the one hand, as we shall see at once, consciousness processes pre-dating the new impression continue to operate, and on the other hand, the consciousness processes are by no means terminated by actions but continue to manifest themselves.

What becomes clear to us, above all, is that as each impression becomes conscious, once the impulse has been transferred to the uptake field, numerous points of departure have already arisen for the further evolution of the impulse that carried the impression. The following question now arises: Why is it that, although each individual element triggers all the elements linked with it, all those elements that were associated with the original consciousness entity are not brought into play in this instance, or why, on the other hand, does the impulse, being dispersed in all directions, not simply dissipate without having any effect? Why is it that in actuality an impression generally produces a well-defined set of consciousness entities, though these sets might be different in different situations? What accounts for the selection of the path that consciousness will take among the many possible "directions," or, as Verworn expresses it, "how can we account for the fact that with this unlimited set of possible associative linkages in a given case, that is, in thought formation, only a single one, one particular conception, takes its place in the chain of conceptions?"[25]

A good part of the explanation, here again, lies in the fact that impressions never act singly on the organism; rather, they manifest themselves in the company of others, or at least together with impulses stemming from other sources (including the organism's vital processes). We must therefore try to delimit more accurately the concept of impressions for which psychology fails to offer even a vague outline. There are various ways to define a *single* impression with respect to real sensory perceptions: we could define it, first, as a stimulus affecting one single element of the nervous system and, second, as the same kind of intervention, but affecting several elements; third, as the effect on a single sensory organ of an object viewed as a single entity and, fourth, on all sensory organs; and finally, as all stimuli affecting an individual's sensory organs, as long as they intervene either simultaneously or at least within short intervals of each other, so that the later stimuli will overlap with the after-effects of the earlier ones. An additional possibility that might be added to the

---

[24] Ibid., p. 7.
[25] M. Verworn, 1920, p. 24.

many ways of arbitrarily delimiting an impression on the real sensory organs is the inclusion of inner sensations, "frame of mind," sentiments, and "mood" in the total impression. Here it might be preferable to speak only of an over-all state of arousal.

It is of course not legitimate to delimit arbitrarily the impressions that determine the process of thought formation, since the general interpen-etration of the uptake fields allows the triggering effects of all impressions to compete with each other. Psychology, however, presented associations as something resulting from an arbitrarily limited partial impression. This sim-plification of the causes prevented it from doing justice to the resulting multi-plicity of phenomena. But if one takes as one's starting point the multifaceted general impression or the overall state of arousal in analyzing associational processes, one observes the same wealth and variety in these determinants as in the number of the resulting reproductions.

This is how we can best view the influence of this totality of impressions on the process: all components of the overall impression, both elements and nexuses, have uptake fields of their own. This means by their manifestation they excite a huge number of elements, many of which are included in sev-eral uptake fields, so that the tendencies acting on them will be reinforced. The more the composition of stimuli resembles that of a previous impression, the more strongly this combination will activate those elements linked to the previous one. Where the composition of the current impression bears a great similarity to that of the previous impression, the triggering effects of nearly all elements will be merged with those transmitting the associated impression. This will produce such a predominant activation of these elements compared to those produced by only a single or a few linkages that it alone will create an uptake field and it alone will therefore give rise to a consciousness entity.

The impulse will certainly disperse in every direction and to some extent arouse the entire brain, as is required to spark the total linkage in the brain. Every process in our consciousness that receives no external nourishment must necessarily grow steadily weaker and finally fade away. In his waking hours, however, each individual is the recipient of external impressions, which will therefore have their share in helping to determine which course our thoughts will take, which recollections are to be reawakened at any given time.

When nearly all the simultaneous impressions converge to elicit a certain consciousness content with which they were all linked at one time, the multi-plicity of associations evoked by a particular impression will be narrowed down to just one—the one which follows the same direction as the others—and only that one will have an impact. But even when there was no previous instance in which the simultaneously acting stimuli had a comparable com-position, a common relationship will emerge among the components of this combination and a main direction will prevail.

While the impressions acting simultaneously by themselves can affect the selection among the many linkages each of them possesses, even more important is the preexisting general state of arousal of the brain. The impression encounters the preestablished consciousness content (that is, "what one happens to be thinking about just then") or a given mood, and the components of these will inevitably engender other impressions, which will compete with the impression in determining the further development of the consciousness process. Since the preexisting impulses that the impression encounters are usually much richer than the ones induced by the simultaneous impressions, and since those related to thought processes are more coherent and more unidirectional than the often quite heterogeneous elements of this impression, which are likely to elicit widely diverging associations, their significance for the selection of the direction taken will be much greater.

How prior processes affect uptake is very clearly illustrated by the way in which a particular context helps to understand an impression. This context almost invariably serves to complement what is only imperfectly grasped, with the result that even an incomplete impression can produce a correct interpretation. Conversely, by making a different meaning more plausible, a context may well induce an erroneous complementation, as is best exemplified by mishearing, misperceiving, or misreading as best matches for a preceding train of thought. Everyone is familiar from his own experience with the fact that the same impression can evoke entirely different associations, depending on our different moods or our train of thoughts. No need to cite any particular examples.

One other factor helps explain this phenomenon. Multiple physiological processes carry the activated consciousness content, and their elements in turn are closely interrelated. Hence all the elements that belong to one consciousness content have common uptakes and reinforce each other when they are called into play, while isolated elements that do not share the direction taken by most of the other elements cannot prevail against them.

It is not my purpose here to describe what determines the entire trajectory in full detail, since the difficulty of this undertaking would be beyond my capacity. All that needs to be shown here is how many factors are involved in the determination of this trajectory and why the resulting possibilities are as multitudinous as the actual consciousness phenomena.

Clearly, as long as one took as one's starting point a single, partial impression or at best all stimuli acting simultaneously on a sensory organ, one was faced with an insoluble problem in trying to explain how a selection among the many available associations might actually take place. But the situation changes when one realizes that associative effects emanate from many impressions simultaneously. The basic element corresponding to the consciousness content to be elicited can therefore have access to consciousness only if it is as strongly excited as are each of the elements corresponding to the conscious impressions, so that as many stimulatory pathways must come together there as are propagated by the basic element. Consequently the only element to reach consciousness will be the one that is linked to the largest number of elements.

It is therefore completely misguided to ask which thought is elicited by a particular impression, as is always done in association experiments. Obviously impulses are transmitted to all elements connected with the impression element. All that remains to be seen is which ones then reach consciousness, and this depends on stimuli that act simultaneously (and usually have a different source) as well as on the preexisting state of arousal. How these two elements interact will then determine which associations are released. The question should therefore be phrased as follows: Which thought processes are elicited by a given impression under certain well-defined circumstances? And here the meaning and usefulness of association experiments become altogether questionable, in view of the importance of the preexisting state of arousal—which is impossible to determine—and of the difficulty in ascertaining some impression effects (inner feelings!).

If we maintain that it is essential for the uptake—the access to consciousness of an element—that the element activates all the elements associated with it, then we must also reject physiological hypotheses about "inhibition," and particularly about "chronogenic localization," as an explanation for determining which association has an impact. Sigmund Exner[26] expounded the "inhibition" hypothesis, which Verworn[27] tried to explain in an odd way by the interference of the refraction stages. The hypothesis claims that simultaneous impressions exert an inhibiting effect on associations that are not intended to be activated. Semon is the proponent of the "chronogenic localization"[28] hypothesis, according to which impressions are stored in layers in the cell, as a result of which only "engrams" belonging to the same layer can be elicited. The unfolding of consciousness processes is determined, accordingly, by which layer is reached by the impulse, as the latter must then follow the established course. This is probably an oversimplification of the concept of

[26] Sigmund Exner, *Entwurf zu einer physiologischen Erklärung der psychischen Erscheinungen* (Leipzig and Vienna: Deuticke, 1894), part 1. [Sigmund Exner (1846–1926) was an Austrian physiologist and director of the physiological institute at the University of Vienna. He was one of the first to develop a neural-network outlook of the brain. From 1867–68 he studied with Hermann von Helmholtz in Heidelberg.—Ed.]

[27] M. Verworn, 1914a, pp. 33ff.; 1920, pp. 24ff.; Max Verworn, *Erregung und Lähmung: eine allgemeine Physiologie der Reizwirkungen* (Jena: Fischer, 1914b).

[28] [The term "chronogenic localization" was introduced by the brain anatomist Constantin von Monakow, in whose Viennese institute Hayek spent the winter of 1919–20 (see above, editor's introduction, fn. 31). The term refers to the time-dependent organization of the brain.—Ed.]

an isolated sensation, which can only be explained as a result of the difficulties encountered, upon closer examination, by Semon's interpretation.—It is worth mentioning that we sometimes intentionally activate triggering mechanisms when we wish to recall a certain content into our consciousness. We try very hard to imagine a person's appearance, for instance, in order to be reminded of that person's name.

In this context we must mention a related phenomenon, namely the kind of attentiveness which consists in guiding one's thought in a direction that is preliminary to grasping an impression. This is analogous to the before-mentioned way context makes comprehension easier. Attentiveness is focused on the anticipated element, and thereby the uptaking elements are already activated from a different direction. The result is that the impact is especially intense and the consciousness content particularly well defined. This explains why attentiveness relates only to something that is anticipated, since the only field of uptake that is stimulated in advance is that of the expected element.

In combination with the previously discussed fact that apprehension is dependent on preexisting linkages ("apperception masses"),[29] attentiveness in general can be viewed as a preparation for apprehension. This is a field of investigation for psychology that is most likely to be fruitful for pedagogy. It is quite clear that the processes outlined for the simplest kind of experiences, individual sensations, can be applied quite analogously to multifaceted impressions. The fact that every human being can apprehend only those things that it is capable of uptaking, for which "apperception masses" exist, applies just as much to the apprehension of a set of ideas being communicated as to that of a single stimulus. Everyone knows that each individual person apprehends only those things that suit his character, his nature,[30] and that the same thing may have an entirely different meaning for different people. This is a self-evident consequence of the variability of all uptakes into consciousness, which makes each seem different from one another. It would take us too far afield to elaborate this point. Let us still mention Otto Weininger's[31] pointed remark that the more impact everything has on a person, the greater

---

[29] [Apperception is the mental process by which new experience is, consciously or unconsciously, integrated into an already existing mental framework. The term "apperception mass" denotes the entire system of a person's past experience into which new experience is integrated.—Ed.]

[30] Adolph Stöhr, *Psychologie* (Vienna: Braumüller, 1917). [Adolph Stöhr (1855–1921) was a professor of philosophy at the University of Vienna. On Hayek's recollections of Stöhr, see above, editor's introduction, fn. 29 and fn. 39.—Ed.]

[31] Otto Weininger, *Geschlecht und Charakter, eine prinzipielle Untersuchung*, 17th ed. (Wien: Braumüller, [1903] 1918), p. 161. [Otto Weininger (1880–1903) was an Austrian philosopher whose book *Geschlecht und Charakter (Sex and Character)* gained popularity after the author had committed suicide, at the age of 23, in the house in Vienna where Beethoven had died. Ludwig Wittgenstein was influenced by Weininger's book.—Ed.]

is his impact. Speaking of animals, Ludwig Edinger[32] characterized as "biologically adequate" those impressions for which they have an uptake based on their way of life, which have a significant meaning for their life, and which are relevant to them, a point nicely illustrated by his example of a lizard: "It is as unresponsive to a new noise that it otherwise never encounters biologically as I would be to a warning sign in Chinese that might save me from the abyss."

Apprehension therefore always depends on linkages retained from earlier relationships. An impression can thus become meaningful for an individual (become part of the consciousness content) only if the requisite receptiveness in terms of numbers and type of linkages is present. The significance of everything that was experienced at one time but has been forgotten since then ("an educated person is one who has learned a great deal and forgotten just as much") lies in its contribution to preparing apprehension. Even an experience that has been forgotten contributes to the uptake of the elements it contains as well as to their linkages to higher-level consciousness content. The fact that we can often no longer state anything definite about an experience but are perfectly capable of judging the truth or falsity of statements regarding it corroborates this finding. Attentiveness is stimulated in a special way when a composite impression recurs and is now recognized as *familiar*. In this case the impression has acquired not only the uptake corresponding to its constituent elements and its abstract content determined by specific uptakes (see below), but also certain additional linkages that relate to its first appearance. These linkages provide an "insertion into an earlier, temporally defined experiential context." This means that the "sense of familiarity," as it is generally designated, arises from an expanded uptake of the impression involved and is caused by its association with those impressions that accompanied it at the time of its previous occurrence.

The totality of these linkages, which determine the quality of each impression and the reaction it evokes, constitutes each individual's self, determines his being, his character. Just as our ability to grasp things is a function of previously acquired uptakes, all the other processes taking place in our consciousness are determined by this system. The regulation of consciousness processes is not a function of linkages created by individual experiences. It is a function of the joint action of all experiences, which manifests itself in the uptake and selection processes. To this we owe our ability to make assertions independently of concrete cases embedded in our memory and not merely to

---

[32] Ludwig Edinger, "Die Beziehungen der vergleichenden Anatomie zur vergleichenden Psychologie," Bericht des 3. Kongresses für experimentelle Psychologie, 1908 (Leipzig, 1909), pp. 9f., in which, however, he does try to distinguish between "biologically adequate stimuli" and "stimuli that only act associatively." [Ludwig Edinger (1855–1918) was a German anatomist and neurologist. Appointed in 1914 by the emperor Wilhelm II, he was the first professor of neurology in Germany.—Ed.]

reproduce specific trains of thought rigidly linked to past experiences. Herein lies the difference between understanding and knowledge. The latter term refers to firmly anchored associations, the former to the multifaceted uptake instruments, whose joint action can induce conscious results via intermediate links that do not reach a conscious level—a phenomenon that is called "intuition." It is quite encouraging to think that even knowledge that has seemingly vanished continues to have an impact and that nothing that we have ever acquired is ever completely lost.

The consciousness process set in motion by an impulse remains a mental process as long as the selection resulting from the convergence of impulses acts on experiential elements and thus gives rise to a series of reproductions. However, when impulses act on motor ganglion cells, that is, the brain's motor centers, motion will be contingent on consciousness processes. The decision as to which action to carry out, the act of will, depends just as much on uptake and selection processes as do the changes in consciousness previously described, no matter whether we carefully weigh our actions or act intuitively. An action that takes place under a given set of circumstances is thus determined by the way in which the individual takes up the impressions that he experiences, and this in turn depends on previously acquired linkages. Because of this roundabout causal effect via the whole self of the concerned individual, it is misleading to say that a given impression produces a certain reaction. The reaction is actually determined not only by the conjunction of all simultaneously acting impressions and the current state of consciousness, but also by the previously acquired uptakes. The relationship between impression and act of will is therefore multifaceted, and in addition each element in this chain is determined by an uptake, viz. a selection process. Hence the conjunction of many conditions must be met to produce a given result. In living creatures, memory inevitably introduces complications into the simple causal nexus. The concept of causality, which in this connection would result in a mechanistic interpretation, is replaced here by the concept of uptake, which posits a complex, indirect dependence of all conscious reactions on the triggering impression. In its eagerness to explain mental life by the application of the more simplistic relationships that are generally adequate in the physical sciences, psychology has ended up discrediting all physiological hypotheses. And in general, all scientific attempts to explain biological phenomena tend to founder on this primitive interpretation of causality.

The question of free will depends on what one means by an individual who is the subject of free will. If the individual, as argued here, is identified with his self, his consciousness and memory, the question is easily resolved. The question is: "Who decides an act of will—external interventions or . . . ?" Well, what about this "or"? On the basis of what we have just stated, this "or" is the individual's memory, which means previously experienced impressions.

The individual's memory enables it to respond to impressions in a specific way, according to his individual past and that of his species. But this is precisely what Aristotle already asserted in his remark that free will simply means that human beings are guided in their actions by their own nature.[33] Surely we can want to do only those things that occur to us—and for which of several emerging possibilities we opt, which conception is translated into an action, depends just as much on a selective conjunction of impulse pathways as does the preceding conjunction of elements that become conscious as memory.

Aside from uptakes, which we owe primarily to our past experiences, there is a second category that is of the greatest importance for determining conduct, namely emotions. The James-Lange theory of emotions[34] must be viewed as a precursor of the interpretation advanced by us here. The theory parallels our overall approach to the contents of consciousness: like our theory, it too considers the most important aspect of a sensory excitation that provokes emotion—not the sensory excitation itself but the resonance it evokes. That is what counts for the consciousness quality. James is of the opinion[35] that emotion itself is nothing but the awareness that a change symptomatic of a reaction has taken place. Paradoxical as it may sound, "the more rational statement is that we feel sorry because we cry, angry because we strike, afraid because we tremble and not that we cry, strike, or tremble because we are sorry, angry, or fearful." Just think how easily we can generate all sorts of moods in ourselves by mimicry, how we can make ourselves feel grief by crying, etc., and this assumption ceases to be implausible. Only one rectification of James's theory is required. Resonance does not, as he states, enter consciousness directly; it only accounts for its emotional quality. We are confronted here with an uptake by means of inherited linkages to motor reactions (actually innervations[36] originating in the brain generally), reactions that may in earlier times have served to ward off or reinforce certain impressions.[37]

---

[33] *Nicomachean Ethics*, III. i. 20: ". . . a voluntary act would seem to be an act of which the origin lies in the agent. . . ."

[34] [See above, *TSO*, 4.70, fn. 14.—Ed.]

[35] William James, *Principles of Psychology* (London: Macmillan, 1890), vol. 2, pp. 448ff. He characterizes the core of his own theory in the following terms on pp. 451f.: "If we fancy some strong emotion, and then try to abstract from our consciousness of it all the feelings of its bodily symptoms, we find we have nothing left behind. . . . What kind of an emotion of fear would be left if the feeling neither of quickened heart-beats nor of shallow breathing, neither of trembling lips nor of weakened limbs, neither of goose-flesh nor of visceral stirrings, were present, it is quite impossible for me to think. Can one fancy the state of rage and picture no ebullitions in the chest, no flushing of the face, no dilation of the nostrils, no clenching of the teeth, no impulse to vigorous action, but in their stead limp muscles, calm breathing and a placid face?"

[36] [The term "innervation" denotes the stimulation of a muscle or organ by nerves.—Ed.]

[37] In the section on the genesis of emotional reactions, James (ibid., p. 478) states: "Some movements of expression can be accounted for as weakened repetitions of movements which

Since different impressions may have provoked similar reactions, the same network of reactions is linked to different impressions and has thus become a generalized consciousness content, which may be released by stimuli that otherwise provoke quite dissimilar uptakes. We again encounter this phenomenon of a *generalized consciousness content*, under which experiential contents of various kinds are subsumed, when dealing with abstraction and conceptualization. Because of the fact that abstraction and conceptualization are difficult to explain in any other way, the phenomenon has given rise to a theory related to ours. The reason that the recognition of similarities or abstraction is fraught with difficulties is because the consciousness quality of each individual element fails to explain how a constellation of elements (such as a Gestalt) can possess a completely new quality that differs from the sum of the individual impressions, a quality that may even belong to some other constellation, which is independent of these impressions. What gives rise to this creative synthesis (Wundt), which underlies abstraction? The hypothesis of identical associated phenomena, of which E. Mach is the leading proponent, offers the explanation that, as Kries formulates it, "the essential feature of a visible shape, for instance, does not lie in the specific nature of the optical sensation as such but rather in evoked changes in motor mechanisms, which have been designated as innervation stimuli, muscular sensations, etc."[38] E. Mach elaborates this point by his comment that "the same muscular sensations must manifest themselves when shapes that are identical appear in different colors, if the shapes are to be recognized as identical. In the same way, specific conceptions must underlie all shapes, not to say all abstractions. This applies to space and shapes, as it does to time, rhythm, pitch, melody, intensity, etc."[39]

Here too an effort is made to shift psychic qualities from the basic triggering stimulus to its resonance, which can of course be acquired in the same way from physiologically different impulses. This automatically answers the question whether dissimilar consciousness uptakes can be subsumed under one

---

formerly (when they were stronger) were of utility to the subjects. Others are similarly weakened repetitions of movements which under other conditions were physiologically necessary effects." James also gives interesting examples from Spencer, Darwin, Wundt, and Mantegazza. [Paolo Mantegazza (1831–1910) was an Italian neurologist, physiologist, and anthropologist. He was a pioneer in psychopharmacology, carrying out experimental research on the effects of coca and other psychotropic drugs.—Ed.]

[38] J. v. Kries, 1898, p. 35.

[39] E. Mach, 1903, p. 122. [It may be worth mentioning that Mach had dedicated his *Populärwissenschaftliche Vorlesungen* to William James with "sympathy and respect."—Ed.] On the whole, despite E. Mach's totally different views, his works must be designated quite specifically as precursors of the theory advanced here. Mach came very close to it by his way of dissociating the various mental formations. His general philosophical approach, in which sensations constituted the sole firm elements of existence, was undoubtedly what held him back from taking this final step.

heading. Abstraction constitutes a special problem only if consciousness characteristics are specifically attributed to and considered dependent on physiological elements. It is, in particular, the *Lokalzeichen* theory that stands in the way of a physiological explanation of Gestalt perception. If we assume a relative spatial quality, as we do, the problem is automatically solved.

Constellations of elements, which always represent the impressions underlying abstractions, can of course yield uptakes as easily as do individual elements. A similar sectional sample of the uptake field of these constellations, such as motion associated with it, is then responsible for conveying similarity and represents the content of an abstract concept. Adolph Stöhr[40] elaborates Mach's hypothesis by explaining the formation of concepts by identity of reactions. He explains concept formation itself as a reaction that extends to all the impressions constituting the conceptual field. It can thus be viewed as a common component in their field of uptake, once they have been summated or "grasped." This solves the puzzle of how entirely different representations or experiential contents can be subsumed under a single concept, since the linkage with the one reaction in question, which (contrary to what Stöhr says) must itself always be conceived as a constellation, can perfectly well be shared by impressions with quite different uptakes. In this respect it makes sense to envisage concepts and emotions alike as a generalized consciousness content. In both cases the relationships to the organs of motion constitute the main shared component selected in the uptake. The latter can also become an autonomous consciousness content by its connections with the impressions in whose field of uptake it appears. In the case of emotions, however, associations are always induced by inherited associations, so that experience can at most contribute to its linkage with eliciting impressions. Reactions determining concepts, by contrast, must be acquired individually or are at best indirectly inherited through the acquisition of language, etc. One might therefore call emotions inherited concepts as well.

Let us now, on the basis of the previous findings, attempt to establish the conditions for the development of consciousness of a subject. At this point it becomes self-evident that the contents of consciousness can solely arise from excitatory processes in the brain, since this is the only place where the necessary connections can be established with the totality of excitations. Consciousness presupposes the existence of a central nervous system, in which information about all stimuli received by a living being aggregates. Such an organ does not exist in primitive organisms. At the lowest developmental level, there are no special mechanisms for transmitting stimuli, so that excitations can only be transmitted from tissue to tissue, or else transmission is limited to the connection of certain organs, but without a centralized system. Such a sys-

[40] A. Stöhr, 1917, p. 357.

tem can arise only when nerve impulses are organized around a central pathway, but here too, at this developmental level, linkage is limited to individual impulse tracks; there is no central organ where interconnections can be established. The nerves of individual organs merge their ganglion cells in small centers, through which the excitations of that particular organ acquire a joint meaning, that is, a joint influence is exerted by reciprocal links to the reactions (reflexes) that are connected with them. It is only in the case of vertebrates that the special centers of vision, hearing, smell, and taste, which are located at one end of the central nervous pathway, are converted more and more into a generalized center where all stimuli that have been received are recorded. The cerebrum, which assumes this particular function within this part of the central nervous system, becomes the most powerful component of the whole system. Its size serves as an approximate yardstick for the advances made in this centralization process and for this particular living organism's capacity to develop consciousness.[41] The fact that this development, which goes hand in hand with centralization, is among the preconditions for consciousness is further evidence that the essence of memory must be sought not in the individual cell (the "engram") but in the connections between cells. "Consequently the concept of an 'atomic unit of consciousness' [what we have designated here as the concept of an isolated sensation] is self-contradictory. Only the connectedness of life is responsible for and maintains consciousness, which is largely connectedness, unity within multiplicity."[42]

To clarify the basic features of the development of consciousness, one must revert to the ideal preconditions for its original manifestation, that is, the existence of a central organ of this sort, in which all stimuli arising simultaneously have an equal chance to create connections between the appropriate ganglion cells, but where the central organ itself has not yet received any stimuli, so that a new stimulus remains completely isolated for lack of any preestablished connection. Here a network encompassing the linkages between all the elements of the nervous system could take shape purely on the basis of

[41] In 1809 Lamarck already pointed out the parallelism between the development of the nervous system and the development of consciousness. [Jean-Baptist Lamarck (1744–1829) was a French naturalist and an early proponent of a theory of organic evolution. In his main work, *Philosophie zoologique, ou exposition des considérations relatives à l'histoire naturelle des animaux* (Paris: Dentu, 1809), 2 vols., he argued that evolution is propelled by two forces: a "complexifying force" that leads to more complex forms in the living world, and an "adaptive force" that causes animals to adapt to the challenges they face in their respective environments, due to the use or disuse of certain organs. Lamarck claimed that characteristics animals acquire through such use or disuse of organs are inheritable, a claim that is in contrast to Charles Darwin's theory of evolution by natural selection.—Ed.]

[42] Alois Riehl, *Zur Einführung in die Philosophie der Gegenwart, Eight Lectures*, 5th ed. (Leipzig and Berlin: Teubner, [1903] 1919), p. 139. See also the same author's *Der philosophische Kritizismus* (Leipzig: Engelmann, 1876–87), 2 vols.; F. Jodl, 1908; and B. v. Carneri, 1893.

individual experience. In its wake every single impression would induce an increasingly well-defined uptake. No living organism, however, can ever experience such a starting point for its individual development, because the evolution of its progenitors has already shaped its brain in such a way that certain pathways have been smoothed in advance or perhaps even from the very start guaranteed the transmission of impulses between certain elements. This should not prevent us, in a theoretical exploration of the development of consciousness, from starting out at its original creation, even though, through the genetically acquired foundations of consciousness, heritable pathways and hence uptakes are always present from the very beginning.[43]

The problem of consciousness must be approached by a developmental theory, as has already been frequently observed.[44] It is the task of a theory of the development of consciousness to explain how a system of qualities that encompasses the impressions of all sensory organs is formed by experience, given the preconditions cited above. It must explain how its fundamental, ever reasserted makeup is a function of the regularities of nature, and how its specific elaboration in individual beings results from the kind of experiences encountered and the order of their appearance. The theory will have to concern itself primarily with repetitive experiences, be it those that each individual encounters in the same way, or be it uptakes that may have been acquired once and for all in the history of the species and which constitute the basis of all consciousness activity. The theory must also demonstrate how physiological elements are converted into relatively simple consciousness uptakes and how these are linked together by experience into ever more multifaceted and differentiated uptakes. We have made a modest attempt to show that it is the same process which links together simpler consciousness contents with more complex ones and which also elevates to psychic events those that the individ-

[43] It is a different question, however, whether, as a result of the anatomic construction of the human brain, especially through the position of the various sensory centers, certain connections can arise at an earlier stage and therefore receive preferential treatment, whereas other connections are harder to establish or must rely on indirect means, perhaps only through connecting ganglions.

[44] As to the need for a developmental psychology, see the following in addition to the passage from Wundt quoted in the text: Carneri, 1893, p. 16: "The only way we can learn the circumstances under which consciousness arises is genetically"; O. Weininger, 1918, p. 159: "What has been attempted here is a mere hint of what can be done by ontogenetic psychology or theoretical biography, which will sooner or later supplant today's sciences of the human mind." Literature is particularly abundant with respect to specific psychological developmental problems. Let us mention particularly F. Krüger (ed.), *Arbeiten zur Entwicklungspsychologie*, 1915, notably the first issue of the collection *Über Entwicklungspsychologie, ihre sachliche und geschichtliche Notwendigkeit*, authored by Krüger himself; further M. Verworn, 1920. Georges Bohn, *Die Entstehung des Denkvermögens: Eine Einführung in die Tierpsychologie* (Leipzig: Thomas, 1910), translated from the French original *La Naissance de l'Intelligence* (Paris: Flammarion, 1909), informs about related problems of animal psychology. [Georges Bohn (1868–1948) was a French biologist.—Ed.]

ual is unable to recognize as such. If I have succeeded in making the process of consciousness uptake comprehensible, the next task will be to classify the immensely rich material that science has collected about the development of consciousness according to the principle underlying this process. It will then be possible to fulfil, as Wundt[45] expresses it, "the only task which at present psychological theory can tackle with any hope of success, a synthetically presented developmental history." Yet it will have to be not a history of the development of consciousness, but only its theory, a schema for the development of all consciousness processes, which allows one to grasp the essence of each individual process. A precondition for such an attempt was the resolution of the one question that confronts us with all consciousness phenomena: How does consciousness arise at all? When I first recognized that the problem of the development of consciousness held the key to the questions about consciousness, I had the intention of presenting this development, starting with the simplest existing consciousness uptakes, until I recognized, in the course of these investigations, that the process whereby consciousness as a whole is created from "psychic elements" is identical in nature to the physiological process whereby consciousness uptake is created. Up to a point the old associative psychology was right in trying to explain all psychic phenomena from associations, since it turned out that the "primordial" qualities of sensations and feelings, and hence all consciousness uptakes, are based on association—in a different way, to be sure, than the upholders of this theory believed. It is not the psychic capacity of association to deal with psychic qualities, but rather a process that is part of the natural order of things as a whole, which enables physiological processes to induce consciousness uptakes.

It may be carrying empiricism to extremes to derive even the interrelationship between sensations from experience, yet at the same time this interpretation serves to mitigate the abrasiveness of empiricism, inasmuch as experiences conveyed to us through sensations must always stay within these interrelationships and thereby acquire a certain aprioristic character. These aprioristic laws are then the inherent interrelationships that govern all our experiences, so that our thinking, which is created by them, is in turn subjected to them. It would, however, be extremely presumptuous for man to equate this world with the totality of all that has ever happened and to try to impose thereon the laws of his own thinking. This would mean pitting his mind—which merely reflects his own consciousness—as an independent or even superior entity against this totality, just as he pits his own body—which he experiences only indirectly through his sensations—against the psychic processes that he experiences directly. This represents a residual anthropo-

---

[45] Wilhelm Wundt, *Grundzüge der physiologischen Psychologie*, 5th ed. (Leipzig: Engelmann, [1874] 1902–3), vol. 2., p. 641.

morphism, which is deeply rooted in human thinking. After endowing each little particle of nature with a manlike spirit, then limiting itself to the organic realm, anthropomorphism has had to give more and more ground. Here there remained a final opportunity to contrast nature as a whole with something in keeping with man's soul. As long as our knowledge was considered to be absolute and our worldview to encompass all existence, a materialism regarding all existence that, after all, can be grasped only in a form that is compatible with our mind, must have seemed a dreary theory. Once we recognize, however, that the totality of existence is the infinite source from which a miniscule segment—a living being—acquires uptaking relationships with those aspects of existence that concern it, we will cease to think of our limited minds as standing outside of or even above existence. Thus all the solid components from which an autonomous mind was to be constructed have now been demolished. The a priori structures of apperception (*Anschauungsformen*) posited by Kant have been overturned primarily by Ernst Mach, and now Mach's elements, sensations, may have suffered the same fate in the light of the reflections presented here.

Addendum

Since the completion of this study a year ago, in September 1920, the following publications concerning the above problems have been published and have come to my attention. Let me refer to them expressly here.

Bleuler, Eugen. *Die Naturgeschichte der Seele und ihres Bewusstwerdens: Eine Elementarpsychologie.* Berlin: Springer, 1921.

Hoffmann, Franz Bruno. "Die physiologischen Grundlagen der Bewusstseinsvorgänge." *Die Naturwissenschaften*, vol. 9 (1921): pp. 165–72.

Matthaei, Rupprecht. "Von den Theorien über eine allgemein-physiologische Grundlage des Gedächtnisses." Reprint from *Zeitschrift für allgemeine Physiologie*. Vol. 19(1/2). Jena: Fischer, 1920.

WHAT IS MIND?

It may seem presumptuous for a mere economist to address a problem over which philosophers and psychologists have labored for so long and with so little success. Yet the subject of my talk is nothing less than the old problem of the relation between body and mind, between the material and the mental—a problem that has gone somewhat out of fashion today because specialists consider it as either nonexistent, unsuitable for scientific investigation, or insoluble. Yet when a social scientist takes up such a question, he is infringing less on other disciplines than might appear at first sight. Any serious reflection on the nature of the methods of the social sciences and particularly on the relationship of these methods with those of the natural sciences must inevitably lead to this basic question. This applies all the more to someone like myself who, for the last thirty years, has coupled his work in one of the social sciences with a strong interest in physiological psychology. Under these circumstances, you may find it less mystifying that I have chosen this topic for a conference on the frontiers of science.

In this connection, I should tell you at once that the title that I have chosen for this lecture is actually misleading and inappropriate. In my view, in raising the question about the nature ["*Wesen*" in German] of a phenomenon you are not addressing a genuine scientific problem at all. My excuse for using this expression, for lack of a better short title, is that the main difficulty, in my opinion, lies in the failure to state the problem clearly up to now. As is often the case in science, what is most crucial is a proper formulation of the ques-

[The original unpublished German version, "Das Wesen des Geistigen," had been prepared for the fifth Internationale Hochschulwochen in Alpbach, Austria, August 20 to September 9, 1949. The undated typescript is kept in the Hayek Archives at the Hoover Institution, box 104, folder 20. Dr. Grete Heinz has translated the article for the present edition. As Hayek indicates at the beginning of the second paragraph of the essay, he had misgivings about the German title. It seems likely that he chose it for want of a better translation of the title of his 1947 typescript, "What Is Mind?," which was to become *The Sensory Order* (see above, editor's introduction, p. 11). This is the reason why translator and editor decided to adopt "What Is Mind?" as the title for this essay instead of trying for a literal translation of the original German title, "Das Wesen des Geistigen."—Ed.]

tion, and I hope to be able to show you that once we can agree on what we really want to know, it will not be so difficult to find an answer, at least in principle. My lecture will therefore be primarily concerned with how to formulate the question. It would have been more accurate, in fact, to choose an awkward title such as "The Nature of the Mind-Body Problem." We must first clarify what we mean by the "relation" between "mental" and "material" and how mental processes differ from material ones before we can profitably undertake an "explanation" of their relationship.

Scientific thinking is always in great jeopardy when we accept everyday concepts as self-evident and take it for granted that they designate clearly distinguishable phenomena. This holds true particularly for our topic. All we know about the material world is the result of our own mental processes; on the other hand, the only way that we can grasp the existence of mental processes that are not our own is through material events. From a certain perspective, the mental and material are always interconnected and our first task must be to determine how we can speak at all about two distinctive realms. It seems to me that only after the most modern advances in the natural sciences, particularly in physics, have sharply defined what we call material or physical are we able to delimit a clear realm of phenomena that we must designate, by contrast to the former, as mental or psychic.

Suppose our nervous system had the exclusive function of perceiving our current environment. We would then lack both the incentive and the possibility to distinguish between the mental and the material. Knowing about the material world only through our perception, we could legitimately conclude that whatever we perceived would match corresponding material events. The two realms would be identical, and there would be no way to differentiate between them. Our belief in a special world of mental phenomena is derived from the fact that our experiences are largely independent of perception. We have visual memories, images, hallucinations, etc.; we think and feel without having the objects of these experiences correspond to our current surroundings. This independent experience of the mental realm—this occurrence of mental processes that represent events in the external world without their being presumed to be present concurrently—is what first gives rise to the distinction between the mental and the material.

But how do we know when our experiences are true perceptions and when they are mere images? How do we differentiate, in other words, between purely mental processes and our experiences in the material world? The answer to this question is of considerable importance because it is essentially an extension of the same basic procedure that originally helped us distinguish between "illusion" and "reality," which later led to the establishment of the natural sciences.

There is a very simple first answer. The way we can determine that something we see is only in "our mind's eye," that it is just an image or an illusion, is by our being incapable of also touching or smelling it. To ascertain whether an experience is "real," we insist on validating it with our other senses as well. What persuades us that a material object is currently present and not merely a figment of the mind is the concurrent imprint it leaves on all our various senses, thus confirming the expectations to which such a sensory experience gives rise.

We have kept refining this conscious verification of whether "appearances" correspond to the expectations we connect with them and have developed it into what we now call science. At first the only objective was to determine whether what we were seeing or hearing was "actually" present. But this is not an intrinsically different problem from determining whether what we believe we are seeing really *is* the very thing that our eyes lead us to believe. Two things may look visually identical but may turn out to be different when we touch or lift them. And to this verification by means of our other senses we soon add control through the observation of how things behave under artificially produced conditions. Two things may seem similar to all our senses, but when we bring them into contact with various other things, they may act differently in relation to them. Experiments are in truth an extension of the method whereby we first distinguish between appearance and reality. Two chemicals may be exactly identical when exposed to all ours senses, but if under certain circumstances they react differently, we learn in the process that two things that look at first alike should be considered as two different things.

In this sense, the entire development of the natural sciences can be envisaged as a continuous process of reorganization or, better yet, of reclassification of objects within our range of experience. Things that seemed identical to us at first now acquire different meanings, and things that at first seemed quite different from each other may turn out to be very similar or even identical. The process of reordering the world in line with scientific findings typically marginalizes those sensory qualities that were at first at the core of our differentiation between various things and eventually eliminates them altogether. While we at first distinguished among various things or classified them according to how they appeared to us in isolation, we gradually learned to distinguish them by the way that they behave in relation to other things. Ideally, in the final phase of this process, salt, for instance, would no longer be a white powder with a certain taste, etc., but something that, in contact with other objects, produces certain results. And inasmuch as all these other objects are similarly identified only by their relations with other objects and not by their sensory qualities, and so forth, eventually sensory qualities of objects would disappear from our worldview. From the purely scientific perspective, from this physical view of the world, objects would be defined exclusively by their interrelations with each other, not by their relation to us, that is, by their sensory qualities.

The development of the natural sciences in the direction of this ideal presents psychology with a totally new set of problems that it has not yet fully recognized. We are familiar with two different organizations of the same world: the order of our world of sensory experiences, in which things are red, warm, sweet, etc., and the order of the physical world. Here objects are distinguished from one another in an entirely different way: what is the same for our senses turns out to be different, and what seems distinctive to us must be considered identical.

The elimination of sensory qualities from the physical worldview does not simultaneously eliminate them as a scientific problem. If the world looks different, from the point of view of physical observation, than it looks to us, the problem remains why this is how it appears to us. At the same time that the system of sensory qualities disappears from physics, it becomes a problem in psychology. In the face of the order of physical objects that natural science reveals to us, what is the proper place of that other order of sensory experiences, with whose help the human organism orients itself in this physical world?

By highlighting the nature of sensory qualities as a characteristic problem of mental processes, I do not wish to imply, of course, that sensory responses to colors, sounds, forms, etc., are the only kind of mental processes with which we have to deal. All I mean to say is that they belong to the same mental realm as images, concepts, feelings, etc., and that the typical problem with respect to mental processes already manifests itself in the fact that the world *appears* to us in a certain order that, on closer inspection, proves to be different from the order in which things manifest themselves by their interactions. Once we succeed in explaining the structure of the sensory world, once we manage to show how an organism within nature learns to differentiate or organize in a particular way what goes on in his surroundings, as we do with our senses, the larger part of our problem will have been solved.

The concept of two different orders by which we grasp what happens in the world is of such great significance that it deserves fuller presentation. It implies no less than that in referring to mental and to physical aspects we envisage the same events, on the one hand, as elements of an order or a system within which these elements differ in a particular way from the other elements of the same order, and, on the other hand, as elements of a different order within which they differ from each other in a manner different from the first. It is beyond doubt that we are in fact confronted by two such differing orders. Psychologists exploring sensory perceptions organize them in terms of their similarity and dissimilarity in a multidimensional edifice that is very different from the way in which physicists organize the corresponding stimuli. For physicists events in the external world are evaluated in terms of the similarity or dissimilarity of their effects on other events. The color octahedron, the touch pyramid, and the smell prism,[1] with whose help psychologists represent the different dimensions along which the related sensory qualities can vary, reveal a structure that is in many ways similar to that of the system by which physicists organize the corresponding stimuli, but there are also differences. Visible light waves, for instance, vary along a continuum in an increasing linear order going from 400 to 760 millimicrons. The color sensations they evoke, on the contrary, vary not only stepwise but circularly, because, as far as the eye is concerned, violet at one end of the spectrum is a transition to red at the other end of the spectrum.

The only relative novelty of this approach is the recognition that the ordering of the sensory world or of the phenomenal world as such—the ordering of sensory qualities—ceases to be a physics problem and turns into a psychology problem. It is converted into a problem of how the mental order, which also encompasses our abstract concepts, our feelings, etc., comes into being.

But what constitutes this "order" of mental events or qualities, and in what sense can we "explain" this order or how it comes into being? This is the point where I anticipate the strongest disagreement and where I hardly hope to be able to present an adequate argument in favor of my point of view in a short lecture. It is my contention that there is a parallelism between physical processes and mental processes. In both cases, distinctions between identical and different events are based on the difference or similarity of their interactions. Therefore, if we can explain in what way and why given mental processes differ from other mental processes in that, in combination with different mental processes, they trigger further mental processes, we will have explained not only everything susceptible to explanation but everything requiring an explanation.

To make things as easy to understand as possible, I will restrict myself to certain sensory qualities as examples of mental processes. Effectively, I am asserting that the only things that need to be explained about the experience of a certain red color or of a certain sound are the differences in the impact that the appearance of this specific sensation, rather than some other sensation, has on all other mental processes, under every conceivable circumstance. In this sense the order of sensory qualities is a causal order, an order that is based on the various effects of sensory qualities; and there is no question about the "nature" or the "character" of sensory qualities that cannot also be formulated as a question as to how their effects differ from all other sensory qualities. In this sense, all differences between the many sorts of mental processes are relative, and, once we have explained their difference from each

[1] [See above, *TSO*, 1.45, fn. 26, 27, 28.—Ed.]

other in the effects they exert on each other, we have explained everything in need of an explanation.

So far, however, I have not given even a clue as to how we can possibly explain this order. I have addressed myself only to the question of what needs to be explained. The answer to this question is that we are dealing with a structure, an order in which all the different elements are exclusively defined by their relations to each other. From that we must conclude that we are dealing with a closed system, that we define the character of certain mental processes entirely by its relation to other mental processes, but that we never go beyond the mental realm. Yet how shall we "explain" these mental processes? Only by breaking out of the vicious circle in which we are locked. Is it possible to make such a transition from the mental to the material realm?

We find the key to the answer in our description of the mental realm as an order or a structural linkage in which relations between mental elements are causal relations. Having thus defined the nature of the mental realm, we can now in principle construct strictly equivalent structures from known physical elements that accomplish exactly the same thing in all relevant relationships that behave exactly like the order that we know as the mental realm. The identity of two structures, based on the relationships between elements that are intrinsically quality free, is called "isomorphism" in the mathematical disciplines that deal with this problem. What I am asserting is that, if we succeed in demonstrating the presence of structural relationships in human organisms that are isomorphous with the structural relationships in the mental realm, we have gone as far as we can in "explaining" the mental realm. If we can construct a system of physical events in which the manner that the various constellations of mental experiences interact with each other can be copied or reproduced exactly, this system will then allow us at the same time to explain everything that we usually explain with reference to mental processes as a result of physical processes.

In truth, in the vertebrate central nervous system and particularly in the highly developed human cerebrum, we find precisely an organ that is suitable for maintaining and reproducing extremely complex structural relationships between a huge number of elementary physiological events. There is no need for me to go into the physiological details here, and I will do no more than outline here the following two major points:

1) Between the millions of sensory nerve fibers by means of which impulses triggered by external stimuli are conducted to the brain and the millions of motor nerve fibers by means of which, conversely, impulses that trigger motion are conducted from the brain to the periphery, there exists a system of additional tens of thousands of millions of nerve cells whereby the differentiated human actions are transmitted.

2) In a way that is still entirely unexplained, connections are created between nerve cells in which impulses appear simultaneously with the effect that when an impulse later appears in only one of the cells, it is transferred to the cells with which it is connected.

This is all we need to know to be able to sketch out how, as a result of external inputs experienced by the organism, a system of relations between the impulses acting on the various cells can be built up, in which the significance of specific impulses is distinguished from that of other impulses exactly in the way that we need to build up a system of sensory qualities.

It will certainly not come as a surprise to you that any further attempt to give you a detailed and realistic representation of this apparatus would be extremely complicated and cumbersome, and that I must therefore limit myself to an extremely crude simplification. For this purpose I think it is most useful to view the central nervous system as a mechanism for "classifying" the impulses that it receives and the nerve impulses that are triggered by them. You will grasp immediately in what sense I am using the term "classification" and how, in the process of this classification, the "order" of impulses that I wish to explain manifests itself.

It may seem to you at first that the term "classification" introduced here is nothing more than an overblown name for triggering a nerve cell's excitation by the excitation of another nerve cell. It is true that this definition applies perfectly to the simplest possible case—namely, when several cells establish connections with one or several similar other cells. When any one of the former cells is excited, this excitation will be transmitted to the similar other cells, and thus the former cells must belong to the same "class." This way of putting it is correct but not particularly revealing. It is true that if a group of cells has all its connections with these same other cells, excitation of any one of them obviously has the same functional meaning and is indistinguishable in its effect from the excitation of any other cell belonging to the group.

The story becomes interesting only when we take into account that (1) a given cell may belong not only to one "class" but to a large number of different "classes" because it has not just one connection but a multitude of connections with additional cells, which may in turn have many connections with various other cells, which it may then have in common with many other cells; (2) not only the excitation of individual cells but the excitation of various groups of cells can similarly form well-defined "classes"; and (3) the excitation of additional cells, which constitutes in a way the act of classification— because their being triggered by excitation in any one of a group of other cells converts them into a class—in turn can become the object of an act of classification, so that we obtain classes of classes and classes of classes of classes. I find this interpretation of the whole system as a classification device particularly useful as a way of obtaining an overview, at least in principle, of the many forms of connection that can exist between individual events and the order that these connections between them create, or the functional differentiations that they create.

Does this bring us any closer to our objective? I believe it does. If, as I asserted earlier, it is possible to represent the order of sensory qualities and other mental events in a truly exhaustive way by summarizing all the differences in their impacts on other mental events and on human behavior, we can conceptually build a strongly equivalent physical system from the material that the central nervous system offers us, such that the latter can unequivocally be seen as a copy of the former and can accomplish everything that the former accomplishes. These two systems or orders are identical exclusively with respect to their structural equivalence. However, since the significance of individual processes lies entirely in their position in this structural connection and does not in the least depend on material properties they possess on their own and in isolation, structural identity as such is sufficient to explain one system on the basis of the other. For our purpose, for instance, it is quite indifferent what material properties the individual excitation processes in the nervous system possess, whether they are chemical or electrical in nature. In theory, we could also envision other physical systems rather than specifically the central nervous system, systems that are constructed of other kinds of elements, but which, because they have the same structure, will also achieve the same result. This is precisely what I meant at the beginning of my talk when I emphasized that the nature of mental processes lies in a certain order of events and that, when we can explain how such an order is created, the properties of the elements between which the order exists are uninteresting. We can also express this same idea by stating that only those "properties" of the elements that are determined by their position in the structure of the whole edifice are relevant and that other properties that they "intrinsically" possess and that we usually describe as their "material" properties are insignificant.

All this has very interesting consequences with respect to sensory qualities. Psychology remains strongly under the sway of the old concept that the appearance of certain "elementary" sensations corresponds to the stimulation of certain nerve cells. This attribution of presumably isolated sensations to presumably isolated stimuli inevitably presented an insoluble problem. If my view is correct, however, there is no such thing as simple and pure sensation that can be attributed to the stimulation of specific nerves. A specific nerve stimulation acquires links with other stimulations of the same kind only gradually, after they have been incorporated into the structural relationship; they achieve a certain quality only after this incorporation has taken place. It is not the case that we initially have isolated sensations that are organized into a system by experience. "Experience," in the physiological sense of creating connections between nerve stimulations occurring simultaneously, precedes the appearance of sensory qualities and first has to create this very relational system that determines sensory qualities. It is of the greatest philosophical importance—to whose significance I will revert at the end of my talk—that we are faced with a sort of pre-sensory or pre-perceptive experience that precedes the qualitative differentiation of sensations and therefore all conscious experience, so that the system of sensory qualities is itself founded on experience and in a constant state of flux.

Before I turn to these philosophical conclusions resulting from this whole approach, I must still try to show that this classification apparatus (my simplified interpretation of the nervous system) gives rise not only to "concrete" perceptions related to sensory qualities but also to the creation of abstract mental experience, as seen in the perception of configurations (*Gestalten*) and in the formation of concepts. On the basis of our interpretation, these "higher" mental processes actually do not raise any new problem. Once sensory experiences are not viewed as inexplicable "reproductions" of external objects but as acts of classification undertaken by the brain or mind on the basis of prior experiences, there is nothing basically new about the fact that this same apparatus is capable of further organization of not only individual events but also groups or classes of events. Abstractions such as configurations (*Gestalten*) or concepts are a novel problem only when we envision them as somehow composed of elementary sensory experiences or as having been derived from them. Once we have accepted the fact that the so-called "simple" sensations are the result of a classification process, nothing stands in the way of accepting that, just as individual nerve stimuli correspond to specific stimuli, groups of such stimuli can be classified analogously and can assume a group meaning that is in no way dependent on the meaning of the individual stimuli arising in isolation.

I pointed out earlier how the kind of classification apparatus that I envisage can form not only classes, but classes of classes and classes of classes of classes and so on. We know from logic that we can thereby erect ever more abstract edifices—and it is probably no accident that our psychological disquisitions about the nature of mental processes quite naturally led us to use the same concepts as those that logic applies to the process for reaching conclusions.

All this is of course only a very incomplete sketch of a theory of which details still need to be fully worked out before it can be convincing or even more than very partially understandable. But instead of bothering you with a few further details that could contribute little to round off the picture within the time at my disposal, I prefer to draw your attention to various philosophical consequences that the confirmation of the theory I have outlined here would imply. These consequences are much more far-reaching and interesting than you are likely to expect at first thought. In fact they are so far-reaching that I will limit myself to the most important ones, and, even in their case, be extremely brief. I will start out by outlining the consequences of this theory for assessing the basic claims of pure empiricism, phenomenalism, and dualism. I will then explore quickly in what sense and to what extent the theory that I have presented offers an "explanation" of mental processes and to what extent any such complete explanation is attainable. In all these respects the result will be paradoxical. In a sense, the theory I have outlined can be viewed as purely naturalistic, maybe even as a sort of extreme naturalism some of you might find repugnant. The strange thing is that the philosophical conclusions that result from this consistent naturalism lead to almost diametrically opposite conclusions from those that are commonly drawn from it and are more similar to those that are usually drawn by the opponents of naturalism.

First of all, let us consider the significance of our interpretation for the basic tenets of pure empiricism. It agrees with empiricism in assuming that all our knowledge stems from experience. But according to our interpretation, a large part of this knowledge stems from a strange kind of experience: one that antecedes conscious sensation and perception and that first creates that order of nerve stimuli that gives them a conscious value or significance. Conscious experience thus presupposes the existence of an order that is indeed created by a sort of pre-conscious or pre-perceptive experience, but which itself is not accessible by conscious experience. Every experience thus implies an inclusion into an existing system that must be considered as given and that is incapable of being falsified by experience. Kant's categories are here resurrected as ordering principles that the organism does indeed acquire via the kind of impact of the outside world that I call pre-perceptive experience, but which themselves then become a condition of any conscious experience and cannot on their part be verified thereby.

However, the whole order that we call mental as well as the values of the various mental qualities that are exclusively determined by their position in such an order are continually, though slowly, altered by all new experiences. That means that sensory qualities in particular do not remain constant, but on the contrary are subject to constant change (in their interrelationships). As a consequence, the phenomenal world shown by our senses is itself not constant but subject to constant change. This negates the ideal goal of phenomenalism (positivism) to turn science into a pure description of nature. Every new experience incorporates a change in the way we "see" nature, by a reclassification of objects, thereby influencing all our subsequent experiences. The fact that the abstract picture of nature erected by science changes even faster than the image presented by our senses should not make us forget that the latter is not constant either but changeable in turn.

The third point that I would like to mention briefly is the relationship of my theory to dualism. My theory is antidualist and could therefore be described as materialistic, but that would be an erroneous way of looking at it. It is dualism that actually thinks in materialistic terms by viewing the mind as a special "substance" that is different from matter. Not only does this not get us anywhere, but it also forces us to incorporate materialistic elements into the way we visualize the mind. Irrespective of how we define the concept of "substance," if it is not entirely empty, it inevitably contains conceptions referring to the properties of material things. It is much less materialistic to recognize that the mind is not a substance that differs from matter but an order that reveals itself in the relations between material things.

And let us now come to the last big question: How far have we explained mental processes at all, and how much further can we progress? In attempting to answer this question, I must first introduce an important distinction. My answer is that we can explain in principle how known natural forces can give rise to an order of the sort we call mental, but that it will never be possible for us to explain or predict why we think exactly as we do rather than differently, or why the human mind under certain circumstances will lead us to certain actions rather than to others. Our answer thus depends on the distinction between an explanation in principle for the unfolding of a process and its full or detailed explanation, which would allow one to predict the results of a certain situation. We must therefore turn to the significance of this distinction.

It is basically a distinction with which we are familiar, though we have no specific name for it. We all know the principle underlying the functioning of a clockwork, an internal combustion engine, or the tides, without our being necessarily able to build a clock, predict how fast an internal combustion engine will be running under specific circumstances, or predict the lowest tide on a given day. In some cases this incapacity is not limited to us individually; sometimes there exists nobody at all who can transform the explanation of a principle into a detailed explanation, simply because the number of implicated circumstances is too large for our intelligence ever to master it completely: we know the mechanism of the formation of waves on the surface of a body of water, for instance, yet it is probable that nobody will ever be able to explain why the wave that is forming at a specific point and at a specific moment in the ocean has a particular shape and no other. Generally we refer to practical difficulties and assume that we will gradually surmount these practical difficulties by progressive refinements of our methods of observation and calculation and that we will eventually be able to extend an explanation of the principle to a detailed explanation of concrete phenomena.

There are other cases, however, in which this difficulty is not only of a practical nature but is also a matter of principle, so that it is unthinkable that we can ever refine the "explanation" of the principle into a detailed explanation permitting a prediction of concrete phenomena. Such is the case—it may be the only case—with the explanation of our own mind or of mental activities that strongly resemble our own. That is what I will now try to demonstrate.

Let me start out by stating that an "explanation," like all mental activities, incorporates a classification process. It would take too long to try to show how the simultaneous classification of various objects leads to the construction of "models" and how these "models" serve as instruments for an explanation. I must ask you to take this on faith and must limit myself to pointing out to you that a classification apparatus must have a higher degree of complexity than what it classifies and can therefore never classify objects of its own kind. That may seem quite plausible on first inspection; if the assumption is correct, it would naturally imply that the brain can never explain itself. But to be truly convincing, I will have to be much more accurate in my formulation and specify more completely the vague concept of degrees of complexity.

The degree of complexity in question is essentially determined by the number of variable properties according to which the objects are to be classified and the number of "values" that each of these properties can assume. We might wish to classify apples, for example, according to five different criteria: shape, size, color, aroma, and degree of sweetness. Thus each apple would only have five properties, but the machine that classifies apples according to these five properties must distinguish between 5 to the fifth power or 3,125 possible combinations of these five properties; it must hence display not just 5 but 3,125 different headings to register differences between two apples. There are, moreover, many different ways in which 3,125 different units can be classified, and a machine capable of ordering all possible classification schemes for 3,125 units must therefore have a number of possible variations that is some power of 3,125. This is what I have in mind when I claim that each classification apparatus must have a degree of complexity that is of a higher order of magnitude than the objects to be classified. Here is an analogy to my assertion, which I just mention in passing without further elaboration: no calculating machine is capable of calculating the number of different operations that it can carry out.

I believe that when we apply these considerations to explaining our mind—or the functioning of our brain—one thing becomes clear: the mind can never explain itself! To explain the functioning of our brain or of our thinking, we would need a higher-order brain. And since the connection between mental processes is, strictly speaking, a whole (i.e., since the essence of mental processes lies in the structure, the mutual relationship of all mental processes), we are also unable really to explain individual mental processes, that is, to derive them from structural connections of material things, without explaining mental processes as a whole, something that happens to be impossible.

As a matter of curiosity I want to mention that the human mind's categorical inability to explain its own functioning, or what amounts to the same thing, to derive certain mental processes from well-defined material processes, does not necessarily mean that someday a machine, an artificial brain, could not be built to accomplish this feat. The knowledge of the principle underlying the operation of the brain should basically make this possible. Similarly, in principle it is feasible to construct calculating machines that can solve systems of equations, with whose help we can for instance solve systems of equations that we cannot solve on our own. I leave open the question whether the construction of such a machine is practically feasible.

In conclusion, I would still like to mention briefly some important consequences resulting from our inherent incapacity to explain mental processes in detail or to derive them from material processes. The first conclusion is that, since we will never be able to reduce particular mental processes to specific material processes, it will never be possible to achieve a unification of science of the kind the advocates of a physicalist unitary science dream of. Even if we could ever show in principle how mental processes are governed by the same forces or regularities as those that are known to exist in nature, *for us* the two realms of nature and mind must always remain separate. In the social sciences in particular the mental experiences known to us directly must always remain for us the inescapable point of departure, which we can never replace by a description of whatever kind of material processes. Even if we give up the dualist view of mind and matter in theory, in practice we must still adhere to a dualist view of the world. Attempts of the kind that, under the influence of nineteenth-century views of the natural sciences, were undertaken by the materialist account of history and the sociology of knowledge that derives from it must turn out to be impossible in principle: we will never be able to explain mental processes by specific material processes.

The problem of man's free will is closely associated with the above problem. We may be in a position to demonstrate that, in principle, human decisions are determined by material processes, but we will never be able to identify the material processes that cause particular decisions. It is, however, senseless to talk about the human will being predetermined if we can never specify by what material processes a given decision was determined. All we can say is that an assumed intelligence of a higher order than ours could say why we must act as we do.

And finally I would still like to observe that, strictly speaking, denial of free will is in any case senseless. For the use of the word "free" implies the very state in which we make a decision based on our will. There is no other definition of "free." If we deny that our will is free, then the word "free" is meaningless, and in that case the denial of free will is as senseless as its affirmation.

WITHIN SYSTEMS AND ABOUT SYSTEMS
A Statement of Some Problems of a Theory
of Communication

Man is a classifying animal: in one sense it may be said that the whole process of speaking is nothing but distributing phenomena, of which no two are alike in every respect, into different classes on the strength of perceived similarities and dissimilarities.[1] —Otto Jespersen

I

1. This paper will be devoted to a task which many will regard as futile, namely to deriving from the study of certain kinds of causal systems conclusions concerning the character of our possible knowledge of our mental pro-

[This is a previously unpublished and unfinished paper that Hayek left as a fragment. The typescript is kept in the Hoover Institution Archives (HIA), Stanford University, California, Hayek papers, box 104, folder 22. On December 7, 1952, Hayek wrote in a letter to Karl Popper (Hayek papers, box 12, folder 4, HIA): "I am now for months puzzling about what just now seems to me the most general problem of all and which at the moment I describe for myself as the distinction between what we can say 'within a system' and what we can say 'about a system.' I am convinced that this is a most important problem, ever since I began to see it clearly I meet it constantly in all sorts of different connections, but though I have made some little headway it is one of the most difficult and elusive problems I have ever tackled." Three decades later, in a letter to Walter Weimer (December 29, 1983, Hayek papers, box 57, folder 2, HIA), Hayek wrote in reference to a conference paper Weimer had sent him: "It . . . has reminded me . . . particularly of the problems with which I attempted to deal immediately after I had published *The Sensory Order* but which I found excrutiately difficult at that time. I abandoned the attempt when I found that even the one man who had understood—and helped me to publish—*The Sensory Order* (Heinrich Klüver) found my draft of the first part unintelligible. I have now again looked at that 30 years old fragment and though I know now even less than I did then how to complete it, I wonder whether for a specialist in these problems like yourself it does not still offer something." See also Hayek's remarks on the subject in "*The Sensory Order* After 25 Years" (this volume, p. 385f.). In *Hayek's Challenge: An Intellectual Biography of F. A. Hayek* (Chicago: University of Chicago Press, 2004), 301, Bruce Caldwell reports that, in a "Memorandum on Plans for Work, 1955" (Hayek papers, box 72, folder 11, HIA), Hayek "states that he plans to break up the 'Within Systems' paper into parts, the first of which was to be 'Degrees of Explanation.'"—Ed.]

[1] [Otto Jespersen, *Language: Its Nature, Development and Origin* (London: Allen & Unwin, 1922), 388f.—Ed.]

cesses. Those who feel that such an attempt is absurd on the face of it may perhaps be persuaded to consider the argument if I state at the outset the main conclusion to which it will lead: it is that for any causal system there is a limit to the complexity of other systems for which the former can provide the analogon of a description or explanation, and that this limit necessarily excludes the possibility of a system ever describing or explaining itself. This means that, if the human mind were a causal system, we would necessarily experience in discussing it precisely those obstacles and difficulties which we do encounter and which are often regarded as proof that the human mind is not a causal system. In particular we shall find that to such a system the world must necessarily appear not as one but as two distinct realms which cannot be fully "reduced" to each other.

2. The reason for approaching these problems via the study of causal systems is precisely that in all our relations to mental phenomena certain general problems arise which can be shown up and clearly defined only if we reproduce the same type of relations for the case of very much simpler systems, so that one system which we can still fully encompass and represent stands to a system which it can be said to describe in the same sort of relation in which the human mind stands to what it can describe. It will then be seen that the basic difficulty in talking about our own mental processes is that we can describe (or explain) anything only by moving within a given system which must be roughly the same for the describing agent and for him to whom the description is addressed, and that we can therefore never describe this system itself.

3. Although most of our discussion will have relevance to most types of mental phenomena, we shall here concentrate on communication and particularly description, because these raise in the clearest form the problems involved when we talk about mental phenomena, and because it is for this case comparatively easy to state a test by which we can decide whether a description has been communicated by one system to another. Provisionally we shall define this by saying that a description has been communicated by one system S_1 to another system S_2, if S_1, which is subject to certain actions by the environment which do not directly affect S_2, can in turn so act on S_2 that the latter will as a result behave, not as S_1 would behave under the influence of those causes, but as S_2 itself, in its peculiar individual position, would behave if these causes which have acted on S_1 had acted directly on S_2. A fuller discussion of this relation with a concrete illustration will be given in section II below.

Schemas or Models Exhibiting a Principle of Explanation

4. A few remarks should he made here about the significance of the use of "simplified models" in order to derive certain general properties appertain-

ing to a certain class of phenomena—especially as the models we shall use can admittedly never be used to provide a full explanation of (or lead to precise predictions about) the phenomena of the kind in which we are mainly interested. So far as these particular instances are concerned, our models provide merely an "explanation of the principle" of a "schema" which enables us to construct, by inserting appropriate assumptions, instances of the same kind, i.e., phenomena sharing certain significant features with the former. They show that the observed phenomena of the kind are within the range of what may result from the combination of known forces and thus show us at least one possible way in which instances of the kind of phenomenon may be brought about, without enabling us to say that it was actually this rather than some other manifestation of the same principle which has brought it about.

5. If our aim is to be achieved, we must succeed in producing models which produce *in kind* such mental functions as "thinking" or "having an intention", or "naming", or "describing", or "communicating a meaning", or "drawing an inference" and the like; but for our purposes we need not reproduce all the features of any one particular instance where a human mind is said to perform any of these activities. It will be sufficient if we can construct an instance which possesses all the characteristics which are common to all the instances to which we commonly apply any one of these terms.

6. The most familiar example of such an "explanation of the principle" is probably the general theory of evolution of living organisms. In so far as this theory is successful it provides us with a schema which allows us to state a set of conditions under which known forces could have led to the appearance of any one particular kind of organism (say, such and such an animal). But it does not place us either in the condition to say that this possible course of events was in fact the one which has resulted in the particular species, or to say that the factors enumerated were sufficient to determine that this particular organism would emerge. It indicates merely a range of possible ways in which known forces might have combined to bring about the particular result, and at the same time excludes the possibility of certain other events which do not fit into the scheme (such as, for instance, the inheritance of acquired characteristics).

7. Another field in which the general properties of a class of phenomena are derived from the general principle by which they are defined, a field to which indeed our particular problem belongs, is the general theory of machines or, as J. von Neumann has recently called it, the "logic of automata".[2] This theory

[2] John von Neumann, *Functional Operators* (Princeton: Princeton University Press, 1951), p.17. [John von Neumann (1903–57) was an ingenious Hungarian-American mathematician who made major contributions to a broad range of scientific fields, including, besides mathematics, physics, computer science, and economics. After receiving his PhD in mathematics from the Catholic Péter-Pázmány-University in Budapest, he taught from 1926 to 1930 as the young-

also is able, on the one hand, to indicate the range of phenomena which can be produced, and therefore be accounted for, by the operation of certain basic principles, and, on the other hand, to show that certain other conceivable operations lie outside the range of what a machine so defined can possibly do. The general theory of classifying machines in particular, with which we shall be concerned, may not be sufficient to specify in detail the operation of any such classifying machine of a sufficient degree of complexity to be of practical interest; but it will indicate the range of phenomena which may be produced by machines of this type.

8. For the purposes of our discussion where we want to include what is commonly described as an "organism" as well as what is understood by the terms machine or "mechanism" in the narrower sense, it will be advisable to avoid the latter two expressions and to employ the more neutral expression: "system" in the sense of a coherent structure of causally connected physical parts.[3] The term system will thus be used here roughly in the sense in which it is used in von Bertalanffy's "General System Theory".[4] We need not enter

---

est ever Privatdozent at the University of Berlin. In 1930 he joined the faculty of the Institute of Advanced Study at Princeton University, where he remained for the rest of his life. Jointly with Oskar Morgenstern (see above, editor's introduction, fn. 110), he wrote *Theory of Games and Economic Behavior* (Princeton, NJ: Princeton University Press, 1944), the founding treatise in the field of game theory. With his reference to the "logic of automata," Hayek alludes to the model of cellular automata or self-reproducing machines that Neumann conceived in the 1940s (see John von Neumann, *Theory of Self-Reproducing Automata*, edited and completed by Arthur W. Burks [Urbana: University of Illinois Press, 1966]), anticipating the reproduction process of living cells before the discovery of the structure of DNA in 1953. Recalling an encounter with von Neumann, Hayek notes: "I wasn't aware of his work, which stemmed from his involvement with the first computers. But when I was writing *The Sensory Order*, I reasoned that I could explain to people what I was doing. Usually I found it very difficult to make them understand. And then I met John von Neumann at a party, and to my amazement and delight, he immediately understood what I was doing and said that he was working on the same problem from the same angle. At the time his research on automata came out, it was too abstract for me to relate it to psychology, so I really couldn't profit from it; but I did see that we had been thinking on very similar lines." (See "Weimer-Hayek Discussion," in *Cognition and the Symbolic Processes*, vol. 2, ed. W. B. Weimer and D. S. Palermo (Hillsdale, NJ: Lawrence Erlbaum, 1982), 322.)—Ed.]

[3] [In Hayek's typescript a reference to "L. S. Stebbing, 1933, p. 198" appears without corresponding placement in the body of the text and without further specification. The reference pertains most likely to a paragraph in the chapter "System and Order" in Lizzie Susan Stebbing, *A Modern Introduction to Logic*, 2nd. rev. ed. (London: Methuen, 1933), 196–209, in which Stebbing comments on the concept of a "coherent system": "A system is said to be *coherent* if *every* fact in the system is related to every other fact by relations that are not merely conjunctive." This suggests that the reference was meant to be placed at the chosen location. L. Susan Stebbing (1885–1943) was a British philosopher who taught at Bedford College, University of London. She introduced Karl R. Popper, whom she had invited to give lectures in London, to Hayek (see above, editor's introduction, fn. 134).—Ed.]

[4] [The reference in Hayek's typescript is to page 19 of an undated edition of this work. In Ludwig von Bertalanffy, *General System Theory—Foundations, Development, Applications*, rev. ed. (New

here into all the difficulties of a precise definition of this term and may content ourselves with saying that by a system we shall throughout understand a persistent structure of coherent material parts which are so connected that, although they can alter their relations to each other, and the system thereby can assume various states, there will be a finite number of such states of which the system is capable, that these states can be transformed into each other through certain orderly sequences, and that the relations of the parts are interdependent in the sense that, if a certain number of them are fixed, the rest is also determined.

Classifying Systems

9. The particular kinds of causal systems which we will consider here will be systems capable of "classifying" external actions upon them and of responding to any one of the external events belonging to the same class (or class of classes, etc.) by the "appropriate" one among the class of responses to which the state of the system at the time disposes it. For a full discussion of this kind of system I must refer to my book *The Sensory Order*. For the present purposes it must suffice if I briefly sketch in the next few paragraphs the most important characteristics of such a system, without attempting to show how these characteristics follow from certain properties known (or generally assumed) to belong to the central nervous systems of the higher animals.

10. The systems will be assumed to be so organized that certain kinds of external actions on some of its parts will give rise to signals conducted to a center (or, rather, to a series of successive and progressively more comprehensive centers) at which any one of a class of such signals, and any one of a class of certain groups of such signals occurring simultaneously, will give rise to further signals representative of such classes; and where these representative signals will in turn be subject to a similar process of classification, and so on. Starting from the initial signals evoked by the action of the environment upon the system, the "classification" which the system performs will therefore include the following types of events: a) any one of a certain class of initial signals evoking by its occurrence the same representative signals standing for this class; b) any one such initial signal being able to evoke several groups of representative signals which it has in common with different other initial signals, which will mean that it belongs to as many different classes; c) particular groups of initial signals in the same manner, if they occur together as groups, forming the elements of classes of such groups; and d) all these three forms of

York: George Braziller, 1968), 19, a system is defined as a complex of interacting elements. On L. v. Bertalanffy, see above, *TSO*, preface, fn. 14.—Ed.]

classification being capable of being repeated on the representative signals, on the representatives of classes of representative signals, and so on in relay fashion. The whole of this process will be referred to as "multiple classification".

11. It should be specially noted that a process of multiple classification as here described also involves an apparatus of selection among the numerous further signals to which any one (initial or representative) signal might give rise: this is provided by c) above, namely by the fact that in some instances not individual signals but only groups of signals occurring together will evoke further representative signals; or, in other words, the fact that the mutual reinforcement of many signals may be required to evoke certain further signals. We shall here merely note that, so far as the special case of the central nervous system is concerned, this apparatus of selection is supplemented by a further factor, namely special inhibiting signals, which, however, will play no role in the models we are going to construct here.

12. This multiple classification of the signals representative of external actions on the system ("stimuli") will be assumed to "parallel"[5] or "model" sequences of events in the environment. This means that the representatives of a group of external events which have acted upon the system will tend to evoke (more or less directly) representatives of the events which the group of external events will produce in the environment. The classifying system may in this sense be regarded as embodying a theory of the external world which enables it to predict (= produce the representatives of) the events which the former will cause in the environment. The nature of this correspondence between the model formed inside the system and its object will be one of the main subjects of the following discussion.

13. In *The Sensory Order* it has been shown how the formation of connections ("linkages") between simultaneously occurring representatives of external events will build up such a structure which is capable of classifying external actions according to the effects which the corresponding external events will produce in the environment. For our present purposes we shall not be much concerned with the process of learning which produces this structure.

[5] The expression used by Kenneth J. W. Craik, *The Nature of Explanation* (Cambridge: Cambridge University Press, 1943). [On K. J. W. Craik, see above, *TSO*, 5.68, fn. 12. Craik is credited for having first used the terms "internal working model" or "mental model." As he explains: "By a model we thus mean any . . . system which has a similar relation-structure to that of the process it imitates . . . [and] works in the same way as the process it parallels. . . . If the organism carries a 'small-scale model' of external reality and of its own possible actions within its head, it is able to try out various alternatives, conclude which is the best of them, react to future situations before they arise, utilize the knowledge of past events in dealing with the present and future, and in every way to react in a much fuller, safer, and more competent manner to the emergencies which face it" (ibid., 61).—Ed.]

We shall in general simply assume this structure to exist and to operate in a constant fashion. For much of our argument it will even be irrelevant whether this structure has formed itself as a result of the experience of the system, or whether it has been given to the system by a designer. In other words, we shall largely disregard the factor of experience or learning which changes the structure of the system of classification.

14. While for our present purposes it will therefore be expedient to assume, in effect, that the process by which changes in this structure (or long-term memories) are acquired is so slow as to be negligible in the present context, it must be remembered that this long-term memory is not the only kind of memory which such a system will possess and that another, short-term kind of memory will be very relevant for our purposes. This is the continued effect which an external cause will have upon our system so long as the chain of signals continues which has been started by it. (This may, in the case of the nervous system, in consequence of the reverberating circuits which it appears to possess, amount to an appreciable interval of time).

15. The ultimate significance of the signals caused by external action on the system is the effect on further signals determining action by the system itself. Such action may, in the extreme limiting case (of "reflex" action) be caused directly by a signal evoked by external influences. But as a rule we shall have to assume that the initial cause producing a signal for a kind of action will be some change in the internal state of the system itself, a change in the "internal environment" of the classifying apparatus, which, like an external action, is reported to the center and there classified by evoking further signals, representative either of external events or of actions to be taken. As is the case with signals recording external events, there will be two aspects of this classifying process: many different initial signals caused by a change within the system may belong to the same class because each of them gives rise to the same further signal or signals; and each may give rise to the same class of further signals, each of which would tend to evoke a different kind of action, so that the result is that the system becomes disposed towards a class of actions, and the particular action taken will have to be selected from it by the coincidence with other signals tending in the same direction.

16. It is necessary here clearly to distinguish between the signals which represent actions (or classes of actions) as part of the classifying apparatus representing the environment, and the signals sent out from that center which cause or release the actions thus represented. An explanation of how the representation of the environment and of the effects of different actions on that environment will lead to a particular course of action being taken implies that the representation of a pattern of action involves at the same time a disposition to perform these actions whenever some additional signal releases this tendency.

States, Dispositions, and Dispositions to Assume Dispositions

17. The interaction between the representative signals and the action signals at any moment will determine the *state* of the system which is characterized by its disposition to respond by various actions to different further events acting upon it. The representation of the environment must in this connection be conceived as a sort of "general modifier" of the patterns of action to which the state of the system disposes it. The two concepts of the different "states" in which the same system may find itself, and of the various "dispositions" which correspond to any one state, require some further elucidation.

18. The concept of the *state* of a certain system must be carefully distinguished from the changes in a collection of elements which turn it into a different system. Different individual systems may be instances of the same kind of system (or possess the same structure) if they are capable of assuming the same states; and any one individual system remains the same system only so long as it remains capable of assuming any one of the same set of states, but not if it is, e.g., broken and ceases to be capable of some states, in which case it would become a different system in our sense. A full description of any system would have to include sufficient information to derive from it descriptions of all possible states of that system and of their relations to each other, such as the order in which it can pass through the various states and the conditions in which it will pass from one state into another.—It will be noted that strictly speaking a change in the permanent structure of one of our systems such as would be produced by long-term memory (the acquisition of new connections or linkages), being an irreversible change, implies a change of the system rather than a mere change of the state of a given system.

19. By the *dispositions* of a system, on the other hand, are meant all the different responses which that system will show, *if* certain further events act upon it. In their simplest form such dispositional properties of a system, which define its different states, present no serious difficulty.[6] For our purposes however, we need not merely dispositions to a definite range of actions, so that any given state is defined by the overt response of the system to any one of a set of external actions upon it; but we need, corresponding to the hierarchy of classes, dispositions to assume new dispositions, dispositions to assume new dispositions to assume new dispositions, etc., etc. It is mainly because of its neglect of this hierarchy of levels of dispositions that the usual "mechanical" models of mental processes, and particularly any simple attempt to construct

---

[6] For a general discussion of dispositional properties, see Gilbert Ryle, *The Concept of Mind* (London, New York: Hutchinson's University Library, 1949). [On G. Ryle, see above, *TSO*, 1.49, fn. 31.—Ed.]

unambiguous relations between "stimulus" and "response" of the behaviorist type, are so very inadequate.

20. There is nothing mysterious in these concepts of a "state" or of a "disposition", or of a change in either. One of the most familiar instances of a change in the state of a system, which will manifest itself in altered responses to a multiplicity of causes acting upon it, is the effect of depressing the shift-key of a typewriter: the result is that on striking any other key the typewriter will print a capital instead of the corresponding lower-case letter. Another familiar instance is the shift of the gear of an automobile with the result that it will respond in a different manner to the action of the accelerator pedal. An illustration of the higher-order relation of a disposition to assume a disposition is provided by the special "transfer gear" which some cars designed for rough country, such as the Jeep, possess. Here a shift of the transfer gear changes the rate of transmission for each of the positions of the ordinary gear lever, which in turn determine the response of the car to changes in the gas supply.

21. The response of a system of the kind which we are considering to actions of the environment will thus frequently not be an overt movement but may merely be a change in its disposition to respond to further external causes. And the disposition produced by the latter may in turn not be a disposition to particular movements but a disposition to assume other and still different dispositions in response to still further events. The connection between an external cause A and an overt action l of the system may therefore be that in the state α the system will respond to A by changing into the state β in which it will respond with the actions b, c, d, to the causes B, C, D respectively, while to the causes E, F, G it will respond by assuming respectively the states γ, δ and ε; and that in the state ε it will again respond to some causes by certain actions and to others by further changes in its disposition, until finally it reaches a state λ in which it will respond to the cause L by the action l. However indirect the connection between A and l, the former still contributes in determining the latter.

Response to Representations

22. The peculiar character of such a classifying system consists in the fact that in a clearly definable sense it will respond, not to the external facts, but to the representations of these facts. This means, in the first instance, that the response to a given event will depend, not on how this event differs for an observer of both the representing system and of the represented fact, but only on how its representation within the representing system differs from the representation of other facts. Events which are either represented within our sys-

tem by the same signal or which are represented by signals which are related to all other possible signals within the system in the same manner will necessarily have the same effects upon the system. And the effects of different external events upon the system will differ only in so far as the positions of their representations in the whole structure of possible representations differ from each other. All this is of course merely a consequence of the fact that the effects of an external event pass through a series of connecting links and that the effects of different events will be the same or different according as their consequences pass through the same or different connecting links.

23. From the fact that a classifying system will in this sense respond not to the external facts but to their representations follows, however, more than is apparent on a first glance. It implies that the response of such a system will not be uniquely determined by a singular event but will always depend on such generic features of its whole environment as the classes, classes of classes, to which any parts of the environment belong for the system, or the relations between and patterns of the events in the environment which it classifies as the same. And, secondly and equally important, since the classification of the events and groups of events in the environment consists in evoking representations of other events which they will produce in various combinations, or in building models of the course of events which may take place in the environment, it will not only be representations of actual or present events in the environment but also representations of potential or future events in that environment which will determine the responses of the system.

24. That the structure of representations which is the immediate determinant of the responses of a classifying system includes representations of possible future events as well as representations of the events of the immediate past, or to put it differently, that the map of the environment (as it has been called in *The Sensory Order*) which guides the action of the system, is, as it were, a four-dimensional map which includes a time-dimension, is of crucial importance for the causal explanation of a feature which appears to be common to all structures which we describe as "minds". This is the property to which we refer by such terms as "intention", "purpose", "aim", "need", or "desire". Though we must not use any of these "mental" terms until we have succeeded in adequately defining them in terms of our causal system, this is clearly necessary if we are to substantiate the claim that we can supply at least an explanation of the principle on which "mind" operates.

Selection of Action Appropriate to the Environment Represented

25. The decisive problem, the solution of which provides in principle the explanation of all the more complicated problems, arises already in instances

of the kind which seem so simple that at first neither the future nor "intention" seem to be at all involved. Such instances are provided by all those cases where, e.g., an optical action upon a system evokes a particular kind of movements of the system because the immediate optical effect produces within the system representations belonging to a class which, in the state in which the system happens to be at the moment, dispose it to a certain class of movements while the optical action determines which among this class of movements will be selected. For our purposes it makes here little difference whether by "movement" in this connection we mean literally a single external move of some part of our system or a more or less complicated chain of actions, particularly, as with the kinds of systems in which we are primarily interested even the simplest kind of movement is the effect of a most complex spatial or temporal pattern of signals.

26. It is useful at this stage to remind us of the sense in which biologists have found themselves under the necessity of re-admitting the concept of "purpose" into their thinking as meaning something like the "use of variable means to an invariable goal", and to ask how far we can construct causal systems which will show this property. Let us for this purpose consider a mechanical classifying system which derives its power from a petrol-engine and which is so constructed that when its internal store of fuel falls below a certain level it will start to act in such a manner that, firstly, in the sort of environment to which it is adapted, it is likely to meet external influences indicative of the presence of petrol, and, secondly, when this happens it will take such action as will lead to the replenishment of its stock of petrol. By what kind of causal connection between the apparatus classifying external effects on such a system and the apparatus disposing it to certain classes of actions can such a behavior be brought about?

27. There is no great difficulty about the manner in which an internal change of a system (such as the falling of the petrol-level) may put it into a state in which it will respond to any one of a class of external events by a particular response. Only slightly more difficult seems to be the case where the disposition produced by the internal change is towards a *class* of responses from which the one appropriate to the environment will be selected, though even this would not appear to raise fundamentally new problems so long as the class of responses is limited to definite types of action to which the system becomes disposed as a result of the internal change. But greater difficulties evidently arise where the disposition required for an explanation is not a disposition towards *particular kinds* of actions (definable by their physical characteristics) but a disposition to take *any* action which the representation of the environment shows to produce one of the class of results which will cause the system in its existing state to act.

28. Basically the same problem, however, which assumes great magnitude

in the third case, arises already in the second case which includes that of our machine replenishing its stock of fuel (or of a thirsty animal getting a drink, etc.). This involves not merely that the low stock of fuel triggers a mechanism which makes the system responsive to certain cues, but that the response is adapted to the environment: the state caused by the deficiency is not a disposition to one particular response but to a class of responses among which the one corresponding to the external conditions existing at the moment will have to be selected. The system will not merely have to move but to move in a particular direction, perhaps avoiding obstacles, and when arrived at the supply, will have to take further actions adapted to the particular circumstances in order to ingest the substance in question.

29. The conception that a system selects a particular course of action because this course of action is represented as producing an effect towards which the system is disposed at the moment implies that this course of action and its successive effects must first be represented in their temporal order; secondly, that when one of the effects towards which the system is disposed appears as a link in this chain, this whole pattern is temporarily locked or frozen; and finally, that the process can then, as it were, go back to the beginning of this chain and retrace the course in a manner which will evoke the action represented.

30. The intellectual difficulty which we experience about this is due to the fact that the process sketched appears to involve a sort of reversal of causation: the effect which is at first represented as the end of the represented chain of actions is then assumed to become the cause of this same chain of actions being actually carried out. The difficulty would be indeed serious if we had to think of the chain of representations as a series of strictly successive events which did not overlap in time, and could not conceive of them as a pattern of events coexisting during a short period of time. Such a simultaneous existence of the signals making up the pattern is clearly mechanically possible, and so is some arrangement by which such a preformed pattern is translated into action whenever a representation of one of the effects singled out as significant by the state of the system appears as part of the pattern.

31. Although this has not been explicitly considered in *The Sensory Order*, there are in fact also other reasons which make it necessary that our system possess some mechanism of this sort. If it is to try out representations of alternative courses of actions which are possible in a given situation, these representations must clearly occur not simultaneously but successively, since otherwise different and mutually contradictory positions would have to be represented at the same time, which is impossible (cf. *TSO*, 5.72). There must exist a kind of mechanism which ensures that at any one time only one of these alternative chains of associations is effective and all the others are blocked. But once each channel is opened only for a limited time, there is no difficulty in conceiving that signals enter into this channel continuously until

they will be proceeding at the same time in all its parts. (It would seem at least plausible to assume that in this respect the rhythmical character of the activities of the brain may make a sort of internal scanning process possible by which the various alternatives are tried out successively.)

Intention

32. Whatever the actual mechanism involved in the case of the vertebrate brain, we can thus clearly conceive of a kind of causal system which will respond to any one of a certain class of external effects by such a set of responses which in the situation which is represented within it will in fact produce the result (or one of the class of results) towards which it is disposed by its existing internal state. Such a general state or disposition of a system as we have just described is, however, precisely what we mean and all that we mean if we ascribe to any of the familiar organic systems, such as animals or men, the *intention* of achieving a particular *goal*.

33. The purpose of our discussion has made it imperative that in discussing causal systems we should scrupulously avoid any mental terms such as "need", "purpose", "intention", "desire", "pleasure", "pain", "search for", etc., unless we were able to define the expression in causal terms and at the same time in such a manner that the definition will cover all the features which are common to the different instances in human and animal life to which in ordinary language we unhesitatingly apply it. We are now in a position to give such a definition to the term "intention" and to the related term "goal" which will entitle us henceforth to use them in our discussion of causal systems.

34. By *intention* we shall mean such a state of a system that, whenever its classifying apparatus represents a chain of actions as producing a result which at the same time the internal state of the system singles out as appropriate to that state, it will perform that chain of actions. And we shall describe the result or class of results which in any such state will activate the chains of actions which will produce them as the *goal* or goals to which the intention is directed. It should be noted that the goal in this sense may be either a particular event or any one of a class of events, or, in other words, that the goal may be concrete or more or less abstract. (We will not enter here into any discussion of the further problem of selection which arises when in any situation more than one chain of actions should be represented as achieving the goal. See on this *TSO*, 5.74.)

35. In thus offering a definition in physical terms of a state which possesses all the properties common to all human and animal instances to which we can legitimately apply the term "intention", we do of course not claim that we are therefore able to provide a full physical explanation of any one particular instance of a human intention. We shall, on the contrary, maintain that

this is basically impossible. But there is a great difference between providing a simplified model of the kind of state of a causal system which will exhibit all the characteristic properties described as "having an intention" and showing what this would involve in the case of a much more complex system. But, as has been suggested before, if we claim to have supplied an explanation of the principle of the manner in which the kind of order which we call mind can arise in a physical system, it would seem essential that we should also supply such explanations of the principle for all the characteristic properties which we meet wherever we find what we call mind. An "intention" would seem to be one of the most general attributes of which all that we call "mind" is capable.

Program of Further Discussion

36. The introduction of "intention" as one of the properties which a classifying system of the kind described will possess has completed the setting up of the framework within which we wish to consider the main problems to which this paper is devoted. In the next section we shall take up the question how such a system can transmit to another similar system information about the environment so that the second system will as a result behave in some respects as if it had directly undergone those effects of the environment which in fact have affected only the first system, but which have become the object of the description transmitted by that system to the second.

37. Any answer to this first question will at once raise certain further questions of wide significance: we shall next ask how much information a system of a given structure can transmit and, in particular, in what manner both the structure of the system itself and the character of the system of symbols used in transmission will limit the character and amount of the information which can be transmitted. If it should prove, as we should expect, that there will be information about the character of the environment which must be implicit in the structure both of the transmitting and the receiving system in order that communication between them be possible, this would mean that there is "information" about the environment which both systems use in their actions but which can never become the object of communication between them. Some rather far-reaching implications of this will also be briefly considered in the later sections of this paper.

II

38. The problem of communication will arise only if we have to deal with at least two similar systems of the kind we have described. In order to avoid cer-

tain exceedingly difficult problems we shall assume for the purposes of the following discussion that the structure of the communicating systems is not merely similar but identical. This means, strictly speaking, not only that the initial physical structure of the systems was the same but also that the long-term memories accumulated by them up to the moment we are considering are undistinguishable. But we must assume of course that they are capable of undergoing, and for short periods retaining, different experiences. (How far and to what extent a succession of necessarily somewhat different experiences can create in different systems structures which are at least sufficiently similar to make some communication possible, and how far different degrees of mere similarity of structure limit the possibility of communication are very important questions which, however, will not be further considered here.)

39. No special problems arise in so far as one system learns to regard certain actions of other similar systems as *symptoms* of further actions to be expected from these systems. Such instances of what K. Bühler has described as the first, "expressive" or "symptomatic" function of language[7] do not differ

---

[7] [Hayek's typescript provides only the following incomplete reference: "K. Bühler, 19, p.; the English expressions are taken from K. R. Popper, 19, p." From his correspondence with Popper (Popper to Hayek, December 2, 1952; Popper to Hayek, January 19, 1953; Popper to Hayek, November 30, 1953; Hayek to Popper, January 26, 1953; Hayek to Popper, January 27, 1954. All letters in Hayek papers, box 44, folder 1, HIA) one can conclude, however, that the reference is to Popper's article "Language and the Body-Mind Problem," originally published in 1953 and reprinted in Karl R. Popper, *Conjectures and Refutations*, 5th rev. ed. (London: Routledge, 1989), 293–98. In this article Popper cites Karl Bühler's distinction between "three functions of language: (1) the expressive or symptomatic function; (2) the stimulative or signal function; (3) the descriptive function" (ibid., 295). He notes that Bühler introduced this distinction in his *Die geistige Entwicklung des Kindes* (Jena: Gustav Fischer, 1918), 107f., and returned to it in his *Sprachtheorie: Die Darstellungsfunktion der Sprache* (Jena: Gustav Fischer, 1934), 24ff.

On "Bühler's theory of the lower and higher functions of human language," Popper comments: "Briefly, Bühler points out that animal and human language are alike in so far as they are always *expressions* (symptoms of a state of the organism) and *communications* (signals). Yet human language is also different since it has, in *addition*, a higher function: it can be *descriptive*. I have pointed out that there are other higher functions, and especially one which is of decisive importance: the *argumentative or critical function*." (See *Objective Knowledge—An Evolutionary Approach* [Oxford: At the Clarendon Press, 1972], 160, fn. 9, and 235ff.) Popper opens his essay "Language and the Body-Mind Problem" with the statement: "This is a paper on the impossibility of a physicalist causal theory of the human language." As a footnote he adds: "This issue was first discussed by Karl Bühler" (ibid., 293). Popper did his doctoral dissertation with Karl Bühler (1879–1963), who became professor of psychology at the University of Vienna in 1922. Bühler emigrated to the United States, where he taught from 1940 to 1945 at the University of Minnesota, and from 1945 to 1955 at the University of Southern California, Los Angeles.

As its subtitle indicates, Popper's challenge seems to have prompted Hayek to make the "theory of communication" a focus of his "Within Systems" paper. Responding to a letter from Hayek of October 30, 1953, Popper writes in his letter to Hayek of November 30, 1953: "I was extremely pleased to hear that with 'the challenge' of my article . . . , I have done you 'a great service.' I am really happy about this remark." On this issue see also Bruce Caldwell, *Hayek's Challenge: An Intellectual Biography of F. A. Hayek*, 300f. For a more detailed account of the exchange

essentially from any other instance in which a classifying system learns to predict events in the environment. The correct interpretation of such a "symptom" is not fundamentally different from the interpretation of any other situation in the environment and requires only a very limited similarity of parts of the structure of the two systems.

40. The same applies at least to the simplest instances of what Bühler has described as the second, "stimulative" or *signal* function of language where a given event regularly triggers a particular response of a system or, according to its momentary state, one of a limited number of responses. For this to be possible there is again no need for more than a very limited partial similarity of the two systems, and indeed, as in the first case, only one of them (the receiving system) need be a classifying system in our sense in order that all the characteristic elements of a signal in this sense be present.

41. It will be useful, however, briefly to consider certain kinds of simple communications between systems which probably still ought to be regarded as belonging to the mere symptom-signal range but which derive their special significance from a great similarity of the structure of the communicating systems. Certain persistent groups of individuals, such as a swarm of bees or a flock of geese, persist as groups only because the external symptoms of a disposition to a certain kind of action act as a signal which puts other individuals of the group into the same disposition. K. Frisch's[8] account of how bees influence each other to swarm in a particular direction, or K. Lorenz'[9] description

---

between Hayek and Popper on the issue of a physiological theory of the mind, see also above, editor's introduction, pp. 53ff.—Ed.]

[8] [Hayek does not provide a reference. He was most likely familiar with the German original, Karl von Frisch, *Aus dem Leben der Bienen* (Berlin: Springer, 1927), which was translated into English as *The Dancing Bees: An Account of the Life and the Senses of the Honey Bee* (Harcourt: Brace Jovanovich, 1953). Karl von Frisch (1886–1982) was an Austrian ethologist whose principal research was on the sensory perception of honeybees, their methods of orientation, and their means of communicating information about feeding places (Karl von Frisch, *The Dance Language and Orientation of Bees* [Cambridge, MA: Harvard University Press, 1967]). After graduating from the University of Vienna in 1910, Frisch spent most of his academic career at the University of Munich until his retirement in 1958. Jointly with Nikolaas Tinbergen and Konrad Lorenz, he was awarded the Nobel Prize in Physiology or Medicine in 1973.—Ed.]

[9] [Hayek does not provide a reference. A likely source on which he may have drawn is Lorenz's 1935 article "Der Kumpan in der Umwelt des Vogels (Der Artgenosse als auslösendes Moment sozialer Verhaltensweisen)," *Journal für Ornithologie* 83: 137–213, 289–413. An English version, entitled "The Companion in the Bird's World," appeared two years later in the organ of the American Ornithologists' Union (*Auk* 54 [1937]: 245–73). In this article Lorenz applies his principal research interest, namely the study of genetically evolved, species-specific, innate behavior patterns, to the issue of how social animals manage to coordinate the behavior among individual members of a flock or herd in situations in which such coordination is of survival value. According to Lorenz, such coordination is based on innate behavior patterns that are activated by a "releasing set of stimuli" that, stated in terms of the "key-lock" metaphor, provide the "key" that

of how the behavior of some geese will dispose the rest of the flock to rise into the air presupposes no more than that a disposition to a kind of action is regularly accompanied by certain external actions of the system, *and* that this kind of action on the part of one system will evoke the same states in other similar systems.

42. This case, in which the same external action of a system acts both as a symptom of a certain state and as a signal evoking that state in similar systems, is of great importance of what follows and requires some further examination. As a generic term to describe such actions which may serve as symptom and/or signal (and later also as "symbol") we shall use the word "sign". Where a sign acts on the system which emits it in the same manner as on other systems which it reaches, as might be true of an acoustic sign, there is little difficulty about explaining how the act of emitting the sign and its perception may become so closely associated that they will mutually evoke each other. This result is however somewhat more difficult to account for where the symptom consists in some movement which will act optically on other systems but which cannot act in the same way on the emitting system itself.

43. Before considering this further it is worth mentioning that, so far as animal societies are concerned, some sort of symptom-signal action must be presumed to make groups even temporarily act sufficiently in unison to continue as groups. It is not as if we could assume that the groups were formed first

---

fits the "lock" of an "innate perceptory pattern" (ibid., 247). While evolutionary selection works in general "to adapt the innate perceptory apparatus as closely as possible to the preexisting sets of key stimuli" (ibid., 248), social coordination requires, as Lorenz argues, "the parallel differentiation of releasers and innate perceptory patterns" (ibid., 259), in the sense that certain activities exhibited by one member of a flock or herd serve as a releasing stimulus that activates corresponding innate behavior patterns in other members. Lorenz uses the example of a flock of geese synchronously rising into the air to illustrate the interplay of "releasing action"—as a "private signaling code of the species" (ibid., 254)—and "corresponding innate perceptory patterns" on which the social coordination of behavior is based (ibid., 257). As a general observation he states: "In social animals the transmitting of specific excitation may clearly become of very considerable survival value. All those functions of coordinating the behavior of the individual members of society which, in the human species, represent one of the chief tasks of speech, are performed by releasing ceremonies or by the transmitting of specific excitation. . . . We have, therefore, to assume the existence of innate perceptory patterns corresponding to certain sets of stimuli emanating from the individual first showing the reaction. . . . By the evolution of this kind of innate perceptory pattern, almost any instinctive reaction in a social species may be appointed to the secondary and purely social task of releasing like reactions in the fellow-member of the flock or herd" (ibid.). In the present context it is worth mentioning that Lorenz studied psychology in Vienna with Karl Bühler, to whom he refers in an autobiographical article as "my teacher." (See p. 264 of Konrad Lorenz's "My Family and Other Animals," in *Leaders in the Study of Animal Behavior: Autobiographical perspectives*, ed. D. A. Dewsbury [Lewisburg, PA: Bucknell University Press, 1985], 258–87). On Lorenz see also above, editor's introduction, fn. 169, and *TSO*, 1.70, fn. 46.—Ed.]

and life in the group led then to the first development of communication. It is rather the capacity of responding by similar action to the actions of other individuals of the same species which leads to the formation of the group. This does, of course, not exclude the possibility that, in instances where external conditions bring it about that numbers of individuals will frequently assemble in the same place, a common response to external events (e.g., the flight response) may in due course (as "conditioned reflex") become attached to the perception of the same response by other individuals, and that in this manner the accidental congregation in space may develop into a continued association of the group.

44. Once, however, similar systems happen to be frequently in spatial proximity, the similar responses to any class of events which all the systems have in common with every one of them will for each system become so associated with the class of external events eliciting them (and with its own response to them) that the response will come to "stand for" that class of events in the sense of both, being evoked by any one of them and of evoking all those other responses by each of them. This relation is most conveniently represented by a diagram.

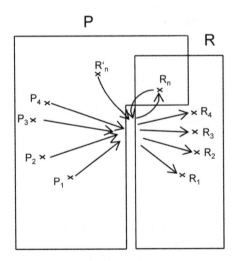

If P_1, P_2, P_3; . . . are the group of external events P, to any one of which any one of our systems will respond by the class of actions R (consisting of R_1, R_2, R_3 . . . which includes merely internal changes of the system such as changes in its disposition), there may be an R_n which also acts in turn as an external event and, being regularly associated with P_1, P_2, P_3, etc., becomes a member of the class P. This will apply not only to a given system's own R_n, but also to the R'_n, R''_n . . . of those other similar systems among which the first regularly moves. It does not matter for this that the physical character of the effects of R_n and R'_n on the first system may be quite different: that, e.g., if R_n is a movement, the system may have its own R_n reported by what we call a kinesthetic signal, while the R'_n, R''_n, etc., of other systems will affect the former as optical signals; they will nevertheless become associated both with each other and with the class of external events which they come to represent.

45. We shall not here concern ourselves further, however, with the genetic question *how* a classifying system can come both to show a definite symptom of the classes it forms at any moment, and treat the same symptoms if shown by other systems as elements of this class, but we shall for our purposes be content with the fact that we know how we could build systems which at least for some of the classes they can form will both show a distinct sign and respond to that sign if emitted by other similar systems by the same responses which are evoked by any one of the events belonging to the class.

46. The important point here is that the same external action, performed by any one of the similar systems, whether performed by it or whether it is affected by the action being performed by one of the other systems, will *for* it and for the other systems in the same sense stand for the same class of events, or have the same effects on them as are common to this class of events. Although we have yet to justify this usage, we shall henceforth apply to such kind of signs passing between systems the term *symbol* by which Bühler describes the third function of language, the "descriptive" function. A symbol thus differs from the two other kinds of signs (symptoms and signals) by the fact that it stands for and evokes, both for the emitter and the receiver, the same class of events.

47. Like any other kind of response, the emission of a symbol need not be a necessary effect of the occurrence of any element of the class for which it acts as a symbol, but may be connected with those elements only "potentially" so that it will be evoked only if reinforced from other sources. It may, in particular, merely constitute a link in one among the many alternative chains of action which the occurrence of any element of the class tends to evoke, but which will actually be carried out only if that course of action is selected as leading to one of the results which are within the range of the momentary "intention" of the system as defined.

48. Since these symbols stand for classes of events and their occurrence will produce precisely those effects which are common to the occurrence of the members of the corresponding classes, the simultaneous or nearly simultaneous occurrence of two or more of these symbols will have precisely the same effects as would be produced by any event belonging to the several classes for which these symbols stand. Occurrence of different symbols at the same time (or in rapid succession) would then have the effect which in ordinary language we aim at by conjunction. (We shall not follow up here the

possibility of combining class symbols in other manners but will merely mention that if we could add to conjunction the operation of negation, all the other operations corresponding to the logical constants could be built up by combinations of these two.)

49. The significance of these considerations will be made clearer by an example. Let us assume two similar systems so constituted that they are capable not only of hunting a moving object (which we will call the prey) but also showing symbols of each class they form in observing the movement of their prey and the environment, and of taking appropriate notice in doing so of events which they cannot observe directly but which affect them only indirectly via the symbols shown by the other system. We shall examine such a process where in the initial position two systems are some distance apart and only one of them can see the prey moving at a point concealed to the second system by an obstacle and in a direction which will make it emerge on the side nearer to the second system. The situation assumed is represented in the adjoined sketch. We shall ask whether two systems of the kind described could conceivably communicate such information to each other, and, if so, whether such communication would have to be regarded as true description in the sense defined at the beginning of this paper.

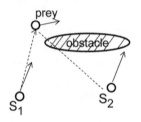

50. There can, in the first instance, be little question that machines could be constructed which in certain states (corresponding to the "intention" of catching the prey) will take such action as their internal representation of the environment indicates as leading to the capture of the prey. Although self-steering missiles are not usually equipped with a sensory apparatus perceptive of anything other than their particular target, there is no fundamental difficulty about equipping them with the capacity of perceiving and avoiding various kinds of obstacles and still reaching their target. What is required for this is sensitivity for signals from such obstacles (we shall discuss this entirely in terms of optical signals) and an apparatus for classifying such signals in a manner which produces an appropriate modification of the movements of the system.

51. We have seen before that there is no difference in principle between simply moving straight in the direction from which optical signals indicate the presence of the goal, and selecting any more complicated chain of actions

which the representation of the whole environment shows as leading to the goal. In particular, there is no generically new difficulty if certain parts of the environment should, e.g., require a different mode of propagation, offer the prospect of faster or slower advance, or indicate the necessity of some preparatory action of a different kind (e.g., removing an obstacle) if progress in the direction aimed at is to be achieved. This will include what we commonly call the "use" of objects of the environment as "means" for reaching the goal, be it merely the choice of a surface on which it is easier to move or the employment of a "tool" (e.g., using a log as a bridge). All that is required is a sufficient richness of the apparatus of sensory classification as to be able to classify the effects of all the alternative combinations of actions and external circumstances which can arise from the initial situation.

52. Among the objects of the environment which will influence the action of S_1 will be S_2. Among the "knowledge" of S_1, i.e., among the alternative courses of events represented in it, there will be included the representation that "if S_2 joins in the chase, the prey will change its direction so as to become easier to catch", that "if S_2 sees the prey, it will join in the chase", and "if I (S_1) show symbols representative of the kind of prey, the place and the direction of its movement, S_2 will act as if it had seen the prey."

53. Finally, every part of the information which S_1 has to transmit to S_2 in order to cause S_2 in the fashion which S_1 expects to be helpful in catching the prey, refers to classes which the two systems must be able to form in order to perform the actions (other than communication) which we have assumed them capable of performing. All that we have to assume to explain the transmission of information is that the representatives of the classes which are formed in evaluating the environment can also be evoked by symbols shown by another.

THE SENSORY ORDER AFTER 25 YEARS

I appear here not just as an old man. So far as psychology is concerned, I am really a ghost from the 19th century. By this I do not refer to the irrelevant fact that I was born in that century. This also does not go back far enough. What I have in mind is that even nearly sixty years ago, when I conceived my psychological ideas, I never had a live teacher in psychology. For a young man returning from World War I to enter the University of Vienna, with his interests having been drawn by those events from the family background of biology to social and philosophical issues, there was at the moment just no teaching in psychology available. To teach the subject was then still part of the duties of some of the professors of philosophy—not an altogether bad arrangement; but one of them (Friedrich Jodl)[1] had recently died, and the other[2] was clearly dying and the few of his lectures I heard, as painful for him to give as for the students to listen to. So I had to get my knowledge of psychology from the books of men long out of fashion, such as Wilhelm Wundt,[3] or long dead, such as William James,[4] Johannes Müller,[5] and Hermann von Helmholtz[6]—the latter, in my opinion, the greatest of them all. But the decisive stimulus for taking up the problem on which I soon started to work came

[Hayek contributed this essay to a conference on Cognition and the Symbolic Process, held in May 1977 at Pennsylvania State University (see above, editor's introduction, p. 3). It was originally published in Walter B. Weimer and David S. Palermo, eds., *Cognition and the Symbolic Process*, vol. 2 (Hillsdale, NJ: Lawrence Erlbaum Associates, Publishers, 1982), 287–93. The conference volume also includes, under the title "Weimer-Hayek Discussion" (ibid., 321–29), a transcript of the discussion that followed Hayek's presentation. The transcript is not included in the present volume.—Ed.]

[1] [On F. Jodl see above, "Contributions," fn. 4.—Ed.]

[2] Adolf Stöhr, a *very* profound thinker who, although I had barely looked in at his lectures, was prepared to read my first rough manuscript and encouraged me to go on. [On A. Stöhr see above, editor's introduction, fn. 39.—Ed.]

[3] [On W. Wundt see above, *TSO*, preface, fn. 8.—Ed.]

[4] [On W. James see above, *TSO*, preface, fn. 9.—Ed.]

[5] [On J. Müller see above, *TSO*, 1.32, fn. 17.—Ed.]

[6] [On H. von Helmholtz see above, *TSO*, preface, fn. 7.—Ed.]

from Ernst Mach[7] and particularly his *Analysis of Sensations* (1902/1959)[8]—the work of an only recently dead physicist to whose writings turned most of the young scientists, who then arrogantly regarded all non-positivist philosophy as absurd nonsense.

Mach's acute analysis of how what he regarded as the elementary pure sensations corresponding to the individual sensory stimuli came to be further organized by such acquired properties as local signs as a result of experience made me, in a sudden flash of insight, perceive that the presumed pure core of sensation originally attached to the afferent impulse was a superfluous assumption, and that all attributes of sense experience (and soon after that, *all* mental qualities) might be explained in some way by their place in a system of connections. I began to see that there were two orders in which we could conceive of the same set of events—two orders that were in some respects similar but yet differed in exactly that way in which our sensory picture of the world and our scientific conception of it differed from each other.

The conclusion that the world of our mental qualities provided us with an imperfect generic map with its own units existing only in that mental universe, yet serving to guide us more or less successfully in our environment, led me to a philosophical view of the relation between the physical and the sensory world that then had been recently revived by the physicist Max Planck, but that really goes back to Galileo Galilei, who in 1623 had written:[9]

> I think that these tastes, odors, colors, etc. . . . are nothing else than mere names, but hold their residence solely in the sensitive body, so that, if the animal were removed, any such quality would be abolished and annihilated.

My conclusion at an early stage was thus that mental events are a particular order of physical events within a subsystem of the physical world that relates the larger subsystem of the world that we call an organism (and of which they are a part) with the whole system so as to enable that organism to survive. Although I did soon see my problem as one raised by the qualitative character of *all* the different kinds of mental events, and was soon aiming at a general theoretical psychology, I thought that I could best demonstrate my conclusions by a closer analysis of the determination of the system of sense qualities only—or what I later called the sensory order. In the final version in the

[7] [On E. Mach see above, *TSO*, preface, fn. 11.—Ed.]

[8] Ernst Mach, *The Analysis of Sensations* (New York: Dover, 1959) (originally published in German 1902). [The original German edition, *Beiträge zur Analyse der Empfindungen*, was published by G. Fischer, Jena, in 1886.—Ed.]

[9] Galilei, Galileo, "Two kinds of properties"[1623], Selection from *Il Saggitore*, in *Philosophy of Science*, edited by A. Danto and S. Morgenbesser (New York, NY.: Meridian Books, 1960), p. 27.

book, of course, I tried to make this fully clear and claimed that in this manner, it should be possible to provide an adequate explanation of all the events that took place between the input of (external and internal) stimuli and the output of actions. But the basic idea was on paper, though in a very amateurish fashion, by 1920.

After I got my law degree in 1921, after 3 years at the university devoted mostly to psychology and economics, I had to think about earning a living and to confine my extracurricular activities to one of those two subjects. I chose economics, perhaps wrongly; the fascination of physiological psychology never quite left me, though for the next 25 years—struggling to get on as an economist (and rapidly forgetting my law)—I could devote no time to following the development of psychology. Only after I had taught for 15 years as professor at the London School of Economics, and had established a certain reputation as an economist—and had made myself thoroughly unpopular with the majority of my fellow economists through an attack on socialism (incidentally, as a result of my recognition of the market as a mechanism for communicating information)—did I feel that I could afford to take out the old manuscript and see what I could do with it.

When I then, about 1946, began looking at the current psychological literature, I found to my amazement that my problem seemed to be in exactly the same state in which I had left it 25 years before. Helpful factual information had of course been accumulated, but on the purely theoretical issue, the muddle seemed to me at least as great as before. Only in the course of the next three years—while using what time I could spare from my teaching and work in economics to put a fuller statement of my views on paper—did there seem to occur some revival of interest in my problem, and some suggestive contributions to it appeared. The point from which I could then start was the conviction that the different attributes of mental entities—conscious or not—could be reduced to differences in effects as guides to human action. But the crudities of behaviorism (which I had in the meantime encountered in the social sciences) had too much repelled me (particularly in the person of the social science specialist of the Vienna Circle of logical positivists)[10] to make the effect on observable conduct more than a final visible outcome of a complex process we had to reconstruct.

In the early 1940s, I had done a study of what I christened "scientism"—that is, an examination of the harmful effects that the physics model had had on the methodology of the social sciences—and in this work had been driven both to rely in some measure on the results of my unpublished work in psy-

---

[10] [On Otto Neurath, to whom this remark refers, see above, *TSO*, 8.88, fn. 15; and editor's introduction, fn. 48 and fn. 58.—Ed.]

chology, and to think further about some of the problems with which I had dealt in it.[11] Having through this become somewhat clearer about the underlying philosophy, I felt that I could at last state more precisely the problem that I had tried to solve in my juvenile attempt. I had also learned to see what, in the case of really complex phenomena, explanation ought to achieve and could achieve.

What I had from the beginning been unable to swallow was the conception that a sensory fiber could carry, or a nerve cell store, those distinctive attributes that we know mental phenomena to possess—know not only by introspection but equally from our observation of other people's behavior. The result of my earlier studies had been a clear perception of the fact that these mental properties could be determined by the place of the impulse in a system of relations between all the neurons through which impulses were passed. This led me to interpret the central nervous system as an apparatus of multiple classification or, better, as a process of continuous and simultaneous classification and constant reclassification on many levels (of the legion of impulses proceeding in it at any moment), applied in the first instance to all sensory perception but in principle to all the kinds of mental entities, such as emotions, concepts, images, drives, etc., that we find to occur in the mental universe. But the only thing I tried fully to show was that the whole order of sensory qualities, all the differences in the effects of their occurrence, could be exhaustively accounted for by a complete account of all their effects in different combinations and circumstances, and that, if we succeeded in this, nothing would be left to explain about them.

As I remembered my exposition after 25 years, the central conception in the argument was the concept of "disposition." But as I discovered to my disappointment when during the last few days I reread my book (I believe for the first time since I had received a finished copy), and although in general I was very much pleased with what I found in it—in that exposition, I actually use the term *disposition* only a few times in connection with my discussion of purpose and intention. Evidently my ideas have unconsciously further developed since; or perhaps while, in the first few years after I had finished the text of the book, I made an effort to complete its formulations of the theory in one respect. I had then endeavored to elaborate the crucial concept of "systems within systems," but found it so excruciatingly difficult that, in the end, I

---

[11] "Scientism and the Study of Society," published in the journal *Economica* (1942–1944) and reprinted in a volume entitled *The Counter-Revolution of Science* (1952a) [Now reprinted as Part I, pp. 75–166, in F. A. Hayek, *Studies in the Abuse and Decline of Reason, Text and Documents*, ed. Bruce Caldwell, vol. 13 of *The Collected Works of F. A. Hayek* (Chicago: University of Chicago Press, 2010).—Ed.], which appeared in the same year as *The Sensory Order* (1952b).

abandoned the longish but unfinished paper that apparently nobody I tried it upon could understand.[12]

It seems to me now that I could have greatly simplified my exposition in the book if I had throughout used the term *disposition*. Perhaps I refrained from doing so because I feared then that it would be understood as referring primarily to dispositions to act or to move, whereas of course what I had in mind were as much dispositions to interpret further stimuli and dispositions to change dispositions, and also various long chains where dispositions succeed other dispositions, with actions coming in at a very late stage only as potential events that might have been produced if certain other stimuli had occurred.

In these terms the mental significance of any impulse (and group of impulses) proceeding anywhere in the central nervous system is determined by the "following" it evokes through "linkages" created by former simultaneous occurrence of these impulses at particular points. I deliberately avoided the term *field* in this connection, because it had been used in other somewhat vague senses; and I used "linkages" rather than "associations" because I wanted to stress that I was speaking of purely physiological connections between impulses and not of associations between mental events, which seemed to me to be produced by large numbers of such linkages. Indeed my "linkages" were assumed to create or determine the content of those mental events on which associations were supposed to operate.

The "followings" of all the impulses proceeding in the central nervous system at any one time are thus assumed to determine the potential or readiness of the system to do new things—internally or externally. Which of these potential neural events (toward which the system is inclined at any particular moment) eventuates would be decided by the partial overlapping of these followings through which, by summation, the potential effects of those linkages would be made actual. Only where a sufficient number of impulses converged on any one neuron would it be made to "fire" and to send out impulses to hundreds or thousands of other neurons.

It is very tempting to represent this graphically by showing a bunched tail of other neurons being affected by the excitation of any one particular neuron, with the overlapping of these tails determining where the impulses are to be passed on further. But any such graphic representation is apt to suggest a local grouping, whereas of course the streams of impulses being sent out by one firing neuron may be spread over the whole cortex, with the ramifications of the impulses spreading from the different neurons being completely interlaced. What perhaps deserves to be spelled out is that in this process, though each neuron may, by the impulses it sends on, "tend" to evoke fur-

---

[12] [The "unfinished paper" to which Hayek refers is now published for the first time in the present volume, above, pp. 361–381.—Ed.]

ther impulses in exceedingly large numbers of other neurons (the effectiveness of this depending on the summation of perhaps as many separate impulses arriving at more or less the same time), this process of a dispersion of individual impulses need not lead to a continuous increase of the number of excited neurons, but may be compatible with this number remaining approximately constant and, perhaps, if no new impulses were brought in by afferent nerves, even more or less the same assembly of impulses in particular neurons being evoked and re-evoked for some time.

Mind thus becomes to me a continuous stream of impulses, the significance of each and every contribution of which is determined by the place in the pattern of channels through which they flow within the pattern of all available channels—with newly arriving afferent impulses, set up by external or internal stimuli, merely diverting this flow into whatever direction the whole flow is disposed to move. Stimuli and responses thus become merely the input and output of an ongoing process in which the state of the organism constantly changes from one set of dispositions to interpret and respond to what is acting upon it and in it, to another such set of dispositions. In my own mind—perhaps naturally, since not long before I wrote *The Sensory Order* (1952b), I published the results of many years' work on *The Pure Theory of Capital* (1941)[13]—I liked to compare this flow of "representative" neural impulses, largely reflecting the structure of the world in which the central nervous system lives, to a stock of capital being nourished by inputs and giving a continuous stream of outputs—only fortunately, the stock of this capital cannot be used up.

I leave it at that, so far as psychology proper is concerned. But I would like to add a few words about philosophical implications concerning the relations of our experiential picture of the world, and that picture of the "real" world that the physical sciences elaborate, and about the nature and limits of explanation.

Perhaps the most basic contention in my book—not original but at the time of its publication, certainly not generally accepted—is that which occurs in the first chapter (Section 1.13), saying:

> The task of the physical sciences is to replace that classification of events which our senses perform but which proves inadequate to explain regularities of these events by a classification which will put us in a better position to do so. The task of theoretical psychology is the converse one of explaining why these events, which on the basis or their relations to each other can be arranged in a certain (physical) order, manifest a different order in their effects on our senses.

[13] F. A. Hayek, *The Pure Theory of Capital* (Chicago, Ill.: University of Chicago Press, 1941).

The relation between these two orders, one of which is a part of the other, is still one of the most intriguing problems of philosophy. I believe that this is a relationship that, in the nature of the case, and forever, we can explain only "in principle" and never in full or in detail. But I believe also that the question of whether there exist "objectively" two different worlds is really unanswerable or perhaps meaningless. The word *exist* loses all definite meaning in this context.

It is a different thing if we assert, as I believe to be true, that it is permanently impossible—because it would involve a logical contradiction—that we should ever be able *fully* to reduce the mental world to physical events. This, however, does not preclude, or make meaningless, the assertion that to a brain of a very much higher order than that which we possess, what our brain does might be capable of explanation in physical or physiological terms. But this suggests to me that the categorical questions of whether there *are* or *are not* two (or three) different worlds really do not have much meaning—at least if we impose upon ourselves the discipline of not talking about what we cannot know. Perhaps it would be sensible to agree not to use in this context the expressions "there is" or "there is not" in any absolute sense, and to understand any use of the term *exist* as meaning "exists for us"—that is, having a definable place in our system of thought.

The proof I have attempted in my book that any explanation—which always rests on classification—is limited by the fact that any apparatus of classification must be of a higher degree of complexity than what it classifies, and that therefore the human brain can never fully explain itself, may be inadequate. To prove it strictly is probably of a degree of difficulty comparable to that of the famous Gödel theorem in mathematics,[14] which indeed seems to me to deal with a special case of the more general proposition that the mind can never fully explain itself. But the conclusion about the absolute limit to our powers of explanation seems to me of considerable importance for some of the basic problems of what used to be called the mind-body relationship and the tasks of the mental and moral sciences generally.

It would take too long, and would probably also exceed my powers of

[14] [Kurt Friedrich Gödel (1906–78), generally considered the most significant mathematician-logician of the 20th century, was born in Brünn, Austria-Hungary (now Brno, Czech Republic). He studied theoretical physics and mathematics at the University of Vienna, where he participated in the meetings of the Vienna Circle, earned his doctorate in 1930, and did his habilitation in 1932. After Austria had become part of Nazi Germany in 1938, he emigrated to the United States, where he became a permanent member of the Institute for Advanced Studies in Princeton. In his 1931 article "Über formal unentscheidbare Sätze der *Principia Mathematica* und verwandter Systeme," *Monatshefte für Mathematik und Physik* 38: 173–98, he proved his famous "Incompleteness Theorems" according to which any consistent axiomatic mathematical system includes propositions that cannot be proved or disproved within the system, and that the consistency of the axioms themselves cannot be proven.—Ed.]

lucid oral explanation, to justify this contention abstractly. But I have recently thought of an illustration, or a fictitious case, that exhibits the essential points.

Assume I could construct a rat—that is, a mechanical model that can do all a rat does. To be a really true model, it would clearly have to do also a great many things we could not predict, even though we know precisely how the mechanism we have built works. It would both occasionally have to respond to external stimuli in a manner that we cannot predict, but also have to act "spontaneously" in response to internal processes that we cannot observe. The reason for our inability to predict, in spite of our precise knowledge of the mechanism that moves it, would be that our mind is not capable of perceiving and digesting, in the same manner as the mechanical rat does, all the particular stimuli that operate upon it and all the processes of classification that proceed in it. The only means by which we could achieve predictions would be to build a computer that imitates all that the mechanism of the rat performs; or, in other words, to build another rat identical in structure with the first one and making it live from the beginning in exactly the same environmental conditions, so that it would perceive and learn exactly what the first rat does. That is, in order to understand what a rat will do and why it does it, we would in effect have to become another rat. Need I spell out the consequences that follow from this for our understanding of other human beings?

In conclusion, let me just say how grateful I am for having been permitted to listen to your discussions. Although my book had at first a few sensible and sympathetic reviews, especially one by E. G. Boring,[15] I have since had practically no indication of any response to my thesis by the psychological profession. All that showed me that some people must be reading it was that it had gone into a third printing. But I had no idea whether its basic approach was accepted or used by anybody else. I need hardly say how gratified I now am to discover how much active work is being conducted on the general lines I then indicated—irrespective of whether it was suggested by my early efforts or not. And I hope some of you may still discover in my books some hints you may find useful.

It seems to me that the young discipline of cognitive psychology is succeeding in showing that "meaning" can be given a meaningful place in our picture of the physical world.

[15] [On E. G. Boring see above, *TSO*, 1.5, fn. 1.—Ed.]

NAME INDEX

SUBJECT INDEX

The entries included in the index of the original edition of *The Sensory Order* are printed in **bold**. Where applicable the paragraphs of the *The Sensory Order* listed in the original index are added in parenthesis.—Ed.

absolute qualities, 123, 162–67 [1.90ff.], 226–27 [5.12]

abstract, primacy of the, 2n14, 40, 44–45, 63n244, 83n305, 104, 116n4, 133n12. *See also* concrete

abstractions, 9, 21n85, 40n154, 45, 116n4, 131, 200 [3.69], 201n12, 202–3 [3.73, 3.77], 228 [5.19], 234 [5.39], 253–54 [6.11, 618f.], 258–61 [6.32ff., 6.46ff.], 263, 321, 332n21, 342–43, 356. *See also* conceptualization

action, causally determined, 66, 302; goal-directed, 59–60, 157n48; intentional, 47, 59, 61; program-based, 60; purposive, 47, 49, 52, 59n228, 60n231, 61–62, 63n242, 64, 205–7, 219–20, 241–45, 252; teleonomic, 59–60; voluntary, 66, 210, 341n33

'all-or-nothing principle', 185 [3.8], 186 [3.13]

Alpbach, ix, x, 11, 83

'apperception', 264 [7.7], 266, 336, 345

a priorism, Mises', 29n117, 30, 33n127, 34, 36, 44n170, 48n189; praxeological, 35, 37–38

assimilation, 265 [7.13], 266n9, 325n5

association psychology, 18n76, 267 [7.16]

associations, 18n76, 53n205, 116n3, 200–01 [3.69f.], 220, 228, 234 [5.50ff.], 242–43, 264, 267, 275–76 [7.45], 280, 321, 323, 326–28, 335–37, 339–40, 343, 346, 372, 378, 386

attention, 119, 125, 220, 252, 255–58 [6.22ff.], 260 [6.41f.]

attitude, 154, 194, 219–21

behavior. *See* action

behaviorism, behaviorist, 47–48, 61, 116, 117n6, 120n12, 123, 149n31, 150, 157–62 [1.74ff.], 172n5, 174 [2.23], 204 [4.2], 213 [4.36f.], 250 [6.1], 369, 384

biogenic impulses, 125, 206 [4.10], 218–20 [4.56ff.]

blindness, congenital, 163 [1.95f.], 269 [7.23]

body-mind problem. *See* mind-body problem

brain. *See* mind

categories, 15n64, 22, 42–45, 235 [5.43], 281 [8.11], 357

causation, 29, 62, 63n242, 64, 67, 372; downward, 84–86, 91, 94, 100

causes, proximate and ultimate, 60, 94–95

choice, pure logic of, 31n121, 32n123, 33–38